THE TEAMSTERS

Steven Brill

Simon and Schuster
New York

LIBRARY OF CONGRESS CATALOGING IN PUBLICATION DATA

BRILL, STEVEN.
THE TEAMSTERS.

INCLUDES INDEX.
1. INTERNATIONAL BROTHERHOOD OF TEAMSTERS,
CHAUFFEURS, WAREHOUSEMEN, AND HELPERS OF AMERICA.
I. TITLE.
HD6515.T3B74   331.88′11′38050973   78-16610
ISBN 0-671-22771-8

2. Labor Unions

To my parents and to Cynthia

Contents

Acknowledgments

More than 300 people were interviewed for this book. Though it is impossible to name them all, they all have my thanks. In this regard I am especially indebted to the officials and the members of the Teamsters union. Most who were asked agreed to talk with me. In a book that attempts, above all, to be about people, theirs is the most important contribution.

Before interviewing anyone, I drew on the excellent work of many who have reported on labor and the Teamsters over the years. My thanks to Tom Joyce, Jonathan Kwitny, Clark Mollenhoff, Ralph Orr, A. H. Raskin, Brian Ross, Russell Sackett, Walter Sheridan, Jo Thomas and many others for the indispensable crash course their work provided, and to research assistant Richard Margolin for his fast, efficient help in compiling these materials. Similarly, my thanks to the Chicago *Sun-Times,* the Detroit *Free Press,* and the St. Louis *Post-Dispatch* for the use of their clip files and morgues.

Two journalists served as consultants on this project. Robert Windrem, when he was with the New Brunswick *Home News,* provided research and advice on Chapter Four. And Jim Drinkhall, who has been a trailblazer in Teamster reporting, provided guidance in most areas and was especially helpful in Chapter Six and in other portions in which the Central States Pension Fund is discussed.

Several friends also helped, especially Floyd Abrams and Sandy Berger, who reviewed the full manuscript and provided critically important advice.

My wife, Cynthia, read more drafts more times than I had a right to ask. She always found ways to improve them. Even that contribution was surpassed by the encouragement she consistently provided and the patience she never lost.

At Simon and Schuster, Robert Stein provided exhaustive but cheerful advice. Gwen Edelman made key suggestions and handled hundreds of details with great patience. And Richard Snyder gave this project unwavering support from beginning to end.

Finally, I cannot express enough my thanks to Alice Mayhew, the ideal editor. Her creativity, energy, skill, and good humor were always there.

May 1978

CHAPTER I

La Costa

The La Costa Hotel and Country Club is what its brochures promise. The rooms are bright, large and well furnished. The weather at its worst in this part of Southern California, about twenty-five miles north of San Diego, is usually good for golf and tennis. Golfers play a 27-hole course that winds its way around horse trails and split-level condominiums, and it is challenging enough for professional tournaments. Tennis players find twenty-five first-class courts and a teaching staff that is headed by Pancho Segura and claims Jimmy Connors among its former students.

The pool is Olympic-sized and nicely tiled. The rolling lawns that cover the 5,600-acre resort complex built in the middle '60s are bright green and manicured. The poolside snack bar serves thick, fresh sandwiches. The cocktail lounge serves generous drinks and lavish vegetable hors d'oeuvres.

For $7 to $65.50 a session, depending on the services required, the famous La Costa spa offers a variety of treatments to exhilarate the most listless body—massages, herbal wraps, whirlpools, saunas, manicures, pedicures, steam baths, exercise classes, bath oils, skin lotions, special shampoos.

Most mornings La Costa wakes up slowly. The maids, bellhops, caddies and car parkers take their posts quietly, showing the same respect for their guests' sleeping habits that the masseurs will show later in the afternoon for the knots and bulges in their bodies. Except at the tennis courts, where by eight o'clock Segura has already started chasing his students to perfection, the loudest intrusion is the spray of automatic sprinklers showering the lawns.

The morning of October 13, 1976, was different. At eight the lobby, the main restaurant, even the golf-course locker room already buzzed with vacationers, mostly men. They were markedly more heavy-set and showed a greater taste for double knits than the usual La Costa crowd.

Whatever they lacked in looks and style they apparently made up in social stature. The President of the United States had sent them a letter of greeting, calling them "labor, business and civic leaders," and commending them for having gathered from across the country to raise money for charity.

They were the leaders, the friends, and the business associates of the International Brotherhood of Teamsters.

They had come to La Costa for the Seventh Annual Frank Fitzsimmons Invitational Golf Tournament, held to raise money for a home for mentally retarded blind children.

Not counting wives, friends, and others on hand just to watch, there were about 150 participants—International vice-presidents, local-union bosses, trucking company executives, Teamster lawyers, and others who had decided that the fun or the good will or both were worth the cost (to them or their organizations) of the trip and the $650 entrance fee for the charity tournament.

At about eight-thirty Frank Fitzsimmons, General President of the International Brotherhood of Teamsters, walked down the spiral staircase from the restaurant toward the golf-course locker room. Crop out the entourage, and Fitzsimmons might be an old Irish waiter who is just off duty. His face—puffy, sullen, pointed down—seemed like that of a man beaten down by years of taking orders, saying thank you with a forced smile, then turning off the smile at the punch-out clock.

Fitzsimmons did not look like someone for whom golf tournaments are named, or like a man who ran what Robert F. Kennedy once called "the most powerful institution in the country, next to the government itself." Kennedy had overstated the Teamsters' power. Still, Frank Fitzsimmons' appearance didn't do it justice.

He did not look like a boss with more $30,000, $40,000, and $50,000 jobs to dispense than any public official except the President of the United States; yet, his two sons held three such jobs between them.

Fitzsimmons had limousines, a private jet, servants and chefs constantly standing by, all supplied by the union. He had an unlimited expense account that provided him and his family first-class entertainment and travel, even on vacations. His $156,000 salary was the highest paid to any union president in the world.

Under his command, directly or indirectly, were 7,000 officers and business agents in 742 local unions negotiating 20,000 contracts a year, or 77 contracts every business day, on behalf of 2.3 million workers.

One of every hundred Americans, one of every twenty American families, and one of every ten American union members is a dues-paying member of Frank Fitzsimmons' union. Teamsters are cafeteria workers at Penn State, sanitationmen in New York City, firemen in Newark, ambulance and armored-car drivers in Chicago, zoo keepers and policemen in San Diego, cartoonists in Hollywood, Hertz Rent-A-Car clerks in Florida, stewardesses and reservation clerks at several airlines across the country, McDonald's hamburger-bun makers in Tennessee, pipeline diggers in Alaska, nurses in Denver, cab drivers in Cleveland and San Francisco, brewers in Milwaukee, egg farmers in California, and 450,000 truckers and warehousemen around the country who drive and store everything from diapers to coffins.

Fitzsimmons' union, with members in the United States, Guam and Canada, is more than 50 percent larger than each of the two next-largest unions—the United Steelworkers of America and the United Auto Workers. The AFL-CIO, with 13.5 million affiliated members, is bigger, but it is a federation of unions, not a union.

In 1902 when the Teamsters were a loose confederation of horse-and-buggy delivery men ("team drivers") a union leader bragged to a reporter that "there is no industry today that can carry on its business if the Teamsters lay down their reins." Three quarters of a century later, when the reins had been turned in for tractor trailers pulling as many as twenty tons of freight in a single load, the assessment was still accurate. Almost everything Americans eat, drink or use at home or on the job is delivered by Frank Fitzsimmons' Teamsters. The Teamsters have organized more than one and a half million workers in hundreds of other fields, but the truck drivers and warehousemen are still the core of their unequaled union power.

The special nature of their work gives these truckers and ware-housemen a strangle hold on the nation's economic lifeline. Much of what they do cannot be delayed. If auto workers go on strike, the cars they are assembling can be finished tomorrow or next week and still be sold. If the Teamsters refuse to store or deliver fresh produce, there is no tomorrow.

Frank Fitzsimmons' men have the power to paralyze apparently unrelated industries. If they refuse to deliver auto parts from the factory where they are made to the assembly line where they are put together, those who make the parts and those who assemble the cars have to stop work.

On the day of the Seventh Annual Frank Fitzsimmons Invitational Golf Tournament, Fitzsimmons was also one of the nation's major banking powers. He was a trustee of the Central States, Southeast and Southwest Areas Pension Fund—$1.4 billion held in trust to cover the present and future pensions of some 450,000 Teamsters who worked in the South and the Midwest. It was then the largest private pension fund in the nation,* with more money than most banks, and income of about $35 million each month from employers obligated by the union contract to set money aside for their employ-ees' pensions. In the years that Fitzsimmons had been a trustee, the Fund had used its financial muscle for investments that were radically different from those made by other funds or banks. Rather than invest in slow-climbing but rock-solid bonds and securities, Fitzsimmons and the other trustees (lower-level Teamsters officers and represen-tatives of the trucking industry selected on Fitzsimmons' say-so) had thrown the money into a series of real-estate loans that were at best reckless and at worst deliberate payoffs to organized-crime interests. As a result, the Teamsters held uncertain mortgages on some of America's most flamboyant real estate—casinos in Las Vegas, Jai Alai in Connecticut, dog tracks in Florida, and well-known hotels and country clubs across the country, including La Costa.

On October 13, 1976, for all his power, Frank Fitzsimmons was fast becoming as trapped as any of the balls he and his friends drove into the sand. He had been reelected president by acclamation at the International's convention four months before. Two months before that, he had negotiated a national trucking contract that gave his members the most generous boosts in wages and benefits ever. Still,

* By 1977, the Teamsters Western States Pension Fund would have more assets, but it was outside Fitzsimmons' control.

the year had not brought him what he had wished for. He had hoped that the press, the rank and file and everyone else would stop talking about him as a man who was where he was only because his predecessor, James R. Hoffa, had been sent to prison in 1967 and then had mysteriously disappeared in July 1975 as he was preparing an attempt to take back the union presidency. That relief hadn't come. He was still regarded as Jimmy Hoffa's lucky, unworthy, even double-crossing stand-in. There seemed to be more stories in the press than ever about how Fitzsimmons had betrayed Hoffa and had perhaps been involved in his disappearance. The government, spurred by the publicity over the Hoffa case and their inability to solve it, was investigating Fitzsimmons and the Teamsters on several other fronts, most significantly the Central States Pension Fund. Nineteen seventy-six had been a year of relentless pressure by government investigators looking to see whether payoffs, trustee breaches of fiduciary responsibility, embezzlement and other misdeeds had been involved in questionable Fund loans.

In June, the Internal Revenue Service had threatened the destruction of the Fund with a simple administrative step; they had decided that the Fund's lending and management practices were so questionable that it did not deserve the tax exemption given to bona fide pension plans. Therefore, it would have to pay back taxes on earnings, while the trucking companies that had contributed to the Fund would owe hundreds of millions of dollars in taxes for deductions they had taken over the years for pension contributions. Subsequently, the government had offered to postpone, or perhaps cancel, revocation of the tax exemption if Fitzsimmons would agree to some changes in the way the Fund was controlled and operated—in the main, removal of the current trustees who had rubber-stamped loans to mob fronts, and an end to risky loans.

That morning, Fitzsimmons was trying to deliver on one of the reforms he had promised the government. Five days earlier he had agreed that eleven of the Fund's sixteen trustees would resign and that a ten-man board, chosen by Fitzsimmons but approved by the Department of Labor, would be constituted.

It was a compromise. Fitzsimmons and four other current trustees would remain on the new board. It was so much a compromise that four months later the new Carter administration would review the deal and veto it. Nonetheless, that morning Fitzsimmons was having trouble selling even that to his side. Some of the trustees didn't want to resign. Top Teamsters, including Fund trustees, had been investigated and threatened by the government for more than two decades. They had survived this long by fighting, not negotiating. "Jimmy would never have given in," one of them had reminded Fitzsimmons, a comparison that always unnerved Fitzsimmons.

The merits of their arguments aside, these were men whom Fitzsimmons did not like to offend. He was afraid of offending some of them. But his lawyers had warned that if he didn't go along with the compromise there would be a long court fight in which the government would argue for revoking the tax exemption. Or, as a more realistic alternative, they might oust Fitzsimmons and all the trustees and put the Fund under the control of outside parties, charging that it had been mismanaged and corrupted. Not only might the government win its civil case and take control of the Fund away from Fitzsimmons and the other trustees, the lawyers warned, but they might well bring some criminal-court action against the trustees, including him, for fraud or embezzlement. The government kept hinting to Fitzsimmons and his lawyer about the evidence it had to back such charges. They were partly bluffing, but Fitzsimmons couldn't know that. They refused to be specific, a coy game that left Fitzsimmons trying to guess what they might know.

In the year ahead, Fitzsimmons would face mounting pressure from the opposing forces—the government pushing for reform, the old-line Teamsters leadership demanding resistance. As he weighed his choices, Fitzsimmons had to wrestle with his fears that the government could make good on its threats, and that the other side had a track record, including Hoffa's disappearance, that made it unnecessary for them to make threats.

Also, his lawyers were admonishing him that courtroom battles are public. If the government were to go to court to defend the revocation of the tax exemption or to remove the trustees, whatever evidence of wrongdoing it had obtained would be laid out there for the press and the public, day after day. Fitzsimmons knew what that meant: more headlines of the sort that had torn at his pride and his ulcer during the last year—publicity that had made him out to be a fool, a crook, and the beneficiary of a daring murder of Jimmy Hoffa.

On October 13, 1976, Frank Fitzsimmons was also worried about a date he had six days later with a Senate investigating committee staff behind closed doors. They wanted to ask him about a scheme in which his son Donald had been involved, to help a convicted swindler named Louis Ostrer sell overpriced life-insurance plans to local

Teamsters unions. Five weeks later, on November 22, 1976, he was going to have to explain it again, this time to a federal grand jury in Detroit. Both times, he was going to do something no father could enjoy: without warning his sons, he would deny his own role in the scheme. It would contribute to one of them, Richard, being indicted* and putting the other, Donald, under suspicion. Fitzsimmons' damaging testimony was a matter of survival. The government was bearing down on him as never before. If he did otherwise he would risk an indictment for conspiracy to embezzle union funds. The odds of a perjury indictment were much lower.

Since his take-over in 1967 Fitzsimmons had been playing those survival odds better than anyone had predicted. He had been much shrewder than the tongue-tied bore of the newspaper profiles.

Not that Fitzsimmons hadn't himself projected an unflattering image. Early in 1967 in Hollywood, Florida, Jimmy Hoffa had presided over the last meeting of the Teamsters executive board before he went to prison for jury tampering. He had used the occasion to confirm to the executive board and to the press that, as rumored, Frank Fitzsimmons—his hand-picked general vice-president, who had been known since the '40s as Hoffa's gopher—was now in charge while he was away. ("Hoffa used to strike matches against him," a mutual friend later remarked, echoing the exasperation of other top Teamsters, who thought Hoffa had made less than the best choice.) When the board meeting ended, the new leader of the world's largest union emerged to find a crowd of reporters waiting. Recognizing a face among the pads and TV lights, Fitzsimmons delivered his first statement to live cameras and recorders: "I'll talk to you later, Bob. Right now I have to go piss."

Fitzsimmons' way with words hadn't changed much since. But he had grown into the job. Like the executive who disdains first class until the company lets him do it three or four times and he begins to wonder how he had ever survived coach, Fitzsimmons had developed a sweet tooth for luxuries and subservient attention. He also learned to handle the job, not in Jimmy Hoffa's autocratic way, but in his own way. He let his vice-presidents and lesser bosses make many of the decisions on contracts, member grievances and strikes that Hoffa had always made. The great mystery was whether this sharing of power was the shrewd scheme of a clever politician or the capitulation of a weakling hopelessly over his head in a big job. Either way,

* Eighteen months later, a jury would find him not guilty.

it had the same result: by giving some of the decision-making back to International vice-presidents around the country, Fitzsimmons had managed to win their support to keep his job when he came up for election in 1971.

After that, there had been still better days for a while. He was president of the largest union in the world in his own right. The talk about being Jimmy Hoffa's gopher had died down. Soon, he had achieved something that had eluded Hoffa. As Richard Nixon's major union supporter in the 1972 election, he was labor's Mr. Inside at President Nixon's White House. Fitzsimmons had access to any cabinet member, even to the President himself. For a man who had started out as a Detroit bus and truck driver, and had spent much of his union career taking coffee orders for Hoffa, these were heady days—White House invitations, membership on presidential boards and commissions, gifts of presidential cuff links and golf putters.

But by 1973, it had started to fall apart. Government investigators, who had planted an informant among organized-crime figures in California, stumbled onto Fitzsimmons conferring with mobsters on an insurance-fund-fraud scheme; when friends in the Nixon administration quashed an investigation, a disgruntled FBI agent leaked the episode to the press. Other reporters began writing about the way Central States Pension Fund money was being loaned to mob fronts. Nixon began to be enmeshed in Watergate. And Fitzsimmons began to hear Jimmy Hoffa thundering up from behind. Recently released from prison, Hoffa was planning to take back the big leather chair at headquarters by running for president at the Teamsters convention in 1976. In July 1975 Hoffa vanished, the presumed victim of organized-crime forces who felt more comfortable with Fitzsimmons as Teamsters president. Now, as a result of the furor, all aspects of Teamsters business became favorite targets for government investigators anxious to prove they could do something about the Teamsters even if they couldn't crack the Hoffa case. There were investigations of the pension fund and of his sons' involvement in that life-insurance deal. The press was writing relentlessly about corruption in these and other Teamsters activities. And, though it hadn't been reported publicly, Fitzsimmons knew from questions the FBI had asked him that the feds had at least circumstantial evidence suggesting that he had played a role in planning the disposal of Hoffa's body at a private sanitation company near Detroit, where, it was thought, Hoffa may have been incinerated.

It was not surprising that Frank Fitzsimmons looked less than buoyant on the morning of October 13, 1976. It was not a happy time. And things would not get better between then and next year's tournament.

On October 13, 1976, James Hoffa, Jr., went to the five-man law office in downtown Detroit that bore his name. Hoffa was aware that the tournament opened that day at La Costa. He had kept in touch with almost everything going on in the Teamsters world since the next-to-last day of July the year before, when his father had disappeared.

He did legal work for the Teamsters, serving the Detroit local that his father had built three decades before. Occasionally, he had been talked about as a candidate for union president against Fitzsimmons. But though he was interested in everything that was going on at La Costa—who was there and who talked to whom—Hoffa junior stayed away. He couldn't face the men who thrived in the sun over his dad's dead body.

Jimmy Hoffa had bequeathed none of his exterior roughness to his thirty-four-year-old son. Jimmy junior is soft-spoken, good-looking, warm, and quick to smile. His accent, manner, conservative striped suits, and his University of Michigan Law School diploma are far removed from the street world that his father had conquered and died in. But he had his father's pride and toughness of mind. He wasn't about to go to a tournament that was named for a man who had profited from his father's disappearance and who was, he thought, better suited to be holding his dad's coat than sitting in his old chair. He would take some of their local law business, especially since his father's people still controlled much of the Teamsters activity around Detroit. But he wouldn't socialize with them.

By now young Hoffa had given up any thought of trying to pick up his father's mantle. He preferred his own world of secure, lawyerly respectability to the grimy, violent arena where his father had thrived and perished. Besides, as he saw it, even an insurgent with the name Hoffa had no chance in a union that elected its president through indirect area representation rather than by a rank-and-file vote.

Hoffa junior's interest now in Teamsters activities and Teamsters gossip was a matter of keeping tabs on the family's enemies. As in the past fourteen months, most such vicarious involvement left a bitter aftertaste, as he heard of this or that undeserving Fitzsimmons satellite being given a higher union office and more money, or as he became more and more disgusted with the way the FBI kept telling him about progress in his father's case while producing nothing. But there were satisfying moments, as when he learned of the trouble Fitzsimmons and his sons were in, or when he thought he had come across a lead in his dad's disappearance that he could pass on to the FBI.

Teeing off at La Costa just behind Fitzsimmons was Salvatore Provenzano, the sixth vice-president of the International Brotherhood of Teamsters. In Teamsters circles he is known as Sammy Pro. The nickname is a hand-me-down from his older brother, Anthony, known as Tony Pro. Almost everything Sammy Pro had in life came by way of Tony Pro, including three union posts in New Jersey that gave him $94,000 a year in Teamsters salaries.

Tony Pro had not passed along to Sammy his habit of getting into trouble with the law. Except for one 1971 arrest for counterfeiting food stamps, postage stamps, and twenty-dollar bills (later dismissed when one of his business agents confessed to the crime), Sammy Pro's record was clean. Short, low-keyed and good humored, he was thought to be the smoothest and nicest of the Provenzano brothers, the respectable one who could have his picture taken with presidents and governors and handicapped children, as he represented the New Jersey Teamsters at political dinners and telethons.

Tony was the tough one—hard drinking, impetuously violent. If anyone encouraged the popular notion that *Teamster* is synonymous with *gangster,* it was Tony Pro with his silk suits, pinky rings, and waterfront vocabulary. He was capable of atrocities that were right out of grade-B Hollywood scripts—like having one of his loan sharks killed but remembering to send his widow a Christmas card three weeks later. A captain in the old Vito Genovese New York–New Jersey "family," Tony Pro ran his New Jersey Teamsters union as an arm of organized crime. Headquarters was a shabby old building owned by the Teamsters in a New Jersey eyesore called Union City. There, or by telephone from the Florida house he had bought for less than market value by arranging a pension-fund loan for its previous owner, Tony Pro directed the loan-sharking, the numbers running, the cargo pilfering, the sweetheart contracts, and other rackets that were his brand of trade-unionism. Usually, he used respectable, nice Sammy as the front man.

Sammy's front-man role had been a necessity from 1967—when Tony had gone to prison for extorting a bribe from a trucking company—until 1975, when the law's restriction on Tony's involvement with union affairs had expired. (Federal law prohibits those convicted of labor-law violations from holding union office for five years after they leave prison.) Even after that, Tony's public reemergence had been stalled by the heat from the Hoffa case. He was the number-one suspect. Openly taking back power would be too brazen, even by Teamsters standards.

Tony had decided not to come to the tournament today. It was not that he wasn't up there in the pecking order with Fitzsimmons and the others or in constant touch with them. He had to stay off stage because of the renewed notoriety following the Hoffa disappearance and FBI leaks that he was a prime suspect. Also, he had recently been indicted for the kidnapping and murder, in 1961, of a New Jersey Teamsters official who had been challenging his power there. (The 1961 abduction and murder, which the FBI was able to pin on Provenzano fifteen years later, after they had begun pressuring his cohorts for information about Hoffa, bore a striking resemblance in motive and in method to what was known about Hoffa's disappearance.) The bail agreement pending trial on the '61 case prohibited the trip to California except by special request. Also, if he turned up at La Costa, the reporters would swarm over him with questions. He didn't mind, but the stories in the press infuriated his wife and kids. He and his brother had managed to talk their families into a make-believe world in which they and their loan sharks and hit men were the good guys, and all that they did was somehow at one with the rosary beads their women carried.

In the year ahead, Tony Pro would not get off the sidelines. The bad publicity would continue; the government's efforts to lock him up would be intensified. The 1961 kidnap-murder rap would move toward trial, with strong evidence lined up to overcome the problems of proving guilt in a fifteen-year-old crime. Now sixty, Provenzano would grow anxious at the possibility that he might spend his final days back in the pen on this charge, or even on the Hoffa charge if any of his boys cracked under government pressure.

On October 13, 1976, Ron Carey, president of Teamsters Local 804 in New York, was oblivious to the festivities at La Costa. Carey woke up that morning at six-thirty in the modest two-family Queens home that he, Barbara and the five children shared with his father, who lived in the upstairs apartment. He dressed quickly, so that he could be at the first stop by eight, when his men reported to work.

Carey's Local 804 represented 5,500 men and women (mostly men) who pushed appliances, furniture and rugs around the warehouses of department stores like Macy's, kept files at the warehouses, or drove United Parcel Service and other delivery trucks in New York City and its suburbs. Small, wiry and intense, Carey looked like the second-baseman who may bat second instead of eighth because he's so scrappy.

Carey had been elected in 1967 on a reform platform. Until then he had been a United Parcel driver. To win, he first had to brave an attempt by one trucking company, which preferred dealing with the incumbent president, to blackmail him into abandoning the race by threatening to tell his wife about an affair they claimed he had had. Within a year of the election he had turned down bribe overtures from department stores, told the bosses from the International to keep out of his negotiations, and had his phone number changed in a futile effort to stop the threatening calls. Three years after that, he angrily left his first International convention when they turned his mike off as he rose from the floor to speak against a dues increase. Since then his relations with the people in Washington had reached détente: they left him alone and he left them alone. When he took his men out on strike, they sent money. When there was a national convention, he sent a representative.

On October 13, 1976, Carey was drawing a $28,000 salary, about the same as one of Frank Fitzsimmons' pilots. He had never played golf and had taken two weeks of vacation in the last two years. Had he known that morning about the La Costa gathering as he moved through the half-mile-long aisles of a Macy's warehouse pressing flesh and jotting down constituent complaints like a political ward leader, or had he been reminded of the salaries and expense accounts of other Teamsters officials, a knot would probably have formed in his stomach. He is not the kind of man who takes easily to the image of himself as sucker or a naïve kid (he was halfway between forty and forty-one that morning) who sweats out the job and the mortgage payments and the parochial school tuition, while other Teamsters chiefs worry about their diets and their golf scores.

Lately, as negative press coverage of the Teamsters had heightened, he was being reminded of how the other half lived in ways that offended more than his pride or sense of fairness. Three weeks earlier he had been trying to organize a group of women clerks at a millinery factory. One morning the women were greeted by a poster of Frank Fitzsimmons; it had been put up by the company. The caption announced that Fitzsimmons' salary was $156,000 and inquired whether the women wanted to pay union dues for that. By December, the organizing drive was a shambles.

Such things would make Ron Carey an increasingly torn and frustrated man in the coming year, as would his realization that although he had mastered the job he had held for nearly ten years, all the steps on the Teamsters ladder were blocked by the guys with the pinky rings.

Chicago insurance executive Allen Dorfman was cosponsor of the Seventh Annual Frank Fitzsimmons Invitational Golf Tournament. The souvenir book, in which dozens of trucking companies and other corporations had purchased ads to benefit the 180 retarded and blind retarded children at the Little City Home in Palatine, Illinois (which houses, among other facilities, the Frank Fitzsimmons Recreational Complex), had singled out Dorfman's "continuous concern for the mentally handicapped children of Little City."

This morning, Dorfman had other concerns as well. For the past three years the government and the press had been zeroing in on the loans he had arranged as "consultant" to the Central States Pension Fund. It wasn't the possibility of a criminal case that bothered him. Except for a conviction in New York in 1972 for taking a payoff to set up a pension-fund loan, for which he served ten months, the solidly built fifty-one-year-old Silver Star World War II Marine hero had been able to beat criminal indictments accusing him of fraud and bribery in connection with the pension fund. When he was indicted in 1975 for conspiring with Chicago mobsters to defraud the Fund by arranging a loan to a company and then siphoning off its assets until the company went bankrupt, he hadn't even had to interrupt his golf game with Fitzsimmons at La Costa. His lawyer, a former assistant U.S. attorney general, had arranged for him to go back to Chicago to be arraigned two weeks later. He was acquitted the following year after the jury had deliberated a few hours. One of the star prosecution witnesses had been shotgunned to death.

What concerned Dorfman was that his control over loans made by the pension fund that Jimmy Hoffa had bequeathed him when he went to prison had been taken away. Dorfman was a Teamsters Cinderella for whom midnight approached.

In the early '50s, Hoffa had made a deal with Dorfman's stepfather, Paul "Red" Dorfman, a mobster of the Al Capone era. Red had introduced Hoffa to organized-crime leaders in Chicago and elsewhere who had helped him seize control of the union by intimidation, election-rigging, and other deployments of underworld muscle. In return, Hoffa set up Allen Dorfman, who was then a college phys-ed teacher, in the insurance business. The ambitious gym teacher would handle all the Teamsters Central States Health and Welfare insurance. From there, Hoffa had allowed young Dorfman to help him distribute loans from the mushrooming Central States Pension Fund. In 1967, before Hoffa went to jail, he gave Dorfman almost single-handed control over the Fund's loans, making him one of the nation's most powerful financiers. The authority that Hoffa gave him, and the unassertive Fitzsimmons let him keep, over the money made him a one-man insurance-and-loan-consultant conglomerate earning ten million dollars a year.

Dorfman had saved enough money and done enough favors for the right people so that he would never have to trade in the Rolls or the Mercedes or give up golf or handball at the best clubs. He still managed the claims made to the Central States Health and Welfare Fund, even if he had lost the power over the pension fund. He was comfortably set up in an elegant Chicago office in the Central States Fund building, full of testimonial plaques from charities. He had deals in mind that might make up for the lost money. Nonetheless, he hated the idea of Fitzsimmons compromising with the government, agreeing to eleven trustees resigning. He was willing to lie low for a while, but the resignations might egg the government on to aggressive action that could threaten the fund deals permanently, including the insurance policies he sold. Fitzsimmons' willingness to back away before the government's pressure would be Dorfman's major problem in the year ahead.

As he put it later, "I told Fitz to tell the government to go fuck itself." And one reason Dorfman was glad to be at La Costa that weekend was that it gave him a chance to keep up the pressure on Fitz and the others. Also, he loved the golf course. He was the best golfer among the Teamsters powers, and he had a beautiful condominium overlooking the fairway. Everywhere he went at La Costa Dorfman was treated as if he owned the place—which in a way he did; he had arranged the 97 million dollars in loans from the Central States Pension Fund that had built it.

In the early evening of October 13, 1976, Alfred "Al" Barkett stepped up into a tractor-trailer and got ready to drive ten tons of auto parts from Cleveland to Cincinnati.

Barkett's pay, $8.60 an hour, had increased 148 percent in the last ten years, while the cost of living had gone up about 80 percent. In an average week he made about five hundred dollars, depending on how many miles he drove. As a senior man, the husky, fifty-seven-year-old trucker had first call on the long runs from Cleveland to Cincinnati and back—about five hundred miles—that would keep him on the road nearly ten hours.

His earnings were supplemented by a generous benefits package. The company paid $55.50 a week to his pension and health-and-welfare funds. For all the talk about corruption in the Central States Pension Fund, the men Barkett worked with at Local 407 who were retiring were having no trouble collecting their monthly pension checks from the fund. When he quit in a few years, he would be entitled to $550 a month for life. He also had full health-insurance protection and a $16,000 life-insurance policy.

The union had recently won a requirement that all new trucks be air-conditioned, though this didn't affect Barkett much, since he only drove nights. He did appreciate other health, safety and comfort features that the union had won over the years: shatter-proof windshields, better windshield wipers, good air brakes, even better seats to prevent hemorrhoids and back aches. All this and more for $4.50 a week in dues.

Barkett left his house in suburban Cleveland about ten o'clock the night of the La Costa Tournament for work at CCC Trucking, the company that Frank Fitzsimmons had been driving for when Jimmy Hoffa took him on as a business agent in 1937. Barkett had been with CCC twenty-nine years. He liked it. He did not like Fitzsimmons, who he thought "spent too much money on himself" and "couldn't hold a candle to Hoffa." He appreciated the union though, and he liked the way the local bosses ran things in Ohio. They were accessible when needed to handle problems and seemed to do a good job handling grievances that members had against their employers.

Barkett was more involved in the union than most rank-and-filers. He was a shop steward, elected by twenty or thirty of his co-workers to be their spokesman in local union matters or in dealing with the company on small on-site questions. In all his years as a steward he had never been pressured by the union leaders to do anything illegal. The union's books had always been open to him and to any of the men who wanted to check on where the money went. To Barkett, Teamsters corruption was a problem only in so far as the rumors, true or false, sometimes made him feel uncomfortable about being a "Teamster." That, and his indignation over Fitzsimmons' salary and "political dealing" were the extent of it. "Teamster" to him meant work. Steady work. Since the Depression days back in Iowa this had been what counted most in life. As he put it, "Having a job means you are somebody; without one you are nothing."

Things were going equally well for Barkett at home. He had managed to build up $20,000 in the savings account, despite his wife's extravagances (like the $2,900 dining-room set they had just purchased). All three kids had gone through college. Bill was doing well as an engineer in Indiana, and Mary, recovered from a divorce, was talking about getting married again. Florence, his twenty-four-year-old "hippie," who had started a pottery store with "the wife's savings" and then suddenly moved to New Mexico, had returned to Ohio and seemed to have settled down in a serious job.

As Frank Fitzsimmons came off the eighteenth hole at La Costa, Teamster Charles McGuire of Local 617 woke up and packed a box dinner at his small, shingle house across the Hudson River from Manhattan, in Jersey City. By the time Fitzsimmons came out of the shower, McGuire was filling frozen-food orders at a distribution warehouse in Secaucus, New Jersey. It was 10 degrees below zero in the storage part of the warehouse, just as it had been every day since McGuire started working in frozen-food warehouses in 1951. McGuire didn't think much about his union as he pulled together the vegetables and pot pies that would go the next morning to supermarkets in and around New York. Except for the five seconds when the fifty-nine-year-old father of three (and grandfather of four) walked past the bulletin board where the seniority list was posted and he cursed and muttered something about how the company and his Teamsters Local 617 had together cheated him out of five years of seniority by recording his starting date as 1956, instead of 1951. He did that every day.

No doubt this was a better job than the one he had had as a kid in a Pennsylvania coal mine. There the dust had filled up his lungs so badly that they wouldn't let him into the army during the war. It was also better than the job he had had later in a factory in Connecticut, where he was paid 50 cents an hour and had his hand mangled when an iron press came down on it. The $6.62 McGuire made per hour in the Secaucus warehouse, including night differential, was still about two dollars less than the Teamsters' National Master Freight Agreement—the supposedly uniform trucking contract that Fitzsimmons was so proud of having negotiated in April 1976—said he was supposed to be making. His local union had allowed his employer to pay a lower rate.

Soon McGuire would retire, but if he wanted to ask his union president or a business agent about the pension he would get, or about why he had been denied his five-year seniority, he was out of luck. They were never around.

About 50 of the 120 men working the forklifts and the loading docks with McGuire at the warehouse the night of October 13 would be gone the night of the 1977 Fitzsimmons Tournament. They'd be laid off. A fence would be placed across the length of the warehouse, dividing it into two companies. The laid-off men would be replaced by other members of the same Teamsters local, and they would work there under the second company's name at lower wages than McGuire and the others received. There would be no protest from the union.

In the year ahead, men like McGuire and his son Bob, a truck driver, would join a growing minority of Teamsters in a group called PROD—a self-styled Ralph Nader reform movement that would receive press attention often exceeding what its small numbers and occasionally sloppy rhetoric deserved.

For Jackie Presser, the sixteenth vice-president of the International Brotherhood of Teamsters, the 1976 Fitzsimmons Invitational was a coming-out party. A week before, the fifty-year-old Cleveland Teamsters leader had been named by Fitzsimmons as an International vice-president, replacing his father, William, who had resigned the same day for health reasons.

Before resigning, William Presser had been one of the most powerful Teamsters leaders. He had been the only one with whom Dorfman had shared real Pension Fund power. In Ohio, which was heavily organized by the Teamsters, his power was undisputed, and he had been able to keep much of the Teamsters Ohio action in the family. Jackie had been an officer in one or another Ohio local for twenty years; and in 1976 he had received $199,500 from six different union payrolls.

Now Jackie was moving out on his own. As he stood outside the golf clubhouse chatting with three or four other vice-presidents, he looked self-assured and as fit as he had been in years—partly because he was midway through a diet that by February would bring him from a dangerously obese 300-plus pounds (on a 5-foot 8-inch frame) to a stocky 200; but also because he was a man with big plans. He could see the wave of government and press scrutiny that would threaten the Teamsters in the next year. He alone among the Teamsters powers would urge that they ride it out not by ignoring the accusers and critics but by taking them on with the best public-relations and political campaign money could buy—TV and radio ads, candidate endorsements and press conferences.

It was a bold strategy, one that most of his colleagues, including Dorfman, didn't like. In the coming year he would have to fight for it at meetings of the executive board. In the process he would shrewdly carve out his own kingdom as head of a rapidly expanding public-relations operation. That, as he planned it, would lead to bigger things: he would try to use the PR operation to undercut Fitzsimmons and rise above the other vice-presidents and capture the top job for himself. Quietly, he would deliberately give Fitzsimmons bad advice and prepare to pick up the pieces when his "new image" and Fitzsimmons' leadership became incompatible. Presser was already telling close friends that he'd soon be in Fitzsimmons' chair.

For Harold Gibbons, the St. Louis-based second vice-president of the International Brotherhood of Teamsters, an appearance at La Costa was partly obligatory and partly another chance to relive past glories with friends who went back ten and twenty years. This is how Gibbons spent much of his life these days—a mix of going through the motions, doing what was expected, and reliving better days.

There was always one thought. Most times it simply nagged at him; on days like today, when he had to watch the ass-kissers court Fitzsimmons, it hurt. Harold Gibbons, at sixty-seven, could not help stopping to think about what might have been.

It was understandable. Tall, strong, handsomely gray, with a voice that boomed crisp, precise words, Gibbons looked and talked like a president just as Fitzsimmons did not. Politically, Gibbons was a much more likely trade-union leader than Fitzsimmons. Yet Gibbons' position as second vice-president (the sixteen vice-presidents are ranked by seniority) was worlds of power from Fitzsimmons' desk in the marble headquarters in Washington.

He was better off now than he had been a year before, when he was still on the outs with Fitzsimmons because he was the one vice-president to speak out against the Nixon endorsement. Fitzsimmons had retaliated, ousting Gibbons from all the local, regional and national posts he held at the union, except for the elected position of International vice-president. Then, six months before today's tournament, they made a deal: Gibbons wouldn't oppose Fitzsimmons' reelection at the International's convention in June if Fitzsimmons gave him back some responsibilities, including the job of trying to reach a settlement in the Teamsters fight with Cesar Chavez and the United Farm Workers union.

The deal had not buried the hatchet. If Fitzsimmons and Gibbons had anything in common that morning at La Costa other than their 16–18 golf handicaps, it was that they both knew that, but for events which neither man had controlled, their positions might have been reversed. Harold Gibbons had been Jimmy Hoffa's right-hand man and had been far more likely than Fitzsimmons to be Hoffa's choice for a stand-in during Hoffa's imprisonment. Nearly ten years after Fitzsimmons had been chosen over Gibbons, their hatred and fear of each other had not receded.

On October 13, 1976, a second, more dramatic might-have-been dogged Harold Gibbons. In many ways this part of the Gibbons story reflects the role his union has played, and now plays, in American life. Harold Gibbons—socialist, veteran civil-rights activist, lone McGovern supporter among the foursomes of Nixon men—might have been the Teamster who steered the union to progressive social and political activism. He might have been the leader who spoke out against, and was in a position to *do* something about, all the corruption. He was the one man who might have succeeded in challenging Hoffa or Fitzsimmons for control of the union.

That he hadn't done these things was in some measure a matter of physical fear; he had often told close friends that he was afraid he'd exit from the Teamsters world "horizontally." More than that, it was a weakness for money and women. Harold Gibbons was a socialist who drove a Lincoln Continental. One friend claimed that "the real class war he fought was the war to get every stewardess in the country into bed.'' He fought the other class war, too. He had worked hard to redistribute wealth and give workers a larger share of the economic pie, but as he fought those battles he also insisted on the good life. This didn't lead him to extort payoffs or steal union money for himself, but it made him willing to look away and to rationalize stealing by Hoffa and the others so that he could hang on to a paycheck and a high-powered, sexy position in life that no one born into a poor Pennsylvania coal miner's family of twenty-three children had a right to expect, or might be expected to risk losing.

In the 1940s and '50s in St. Louis, Gibbons had built a local union that was a model of what unions as big and powerful as the Teamsters could become. His union had provided free health care and indoor and outdoor recreation centers for all its members. It built rent-subsidized housing for its retirees, and ran a food co-op to cut members' grocery bills. It took a progressive lead on key political and social issues. Gibbons and his union board had proposed school desegregation in the border state of Missouri two years before the Supreme Court's 1954 *Brown* decision.

Now, except for Alaska, where Teamsters leader Jesse Carr had borrowed some of his program ideas, Gibbons' legacy was limited to St. Louis and to the might-have-been wisdom he dispensed over poolside drinks at his Palm Springs home. In the coming year, he would start a new marriage and be allowed by Fitzsimmons to get back into more of his old union activities. But even though Fitzsimmons' star had begun to fall, Gibbons would face a limited future confined to rethinking the big chance he never took to take over the union and make it what it could have been.

CHAPTER II

Hoffa

Just upstairs from the locker room at La Costa is the Tournament of Champions lounge, where a live band plays at night. Frank Fitzsimmons' older son, Richard, spends many of his evenings there when he comes to La Costa for Teamsters functions or to use his father's condominium. On more than one occasion he has made a fool of himself.

According to the bartenders, after a few drinks, Richard remembers that he has always wanted to be an entertainer. At about one in the morning he may grab the microphone and croon away. It usually elicits some embarrassed half-smiles. But the management never protests.

On the morning of the 1976 La Costa tournament, Richard Fitzsimmons was playing in one of the foursomes behind his father's. He was forty-six years old, a Teamsters general organizer and a vice-president of Local 299, making $88,000 a year. Most of the jobs he had held had been arranged by his father. His younger brother, Donald, forty-one, a $48,000-a-year International Auditor for his father's union, had neither accounting experience nor any training.

Richard and Donald fell into the tradition of the sons of powerful Teamsters. Dan Tobin, the Teamsters president from 1907 to 1952, had two sons at headquarters. His successor, Dave Beck, helped his son rather more obviously. The Senate Committee on Improper Activities in the Labor Field—the McClellan Committee—discovered that Beck established a company for Dave junior that produced toy trucks and ordered Teamsters locals to buy hundreds to give away as presents. It also established that Beck pressured a Seattle beer distributor, whose employees were under a Teamsters contract, to let Dave junior buy into the firm and eventually become its president.

Jimmy Hoffa, Jr., the son of the man who followed Dave Beck in the Teamsters presidency, was different. The day of the 1976 Tournament, he was a thirty-five-year-old successful lawyer earning more than $70,000 a year. And while it was true that his specialty was labor law and many of his clients were from his father's Detroit local, it was also the opinion of the legal community that the younger Hoffa was now making it on his own as a damn smart lawyer.

One of Hoffa junior's first memories is of going hunting with his father. He was six or seven, and he remembers being left alone in the Canadian woods for hours with a rifle and a bottle of soda. It was his father's way of teaching him how to make it on his own. Hoffa taught his son other story-book virtues. Sunday family outings with his father and mother and his sister Barbara were lessons in the joy of hard work. They stopped at Teamsters picket lines so that Hoffa could inspect the troops. Physical fitness was stressed. Hoffa looked down on golf but he was a barbells-and-calisthenics fanatic. He put his son through the same drills. But he was arming his son with the virtues of hard work and discipline so that the son could rise above his own tough and scrappy world—a classic American story of evolution by generation.

Hoffa senior was the son of an unsuccessful coal prospector in the small town of Brazil, Indiana, who died when Hoffa was four. Hoffa hauled laundry home in a wagon for his mother to wash, chopped and sold wood, and scraped mussel shells off the bottom of the Wabash River to sell by the ton to button makers. When Viola Hoffa moved her family to Detroit, six years after her husband's death, Jimmy hauled ashes and passed out leaflets for patent medicines at factory gates. Hoffa quit school at fourteen in the middle of the seventh grade, to work full time. Three years later, while unloading boxcars at the Kroger grocery chain warehouse for 32 cents an hour, he organized his first strike.

Hoffa junior, at fourteen, was a middle-class youngster, a few years away from the all-city and all-state high-school football teams and the freshman and varsity teams at Michigan State. His first jobs were the summer pastimes of the middle class—a boat yard in Detroit, driving a truck through Alaska, clerking at a local law firm. He made the high-school honor society, had a B-plus average at Michigan State, got a foundation-sponsored internship to work in the state legislature, and graduated from one of the nation's best law schools, that of the University of Michigan.

Hoffa senior met his wife on a picket line at a laundry where she was striking to get a boost in her 17-cents-an-hour wage. His son met his wife at college football practice. Before the felony convictions that sent him to jail, Hoffa senior had had the kind of career that could get him arrested eighteen times in one day for strike activity. He had, in his own words, "a police record as long as your arm" for picket-line brawls. Hoffa junior's contact with the law was as an attorney representing his clients in federal and state courts. Hoffa senior despised politicians; he claimed they were all for sale. Hoffa junior had run unsuccessfully for state Representative and hoped to run for Congress. The father bragged that he had no political ideology. Hoffa junior was an activist Democrat who eagerly cast himself in the "Scoop Jackson, Pat Moynihan wing of the party." Hoffa senior told a reporter that he always wore white socks because "colored ones make my feet sweat." His son wears white socks only when he plays tennis.

The difference in appearance and style was instantly apparent on that early afternoon when Hoffa junior arrived for the first of a series of interviews throughout 1976, 1977 and 1978. The father, by most accounts, used to move through rooms fast, barking orders and pushing past anyone in the way. His son, arriving for lunch at Detroit's Caucus Club, acknowledged the woman who was checking coats with a quiet smile. He walked calmly to the center table that was reserved for him each midday. He was nearly six feet tall, compared to his father's 5 foot 5. There was confidence in his gaze, rather than combat. If he had been a football star at Michigan State, instead of second- and third-string during his sophomore year—before his father made him quit sports to concentrate on his books—he could have made a shaving-cream ad: smiling blue eyes, boyish grin, neat, regular features, fair skin that takes a perfect shave. He spoke confidently, softly and with precision. As he ate his sole, one fellow lawyer stopped by the table to chat about an arbitration they were involved in, and another to discuss a complicated case that had been decided the previous Monday by the Michigan Supreme Court.

That day and in subsequent interviews, it was difficult to talk to Jimmy Hoffa, Jr., about the Teamsters and his father. Like a detective asking a woman for the details of a rape, I squirmed at dragging him through a world he hadn't chosen but couldn't escape—the accusations against his father, the jailing of his father, the murder of his father.

An obituary that had been prepared by a Detroit newspaper in 1958 observed that with the possible exception of the mineworkers' John L. Lewis, no union leader had ever inspired such loyalty among his followers. His son reflected that loyalty. He defended his father's alliance with mobsters—Tony Accardo and Red Dorfman in Chicago, the Purple Gang in Detroit, Provenzano and his friends in New York and New Jersey—noting calmly, as if he had been through the discussion a hundred times before, that his father had used such people only to gain power and that he had planned to throw them out once he became union president.

Then why hadn't he thrown them out when he got to the top, and why instead had he refused to reform the union when the McClellan Committee, led by Chief Counsel Robert Kennedy, and other investigations put the pressure on?

Because, Hoffa junior explained calmly, he was so busy fighting off continual attacks by Robert Kennedy and other investigators that he hadn't had the chance to consolidate his strength enough to risk a reform purge.

And why had Bobby Kennedy and the others been after him?

Because Kennedy had a personal grudge against Hoffa, who had refused to be intimidated by Kennedy or by anyone else. The real tragedy was that if his father had had the chance to beat Fitzsimmons for the presidency at the 1976 convention elections, he would finally have been in a position to clean things up, because then he would have owed nothing to any of the mobsters. That's why his father had "been disappeared," he concluded.

Jimmy Hoffa, running and winning as an outsider against incumbent Fitzsimmons, might well have capped his career by reforming the union. And it is true that Hoffa used the thugs to climb to the top and that, in fact, his alliance with them had been encouraged by the fact that the employers his union was challenging had recruited muscle from the underworld organizations to break strikes in the old days.

That could not alter the realities that Hoffa junior must have known more intimately than his lunch partner. Another labor leader, Walter Reuther, from the same city in the same era had fought his way to the top of a big union—the United Auto Workers—without taking in organized crime as a partner. Besides, Hoffa not only had used the underworld for power; he also had shared in their crimes. He had made tens of thousands of dollars in extortion schemes that bled innocent, often small and poor, businessmen. He had threatened recalcitrant business with union troubles or violence. He had set up his wife, under her maiden name, in a truck-leasing company that received business from trucking companies eager to get Hoffa to go easy on the wages they had to pay their Teamsters drivers. He had bribed members of Congress with five or more hundred-dollar bills stuffed into a hand-delivered copy of the Teamsters monthly magazine. He had siphoned off millions from Teamsters' pension funds to make fraudulent loans to the mob. He had been convicted of mail fraud for conspiring to lift money from the Central States Pension Fund to bail him out of a failing land deal. He had been convicted of jury tampering.

It seemed too much an intrusion to argue these points strenuously with Hoffa junior. Just mentioning them obliquely—"How do you explain to people?"—invited an insistent, noncombative resistance. The convictions were frame-ups, Hoffa junior explained. The bribes and extortion schemes never happened. There was nothing illegal about his mother running a truck-leasing company. His father had to make pension fund loans to the mob and, besides, the Fund's board of trustees had approved them. Reuther and the United Auto Workers had their share of crooks. His heart was in it more than his head. When asked if *he* would have dealt with a Tony Provenzano, the conversation paused awkwardly.

In 1967, Hoffa junior opened his law office just a block and a half away from the Caucus Club on the top floor of Detroit's once elegant, now aging Guardian Building. Ten years later, he sat at his desk one morning, the successful senior partner of a firm of five lawyers. Hoffa senior had been in the habit of humiliating his subordinates. He had thought nothing of dressing them down in front of a large group for such sins as not having completed a phone call. On one occasion he beat an old assistant who disagreed with him at a meeting. His son was unfailingly polite to the secretary who handled his calls and to the young lawyers who did his leg work.

Going methodically through case files he had pulled to work on that morning, Hoffa placed and received calls from other lawyers hoping to negotiate out-of-court settlements. Most of his work involved unions in some way. Perhaps a union had retained him to fight a member's dismissal or failure to receive a workmen's compensation claim, or maybe a member had been referred by his union for a divorce or a criminal case. Much of this union business was Teamsters business. Among his clients was Local 299, the Detroit local where his father had started and where Hoffa loyalists still competed for power with Frank and Richard Fitzsimmons and their allies. His ties to the local were such that he had been both its counsel and its director of organizing. But there was no question that Hoffa now held these clients because of his own competence. His law firm was a successful, independent enterprise.

Still, as someone who did legal work for the Teamsters, Hoffa was part of a controversial group of lawyers that Teamsters watchers have dubbed the Teamsters Bar Association.

The TBA includes hundreds of lawyers around the country. Present and former members range from Gary Witlin, a slightly built, earnest young assistant counsel at Teamsters headquarters; to Leonard Boudin, the high priest of radical lawyers, whose young assistants had almost gagged one evening when Boudin told them during the Daniel Ellsberg trial that he wanted to take on Jimmy Hoffa as a client to fight his parole restrictions because he thought the constitutional issues were so important; to Alvin Baron, an aide of Allen Dorfman and a notoriously uncouth mobster, who, Teamsters financial reports indicated, had drawn tens of thousands of dollars in legal fees consulting for the Central States Pension Fund; to Payne Ratner, a former Kansas governor who, the McClellan Committee alleged, had used his political friendships to help scuttle an earlier Congressional investigation of the union that was chaired by a Congressman from his state.

There was also Edward Bennett Williams. By 1977 Williams was the most prominent TBA alumnus and America's pre-eminent defense lawyer. Twenty years earlier he had been Jimmy Hoffa's main spokesman at the McClellan Committee hearings. In the summer of 1957 he had also been Hoffa's lead lawyer in a criminal trial that highlighted many of the ethically questionable tactics that were used over the years by some Teamsters and members of the TBA.

In March of 1957, Hoffa had been arrested for attempting to bribe a lawyer, John Cheasty, to become a member of the McClellan Committee staff and obtain confidential committee memos for him. When Cheasty went to Robert Kennedy and told him of the offer, Kennedy arranged for the FBI to take pictures of Cheasty at street-corner meetings as he passed government documents to Hoffa in return for cash. It looked like an easy case. Coming as it did on the eve of Hoffa's planned ascension to the union presidency, it was to have been Kennedy's knock out blow. The night of the arrest Kennedy cheerfully promised to jump off the Capitol if Hoffa were not convicted. Four months later, Edward Bennett Williams offered to send him a parachute.

The trial took place in predominantly black Washington, D.C., where the jury of twelve included eight blacks. Williams attempted to portray the prosecution's key witness, lawyer Cheasty, as anti-black, accusing him of having investigated the NAACP and of trying to break up the Alabama bus boycott. Both charges were groundless, certainly irrelevant to the trial.

A second play to the black jurors involved the publication during the trial in July of an ad in Washington's black newspaper, with the heading, "The Facts Behind The Hoffa Trial." In the ad Hoffa and Williams were pictured as civil-rights heroes (Williams was called the "White Knight" and "Sir Galahad" of the civil-rights cause) and the judge in the case was described as a champion of the Old South. Also included was a picture of Williams and Hoffa with Martha Jefferson, a black attorney. The caption identified her as having joined the Williams defense team. Although on occasion Ms. Jefferson had gone to the front of the courtroom to confer with Williams or Hoffa while the jurors watched, she never said anything on the record in the trial, nor was her role in the case ever clear. The McClellan Committee later discovered that the director of the group that paid for the ad worked for a Michigan politician who had received political contributions from Hoffa-controlled Teamster funds.

A third controversial defense tactic involved the surprise appearance in the courtroom of black former boxing champion Joe Louis on July 15. Telling onlookers that Hoffa was an old friend, Louis greeted Hoffa and wished him well in full view of the jury at the start of the afternoon session. McClellan Committee investigators later found that Louis and Hoffa were mere acquaintances, and that Louis' travel and hotel arrangements had been made and paid for by Teamsters aide Barney Baker. It is not clear whether these events had more impact on the jury than Williams' generally brilliant trial performance, but on July 19 the jury acquitted Hoffa after only a few hours' deliberation.

At the time of the trial Williams asserted in an interview with reporter Clark Mollenhoff that he had nothing to do with the newspaper ad, except to have posed unwittingly for it, nor had he had anything to do with the Louis appearance. Two decades later there was no evidence to the contrary. Williams, however, contradicted his original account, when he explained in a 1976 interview that he had had Louis there because he had planned to call him as a character witness but then had changed his mind. The equally strong denial of another Hoffa lawyer involved in the case as a Williams assistant, William Bufalino, clashed with both of Williams' versions. Bufalino claimed, in a March 1977 interview, that Louis had appeared because he was dating Martha Jefferson, the black lawyer. Indeed, Louis later married Jefferson. To add to the confusion, Williams told me that Jefferson had not been involved in the case as a lawyer, while Bufalino claimed that she had been hired for her expertise in entrapment cases.

Also twenty years later, another potential jury-pleaser revealed that, like Louis, he had been approached by Barney Baker and invited to be seen with Hoffa in the courtroom. Monsignor George Higgins, one of Washington's leading Catholic clergymen, recalled in a 1977 interview that Baker, an old acquaintance, had called during the trial to ask, as Higgins remembered it, "that I come give 'James' some 'spiritual guidance' during a recess. When I told him Hoffa was welcome to come to my office, Barney insisted that he needed the spiritual guidance in the courtroom."

To Jimmy Hoffa, Jr., questions about the conduct of the TBA people who had helped his father over the years were subsumed by the methods of the prosecution. He had a good point. The government effort that sent his father to jail was perhaps the most sustained legal assault against one person our government has ever waged.

Joseph Kennedy, Sr., Robert's father, once told Harold Gibbons in a secret, unsuccessful meeting aimed at achieving peace between the Kennedys and the Teamsters that, "Every one in my family forgives—except Bobby."

When Robert Kennedy became Attorney General he remembered Hoffa's defiance of the McClellan Committee and the way Hoffa had slipped through the bribery case. He organized a special team of twenty lawyers and investigators headed by Walter Sheridan, a former FBI agent and a McClellan Committee investigator. Sheridan and his posse, reporting directly to the Attorney General in an arrangement that defied established Justice Department chain of command, set out to complete the job they and their boss had started. Around the Department they soon came to be called the "get-Hoffa squad."

Using hundreds of lawyers, IRS agents, FBI surveillants, wire tappers and informants, they got Hoffa in the jury-tampering conviction in Tennessee. It had involved springing a convicted felon from jail to plant him inside Hoffa's defense team. The informant learned about Hoffa's attempt to bribe the jurors. When Hoffa appealed his case on the grounds that the government had employed improper means, the Supreme Court allowed the constitutionally shaky strategy to stand, though four of the nine justices voted to invalidate the conviction. Chief Justice Earl Warren, one of the four dissenters, called the case "an affront to the quality and fairness of federal law enforcement." He described the Constitutional problems:

> Here the government reaches into the jail house to employ a man who was himself facing indictments far more serious [and later including one for perjury] than the one confronting the man against whom he offered to inform. It employed him not for the purpose of testifying to something that had already happened, but rather, for the purpose of infiltration, to see if crimes would in the future be committed. The government in its zeal even assisted him in gaining a position for which he could be witness to the confidential relationship of attorney and client.

New York Teamsters leader Barry Feinstein summed up Hoffa's perspective: "Sure he was guilty. But they could put you in jail, too, if they did that number of you—investigating every detail of your life. Who isn't guilty of something?"

For their part, the men involved in the Kennedy effort pointed accurately to Kennedy's unparalleled effectiveness as an Attorney General in fighting organized crime. Kennedy obtained, in addition to the Hoffa case, about two hundred indictments against Teamsters officials, and more than half resulted in convictions, though only a few were sentenced to prison.

But, in the end, the prosecutors' basic defense came down to a "good guys"-versus-"bad guys" rationale—an argument based on rule by men rather than rule by law that has a hollow ring.

"Sure we had a vendetta," one member of the "get-Hoffa squad" conceded ten years after Jimmy Hoffa was sent to jail. "But you have to understand how terrible this guy was . . . We weren't Nazis . . . But I guess in this day and age I'd have problems if other people organized a squad like this specifically against some other guy or group."

"I'd hate to see a group like the Hoffa squad become any sort of precedent," agreed William Hundley, now a brilliant defense lawyer, who had been Sheridan's nominal boss as head of the Justice Department's Criminal Division. "I think in our case it wasn't abused, only because of the people involved."

By 1977 there were enough tough questions involving the work of the TBA and their opponents to fill a law-school text on a lawyer's ethics and responsibilities.

But as the second anniversary of his father's disappearance approached, Jimmy Hoffa, Jr., didn't talk much about these broader issues. Only one question interested him: How could Bill Bufalino, a lawyer who had defended his father for years, now be the defense lawyer for the people who were suspected of murdering his father?

William E. Bufalino was perhaps the most colorful TBA member. In the ten years that Hoffa stood at the height of his power, Bufalino was the lawyer who could always be found at his side. Born in 1918 in the Pennsylvania coal town of Pittston, Bufalino abandoned what he said were his early ambitions to be a priest and became a lawyer. He served in the Army as a trial judge advocate during World War II. He was once named "Soldier of the Week." Afterward he came to Detroit, where he married the niece of alleged underworld boss Angelo Meli. He didn't practice law but went instead into the juke-box business.

In 1954, a Congressional subcommittee investigating racketeering in Detroit alleged that Bufalino had, in 1947, moved over to the union side of the juke-box trade under Jimmy Hoffa, and that his reign as president of Teamsters Local 985 was a

> gigantic wicked conspiracy to, through the use of force, threats of force and economic pressure, extort and collect millions of dollars from union members, nonunion members, and independent businessmen . . ."

Three years later, the McClellan Committee hammered away with similar accusations,with Chairman McClellan concluding that Bufalino's Local 985 "is a leech preying on working men and women to provide personal aggrandizement for Mr. Bufalino and his friends." Bufalino denied all the charges, and no criminal wrongdoing against him has ever been proven.

It was at the time when he was being charged with racketeering that Bufalino joined Hoffa's legal team. In an interview in 1977, Bufalino asserted that he had been a major force in the Hoffa legal battles. The pictures of him and Hoffa entering various courtrooms together on the walls of his Detroit office (he was still president of the still-controversial Local 985) featured the starring role. Others who were close to Hoffa disagree. "He was a clerk," said one Hoffa intimate. "He'd sit there and pull files for us."

Whatever Bufalino's role in defending Hoffa and the Teamsters, his role in defending himself has always been clear: from the 1950s on, Bill Bufalino has been an unabashed fighter for Bill Bufalino.

In 1959, citing among other virtues, his war record, his fluency in several languages, and his past membership in the G. K. Chesterton Poetry Society, Bufalino invoked an obscure Constitutional device to petition the Senate for a "redress of my grievances" brought on by the McClellan Committee's destruction of his good name—"my most cherished property right." The Senate ignored him. He sued Robert Kennedy for libel, but the case went nowhere. When *Life* magazine quoted a McClellan Committee report that had mixed up the details of Bufalino's family connection with alleged organized-crime figures, he sued *Life*. They settled for $25,000. Then he sued *Newsweek* and they paid him $10,000. (According to a *Newsweek* lawyer, they wanted to avoid the higher costs of a trial.) Other lawsuits followed. Soon he acquired a reputation as a lawyer ready and willing to sue at the drop of a bad word.

On at least one other occasion Bufalino's aggressive, flamboyant, lawyering had a liberating effect. In 1959 Bufalino found himself excluded from buying land in the exclusive Detroit suburb of Grosse Pointe, because the community had a "point system" that handicapped minorities. According to the court papers filed in this particular Bufalino lawsuit, to qualify to live in Grosse Pointe, Jews had to score 85 points, Italians 75, Greeks 65, and Poles 55. Points were awarded for education, reputation, neatness, and complexion. A light complexion was worth five points. Bufalino scored 69 points; he said he'd been labeled medium swarthy. Although his libel-and-slander suit was thrown out, the attention of an amused Detroit press was enough to inspire the enactment of a state law forbidding such screening. In 1977, Bufalino had been living at his Colonial, waterfall-adorned house in Grosse Pointe Shores for fifteen years.

In late 1975, Jimmy Hoffa, Jr., watched as Bill Bufalino fought for his father's accused murderers with that same flamboyant aggressiveness and to the same kind of press attention.

The suspects who were called before the Detroit grand jury investigating the Hoffa disappearance during late 1975 and early 1976 were Tony Provenzano and four other New Jerseyans: Salvatore Briguglio, forty-six; his brother Gabriel, thirty-eight; Stephen Andretta, forty-two; and his brother Thomas, thirty-eight. All five were represented by Bufalino, and four took the Fifth Amendment and refused to answer the grand jury's questions. Stephen Andretta was given immunity from prosecution on the basis of anything he said and thereby was deprived of his Fifth Amendment right to silence.

In his representation of Stephen Andretta, Bufalino made a mockery of the rule that forbids a lawyer to be present with his client inside the grand jury room. His client walked out of the room to consult him after almost every question. Stephen Andretta's testimony took about six weeks, during which he logged a record 1,117 trips outside the room to consult his lawyer. When federal prosecutor Robert Ozer criticized Bufalino for the delaying tactics, Bufalino filed a libel-and-slander suit against him. (It was dismissed.) When *Newsweek* suggested that Bufalino's clients were involved in the Hoffa case and identified Bufalino as their lawyer, he sued them too—claiming that a lawyer can be libeled by negative references to his clients. *Newsweek* decided to fight this time, and the case is still pending.

When Ozer tried to put Bufalino's clients in a line-up to be viewed by witnesses who may have seen Hoffa's abduction, Bufalino and his son, also a lawyer, objected so vigorously that a scuffle broke out between the Bufalinos and the feds. Ozer claimed later that, seated across from Bufalino in court, Bufalino muttered curses to him low enough so that the judge, an elderly man who was hard of hearing, could not hear them. "Bufalino was incredibly vicious," Ozer asserted. "But what was I supposed to do—get up and say 'Judge, he just called me a cocksucker.' " (Bufalino denied calling Ozer anything, although he used the same words to describe him to me in an interview.)

As the investigation dragged on, Bufalino had bumper stickers printed declaring: "Bill Bufalino says *'End Grand Jury Abuse.'* " He indignantly asserted his clients' innocence at each opportunity and theorized that the CIA might have had Hoffa killed.

Jimmy Hoffa, Jr., seethed. When he let it get to him one day in early 1976 and attacked Bufalino for being disloyal to his father, Bufalino sued him. Bufalino dropped the case when Hoffa promised not to repeat the accusation and put a letter in the court record praising Bufalino.

Years before, Hoffa junior had hung a color portrait of his father on the wall over the left side of his desk at the law office. Like most such brushed-over photographs it presented a softer, more peaceful version of the real thing. It has smoothed the rough edges of the brass-knuckle–minded union boss. The fire in his eyes simmered to a benevolent glow. Now, with Hoffa senior believed dead in a dump or incinerator somewhere between here and Newark, the portrait took on an eerie quality.

His father hovering over him as he went through his law books and his case files and his phone calls expressed the forces pulling at Hoffa junior in the second year of his father's disappearance. His father had given him the better life; he had pushed Jimmy junior up and away from a grimy, violent world, a pin-stripe world that Hoffa junior had come to treasure for himself and for his wife and their five- and six-year-old sons.

But he loved his father. And his father's murder beckoned him back to that other world. "Avenge and maybe pick up my mantle," the portrait on the wall seemed to say.

His father hadn't shielded him entirely. When times were rough he had expected his son to be there. When he was in prison, he had had Jimmy junior visit him regularly to carry messages out.

But the morning of July 31, 1975, brought the worst intrusion of all from his father's world.

Hoffa junior was asleep on vacation in Traverse City, Michigan, at 7 A.M. when he got a call from his mother—hysterical, crying so hard that he feared it would be fatal to a woman with a heart condition. At last, he had gotten her to explain. His father had not come home the night before. He had been due back at four o'clock that afternoon for a barbecue.

His father was a teetotaler, a boy-scout husband who came home every night; there was no chance he had gone out on a binge. He was meticulous; he phoned home if he was a few minutes late.

Hoffa chartered a plane to his parents' home at Lake Orion, north of Detroit. By about 1 P.M. the news had broken. Jimmy junior, his older sister, Barbara Crancer, and his mother waited, hoping it was a kidnapping and that they would get a ransom demand. The next week was a sleepless blur. Jimmy junior instinctively took over and answered the reporters' questions in the sweltering heat outside the Lake Orion cottage. The family got hundreds of calls from cranks claiming they had Hoffa. The family offered a $200,000 reward, which invited more tormenting phone calls. Eventually there came the horrible realization. They had killed him.

Hoffa junior, in a frenzy, called around the country to all his father's old friends. They said they were sorry. They knew nothing. He arranged for a secret meeting with Dorfman at the Detroit Airport. Dorfman knew nothing.

For the family, the absence of the body was nearly as bad as the loss itself. The murderers had inflicted a special kind of torture on the survivors. It allowed them to conjure up a new form of death every day. There could be no ending, no funeral, no rush of grief followed by acceptance, a rebuilding.

There could not even be a settling of his estate until seven years had passed; until then all his money would be tied up in a missing-persons trust, with his wife, Josephine, receiving some only as she established that she needed it. The man who had told his biographers in 1965 that he would not accede to his wife's desire for a large family, because he expected a violent, early death, had left his small family disarmed.

After a few weeks, Barbara Hoffa Crancer returned to her home in the suburbs of St. Louis, bitter about what she thought was an FBI effort to find her father that scarcely matched their earlier efforts to jail him. At one point, she told a family friend, I. Irving Davidson, that she wished the government "had a Walter Sheridan [the head of Kennedy's 'get-Hoffa-squad'] working on *this* case." Josephine Hoffa, who had cataracts and was in need of surgery, fell into a kind of sustained shock; she spent a good part of her days before the shrine of St. Jude that her husband had given her just before he disappeared.

Jimmy junior tried to pick up his life where he had left it. But he found himself distracted from his arbitrations and court appearances.

He tried to manage things for his mother, making the legal arrangements for her to draw some of the estate's money, shielding her from the press and curiosity seekers, and gradually removing his father's clothes and other reminders from their house. He took the nut calls that still came in. He fenced with the IRS over claims that Hoffa—and now Hoffa's estate, if that's what it had come to—owed thousands of dollars in back taxes. And he badgered the FBI and the state police about what they were doing or what he thought they weren't doing. Looking for clues of his own, he kept up the calls to family contacts around the country and became a kind of information exchange center for reporters investigating the case.

As he dipped in and out this way between his world and his father's, something else began to happen. People started urging him to run for the union presidency at the June 1976 convention. Hoffa thought seriously about it. He was a member of Local 299, so he simply needed to be appointed by one of his father's loyal allies in the local as a delegate to the convention to be eligible to run there against Fitzsimmons. But his mother and his wife both opposed it. They were scared. He was scared, too. Besides, however much the rank and file loved his father and resented his death, the delegates at the convention—who were not rank-and-filers, but local officials—were likely to be Fitzsimmons loyalists, especially now that they had been given such a vivid demonstration of the dangers of boat rocking. He decided not to run.

He didn't entirely retreat to his world either. When the June 1976 convention came, he reacted in a way that typified the ambivalence that would dominate his life in the coming years. The toughness he knew his father would have expected of him demanded that he face these people, just as the loyalty his father had expected demanded that he keep trying to find a way to get even. Yet he wouldn't trade in the life he had built for an all-out fight. So he went to the convention, not as a candidate, but as an observer—to face them down and, he hoped, to gather some more clues talking to people. He brought his mother to show them that the Hoffas were strong.

The trip embittered him further. Tony Provenzano looked him in the eye, smiled and started to console him before Hoffa junior spun on his heels. Fitzsimmons, afraid of the audience reaction, arranged that Josephine Hoffa's presence at the convention not be announced officially to the delegates until she had left the hall one afternoon to get some rest. Hoffa junior stayed through it all. He heard all the unctuous speeches by his father's old subordinates praising Fitzsimmons. He exchanged gossip about the elevation to high power and money of this or that unworthy Fitzsimmons courtier, and watched as they strutted through the lobbies, the restaurants and the casinos. He withstood these and other torments and then returned to his law office.

Through this year and the next this would be his wrenching compromise settlement with that portrait over his desk. He would keep to his world of the courtroom and the Caucus Club. But he would also keep the gossip lines open, stung when he heard of the enemy's good fortune and chuckling with bitter delight when he heard bad news for them. In the back of his mind and in enticing talks with old loyalists, he toyed with the possibility of plunging all the way at the convention in 1981; although his real ambition was to run for election in *his* world—for the Congress. He pestered the FBI and bitched about their incompetence, while passing along tips or possibilities to them, to reporters, or to anyone else who might be helpful in his sidelines fight to settle the score.

For all the agony it caused, the absence of Hoffa's body had positive repercussions. If the body had been found in Michigan, the feds could not have entered the investigation. It would have been a case only for the Michigan State Police. Without a body the FBI could maintain the assumption that Hoffa had been taken across state lines, a federal crime. The FBI had its shortcomings, especially at the beginning, when kidnapping experts had been assigned to the case instead of the organized-crime experts. But in resources, in capacity to conduct the necessary out-of-state investigation in places like New Jersey and upstate New York, and in general ability and perseverance, the feds surpassed the Michigan police. The director of the Michigan police had declared the case unsolvable a few days after the disappearance.

Actually, federal law-enforcement officials knew quite a lot about what had happened to Jimmy Hoffa and why.

On January 27 and 28, 1976, FBI director Clarence Kelley convened a conference of all FBI field-office people and federal prosecutors who had been involved in the Hoffa case. The Hoffa investigation had by then been code-named "Hoffex" and a fifty-page "Hoffex Conference" briefing memo covering all the information gathered thus far was prepared for the conferees.

Much of the Hoffex memo confirmed or recapitulated the bare-bones theory of the disappearance, some of which had been previously leaked to the press. Hoffa had left his house, according to Josephine, at one-fifteen on the afternoon of July 30, 1975. He told her he was going to a two o'clock meeting at the Machus Red Fox Restaurant in Bloomfield, a suburb of Detroit. This was supposed to be a peace meeting between Hoffa and Tony Provenzano, arranged and attended by Anthony "Tony Jack" Giacalone, a Detroit gang lieutenant who was close to Hoffa and the Teamsters. At two-fifteen Hoffa called his wife to say that the men he was to meet were late. That was the last anyone had heard from him. The prevailing theory, as expressed in the Hoffex memo, was that Hoffa had been picked up at the restaurant parking lot by Charles "Chuckie" O'Brien, ostensibly to go to the Provenzano-Giacalone meeting. He had been murdered soon thereafter. O'Brien, the suspected pick-up man, had been raised by the Hoffa family since childhood. Though he had had a falling-out with Hoffa in 1974 and had gone over to the Fitzsimmons camp, he was, as the Hoffex memo put it, "one of the few persons JRH [Hoffa] would get into a car with." The memo described O'Brien as "age 41 . . . brought into Teamsters by JRH and supported by him. Well known by Teamsters officials and Detroit Cosa Nostra and calls Tony Giacalone 'Uncle Tony.' He is known as a habitual liar." The connection between Giacalone and Chuckie O'Brien, the Hoffex memo explained, was that O'Brien's deceased mother had been Giacalone's girl friend, and a close friend of Josephine Hoffa.

The suspected hit men were three of those New Jerseyans who had been Bill Bufalino's clients, described in the Hoffex memo as Provenzano's "trusted associates." The first, Thomas Andretta, thirty-eight, was a tall strikingly good-looking, soft-spoken member of Provenzano's Teamsters Local 560. His criminal convictions included hijacking, loan-sharking, and a 1971 counterfeiting scheme for which he served two years in federal prison. The probation report from his loan-sharking conviction said that Andretta had finished 124th in a class of 126 in high school and that he had put out a "contract" on the FBI agent who had arrested him in the hijacking case. The second suspected hit man was Gabriel Briguglio, thirty-six. He hardly looked the part; he was five feet, two inches tall, with soft, boyish features. Briguglio was a vice-president of the Provenzano-controlled Teamsters Local 84 in New Jersey. The third suspect was Salvatore Briguglio, Gabriel's older brother, forty-five. "Sally Bugs," as he was called, was believed to have several Provenzano-inspired "hits" under his belt, although he denied that he was anything other than a hard-working business agent for Teamsters Local 560. He was five feet seven inches tall, and huskier than his brother.

Provenzano and Hoffa were said to have had a "falling out" while the two were serving time in Lewisburg Prison. (Provenzano was there for a labor-racketeering extortion conviction.) The Hoffex memo reported that the reason for the dispute was that Hoffa had supposedly refused to help Provenzano, a long-time friend, obtain a pension payment from the Teamsters.

Eighteen months after the memo was written, an inmate who was in Lewisburg with Hoffa and Provenzano recalled in an interview that he had broken up a near fist fight between the two in July of 1967 over a much broader issue. He claimed that as both men sat in prison, they were dividing up Teamsters turf. "Tony was explaining to Jimmy how he was going to get right back into things in New Jersey," the inmate recalled. "Well, Jimmy exploded at him. 'Look,' he said, 'I dealt with you guys and it almost got me killed before and it's got me so I'm in here now. And I don't like it in here. When you get out, you guys are going to have to be on your own.' Well, it went on like that for a while, until they were screaming and almost came to blows. Tony's cheeks were red and twitching, he was so mad. Finally, he came towards Hoffa screaming, 'If you don't get out of my shit and back off of me, you'll end up like Castellito. They won't find so much as a finger nail of yours. Jimmy yelled 'Bullshit,' and that's when I broke them up."

Provenzano's reported reference to "Castellito" would not have been lost on Hoffa. Anthony Castellito was the New Jersey union leader who had disappeared in 1961 and for whose abduction and murder Provenzano was indicted five and a half years after he left Lewisburg.

The same inmate who says he saw the Hoffa-Provenzano confrontation and claims he was Hoffa's best friend in jail ("We played handball together, lifted weights together, ran the track together, and ate all our meals together") also recalled that Hoffa and Provenzano had had union arguments before in the law section of the prison library, but that after this "chow hall" confrontation they never talked to each other.

As a convicted bank robber, the inmate has a credibility problem, which is compounded by the fact that at the time of this interview he was trying to sell a book that included these recollections. Also, the story of the 1967 fight seems too perfectly fitted to the events of July 30, 1975. Still, a source who worked at the prison in 1967 did confirm the fight, although he was not aware of the issues involved. FBI sources also said in interviews that they too had heard of a Hoffa-Provenzano prison feud.

More significant, as yet unreported details in the Hoffex memo seem similarly to confirm the Hoffa-Provenzano feud, and Giacalone's self-professed role in patching it up, which might have led to the Hoffa-Giacalone-Provenzano meeting Hoffa thought he was going to on July 30. The Hoffex memo reported that on December 4, 1974, Anthony Giacalone met Jimmy Hoffa, Jr., in the hallway of the Miami, Florida, condominium where both Giacalone and Jimmy Hoffa, Sr., had apartments. (The building was built with a Central States Pension Fund loan.) "During this meeting," the memo recounted, "Giacalone told Hoffa's son that Anthony Provenzano was saying some unpleasant things about JRH [Hoffa], and pressed Hoffa's son to have his father 'get together with Provenzano and settle their differences.' " In a later interview Hoffa would confirm the FBI account of the Florida hallway meeting with Giacalone.

The memo proceeded to report another meeting of Anthony Giacalone, his brother Vito, Jimmy Hoffa, Jr., and Jimmy Hoffa, Sr., that took place in Hoffa junior's law office on May 15, 1975: ". . . the meeting again centered around JRH's meeting with Anthony Provenzano to 'settle differences' and 'clear the air.' JRH advised both Giacalones he did not want to meet with Provenzano calling Provenzano 'a bum.' . . . According to young Hoffa, the Giacalones persisted in their attempts to arrange a meeting, stating 'there's got to be a meeting' and further advising JRH that Provenzano was agreeable to meet JRH any place, any time. The meeting terminated with Hoffa telling both Giacalones he would not meet Provenzano anywhere."

The Hoffex memo went on to report that Hoffa's wife had told the FBI that in July Hoffa had received a phone call from Provenzano and that her husband had told her that Provenzano had asked for Hoffa's help in something and that Hoffa had refused. Also, five days after Hoffa disappeared, Mrs. Hoffa gave the FBI a sheet of paper that he had taped to the lampshade on his desk, listing his appointments that week. Among the eleven notations was "TG 2:30 Wed 14

Mile Tel Fox Rest Maple Road.'' "TG" no doubt stood for Tony Giacalone, and "14 Mile Tel Fox Rest Maple Road" is the approximate address and description of the Machus Red Fox.

Now, a certain Louis Linteau became important to the mystery. A former president of Pontiac, Michigan, Teamsters Local 614, Linteau owned Airport Service Lines, a Detroit airport limousine service. By 1975 he had become, according to the Hoffex memo, one of Hoffa's closest friends, and a "buffer" between Hoffa and people wishing to meet with Hoffa. According to the Hoffex memo, "Linteau revealed that on at least two occasions Anthony Giacalone went through him to attempt to set up a meeting with JRH." Although Hoffa turned down these requests, the memo reports that Linteau told the FBI agents that on July 26, 1975, he went to Hoffa's home at Lake Orion, where Hoffa told him that his meeting with Giacalone and probably Provenzano was set for Wednesday, July 30, at the Machus Red Fox Restaurant.

The FBI characterized Linteau in the Hoffex memo as someone known as a "notorious con man." The remainder of his account of the events of July 30 seems to bear that out. It is known for sure, according to FBI interviews with Linteau's employees at Airport Service Lines, that Hoffa arrived at Airport Service Lines at 1:30 P.M. that day—a half hour before his scheduled meeting at the Machus Red Fox, looking for Linteau. According to one employee questioned by the FBI, Hoffa said that he wanted Linteau to go to a meeting at the Machus Red Fox with him and that the meeting was with Anthony Giacalone.

Linteau told the FBI that he hadn't been asked by Hoffa to go to the meeting. At 3:05, he claimed, he had returned to his office from lunch and some shopping, and twenty-five minutes later, at 3:30, he had received a phone call from Hoffa stating that "the bastards are an hour and a half late." The time of this call—3:30—is important, since it would place Hoffa alive and free at that time, making post-3:30 alibis for the suspected murderers more important than pre-3:30 alibis. This is where the FBI had problems with Linteau's account. The Hoffex memo reported that the feds had interviewed Thomas Carson, a Detroit Airport supervisor Linteau told them he was talking to when Hoffa called. "Carson states," the memo reported, that "he overheard a female tell Linteau that JRH was on the other line. Carson places the time of this telephone call between 1:30 and 2:30 P.M. stating he believed it was closer to 2:30 P.M."

Based on these and other interviews, the Hoffex memo surmised that "Linteau was made aware of the July 30, 1975, meeting with Mr. Giacalone and Anthony Provenzano by JRH during the July 26, 1975, meeting at the Hoffa residence, and more than likely was either told by JRH or at least JRH implied to Linteau that Linteau's presence was expected at the meeting on July 30, 1975." The implication, then, is that somehow Linteau got the message to stay away from the meeting because Hoffa's murder was planned and, further, that someone told Linteau to lie or develop a bad memory about the time of Hoffa's phone call, causing him to say that it was an hour later than it was. For these reasons, the Hoffex memo concluded, "Linteau may remain a key to this investigation." Since then, the FBI has tried repeatedly to shake his story about the 3:30 phone call.

Enter Ralph Picardo. Picardo is a former truck driver in Tony Provenzano's Local 560 who was convicted of murder in 1974 and was in Trenton State Prison the day Hoffa disappeared. The Hoffex memo reveals that on November 5, 1975, more than three months after the disappearance, Picardo contacted federal agents with explosive but uncorroborated information about the role of Provenzano, the Briguglios and the Andrettas. According to the memo, "Picardo alleges that in August, 1975, a few days after the disappearance of JRH, he was visited at the New Jersey State Penitentiary . . . by Stephen and Thomas Andretta . . . regarding a business owned by Picardo. When Thomas Andretta [was] out of the room, [Stephen] Andretta asked Picardo if federal agents had been to see him." According to the Hoffex memo, Stephen Andretta "made admissions and references that Provenzano's group was involved in the JRH disappearance." Also, according to the memo, Picardo told the agents that Stephen Andretta had told him "he was not present in Detroit, but had stayed in New Jersey to provide an alibi for Tony Pro." The memo goes on to note that an FBI check confirmed that Picardo had been visited by the Andretta brothers when Picardo claimed they visited him and that Tony Pro had told the FBI that he was with Stephen Andretta in New Jersey the day Hoffa disappeared. "Picardo speculates," the memo continues, "that inasmuch as the Andrettas and Briguglios are Provenzano's most trusted associates, that it would follow if Provenzano was involved in the disappearance of JRH, they would be also."

Finally the memo plugs Picardo's credibility—a problem, given his criminal record and the fact that he hoped to trade his revelations for a softening of his prison term. "It should be noted," the memo says, "that unrelated information concerning the illegal activities of Teamsters Local 560 [the major Provenzano local] has been provided by Picardo. This information led to a search of Local 560 in which numerous loan-sharking records were obtained, as Picardo had indicated."

Meanwhile, at the Red Fox Restaurant, the FBI had found, according to the Hoffex memo, potentially more solid proof of the Provenzano connection: possible eyewitnesses.

Soon after the disappearance, the FBI had conducted an investigation at the restaurant and the surrounding shopping center so exhaustive that it seems better scripted to the old FBI TV shows than to the FBI's more modest real-world record. Hundreds of employees at the restaurant and surrounding stores in the shopping center were questioned. Reservation lists, credit-card charges and other restaurant records, including time checks on when luncheon orders left the kitchen, were examined so carefully that, according to the Hoffex memo, the Bureau agents were able "to place customers into the restaurant, ordering their food and paying their bills within a much more specific time frame than the witnesses themselves were able to do based on recall." As a result, the FBI found six people who had seen Hoffa. All said they had noticed him there between 2:00 and 2:50 P.M. All said that he appeared to be waiting for someone. Most important, two people seem to have seen two of the suspects in the abduction at the same time they saw Hoffa.

One of these two witnesses told the FBI that he saw Hoffa leave the parking lot in a maroon Lincoln or Mercury, along with three other men, one of whom he identified as Chuckie O'Brien. His description of the car matched that of the maroon Mercury that O'Brien conceded to the FBI he had been driving that day. The car belonged to Tony Giacalone's son, Joey.

Another witness told the FBI on August 15, 1975, that she had seen a white male in a brown or maroon "flashy" car at approximately 2:00 P.M. in the Machus Red Fox parking lot. On December 6, 1975 the FBI brought the Briguglio brothers and Thomas Andretta in to appear for a line-up. After they had refused to be in the line-up and their lawyer, William Bufalino, according to the Hoffex memo, had generated "much confusion," a judge ordered them to participate. The second witness looked out at them through a one-way window and positively identified Salvatore Briguglio as the person she had seen in the car in the parking lot.

The suspects weren't prosecuted on the basis of these eyewitness identifications, and the identifications have never been publicly revealed by the federal authorities, because the witnesses' testimony could not meet trial standards. Although the first witness did identify O'Brien positively, he seemed to the FBI, as one agent later put it, "like he was trying too hard to help us." He had remarked to the agents that he had read in the papers about how "it looked like they were getting away with it." In a trial, a good lawyer like Bufalino would easily have probed those biases and discredited an identification of someone whose picture had repeatedly been in the newspapers before a witness had "identified" him to the FBI. Bufalino would have brought out that, though the man had identified O'Brien, he had not identified the Briguglios or Thomas Andretta as having been at the Red Fox when he viewed them in the lineup.

The second witness readily admitted to the FBI that she had seen Salvatore Briguglio's picture in the paper as a probable suspect the day before the lineup and was about to contact the FBI about him to tell them that he was the man she had seen with Hoffa when they contacted her to come view the lineup. Bufalino could claim that her identification of Briguglio at the lineup was tainted. Constitutional standards might have forbidden her identification from even being introduced at a trial.

The two eyewitnesses gave the FBI independent confirmations of their theory. In the guilt-beyond-reasonable-doubt world of the courtroom, they provided nothing.

It turns out, however, that the FBI did have some important negative evidence that could not be used in court to prove the case against the suspects but could prove that the suspects' claims about July 30, 1975, were false. Unknown to the suspects, information that was gathered both before and since the Hoffex memo had shattered most of their alibis.

The easiest alibi to penetrate was Chuckie O'Brien's. He took the Fifth Amendment at the Detroit grand jury investigating the Hoffa case. But before that, in August, he had given the FBI so many inconsistent accounts of where he was and what he did on July 30, 1975, that the Hoffex memo cited his reputation as "a pathological liar who borders on being totally incompetent." Beyond his own inconsistencies, O'Brien's claims as to where he was during the key ninety minutes of two-thirty to four had not checked out with any of the people he said he was with when the FBI questioned them.

The Briguglio brothers and Thomas Andretta were, at the end of 1977, probably still assuming that their alibis were solid. Not true. A post-Hoffex-memo development in the case in 1976 and 1977 was the steady breakdown of their July 30 account of where they were. Although they also took the Fifth Amendment at the grand jury, their claim, through Bufalino's interviews and through Stephen Andretta— who was given immunity and forced to testify—has always been that on July 30, 1975, they were playing cards at the Local 560 office in Union City, New Jersey, with Tony Provenzano and Stephen Andretta. In an interview in 1977, an outraged Sammy Provenzano told me of the suffering his family had gone through as a result of all the bad publicity, and then explained the form of eight-handed rummy the group and other union associates had played that day. It was not a claim calculated to prove their devotion to their union jobs, but it kept them out of Detroit that day. To back it, they thought they had set up a number of corroborating witnesses—the Local's secretaries, elevator operators and others, many of whom were also represented by William Bufalino at the Detroit grand jury, to verify their whereabouts that day. But, according to key federal law-enforcement officials who talked about the case in 1977 and 1978, at least one corroborating witness has since backed away. Also, Stephen Andretta's grand jury testimony was not consistent in several small but important details with what some of the alibi witnesses had said. One of the witnesses told me in 1977 that he had been told by one of the suspects that "we should refresh our memories and recall we had seen them [the Briguglios and the Andrettas] here that day. He told us they [the Briguglios and the Andrettas] were here, but that, just in case we forgot, we'd better not let the cops pressure us into saying we didn't see them, because that would cause us all kinds of problems."

Provenzano also took the Fifth before the grand jury. The FBI, as part of its organized-crime surveillance effort, had seen and followed him in Detroit a few days before the disappearance. But he had a solid New Jersey alibi for July 30: he was seen there by law-enforcement officials. This would fit a Provenzano pattern—setting up in advance and building an indisputable alibi for the day. His 1976 indictment for setting up the 1961 abduction and murder of Castellito stated that the crime took place on the day Provenzano was married in Florida.

Tony Giacalone also had an airtight alibi. So many people had seen him having a massage and haircut at Detroit's Southfield Athletic

Club, that the Hoffex memo concluded that "almost everyone inter-viewed at the SAC complex revealed that Giacalone definitely ap-peared to be establishing an alibi, inasmuch as he made himself very visible, which is not his normal style." It was only a guess; the FBI assumed he deliberately established his alibi, because it was so un-usually solid.

What the FBI didn't guess about, however, was that Hoffa, dead or alive, had been in the car owned by Giacalone's son that Chuckie O'Brien admits he was driving on July 30.

Soon after the Hoffa disappearance, the FBI impounded the car and examined it with microscopes and four dogs trained to recognize human scents. Although it is not in the Hoffex memo, an FBI affida-vit that was filed in 1975 to support a request for a search warrant of an incinerator company where Hoffa's body is believed to have been taken, stated that the dogs "exhibited positive responses to the pres-ence of Hoffa's scent in the rear-seat compartment" of the car. "The three dogs who are owned and were handled by the two nationally recognized experts," the affidavit continues, "also exhibited positive responses to the presence of Hoffa's scent in the trunk compartment of the said automobile." One federal investigator explained in an interview that the scent in the trunk could have drifted there from the back seat, without Hoffa having been in the trunk, but that Hoffa's presence in the back seat of the car driven by O'Brien that day "was absolutely definite."

The Hoffex memo stated that the FBI microscope hunt yielded still better evidence: a "single, three-inch brown head hair" in the back seat with "characteristics similar to JRH hairs," and "a positive reaction to the presence of blood was found on the chemical located on the surface of the hair" but that "not enough of the substance was available for additional tests." However, a top federal investigator later reported that further tests conducted after the Hoffex memo was written revealed "much more definite signs of Hoffa's blood, hair and skin in that car. . . . We know for sure he was in the back seat."

The FBI has Hoffa in the back seat of a Giacalone car driven by suspect Chuckie O'Brien. Where did the body go?

The FBI affidavit describing the dog scents and asking for a war-rant to search a garbage incinerating company is the most surprising document in the government's case file; it theorizes about what hap-pened to the body, and it claims that Frank Fitzsimmons may have had advance knowledge of the Hoffa murder and something to do with the disposal of the body.

The government's affidavit, filed in August 1975 by an FBI agent and sealed from the public, asked a judge for a warrant to search the premises of the Central Sanitation Services in Hamtramck, Michigan, near Detroit. The company was owned by Raffael Quasarano, sixty-six at the time of the disappearance, and Peter Vitale, who was sixty-eight. Alleging that the two men are "Detroit syndicated-crime figures," the FBI agent said in the affidavit, "I believe that probable cause exists to believe that Raffael Quasarano and Peter Vitale have participated in the killing and disposal of the body of James R. Hoffa, and that Hoffa's body was destroyed at the premises at 8215 Moran Street, Hamtramck, Michigan, by means of a shredder, compactor, and/or incinerator located on the premises occupied by Central Sanitation Services. . . ."

The FBI based its opinion largely on information provided by two FBI informants, and supplemented by FBI field investigation.

"Informant 1," the affidavit reported, "has been an FBI informant for approximately ten years, during which period he has provided information . . . on several hundred occasions, which . . . has been consistently established as reliable as the basis of subsequent physical or court-ordered electronic surveillance or by information independently obtained from other reliable informants or witnesses. More than one hundred arrests and convictions have resulted from the information provided by Informant 1. . . ."

Having laid groundwork for Informant 1's credibility the affidavit continued: "Informant 1 has advised FBI agents, as recently as August 7, 1975, that he has personal knowledge, obtained directly from persons present, that at least ten murder victims have been disposed of by [Raffael] Quasarano and [Peter] Vitale through and by the facilities described herein. Quasarano and Vitale own and operate Central Sanitation Services, on which premises are located an extremely large shredder, compactor, and incinerator . . . utilized commercially . . . for the destruction of . . . refuse. Informant 1 has related that these facilities are also utilized by Quasarano and Vitale for the total destruction of the bodies of murder victims in extremely important syndicate murders. Informant 1 has advised that he believes Hoffa to be a victim of such a murder and Hoffa's body to be totally destroyed by means of the aforesaid facilities. . . ."

Next, the affidavit suggests the possibility of Fitzsimmons' involvement; it states that Informant 1's belief about Hoffa's body being incinerated by Quasarano and Vitale was "reinforced" by the fact that the informant "personally observed" Frank Fitzsimmons "at a clandestine meeting" with the two syndicate garbage men, Quasarano and Vitale, in late July at a Detroit restaurant.

The affidavit cited "Informant 2," who had been an FBI Detroit syndicate informant for "approximately twelve years" and had "provided information with a frequency that averages once a month," that had been "completely reliable." This informant told the FBI the same Quasarano-Vitale incinerator story.

No matter how reliable the FBI claims they are, informants must be regarded skeptically, especially if they are providing information on a case important to the agents who are paying them. Except that Informant 1 says he personally witnessed the Fitzsimmons meeting, the information offered by the two informants is hearsay. By itself the alleged Fitzsimmons meeting with Quasarano and Vitale proves nothing. On the other hand, a top Justice Department lawyer involved in the case who is normally as skeptical about the FBI and its informants as any outsider, said in an interview that "these guys were really convincing. They are two totally separate independent people who came up with the same information. . . ."

When the FBI checked further on Fitzsimmons' activities in Detroit the results, some of which were reported in the affidavit, seemed to add weight to the informants' claims. Fitzsimmons had conceded to the FBI, when questioned on August 12, 1975, that he had been in Detroit from July 25 to July 27. He had given the federal agents a summary of his activities but had not mentioned the alleged Quasarano-Vitale meeting. The FBI had not asked him specifically about it at that time. ("They did a real half-assed job," one top government lawyer recalled.) Justice Department officials in Washington had refused to allow the Detroit lawyers to ask Fitzsimmons anything about the Hoffa case when he appeared at the grand jury to discuss his sons' insurance scheme in November six weeks after the Seventh Annual Fitzsimmons International. However, in a later interview Fitzsimmons told me that such a meeting never took place, and he added that, while he knew Quasarano, he hadn't seen him or spoken with him in twenty years, and that he did not know Vitale.

In their August 12, 1975, interview Fitzsimmons gave the FBI a version of the time he had arrived at his motel in Detroit on July 25 that conflicted with the FBI check of the motel's records. This left a ten-hour gap in his activities, during the time, the informants say, the restaurant meeting took place.

The FBI also found Fitzsimmons' trip to Detroit curiously clandestine. The FBI search warrant affidavit noted that "although Fitzsimmons is a nationally prominent IBT [International Brotherhood of Teamsters] official, FBI interviews with numerous Detroit Teamsters union leaders have disclosed that Teamsters union leaders in Detroit were unaware that Fitzsimmons was coming to Detroit in July 1975 and are, to this day, unaware that he was in Detroit in July 1975." Further, the FBI found that although Fitzsimmons was usually chauffeured in one of the Teamsters local's fleet when he visited a city like Detroit, an official of Central Sanitation Services had been asked by Quasarano at the last minute to lend his car to Fitzsimmons for the weekend for Fitzsimmons to drive himself.

Why the secrecy about the Detroit trip? Why the use of a Central Sanitation Services car, especially if, as Fitzsimmons told me, he had not had anything to do with Quasarano in twenty years and didn't know Vitale? In our interview, Fitzsimmons said that the Detroit trip was not a secret, and that he couldn't remember whose car he had used. He offered that he might have rented a car, but that, if he did, he paid cash and had no record of the rental.

It must be pointed out that when the FBI did get the warrant to search the Central Sanitation Services incinerator in 1975, their scent dogs found no trace of Hoffa. And it seems nonsensical that Fitzsimmons would have to arrange personally for Hoffa's disposal, even if he had been involved in, or knew about, the murder. But FBI sources are quick to point out that they always expected that the dogs had gotten to the incinerator much too late to catch the scent. "It was just an outside shot," one investigator later conceded. And serious questions remain unanswered about the Fitzsimmons meeting as reported by the supposedly "reliable" informants and his alleged use of a Central Sanitation car during his visit to Detroit. By the time of the Eighth Annual Fitzsimmons Invitational in October 1977, nothing more was known about the possibility of Fitzsimmons having had a personal role in the murder, but the Quasarano-Vitale incinerator was the best theory going on what happened to Hoffa's body.

Unknown to the law men working the Hoffa case was another coincidence that linked the Quasarano-Vitale sanitation company to the New Jersey mob and Tony Provenzano. In 1976, federal prosecutors in New Jersey had come across a scheme to deposit union funds in a small bank, the Bank of Bloomfield, in return for which the bank was to make unsecured loans to mob-dominated businesses. It was a perfect way to avoid prosecution under the new labor and pension laws: the unions wouldn't be giving the money to the mob. The banks would—in return for getting union deposits. The case involved major organized-crime figures, including the reputed "boss of bosses" Carmine Galente, who, the prosecutors believed, had come across the Hudson River from New York to work the deal in concert with the old Vito Genovese family, of which Provenzano was a member. In the federal government's prosecution of the bank president (they couldn't establish a case against the mob figures, because no one would testify) one bank executive listed the mob loans that had been involved. Had the Hoffa-case investigators seen the list, they would have seen Central Sanitation Services in Hamtramck, Michigan, on there for an $85,000 loan from the small New Jersey bank in late December 1974 for the purchase of new equipment. Bank records showed that the loan had never been paid back.

The reported Fitzsimmons meeting with Quasarano and Vitale, of course, raises broader questions of Fitzsimmons' over-all involvement in, or knowledge of, the Hoffa murder.

In this regard, there's also the curious case of Chuckie O'Brien. Everyone who investigated the case seems to agree that O'Brien was driving the car in which Hoffa was abducted. The only real question left is whether he was an unwitting dupe in the murder, used to lure Hoffa into the car without knowing what was going to happen, or if he was involved in the planning. Whatever the case, he would still know, and be able to testify about, what happened after Hoffa got in the car and who was there. He took the Fifth Amendment at the grand jury.

The day after the murder, O'Brien started a job given him by Fitzsimmons as a "general organizer" for the International, and he was sent to do organizing in Arkansas, where his wife was living. O'Brien had his organizing job through 1975, '76, and '77 (at $49,000 a year according to the latest available records), although no one has been able to cite any union work he has done in Arkansas or in Florida, where he also lived during that time. In 1976 he was indicted and convicted of accepting a gift of a new car from an employer with whom he had negotiated union contracts in a Michigan Teamsters job that he held before the Hoffa disappearance. He stayed on Fitzsimmons' payroll through his appeals.

Why did Fitzsimmons keep a man on his payroll who had taken the Fifth rather than cooperate with the authorities in the Hoffa case and who had been convicted of a union-related crime? In an interview, Fitzsimmons explained to me that O'Brien was "a good worker" and that "I don't know nothing about his involvement in the Hoffa case." He was unable to provide examples of O'Brien's successful organizing efforts.

The real problem with believing that O'Brien's union job was part of a Fitzsimmons-approved payoff to keep him quiet was that it seemed too amateurishly obvious to be part of a professional plan to eliminate Hoffa. "Oh yeah, lots of things in the case are obvious," one lawyer who had been involved in the case from the beginning observed in 1977. "But you don't see any indictments, do you? Remember, these guys aren't worried about public opinion. They're just worried about what can be proven in court. And all of these 'obvious' things are just circumstantial evidence that proves nothing."

Throughout the investigation there had also been rumors that Teamsters leaders, including Fitzsimmons, had referred beforehand to Hoffa's imminent removal from the scene. According to a federal investigator, several people, including Fitzsimmons, were overheard by an FBI informant, at a La Costa meeting of Teamsters leaders about two weeks before the disappearance, saying that Hoffa would soon not be a problem. A talk with one vice-president about two years after July 30, 1975, also suggests that this may be true. The vice-president recalled that he "got the distinct impression late in the spring that they had some plans for Jimmy. Nobody said it right out. But we got the message." Second Vice-President Harold Gibbons was reported by sources close to him to have been given "a message" to carry to Hoffa several months before the disappearance, that he had better stay out of Teamsters activities or face elimination.

More significantly, by 1977 the FBI had developed what one investigator characterized as "strong evidence" that Provenzano and Giacalone had made "at least two other attempts in the two months before the disappearance" to set up Hoffa's murder. It seems clear that the attempt that finally worked was the play by Giacalone to get Hoffa to a peace meeting with Provenzano on July 30. But this raises another tough question: if murder was the intention, why establish this record of a planned meeting that was certain to draw attention to Provenzano and Giacalone? Why set a time and place that Hoffa might tell his wife and others about, rather than just shoot him on the street? (Hoffa never had bodyguards.) The answer has to do with who actually ordered Hoffa killed.

Enter Pennsylvania-New York-New Jersey mob boss Russell Bufalino. During 1977 Russell Bufalino became an increasingly important figure in the Hoffa investigation. Although his name had rarely been mentioned in the public speculation about the Hoffa disappearance, several top federal investigators, as well as sources close to Provenzano who were interviewed independently, revealed that Bufalino was the linchpin in the case. All those in the cast of characters thought to be involved added to all the known motives and all the evidence compel the conclusion that he was the man at the top who was calling the signals.

By the end of 1977 Bufalino, although not written about as much as other organized-crime figures, was one of the nation's top mob leaders. He had several credits to his name. He had been one of the dozens of elegantly dressed mob bosses chased through the woods by police at the Appalachin Conference of 1957. Soon after that, the government tried to deport him back to Italy, but the Italian government refused to take him. Seventy-three years old in 1977, Bufalino was, in the words of top New York City organized-crime detective Remo Franceschini, "very very active. He's all over the city, and constantly involved in meetings with other organized-crime figures. . . . A few months ago [January 1977] the Los Angeles police asked us to watch a few of their people [organized-crime leaders] who were here. We followed them right to Bufalino. . . ."

Part of Bufalino's power base in 1977 was his control over part of the old Vito Genovese crime "family" that operated in New York and New Jersey. He was also close to the then reputed "boss of bosses," Carmine Galente. To some police officials it was not clear that he was below Galente on the mob totem pole. Bufalino was deeply involved in garment center racketeering in New York City, where he spent three or four days a week, and where he had been indicted for extortion in 1976 by the federal Organized Crime Strike Force. He lived in eastern Pennsylvania, where he still ran his own crime family. This Pennsylvania fiefdom has been extended into upstate New York, where in 1977 he was named, though not indicted, as being involved in a burglary-fencing ring in Buffalo, New York. Directly and solely as a result of Bufalino's alleged involvement in the Hoffa case and because of his activities in upstate New York, the FBI's Hoffa investigation in 1977 was being run not only from the

Bureau's offices in Newark and Detroit, but also out of the Buffalo office.

In early August 1977, Bufalino was in a New York federal courtroom on trial for extortion. He is a squat, perfectly manicured, aging man who wore impeccably tailored suits and talked only in whispers and nods. His codefendants, two younger "enforcers" accused of actually threatening the victim, also looked as if they had been sent over from central casting; one was big and burly, the other a wavy-haired, street-punk type.

One aspect of Bufalino's courtroom demeanor that was more surprising was his look of indignation, a look shared by the other defendants, their families, and their friends in the audience. All wore the faces of the persecuted. As telephone taps were played on tape recorders in court—the two enforcers were heard threatening their victim to come up with the money he owed Bufalino—all glared or shook their heads in disgust. It was done too well to be acting. They had to have really believed it. Somewhere along the way, Bufalino and the others had to have talked themselves and their families into a special version of reality. Bufalino assumed the same glare and indignant half-laugh when I tried to ask him about the Hoffa case during a break in the extortion trial.

According to what federal investigators had learned by 1977, and according to other sources independently questioned, Provenzano and Giacalone could not have carried out the Hoffa "hit" without higher approval. Both were too low on the mob ladder to do something that big on their own. The higher-up was Russell Bufalino.

According to the FBI and sources close to Provenzano interviewed independently, Provenzano was a "captain" in the New York-New Jersey Genovese organized-crime "family" that Bufalino largely controlled at the time of Hoffa's disappearance. In fact, Provenzano was a much more significant Bufalino satellite than rank indicated. "He [Provenzano] is close to Bufalino in everything," one federal Organized Crime Strike Force lawyer observed nearly two years after the Hoffa murder. "Everywhere we find Bufalino we find Tony Pro." A prosecutor on another case involving Bufalino (which had produced the extortion indictment in 1976) noted that Bufalino and Provenzano in 1975 were nightly companions at a restaurant in Hollywood, Florida. "When our people were watching Bufalino in that case," the same lawyer noted, "Bufalino would deal with our guy [an informant] on this deal and then go back to the bar and resume his conversation with Tony Pro."

Federal law-enforcement officials, sources close to Provenzano, and one Teamsters vice-president who was willing to talk about it, all believe that sometime in the spring of 1975 Bufalino and perhaps other mob leaders around the country decided that Hoffa's reemergence as Teamsters president was now too likely. They decided to get rid of him. The reason was the often-reported and obvious one: things were going fine with Fitzsimmons in the top spot. True, Hoffa had always worked with organized crime; he had given them their foothold in the Teamsters in the first place. But he had been pushier and harder to deal with than the easygoing Fitz. And now he was making noises as if he wasn't going to deal at all—that he was going to use accusations of sweetheart contracts and other union corruption as campaign issues against Fitzsimmons. It was intolerable. As one veteran New York City organized-crime detective put it, "Hoffa didn't understand that once you let the Russell Bufalinos and the Tony Pros of the world in, you can't just throw them out. It doesn't work that way. He was naïve."

For Bufalino, keeping Hoffa out of the picture was especially important because of Hoffa's grudge against Provenzano; Provenzano was one of Bufalino's vehicles for getting in on the extortion, pension-fund fraud, bank-loan fraud and other Teamsters rackets in New York and New Jersey that were so profitable.

Also, by the middle '70s a new racket was starting to produce handsome profits for Provenzano, Bufalino and their friends, although it would not be fully revealed until more than two years after the Hoffa disappearance, when the *Wall Street Journal* uncovered it. Under this scheme, companies requiring high volumes of trucking— retail chain stores or furniture manufacturers, for example—would contract with "labor-leasing" companies to drive their trucks for them. The labor-leasing companies would accept a fee and hire their own drivers at pay scales well below the wages supposed to be paid to union truckers under the Teamsters' National Master Freight Agreement. Union members who had previously worked directly for the company needing truck drivers would be out of work and nonunion, lower-paid drivers employed by the leasing company would take their places.

Why were the labor-leasing companies allowed to hire drivers at nonunion wages so as to make the master freight agreement often, in the *Journal*'s words, "a mere illusion"? Because, the *Journal* explained, the labor-leasing companies had the right connections in the Teamsters union so that the union did not try to interfere with them.

Russell Bufalino was the mob boss suspected of being connected with the two major labor-leasing companies that had been allowed by the union to prosper; and Tony Provenzano's New Jersey turf was one of the areas where the labor leasers were most active. If, as he vowed in 1975, Hoffa really intended to get rid of sweetheart deals, these new, large-scale labor-leasing sweetheart arrangements would also be threatened. Even if Hoffa didn't do away with such corruption, there was no doubt that, unlike Fitzsimmons, he would demand a good piece of the action for himself in return.

According to a source close to Provenzano, it was for these reasons—the threatened end to, or the need to cut Hoffa in on, the crooked arrangements—that Bufalino, Provenzano and the others felt they had to prevent Hoffa's return to the union presidency. The same source asserted that in 1973 Provenzano had been aided by Bufalino in collecting some $500,000 from Las Vegas casinos and other mob rackets to give to Nixon aides in a "contribution" to the President (or to his campaign committee) in return for Nixon's restriction on Hoffa's parole that forbade him to go back to union work, a restriction that Hoffa was challenging before his murder.

There has always been a great deal of speculation that the timing of Hoffa's murder was based on the mob getting word somehow that these parole restrictions on Hoffa were about to be overturned and that they wanted him eliminated before this happened. This is half true. In an interview two years later, a source close to the Court of Appeals judges who had heard Hoffa's case suggested strongly that the appeals court was close to deciding in Hoffa's favor. Also, a Justice Department lawyer recalled that a memo on the Hoffa question had been prepared for then Attorney General Edward Levi, and that it urged the government to drop the restrictions no matter what the court did, because they were unconstitutional.

However, it seems unlikely that the underworld could have known certainly that this was imminent. What is more plausible is that they simply feared that Hoffa might win his appeal. Most Teamsters insiders and their lawyers saw the chances as fifty-fifty. Also, they expected that, if he didn't win, Hoffa would run Jimmy junior or an old ally in his place, or that he'd make so much noise from the sidelines in the event of an adverse court decision, possibly testifying somewhere against some of them, that it would be almost as bad as if he had won the appeal.

In any case, it was probable that sometime around May or June Russell Bufalino together with other mob bosses—including Giacalone's Detroit boss, Tony Zerilli—recognized a happy commonality of interests in Tony Pro's feud with Hoffa. Aware of Tony Pro's prison dispute with Hoffa and Giacalone's futile efforts to mediate it, Bufalino and the others reportedly decided to have Provenzano and Giacalone set up the murder.* Another, slightly different version of the same story, put forth by one Provenzano intimate, has Provenzano reporting to Bufalino that Hoffa was not willing to patch things up and "work with them," and urging that he, Provenzano, be allowed to do away with Hoffa. Whoever the originating force, there is no doubt that Provenzano needed little encouragement. He is notoriously hotheaded and was anxious to get on unchallenged with his New Jersey Teamsters schemes.

For Bufalino and the other bosses, Provenzano's feud with Hoffa was the perfect smoke screen. If Provenzano were to be suspected or to get caught, it would simply seem as if he had been settling an old score. Thus, a source close to Provenzano recalled that Bufalino and the other bosses told Provenzano and Giacalone to use the pretext of a meeting with Hoffa to get rid of him. This might have been riskier for Provenzano and Giacalone, because Hoffa might talk about any meeting beforehand. Indeed, as one federal investigator explained, Hoffa, worried about precisely this kind of danger, had altered his old habit of not talking to anyone about his day-to-day activities and now always left word about where he was going to be and with whom. But, from Bufalino's standpoint, this way avoided the public witnesses that a street shooting would risk; the job would be done well (they couldn't afford a miss); it guaranteed that the body would not be found, leaving the police additional confusion; and, if anything, it made it look more like a Provenzano grudge murder rather than a true mob "hit."

Two independent factors add to the evidence that Provenzano acted on Bufalino's say-so and with help from Bufalino and Bufalino's people. The first is the apparent role of William Bufalino in the case. William Bufalino has on occasion denied that he is related to Russell Bufalino, and at other times has said he is a distant cousin. But he has never denied that he is a very close friend of Russell's; he told reporter Dan Moldea in 1976 that his daughter is Russell's godchild and that he "would rather be accused of being his friend and

* By early 1978 the investigators working on the Hoffa case had some reason to suspect that though Giacalone would have participated in the Hoffa setup merely on Zerilli's say-so, he also had been given a specific payoff, perhaps in the form of Central States Pension Fund loans to a motel in Las Vegas in which he was suspected of having a hidden indirect interest.

brother by choice, not by an accident of birth.'' The question now in 1975, 1976 and 1977 was: What kind of accident was it that William Bufalino represented all the suspects in the Hoffa case when they testified before the Detroit grand jury and also some of the alibi witnesses the suspects used to vouch for the fact that they were in New Jersey the day of the Hoffa murder.

In a January 1977 interview, William Bufalino explained that he ended up representing Provenzano when Provenzano appeared before the Detroit grand jury, simply because he happened to be there representing a secretary from Provenzano's local who was appearing before the grand jury to vouch for the presence of the Andrettas, the Briuglios and Provenzano in New Jersey on the day Hoffa disappeared. ''I saw Tony,'' Bufalino recalled ''and said, 'Tony, you're in my town now, I'll represent you. Don't worry about the bill.' '' Bufalino's hospitality does not explain how he came to be representing the alibi secretary, the Briguglio brothers or the Andretta brothers in the first place. He explained this by saying that he was then and now (in 1977) New Jersey Local 560's general counsel. He never made clear why a New Jersey Teamsters local would employ a Detroit lawyer as its general counsel. In a 1977 interview, Salvatore Provenzano, Tony's brother and then the Local 560 vice-president, added to the confusion, telling me that ''Bufalino helps, but he's not our lawyer. Don't write that he's 560's lawyer.'' Yet, union records did list him as the local's counsel.

In 1976, Provenzano and Salvatore Briguglio were indicted for the 1961 Castelitto murder and abduction. The federal prosecutors hoped that this indictment might also force one of them to ''turn'' and talk about the Hoffa disappearance rather than go back to prison. William Bufalino's role in this new case (which was still pending in May 1978) was similarly unclear. He was not their lawyer of record; in fact, Provenzano's real lawyer, Maurice Adelbaum, angrily denied that Bufalino had anything to do with the case. Yet Bufalino appeared in pretrial court sessions with the defendant—in his words, ''to help out'' and also to ''protect the Local 560 records that had been subpoenaed.''

In July 1976 the prosecutors asked the federal judge overseeing the Hoffa case grand jury that Bufalino be disqualified from representing the alibi witnesses at the same time that he was representing the potential defendants. The judge agreed.

In addition to William Bufalino's involvement, federal investigators were intrigued by the interest shown in the Hoffa case by another known Russell Bufalino associate—Francis Joseph "Frank" Sheeran. In 1975 Sheeran was the president of Teamsters Local 326 in Delaware. He had a history of alleged involvement in union-related violence, including an indictment for the murder of a local union dissident. (The charge was dropped when a judge ruled that the government had taken too long to bring the case to trial.) Though Sheeran's only union duties were in Delaware, his car was seen in Detroit on December 4, 1975, when the New Jersey suspects appeared in the line-up. And he had been seen in Detroit by FBI informants on the day Hoffa disappeared. Why was he there? Sheeran refused to comment on "anything having to do with the Teamsters or Hoffa," when I called him two years later, and he hung up when I asked if he knew Russell Bufalino.*

FBI files on Sheeran are more revealing. First they indicate that he was deeply involved with Russell Bufalino in the labor-leasing sweetheart-contract racket, working closely with him in securing contracts for leasing companies in New Jersey and Pennsylvania. The files also note that he frequently met with Russell Bufalino at Bufalino's New York City haunt, the Vesuvio Restaurant. One Vesuvio meeting, according to an FBI memo in the Russell Bufalino file, took place on August 4, 1975, five days after Hoffa's disappearance. According to FBI informants and to New York City undercover detectives who were at the Vesuvio that day, this meeting was called specifically to discuss what the government was doing to investigate the Hoffa case. Salvatore Briguglio, Tony Provenzano, Russell Bufalino and Sheeran were all spotted there. In an interview two years later, Briguglio said he remembered the meeting but that it was just a social visit. He offered no explanation of why Sheeran would drive up from Delaware on a work day for a social luncheon.

According to the same FBI file, on the evening of June 11, 1976, Sheeran was served at his Pennsylvania home with a subpoena to appear before the federal grand jury in Detroit investigating the Hoffa case. The next morning he drove to New York for another meeting with Russell Bufalino at the Vesuvio. Soon thereafter William Bufalino notified the Justice Department that he would be representing Sheeran.

* Sheeran did give the FBI a reason for his being in Detroit on the day of Hoffa's disappearance. He was there, he said, to attend the wedding of William Bufalino's daughter, which, in fact, he did attend. Also in town for the wedding was Russell Bufalino.

Ironically, Sheeran had once been one of Hoffa's biggest boosters. He had been a co-plaintiff in the lawsuit that Hoffa had brought to free himself of the parole restrictions, and he had once vowed that he would be "a Hoffa man till the day they pat my face with a shovel and steal my cufflinks." Hoffa had reciprocated: he had been the guest speaker at a testimonial dinner for Sheeran in 1974.

When the FBI inspected the long-distance telephone bills of those thought to be involved in the Hoffa case, they found several calls between Russell Bufalino and Quasarano and Vitale, the two owners of the suspect Michigan sanitation company. Phone records also showed that Sheeran had been a frequent caller to Hoffa's home in the year before Hoffa disappeared. Apparently, something or somebody convinced Sheeran to change allegiances; the phone logs showed Sheeran's calls to Hoffa became less frequent in the final months before the disappearance and that his calls to Russell Bufalino became much more frequent. Also, the FBI file noted, Hoffa junior had reported to agents that Sheeran had acted "coolly" toward him since his father's disappearance.

For these and other reasons, including informants' reports that Sheeran was actively involved in helping to "control" the New Jersey witnesses who had provided alibis for the Briguglios and for Stephen Andretta, and in making sure no one else in the case broke ranks, Sheeran was suspected of having played an important support role in the Hoffa disappearance—a possibility, which if true would further implicate Russell Bufalino. As one federal investigator put it, "With Sheeran's record of violence and with his strong, continuing ties to Russell Bufalino, his involvement in the Hoffa case is perfectly logical. . . ."

Whatever role Sheeran, Provenzano, and all the possible suspects played in the Hoffa disappearance or in containing the government's investigation of the case thereafter, what makes any involvement they had so significant is that the one man who was connected to all of them through past association, long-distance phone records and current deals and who had the authority as a mob boss to order Hoffa's murder was Russell Bufalino. All paths seemed to lead to him. Perhaps the measure of his genius or his luck was that, despite his apparent role as the impresario of the most notorious assassination of the decade, he still enjoyed relative obscurity compared to the mob overlords who dominated the daily headlines of the '70s.

What, then, really did happen to Jimmy Hoffa?

Based on a study of the government's investigation and on dozens of other interviews, including talks with sources intimate with those involved in the Hoffa murder and discussions with Salvatore Briguglio,* this is the most likely sequence:

1. Hoffa went to the Machus Red Fox Restaurant on July 30, 1975, to meet, he thought, with Tony Giacalone and Tony Provenzano.

2. He got there at about 2 P.M.

3. He expected to be picked up outside the restaurant and taken to a meeting elsewhere. *He had already had lunch, and he never went inside to wait for the others.*

4. Giacalone and Provenzano never showed up. *Their alibis are definite.*

5. Giacalone and Provenzano had set up the meeting and the subsequent murder on the say-so of higher-ups in organized crime, including Russell Bufalino.

6. Hoffa was picked up by Chuckie O'Brien and at least two other men in Tony Giacalone's son's car. *Witnesses saw Hoffa and O'Brien there. In addition to the driver, O'Brien, there had to be at least one more man; otherwise Hoffa would not have sat in the back seat— where the dogs found his scent. He was not the kind to sit in the back if the front passenger seat was empty. And if he sat in the back seat, there had to be a third man in the car to sit back there with him to knock him out, as described below.*

7. Hoffa was picked up at about 2:45 or 2:50 P.M. *This is when the last witness saw him, and it matches the time of his last phone call.*

8. The two men in the car with Hoffa along with O'Brien were Salvatore Briguglio (who was identified by the eyewitness at the December 1976 lineup) and either Gabriel Briguglio or Thomas Andretta. The one of the three who was not there—either Gabriel Briguglio or Thomas Andretta—was left at the chartered plane they had waiting to take them back to New Jersey, or was otherwise engaged in securing a getaway.

9. At this point Hoffa still thought he was going to the meeting. *He*

---

* Salvatore Briguglio and I talked in 1977 with the ground rule that I would not reveal our discussions. On March 21, 1978, he was murdered—see page 74. Our talks, which were conducted privately, were rambling and touched on the murder only occasionally. Even then, he only passively confirmed with a nod of his head certain relatively minor aspects of the crime that I put before him. He offered no elaboration and never revealed enough to implicate anyone except possibly himself.

knew the Briguglios and knew they were Tony Pro's men. He simply assumed they had been dispatched with O'Brien, a Giacalone ally, to pick him up.

10. One of the Briguglios or Thomas Andretta, sitting in the back seat, knocked Hoffa out with the butt of a gun during the first minutes of the car ride. *This was implied to me by Briguglio, and it makes sense. They couldn't just pull a gun on Hoffa to get him to go somewhere. Hoffa was notoriously fearless, hardly the kind of man to go to his execution without putting up a fight that would have challenged all three men. Once, in a Tennessee courtroom, he lunged right at a would-be assassin who had pointed a gun at him. Nor could they shoot him right there, since that risked leaving a bullet hole or blood in the car. Their knocking him out would explain the Hoffa hair particle with just the trace of blood that was found in the back seat. And it would match exactly what police believe happened to Tony Castellito, the New Jersey Teamsters official who disappeared in 1961 and for whose abduction and murder Provenzano and Salvatore Briguglio were indicted in 1976. He too was knocked unconscious before being killed.*

11. Next they took Hoffa to some location where they strangled or shot him. *The FBI suspects the location might be a mob-connected catering establishment near Detroit. Also, they could have strangled him right in the car.*

12. Then the dead body was turned over to someone else—maybe Sheeran—who took it in some other car for the trip to the Quasarano-Vitale incinerator. *Investigators believe this was far more likely than what Picardo, the New Jersey informant, speculated about the body being shipped in a 55-gallon drum in a truck to a New Jersey dump. For Picardo it was a logical guess, since he knew that other New Jersey mob victims had been disposed of in that dump; but, as the Hoffex memo put it, "it is unknown why the body would be transported back to New Jersey when Detroit organized-crime people have proven in the past that they are capable of taking care of such things."*

13. The Briguglio brothers and Thomas Andretta then returned to New Jersey. *One of the big unanswered questions is how they got to and from Detroit. The FBI thinks it was by private plane, rather than by car or bus, since the three each have seemingly good alibis for the days before and after July 30. However, a drive shared by three people would not have been that difficult. No records of a private*

plane trip have been found, nor are they likely to be found even if there was one. There are thousands of planes and charter services available that could have made the trip, and the airports in New Jersey or Michigan that might have accommodated them don't necessarily keep a record of all planes that take off or land.

None of this will be proved until there is a real "break" in the case that brings conviction in a court by a jury that finds guilt beyond a reasonable doubt. In this regard, by mid-1978 there had been nothing but a few tragicomic false alarms. Soon after the disappearance, publicity-hungry 1976 presidential candidate Henry Jackson and his Senate investigators were duped by a phony tipster (to whom they gave $25,000 in cash) into digging up a swampy, rattlesnake-infested field north of Detroit for Hoffa's body. They found nothing. Then, CBS Television was taken for a ride by an "informant" who promised that he would find the body for their newsmen in the ocean off Florida.

By mid-1978 the FBI expected that the real break would come, if ever, from those who had been involved. Since the disappearance, the government had conducted an intensive investigation of suspects in the case with the hope that by finding evidence to prosecute on other grounds, one of them would be encouraged to tell the government what he knew about what happened to Jimmy Hoffa in return for leniency.* Tony Giacalone had been tried and convicted of tax evasion, and sentenced to prison. Although he was known to hate prison and to fear at his age, fifty-nine in 1977, that he would never get out alive, he hadn't broken the code of silence. Tony Provenzano, along with Salvatore Briguglio, had been indicted in 1976 for the Castellito 1961 murder. By 1977, the federal charge in that case had been thrown out, because the case was brought after the statute of limitations had expired. The State of New York's case on the same charge against Provenzano and Briguglio did not look completely promising either, because a key witness had begun to develop cold feet. Whatever its potential, it had done nothing that could budge Provenzano or Briguglio into talking about the Hoffa case. Provenzano had also been indicted on a federal kickback-conspiracy charge.

---

* Some federal prosecutors asserted a different causal relationship, saying that in the process of investigating the backgrounds of the suspects they had come across evidence of other crimes. They prosecuted those crimes, they insisted, on their own merits. A by-product of such a prosecution might be that the suspect would cut a deal and reveal information in the Hoffa case.

By Easter of 1978 he had been convicted, but there was still no sign that he was going to talk.

Another key figure in the Hoffa mystery, Stephen Andretta, had refused to answer the Detroit grand jury's questions in December of 1975, even after he was given immunity from prosecution for any of his answers, which eliminated his right to take the Fifth Amendment. Andretta, represented by William Bufalino, balked at talking and spent sixty-three days in a federal prison for contempt of court. Finally, he agreed to testify. Then, taking those famous 1,117 trips outside to consult with Bufalino during eleven days of testimony, he backed up the suspects' claim that they were all in New Jersey on July 30, 1975, playing cards at the union hall. Although the federal prosecutor had statements from union secretaries and other New Jersey witnesses who denied this, the prosecutor didn't have a case, excepting perhaps a minor one against Andretta for perjury. When Andretta finished his grand jury testimony in January of 1976, he returned to New Jersey to find a new union-leased car waiting for him at the airport. That night they threw a party in his honor.

One hope seemed to be Chuckie O'Brien. From the day after the disappearance, when he ran away from Jimmy Hoffa, Jr., after Hoffa junior accused him of having been involved in his father's murder, O'Brien had seemed terrified. Federal prosecutors later recalled that within a few weeks he would become less scared of the police than of the people behind the murder, who, he feared, were going to silence him rather than risk his talking about whom he had driven off with on the day he allegedly picked up Hoffa.

By the time of the Teamsters Las Vegas convention in June 1976, O'Brien's fear had become a joke. He made a laughing stock of himself at the convention, hiding under a friend's bed for two days when he heard Provenzano was looking for him. By mid-1978 O'Brien's appeals of a union-related extortion conviction were nearly exhausted and he would soon have to go to prison. By May, he had been convicted of a new crime—filing a false loan application. But he still hadn't broken. Both FBI men and Teamsters insiders were predicting that he would be killed in jail or soon after, to make sure that he would not go over to the government.

Even if O'Brien were to break ranks before going, as one federal agent put it, "to that great Teamster building in the sky," he could never implicate anyone beyond Giacalone and certainly not Russell Bufalino or the other real bosses believed to be involved in the murder.

One man who the FBI thought could reach higher was lawyer William Bufalino. Through 1977 the government had been pressing him. By the summer it appeared that they had found a good pressure point: Bufalino had, as he claimed to me, indeed been employed as a lawyer for Provenzano's New Jersey Local 560. And, he had been receiving a monthly retainer of $1,350. However, it seemed to the FBI that the only work he had done for the money was to represent the Hoffa case defendants—and the federal Landrum-Griffin Act prohibits the expenditure of union funds for legal services for union officials prosecuted for criminal acts.

In this instance the feds' pressure seemed to work well. In October 1977 Bufalino was hospitalized for heart trouble; then, a few weeks later, he was hospitalized for what was reportedly nervous exhaustion. When the FBI heard about his hospitalization, they swooped down on him, hoping he would blurt out all the details they had been waiting for. All they got was a spirited, somewhat rambling version of his often repeated protestations that he and everyone else involved were being framed.

Frank Sheeran too seemed unbreakable. His dealings with the labor-leasing companies were intensively investigated in late 1977 and early 1978, and there was even talk about bringing him and some of the other suspects before a new Hoffa-case grand jury. But he refused to talk about the Hoffa case.

Nor would Russell Bufalino himself say anything about it, even after October 21, 1977, when he received a four-year prison term for his extortion conviction. Given the crime, the age of the defendant, and the fact that he had no prior felony convictions, this was an unusually stiff sentence. It was handed down by District Court Judge Morris Lasker, after Assistant U.S. Attorney Barbara Jones argued that Bufalino was an organized-crime boss with influence and a criminal resumé that far exceeded his relatively modest press clippings.

In an interview more than two years after Hoffa vanished, a Teamsters vice-president summed up the case this way: "We all know who did it. It was Tony [Provenzano] with those guys of his from New Jersey. It's common knowledge. But the cops need a corroborating witness, and it doesn't look like they're about to get one, does it?"

Through 1977 and into 1978 the FBI was still grabbing for straws. Agents working in Detroit as well as in Russell Bufalino's and Provenzano's strongholds of Buffalo, Newark and New York continued to work the case. Occasionally they dropped in at Teamsters offices around the country, passing the word, often with amusing disregard for subtlety, that the government had an airtight program for relocating helpful witnesses and assuring their safety. According to Fitzsimmons, in an early 1978 interview, "these fellows from the FBI have been to see me every few weeks lately, asking me about Hoffa." Meanwhile, federal investigators continued to watch the Briguglio and Andretta brothers, William and Russell Bufalino, Provenzano, Sheeran and others, looking for any other possible crime, while sending signals to them individually that the heat might be turned off if they would cooperate in the Hoffa case. Reporters, including this one, working on the Teamsters and the Hoffa case also were questioned. There was no progress.

It began to look as if the only break would come by some fluke. One top prosecutor speculated that "we've heard rumors that there are contracts out on one or more of the insiders in the case, like the Briguglios. Well, if they try to kill one of them and they miss, he'll come to us and talk, because it's his only chance, however slim, to live. And if they succeed in killing him, then maybe one of the others will get scared and cave in. Other than that, we're finished until we or some local prosecutor gets lucky and nails one of the gang on a twenty- or thirty-year conviction, and that could happen next year or six years from now."

On the evening of March 21, 1978, it seemed that just that kind of break had come: Salvatore Briguglio was gunned down by two hooded men outside a restaurant in New York's Little Italy. Presumably, his higher-ups believed that he was becoming vulnerable to the government's pressure in connection with the upcoming trial on the 1961 murder charge.

The next day, FBI agents went to O'Brien, Gabriel Briguglio and the Andrettas, urging them to come in and talk. "We're your friends," the agents who appeared at O'Brien's doorstep told him, according to Detroit reporter Ralph Orr. "We're your only chance." Maybe, but by June no one had broken the silence.

It seemed likely that sooner or later the government would be able to use a combination of its own prosecution threats and the specter of the Salvatore Briguglio murder to get someone to talk. Then again, it was at least as possible that all those underlings who were in a position to talk would also be murdered before they got the chance. Or perhaps the Briguglio hit had worked the other way and made them more scared than ever about breaking the silence. (For that to happen, the word simply had to be passed that Salvatore Briguglio had already been talking when he was murdered.)

Through 1977 and the first half of 1978, Jimmy Hoffa, Jr., waited for the break that never came. He still spent more hours than he liked to admit, on the phone at that desk under his father's portrait, exchanging ideas about possible new evidence with reporters and family friends.

Once in a while, now, he found himself discussing theories about his father's body being in a garbage dump or in an incinerator with a measure of dispassion that knotted his stomach the moment he noticed it.

On the second anniversary of the disappearance, he spent the day with his mother while she prayed. And he answered the phone calls from the press asking him how he and his mom had spent the day, and if he still had hope, and where he thought the body was, and on, and on.

A few weeks after that he was jolted by a terrible false alarm. The last week in October 1977 the news carried reports that a body discovered in northeastern Pennsylvania (coincidentally, Russell Bufalino's home base) was suspected by local officials to be the remains of Jimmy Hoffa. Although the FBI assured Jimmy junior almost immediately that the body probably wasn't his father's, it took forty-eight hours of steadily larger headlines before an examination of dental records confirmed that the skeleton belonged to another gangland victim. Five months later, he was jubilant on hearing the news of the Briguglio murder, then soon depressed when it didn't yield the quick break that he had anticipated.

As the third anniversary of the disappearance approached, the FBI would still call Jimmy junior once every few months with some new name, although he knew—and he knew they knew—that the only important names in the case were the old names. And always the FBI agents would say they were trying and they were making progress.

CHAPTER III

Fitzsimmons

Frank Kierdorf is still a legend among Detroit Teamsters officials. They remember how he died, on Thursday, August 7, 1958, in St. Joseph Mercy Hospital, in Pontiac, Michigan, with burns over 85 percent of his body. Police records show that at ten-thirty that Sunday night, Kierdorf, his uncle, Herman Kierdorf, and a third man had been planting a fire bomb at the Latrielle Cleaners near Flint. The dry-cleaning store had refused to go along with one of Jimmy Hoffa's protection rackets, in which a retailer would pay cash in return for assurance that the workers would not be unionized and new competition kept clear of the area.

Frank and Herman Kierdorf had been recruited by Hoffa as Teamsters "business agents" straight from prison, where they had served time for sticking up a variety store in Akron, Ohio. Their agent work was as "torches." A reluctant store owner was paid an after-hours visit, and the next morning the place was ashes.

The job at Latrielle was routine, but Frank dropped his flashlight as they were leaving. When he bent over in the darkness to grope for it, he caused the fire bomb to ignite prematurely. Seconds later he was caught in the flash.

Though his screams woke the neighborhood, police records state that only one witness came forward to say he had seen two men drive Frank away, still smoldering in a station wagon. For two hours at his home, his uncle and the other man had tried to treat his burns themselves. The police were to find bits of his burnt flesh in his car, in his driveway, on his porch, and in the kitchen and bathroom. At 12:55 A.M., Monday, Herman dropped Frank on the hospital lawn, and from there Frank staggered into the emergency room and collapsed. His body was burned beyond recognition and he would tell the staff only that his name was John Doe. Hospital officials used a still-intact fingerprint to identify him.

Frank Kierdorf hung on for four days. From Monday morning on, Assistant Chief County Prosecutor George Taylor tried to get him to tell how the fire had happened. By Thursday, two things were clear to Taylor. Information he had received from aides of Robert Kennedy at the McClellan Committee indicated that Kierdorf was involved in a Teamsters-run group extorting payoffs from small merchants throughout the Flint-Pontiac area. Kennedy had planned to question Hoffa about Frank and Herman Kierdorf before the Committee that very morning. Taylor knew that any information from Kierdorf would be significant. Also, it was clear that Kierdorf was dying.

Robert Kennedy wrote in *The Enemy Within* that, as Kierdorf lay there, the prosecutor, a religious Catholic, decided in desperation to try to get him to talk by invoking fear of God. "You have only a few hours to live," Taylor began, "you are about to face your Maker, your God. Make a clean breast of things. Tell me what happened." There was a silence, and then Kierdorf pressed his charred lips and whispered. "Go fuck yourself." About an hour later he died.

The day after Herman Kierdorf dropped Frank Kierdorf at the door of the emergency room, he disappeared. In Washington, Kennedy's Senate committee investigators fast discovered that Herman had made the first leg of his escape in a Cadillac. Then he sold the Cadillac for $1,700, which he used to get further away. The committee staff found that the car was registered to Teamsters Local 299—the giant Detroit local that was Jimmy Hoffa's original power base and where he still held the title of president, along with his presidency of the International union. Teamsters officials, reacting to allegations that they had helped Kierdorf get away, claimed that the car had been sold to Herman Kierdorf just before the fire-bombing. Frank Fitzsimmons, the vice-president of Local 299, had authorized the sale.

The investigation by the McClellan Committee was among the most significant and controversial Congressional hearings of the century. Senator John F. Kennedy as a committee member and Robert Kennedy as chief counsel both made national names for themselves. As veteran Teamsters Capitol Hill lobbyist David Sweeney remembered it over lunch twenty years later, "Those cocksuckers really worked us over."

Jimmy Hoffa had also become a household name. As witness after witness took the Fifth Amendment under Robert Kennedy's searing, frequently intemperate questioning, *Teamsters* became synonymous with *gangsters*. It was unfair, but it was an inviting generalization as the younger Kennedy paraded intransigent witnesses and provocative evidence before the Senators and the TV cameras from 1957 through 1959.

Three hundred forty three of 1,525 witnesses in 20,432 pages of testimony took the Fifth Amendment before the McClellan Committee. Robert Kennedy wrote, "Without question, we heard the expression 'I refuse to answer on the grounds that a truthful answer may tend to incriminate me' more than any other group in the history of the United States."

One man who did not take the Fifth Amendment was Jimmy Hoffa, at least technically. A ritual had become established: Kennedy would ask a question about a financial transaction by the union that could incriminate Hoffa. Hoffa would chuckle, say he couldn't remember the details, but that Kennedy should "ask Bert Brennan" (a close Hoffa associate) or someone else, about whatever it was that Kennedy was interested in. Brennan or whoever, would be called to testify. As the witness approached the stand, Hoffa would hold up five fingers, a signal to take the Fifth. Sometimes he even whispered, loudly enough to be heard, "Take five."

Frank Fitzsimmons never "took five" for Hoffa, but the evidence indicates that he did protect him. That's what his involvement in the Herman Kierdorf union-car-escape investigation was all about.

Fitzsimmons told the McClellan Committee that it was he, the vice-president of Local 299, and not Hoffa, the president, who had approved the claimed sale of the union car to Kierdorf the day before the Sunday night accident. All Fitzsimmons had received for the alleged sale, he testified, was a "demand note." He couldn't produce the note, nor could he remember exactly how much the note was for, except that he thought it "was $1,400 or $1,500 dollars." A while

later in the testimony, Fitzsimmons' lawyer George Fitzgerald, who
was also Hoffa's lawyer, said the note was for $2,000. But this was
after Kennedy had cast further doubt on the alleged transaction,
triumphantly noting that a researcher had just checked the "blue
book" price of a two-year-old Cadillac sedan (the car in question)
and found that the going price for the cheapest model was $2,895.00.

Describing Hoffa's role in the affair, Fitzsimmons' testimony was
equally tenuous:

> KENNEDY: Did he [Hoffa] instruct you to transfer the title of the
> automobile?
> FITZSIMMONS: I didn't have an opportunity to discuss it with him.
> KENNEDY: Did you discuss it at all with Mr. Hoffa?

Fitzsimmons leaned over to talk to Fitzgerald. Chairman McClellan
urged him to "move along."

> FITZSIMMONS: I think I did. Yes I mentioned it to Mr. Hoffa later
> that day.
> McCLELLAN: Before or after you sold the car?
> FITZSIMMONS: Well—
> McCLELLAN: It was just last Saturday?
> FITZSIMMONS: I understand Mr. McClellan—
> McCLELLAN: Well, all right, did you mention it to him before you
> sold the car or after you sold the car?
> FITZSIMMONS: I think it was discussed with him before I sold it,
> and I didn't know whether we had gone ahead and transferred it
> or made arrangements for Mr. Kierdorf to buy the automobile.
> McCLELLAN: When did you discuss it with him, Saturday?
> FITZSIMMONS: Saturday morning.
> McCLELLAN: Where?
> FITZSIMMONS: In his office.
> McCLELLAN: Was Mr. Hoffa in your office Saturday morning?
> FITZSIMMONS: Yes, he was.
> McCLELLAN: Was he there when Mr. Kierdorf came in and said he
> wanted to buy the car?

Fitzsimmons hesitated, leaned over and again consulted with Fitzgerald. He resumed, this time taking a different course.

> FITZSIMMONS: I beg your pardon. Mr. Hoffa was not there before
> he came in. He came in afterward.

McClellan: Mr. Hoffa came in after you sold the car?
Fitzsimmons: Yes, sir.
McClellan: You are pretty positive now. A minute ago you said you discussed it with him both before and after.

Robert Kennedy picked up:

Kennedy: Did you contact him [Hoffa] about it?
Fitzsimmons: I said I contacted him after the transaction.
Kennedy: Well, before the transaction?
Fitzsimmons: That morning, no.
Kennedy: The day before, Friday?

Fitzsimmons stopped to consult Fitzgerald, which displeased Kennedy.

Kennedy: Mr. Fitzsimmons, you would know whether you talked to Mr. Hoffa about it or not. Mr. Fitzgerald can't help you. This is just last week. You know whether you talked to Mr. Hoffa or not.

Fitzgerald denied trying to help the witness. To which McClellan replied:

The witness has a right to consult with counsel as to his legal rights. I don't know whether he is getting close to where he wants to exercise the legal right [to take the Fifth Amendment and refuse to answer] or not . . . But as to the facts . . . they are within his information, I am sure . . . Proceed, Mr. Kennedy.
Kennedy: Did You discuss it with Mr. Hoffa?
Fitzsimmons: No, I did not discuss it with Mr. Hoffa.
Kennedy: What took you so long to figure that out?
Fitzsimmons: Well, I was asking Mr. Fitzgerald as far as the designation of the duties and bylaws and as far as discussion was concerned.

Fumbling through televised testimony like this to protect Hoffa was worth it to Fitzsimmons, because Hoffa had given him so much. He was, as Hoffa later wrote, "a guy I took off a truck and hand-carried all the way from shop steward."

Fitzsimmons, the fourth of five children, was born in 1908 in Jeannette, Pennsylvania, a small town just east of Pittsburgh. When Fitzsimmons was sixteen, his father, who owned part of a precarious brewery in Jeannette, moved his family to Detroit in search of greater opportunity. That same year the elder Fitzsimmons suffered a nearly fatal heart attack and had to stop working. Frank was forced to quit high school after only one year to take a job in an automobile hardware plant. Eight years later, he became a city bus driver. Three years after that, by now twenty-seven, he took a 22-cents-an-hour job loading trucks at a terminal. Soon he worked his way up to an over-the-road (long distance) truck driver, driving ten hours or more at a time, often through the night, to bring goods from Detroit to cities all over the Midwest for the CCC Trucking Company. In 1937 he became a shop steward—the rank-and-file union man who speaks for two dozen or so of his fellow workers on union matters.

It was during a meeting of shop stewards that year that Fitzsimmons met Jimmy Hoffa. Hoffa, then twenty-three years old, had just been elected president of Local 299. He was fresh from two years of working with a group of avowed Trotskyite Teamsters in Minneapolis on the first really successful strike the truck drivers had ever run. Young as he was, he already had his eye on bigger and better things. Hoffa had never driven a truck and what he needed most was to get some drivers on his side as he made his moves up the Teamsters ladder. So, he befriended Fitzsimmons and signed him on for the ride to the top.

Even then, the contrast between the two was striking. Hoffa was strong, tough, brash, and always, as his son later recalled, "thinking of his next move." He had never stayed at any job more than a year or two. Fitzsimmons, on the other hand, was pudgy, forgettable, a quiet plodder who had already spent eight years at one job in the hardware plant, and three years at another. At twenty-nine he was more than willing to follow a kid six years his junior.

Except for his rare and unenlightening appearances before the McClellan Committee, Frank Fitzsimmons never got near center stage until the day in 1966 that Jimmy Hoffa announced that Fitzsimmons would be his stand-in if he went to jail.

"Jimmy and I were partners," Fitzsimmons would later assert in an interview. Recent Teamsters publications, printed under Fitzsimmons' stewardship, describe his role the same way. "At Hoffa's right hand," one Teamsters history published in 1976 reads, "in an energetic thrust toward greater strength and solidarity was Frank E. Fitzsimmons."

Most Teamsters officials, shocked when Hoffa chose Fitzsimmons as his stand-in, remember it differently. In their view, if Fitzsimmons was at Hoffa's right hand, he was more likely to have been pouring coffee than thrusting forward toward greater strength and solidarity. A 420-page analysis of the Teamsters and Hoffa that was published in 1965 supports this version. The authors, Estelle and Ralph James, mentioned Fitzsimmons in only one footnote.

"Sure. I remember Fitz in those days," a former Teamsters lawyer who was close to Hoffa later recalled. "Jimmy and I would get off a plane in Detroit and he'd be there to meet us. . . . My most vivid memory was one day in '61 or '62. We had a meeting out there. Jimmy decided we needed some lunch. So he had Fitz, who was the Local 299 vice-president, take all the sandwich and coffee orders and go out and get them. Well, when he came back it was pathetic watching him. Maybe he was just nervous around Jimmy. But whatever it was, he was spilling coffee and dropping sandwiches all over the place."

Another Teamsters leader who was close to Hoffa had similar memories: "Jimmy treated him like a gopher or a servant. We'd be in a meeting and he'd tell Fitz to get so-and-so on the phone. Fitz would go out to the next room to place the call. Five minutes later, he'd come back to tell Jimmy there was no answer at the guy's office. Jimmy'd go crazy. 'Call him at home, you stupid cocksucker,' he'd scream. 'Don't you know it's nighttime and the guy's at home?' "

"You have to remember that Jimmy was a macho kind of guy," a long-time New York Teamsters organizer, Nicholas Kisburg observed. "He'd walk into a room, take his coat off, and expect someone to catch it before it hit the floor. That's what people like Fitz were for."

Even before Hoffa put Fitzsimmons in the top spot, there were other rewards that kept Fitzsimmons standing ready to catch the coat. A review of the McClellan Committee records and a series of interviews with long-time friends of both Hoffa and Fitzsimmons, indicate that in Fitzsimmons' gopher days, he set up, with Hoffa's approval, schemes to make money for himself by taking advantage of his union position.

Kennedy's staff found records that showed that Fitzsimmons had been on the payroll of a Chicago beer distributor for two years at $75 a week. The company's main work force were Teamsters drivers, and smooth union relations were a key factor in the business. In 1957, when he was asked what kind of work he did for the company, Fitzsimmons testified that "I consulted with them on their sales program."

"Jimmy didn't set him up in that," a mutual friend remarked. "Fitz was friendly with the guy who owned the company. So he got himself on his payroll in return for easing up a little on the contract. He told Jimmy about it and Jimmy approved."

Allegations against Fitzsimmons also include a trucking company owner's testimony that he gave Fitzsimmons 90 percent of his profits in 1944 in return for Fitzsimmons' promise that he would have exclusive rights to haul lithograph paper in the Detroit area. (Anyone who tried to compete would be paralyzed by strikes.) The trucker testified that he had paid Fitzsimmons three to five thousand dollars or more, in cash or in checks made out to his son or to a middleman truck driver. When Fitzsimmons grew dissatisfied with the receipts, the trucker claimed, he ordered him to let his own accountant audit the books. A Congressional committee that investigated this case four years before the McClellan Committee, concluded that "In the process the . . . owner lost a $30,000-$40,000-yearly enterprise, was forced out of a specialized enterprise where he had twenty-five years' experience and was reduced to employment as a janitor at fifty dollars a week." Fitzsimmons denied the allegation and insisted that it was coincidence that his accountant had audited the trucker's books. He said that his name was endorsed on a five-hundred-dollar check from the trucking company to the driver who was accused of being the middleman only because Fitzsimmons happened to be there when the check was written and had cashed the check for him. Nothing to the contrary was ever proved, and Fitzsimmons was not indicted.

The one case in which Fitzsimmons was indicted, in 1953, was an alleged extortion scheme involving shakedowns of Michigan construction firms. In return for what the government's indictment alleged had amounted to thousands of dollars in systematic payoffs, Fitzsimmons and four other Teamsters leaders agreed to go easy on enforcing union contracts. Ultimately, the charges against Fitzsimmons were dropped. But McClellan Committee testimony, rechecked twenty-four years later with some of those involved, suggests that Hoffa arranged a deal in which the other defendants pleaded guilty in return for a dismissal of the case against Fitzsimmons. Kennedy's McClellan Committee staff found records that showed that the judge who dismissed the case had been the beneficiary of $22,000 of

Hoffa-controlled Teamsters money that financed a thirteen-week television series featuring the judge during his reelection campaign. In fact, $1,300 of the money had been paid directly to the judge by the television production company for his appearances on the shows. The prosecutor in the same Fitzsimmons extortion case testified before the McClellan Committee that Hoffa had approached him and had threatened that he could have him "framed in ninety days," and had then asked him to "lay off Fitzsimmons because he was a very fine gentleman" who "could lose an opportunity" to become a member of the Teamsters International executive board, because of the indictment.

If the allegations against Fitzsimmons are true, they are still penny ante compared to what Jimmy Hoffa was up to during the '40s, '50s, and early '60s. Even so, the fact that Fitzsimmons was cutting deals of his own, however small by Hoffa's standard, should have tipped his boss off to the fact that Fitzsimmons was smarter and more ambitious than the average gopher. Hoffa, as all the others, even the reporters who have covered Fitzsimmons since, have confused style with substance. They read Fitzsimmons' clumsy speech and appearance as signs of stupidity and incompetence.

The rumors that began in early 1966 that Hoffa was going to pick Fitzsimmons to stand in for him while he was in prison shocked the union hierarchy. "My God," remarked one former top Teamsters official, "I figured maybe you'd make Fitz a business agent if he was your brother-in-law. But putting him in charge—that was crazy."

For Hoffa it wasn't crazy at all. Choosing a man he thought was both loyal and incompetent was the best way to make sure he could run the union from prison. "The arrangement was that I was to take the orders from Hoffa during my visits and deliver them to Fitz," William Bufalino, Hoffa's lawyer, explained more than ten years later. Although Fitzsimmons claimed that he alone ran the union from the beginning of his tenure as acting president, Bufalino's description of the arrangement was confirmed a decade later in interviews with a half dozen others who were close to Hoffa, Fitzsimmons or both.

On March 7, 1967, Jimmy Hoffa exhausted his attempts to appeal the Tennessee jury-tampering conviction. He had, according to one lawyer involved in the case, succeeded in "tunneling his way into jail." He had converted a relatively minor misdemeanor charge— taking money from employers, for which he was never convicted— into a felony conviction for fixing the jury that was hearing the misdemeanor case.

For a while all went according to plan. Fitzsimmons concluded a new nationwide Master Freight contract covering more than 300,000 Teamsters truck drivers and warehousemen in much the way Hoffa would have done it, building on the groundwork of the negotiations that Hoffa had begun just before prison and using advice that Hoffa furnished through couriers thereafter. Hoffa's messages on these and other issues were sent through his son, Jimmy junior, and through Bufalino. Meanwhile, Allen Dorfman had been left in charge of the Central States Pension Fund, and by all accounts he faithfully exercised Hoffa's proxy on who got loans from the pot that seemed to be expanding geometrically as both benefits and numbers of members increased.

Three months after he went to Lewisburg, Hoffa's presence was very much felt at headquarters. His gold name plate still sat on what had become Fitzsimmons' desk, and all the Hoffa plaques and family pictures were on the walls and along the shelves. It was as if the night cleaning man had decided to sneak a feel of power by sitting at the boss's desk.

Then things started to change. Like Chester Arthur in another century or Harry Truman and Gerald Ford in this one, Frank Fitzsimmons started to become "presidential." He began to feel comfortable with the power, to look as if he knew how to handle it, and to like it enough to want to keep it. The evolution was subtle enough so that none of those who were closest to Fitzsimmons were able to look back years later and put a finger on when and how. It could have started the first time Fitzsimmons remembered not to grab a tray when he walked into the headquarters' dining room because he was now one of two people (the General Secretary-Treasurer John English was the other) who had their food brought to them. Perhaps it was the first Friday he was not surprised when he opened his paycheck envelope and saw a gross of $1,923.00 instead of $1,057.00 because his salary had jumped from $55,000 to $100,000. Maybe it began the third or fourth time he noticed that people stopped talking whenever he did, or that big shots who had barely tolerated him before now stopped in the halls to offer him their latest jokes or to ask about the wife and kids and the golf game. Or, it might have begun when he noticed that he, Frank Fitzsimmons from CCC Trucking, was actually doing the job—that you didn't have to be god, as he used to think Jimmy Hoffa was, to handle it.

While thoughts and events during the spring and summer of 1967 were turning Frank Fitzsimmons from seat warmer to seat holder,

Hoffa was suffering continuing setbacks in the courts. His lawyers' attempts to reopen the jury-tampering case and intensified efforts to buy changes in witnesses' testimony (documented in Kennedy aide Walter Sheridan's *The Fall and Rise of Jimmy Hoffa*), were going nowhere. And Hoffa's appeals in a later pension-fund-fraud conviction were rapidly being exhausted.

Soon there were signs that Fitzsimmons had decided he was there to stay. In July he sent some of Hoffa's closest headquarters assistants back out to the field and brought in his own men to take their place. According to people who were there, he walked into an executive board meeting of the twelve International vice-presidents in August, swallowed hard, looked up and issued a gruff challenge to those seated around the table who, he had heard, were complaining privately about how the union was being run and were plotting to push him aside. "If you have any complaints," Fitzsimmons told them, "lay them on the table now, because I'm in charge and I intend to stay in charge unless Jimmy comes back." Several minutes of silence followed the speech. Then someone broke the ice to praise the new leader. The rest followed, one by one. In September, Fitzsimmons' own name plate appeared on his desk and pictures of his wife and kids replaced Hoffa's.

Also that month, according to William Bufalino, Fitzsimmons told him he wasn't going to follow Hoffa's orders from prison. Bufalino got the message; soon he stopped visiting Hoffa altogether. "He felt like a prisoner of war when he went to Lewisburg," a family friend later remembered. "But he could accept that as just another condition of life, and just wait it out till he was freed. But when he saw his friends turn against him—well, that was rough." A prison friend similarly remembered that "As time went on, Hoffa became louder and more bad-tempered. He talked more and more about what would happen when he got out. He was really bitter."

There is no evidence that Hoffa had made Fitzsimmons promise in so many words that he would follow his orders from prison. But no one who knew the two men well doubted that if an explicit arrangement hadn't been discussed, it was only because Hoffa assumed on the basis of his relationship with Fitzsimmons that the facts of life need not be spelled out.

This early, in the fall of 1967, Hoffa may have been angry and frustrated about being ignored from the sidelines, but he wasn't yet desperate. It was only a matter of time, he assumed, before he would be back issuing orders from the white leather chair at headquarters. But soon a new fear began to form in the back of his mind. At first it seemed ridiculous. Even two or three years into his jail term it seemed too far-fetched to mention except, half-laughingly, to his son. Was it possible not only that Fitzsimmons wasn't going to listen to him from prison but also that he might try to keep him from coming back when he got out of jail?

As Hoffa grew increasingly uncomfortable with thoughts like these, his twelve vice-presidents began to see a silver lining. Fitzsimmons' challenge to them that July at the board meeting was more significant for the fact that he made it than for the implication that an insurrection was being planned. There was no revolt brewing. Together the vice-presidents had begun to see that losing a charismatic, overbearing president was liberating. What they lost in security they gained in independence, and the more they got used to it, the more they began to like it.

In theory, the Teamsters union, under Hoffa or Fitzsimmons, is a model of constitutionally decentralized power. Delegates representing the 742 local unions meet every five years to choose a general president and an executive board consisting of a secretary-treasurer, sixteen vice-presidents from different areas of the United States and Canada, and three trustees (who are a rung below vice-president in the International hierarchy). Most of what the general president does has to be approved by this executive board. Issues that do not have national import are decided at lower levels, either by one of the five area conferences, by forty-eight joint councils, which consist of several unions in the same area of one state or of neighboring states, by the local unions, by the local business agents who handle a particular employer, or by the local shop steward who represents two dozen people who work with him on a job site.

Under Jimmy Hoffa this was all theory. He had been involved in every detail of the union throughout the nation. The men who worked for him have different sets of stories about Hoffa, sitting in Washington, taking a phone call from a rank-and-file driver about a small grievance in some far-off truck terminal and then calling the trucking company about it—thus bypassing or undercutting the vice-president from that region, the joint council president in charge of that area of that state, or the local president, not to mention the business agent or shop steward.

That changed with Fitzsimmons. Letters or calls to the general president from rank-and-filers were automatically bucked right back to the vice-president who came from the appropriate region or conference. Executive-board meetings, ceremonial under Hoffa, became the place where major issues and even minor ones got decided.

Spreading the power around may have been the secret of Fitzsimmons' success in holding off those who might otherwise have sent him packing when it came time for him to run for election in 1971. But it was no shrewd master plan. It was simply a matter of personalities. By dint of his brains, his sheer energy and his special power to make people believe they should be led by him, Jimmy Hoffa centralized power far beyond the constitution's apparent limits. For lack of the same qualities, Frank Fitzsimmons decentralized it.

Everyone, including the International vice-presidents, naturally fell in line behind Hoffa. Not so with a man like Fitzsimmons, who had begun his union work as a twenty-nine-year-old functionary for a twenty-three-year-old. Nor did Fitzsimmons have the organizational genius that enabled Hoffa to keep everything under his control. Fitzsimmons and most others could never approach Hoffa's ability to remember details (including names of people he had met over a handshake years before), to keep track of a hundred different problems at once, and to psyche out the opposition's thinking so consistently. Beyond that there was the difference in the way the two men approached the job. Most weeks Hoffa worked seven days. Vacations and diversions such as golf were alien to him. Fitzsimmons was the opposite: three vice-presidents and two personal aides estimated in 1977 that he played golf an average of four or five days out of seven. A random check of his calendar for 1976 scanned by a source at union headquarters indicated that he was out of town an average of twenty days a month. There may have been some business or a speech involved in most of the trips, but there was usually some golf and sun involved, too. A check of La Costa records by a source in the accounting department there indicated that Fitzsimmons came to the California country club an average of once a month throughout the middle '70s. These frequent absences from headquarters and the leisurely pace of his working days had to limit Fitzsimmons' ability to keep up with union business.

That Frank Fitzsimmons was not Jimmy Hoffa did not mean that on the day Fitzsimmons appeared for his Seventh Annual Invitational Golf Tournament he didn't have any work to do. That much of the decision making had been delegated to the field did not mean that on that October morning in 1976 most of it wasn't under Fitzsimmons' control.

In August 1940 Dan Tobin was completing the thirty-third of what would be his forty-five years as the Teamsters president. Although union headquarters was in Indianapolis, Indiana, that year he called the membership to a convention in the nation's capital. "Send only the finest type of men as delegates," Tobin warned his local union leaders. "Washington is no place for hoodlums or undesirable characters. There is no such thing as fixing anything in the city of Washington."

Beyond the quaint virginity of his call to the troops, there is about Tobin's timid first approach to Washington an irony that is inescapable to anyone who confronted the Teamsters' flamboyant presence there four decades later. Built in 1955, the Teamsters headquarters was four stories of white marble and occupied a full block of Louisiana Avenue. (A five-million-dollar annex has, since late 1977, nearly doubled its size.) It is one of the more impressive privately owned buildings in the capital, and it sits on the best piece of property on Capitol Hill, with the lawns of the Capitol just across the street serving as a front yard and a marvelous vista for the windows off to the left of Fitzsimmons' desk.

As he approached the first tee to begin the tournament named for him that October morning, Fitzsimmons controlled a complex organization in Washington of more than five hundred employees in fifteen different departments. These included an electronic data-processing department that supplied computer services to hundreds of Teamsters locals through a nationwide terminal network; a legal department that provided advice to, and kept track of the work of, the several hundred lawyers who served the union's locals and joint councils; a research unit that provided Fitzsimmons and his executive board with analyses of contracts and various negotiating strategies; an organizing department that dispensed money and manpower to unions involved in recruiting drives; a lobbying arm that kept track of legislative happenings across the street; a department specializing in health and safety issues; an education department that ran the headquarters' 15,000-volume library; and a communications department that, among other things, published a glossy monthly magazine sent to all 2.3 million Teamsters families.

Many of the International's more routine chores were managed for Fitzsimmons by General Secretary-Treasurer Ray Schoessling. These included hiring, firing and setting salaries for headquarters staff and keeping track of the one million dollars a week in dues money that rolled in. A colorless former vice-president, Schoessling was appointed earlier in 1976, to the great relief of the headquarters employees. His crusty old predecessor, Murray W. "Dusty" Miller, also at La Costa today, had been disliked by the staff, clerks and secretaries, who claimed that he had treated them with contempt when they came to him with requests for salary raises, vacation days and the like. "I knew a guy here who went in and asked Dusty for a raise once," one department head later remembered. "Dusty didn't say anything or even look up from his mail for a minute or two. Then he looked up and told the guy to clear out his desk by five o'clock because he was fired."

Things had improved under Schoessling. But the antipathy toward Miller was a reminder that the "marble palace," as many staffers called it, was peopled with men and women who by and large were concerned more with their work and with salaries, parking permits for the basement garage, or getting on line early in the dining room for the great fish buffet on Fridays, than they were with gangster intrigue or other aspects of the swollen Teamsters image. While at times, like the day Hoffa disappeared, the corridors and dining hall buzzed with rumors, all but a handful of the men and women at 25 Louisiana Avenue knew nothing more than what they read in the papers about the underside of the Teamsters story.

Not that they weren't sensitive to the bad publicity. The accused, including Fitzsimmons, were seen around headquarters as nice, pleasant people, and almost everyone at headquarters seemed to feel the Teamsters had gotten a bad rap in the press. Most staffers were embarrassed by the negative Teamsters image. "When I go to a cocktail party," one assistant in the legal department explained several months after the Fitzsimmons Invitational, "you have to ask me five or six really specific questions before you box me into admitting that the 'labor law' I practice is for the Teamsters."

On October 13, 1976, Frank Fitzsimmons had done little to raise the drooping morale. When Hoffa was in charge, the bad press had been a kind of stimulant for troop unity and fight. With Fitzsimmons usually absent as he was today, and without the force of a Jimmy Hoffa even when he was there, a bunker mentality had set in. Most of the troops whispered among themselves and left eagerly and promptly at 5 P.M.

The only thing that worked the other way for Fitzsimmons by then was that he was genuinely liked by most of the headquarters staff, who saw him as a nice, underbearing guy. From janitor, to cook to lawyer (to caddy at La Costa), those who worked for him agreed that while Fitzsimmons had none of Hoffa's flair he also had none of Hoffa's arrogance toward the hired help. Perhaps because he had been on the receiving end for so long, he didn't expect people to dive for his falling coat when he walked into a room.

Fitzsimmons may have been nice to his subordinates, but he was no patsy. He had refunded some of the old power once concentrated in the General President's in-box, but he had also learned to use the considerable powers that he kept.

This is something that many Teamsters watchers had trouble believing. Nine years after his ascension, rumors of Fitzsimmons' subservience to some hidden power were as common as the jokes about his troubles with the spoken word. One story had it that his executive assistant, Walter Shea—tall, relatively young, with a cold steely look—actually called the shots. Another put William Presser at the hidden helm. A third strand of Teamsterology had Roy Williams, vice-president from Kansas City, in charge. It was indeed true that Shea was the man to see on most administrative matters. But he still cleared anything that was even remotely important with the boss. Presser, along with Allen Dorfman and various silent partners from the mob had had much more to say than Fitzsimmons had about what happened at the Central States Pension Fund. But that was the pension fund, not the union. And Williams had been a major force in negotiations for a new nationwide trucking contract completed the past spring. But Fitzsimmons had been there around the clock, too, and he had had the last word on the Teamsters side of the table. In short, rumors that Fitzsimmons was on puppet strings were exaggerated. Teamsters vice-presidents relished the power he had ceded to them, and many had status as advisers that no one had had under Hoffa. Most still chuckled over his golf schedule or about the way he would skip a line or a page of a ghost-written speech and go obliviously right on with it. But he was still the top dog, and they recognized it.

Fitzsimmons' relationship with one local union president and the International vice-president in the local's area illustrated the special powers of the presidency that he had learned to use. In 1976 Barry Feinstein was the president of Local Union 237 in New York City, which represented some 15,000 municipal workers. In 1971, Feinstein's bridge attendants walked off their jobs. Before they left they opened the drawbridges that took commuters in and out of Manhattan. When the chaos produced a barrage of lawsuits against the union, Feinstein asked Fitzsimmons for a loan to pay the lawyers. Fitzsimmons sent him $90,000. After that, Feinstein was given funds from Washington in the form of an organizing grant to recruit new members. "The General President can do a lot of things to help a local if he wants," Feinstein later noted.

Four months before the La Costa golf tournament, Feinstein had been picked by Fitzsimmons to be a member of a constitutional committee at the national convention—a position that carried prestige and $2,000 in extra compensation. (At the 1976 convention, Fitzsimmons gave out more than a hundred such committee and sergeant-at-arms appointments worth an average of $3,000 each.) Feinstein's committee was the group that approved Fitzsimmons' recommendation for a constitutional amendment allowing his salary to be raised 25 percent. Before the convention, when Feinstein had gotten word of a possible challenge by Gibbons to Fitzsimmons' unanimous reelection, he offered, as he described it later, "to bring our people out there to help him, because I'm a team player." Feinstein's relationship with Fitzsimmons was a matter of a convenient, simple trade-off. There was nothing corrupt about it; Feinstein, in fact, enjoyed a reputation for exceptional honesty. It was simply a pragmatic marriage of interest governed by the fact that Fitzsimmons as president held enough in the way of patronage plums, lending authority, and other discretionary powers to encourage almost unanimous team play.

Feinstein's area vice-president was Joseph Trerotola, the genial former milk-wagon driver who was the International's first vice-president and the president of New York's Joint Council 16. He too was a team player. According to a top Teamsters leader, on at least one prior occasion Trerotola had rejected Harold Gibbons' urging that they try to overthrow Fitzsimmons. His support for the incumbent was no doubt encouraged by the fact that his son Vincent, also playing today at La Costa, was on Fitzsimmons' International payroll for 1976 as "general organizer" for $35,600. Combined with his $17,000 job at his father's joint council, a $14,000 job at his father's Eastern

Conference, a $3,600 job at the joint council pension fund, and a $13,800 job at another New York Teamsters local, Vincent grossed $84,000 that year. He would collect another $10,000 to $15,000 as an agent selling insurance to local unions in his father's joint council. Those interviewed who knew Vincent well and worked with him claimed that he did little more than handle phones and other minor details in his father's joint council offices.

Under the constitution Fitzsimmons had the power that morning to hire and fire any number of such general organizers. He used it well. In 1976 there were forty-five on the payroll, most of whom, like the younger Trerotola, held other supposedly full-time jobs at an area, joint council, or local union. As in the case of Vincent Trerotola, Fitzsimmons had carefully doled out these patronage plums to the men in the union or to their families or friends who could help him, or hurt him, the most. Using the leverage he had over people like Trerotola or Feinstein, he could also influence, or on occasion dictate, the hiring of organizers or other employees by the 742 locals and the 48 joint councils. With no civil-service system to stop him, this gave Fitzsimmons and his allies patronage powers probably surpassed only by the President of the United States.

His appointment power went right up to the vice-presidents. Although the vice-presidents sitting as an executive board theoretically had to approve much of what he did, Fitzsimmons held trump cards by way of appointments he could give to them that made their opposition unlikely. At Fitzsimmons' sole discretion, any vice-president could be named an International organizer or representative for an additional $25,000 or $30,000 in salary, or a conference director for an additional $25,000. Joseph Trerotola in 1976 was both an International representative and a conference chairman, giving him an extra $48,000 beyond his vice-president's salary. As Harold Gibbons had found out in 1972 when he hadn't gone along with Fitzsimmons' and the others in supporting Richard Nixon for reelection, Fitzsimmons could take away these extras as easily as he dispensed them.

Fitzsimmons also controlled who became a vice-president in the first place. The constitution directed that when there was a vice-presidential vacancy between conventions, the president filled it. Because conventions were held only every five years and because through his other appointment powers Fitzsimmons could persuade a veep who wanted to retire to do so just after a convention, most vice-presidents had first been appointed to vacancies.

Ultimately the appointed vice-presidents had to run for election at a convention. History shows that the only way the delegates were likely to vote for a veep candidate was if he was running at the convention with the Fitzsimmons slate of vice-presidents. The bottom line was that as of 1976 no vice-president had ever been elected under Hoffa or Fitzsimmons who hadn't been first appointed by the president and hadn't run on the president's slate.

In spite of the decentralization written into the union constitution, Fitzsimmons also had strong influence over the local unions. He alone had to approve a local's by-laws. In theory, he had the power, although it was rarely exercised, to approve or reject a local's decision to strike. As in Feinstein's case he could make loans and give "organizing grants" to locals. In circumstances where he could establish mismanagement or corruption he could also order a local union into trusteeship, a takeover by headquarters that threw the local's officers out of work. Trusteeship had rarely been used to combat corruption, but it had often been used to bring dissident locals into line. The president also had the power to approve or disapprove any local organizing effort if it involved "raiding" another union, and to appoint a board to investigate and act on any charges of misconduct against local officers—another prerogative that had been used more often to threaten dissenting local leaders than to curb corruption.

Finally, Fitzsimmons had the singular power to spend union-raised money on political contributions. He also controlled the union's two-million-dollar-a-year communications, lobbying and public-education efforts, including the monthly magazine. With a circulation of more than two million, it is among the most widely read special-interest publications in the country.

When Frank Fitzsimmons stepped toward the first hole at La Costa he had learned to use these levers of power well enough to assure him of reelection by acclamation at the convention four months before.

He had also learned to use the perquisites of that power to build a life style he had never dreamed of back on the loading dock at CCC Trucking. He was drawing $156,000 in salary and allowances. His green Lincoln, with its green velour interior, was paid for by the union, and so was the ranch house he kept in suburban Washington. (This was a tradition begun by Dan Tobin, who had his union buy two homes for him; continued by Dave Beck, who sold his house complete with water falls, formal gardens, and swimming pool, to the union for $160,000 and then lived in it rent free; and improved on by Jimmy Hoffa, who had union-paid carpenters reconstruct his Michigan country place.) When Fitzsimmons wanted to get to his other home, the $250,000 split-level here at La Costa, his union-paid private jet took him there. There was no need to play with the travel records since it was all legally part of his fringe-benefit package. The union constitution gave him travel and expense-account discretion that rivaled the fringes of any corporate executive.

A section of the constitution provided that

> the General President, for the purpose of promoting the interests and welfare of the International union . . . and for the purpose of conserving his health, may at his discretion travel . . . and take periodic rests. The General Executive Board shall provide for all expenses and allowances of the General President when performing the services mentioned herein or when taking periodic rests; the said expenses and allowances shall include . . . the full and complete maintenance of his wife so that she can accompany the General President, and all secretarial help and services which he deems necessary while so engaged.

If this provision has any limits, they aren't apparent; in the late '60s, Jimmy Hoffa's jail term had been construed as a "periodic rest" and he received living expenses and a per diem allowance for it.

Clear abuses like this clouded what to some unionists was the thornier question of just where on the socioeconomic ladder the worker-turned-worker's-representative deserved to be. In all the news articles written over the years about Fitzsimmons' salary and benefits there had been a consistent, if often tacit, expectation that union leaders didn't belong at places like La Costa but should instead be making the same money and living under the same conditions as the people they represented.

This editorial concern for worker–union-leader parity had often spilled over into bad reporting. For example, most papers and magazines had by 1976 made some reference to the sumptuous meals served to Fitzsimmons by the French chef in the headquarters dining room. This infuriated Fitzsimmons. Yes, there was a French chef, who was paid $30,000 a year in 1976. He was a pretty good cook. But anyone at headquarters could have explained that actually he was in charge of preparing meals for all headquarters employees and that his food was more institutional than exotic. (Fitzsimmons favored roast chicken with no sauce, New England clam chowder, and coconut custard.)

There were the snide references to Fitzsimmons' home at La Costa. *Newsweek* had called it "palatial" the month after the previous Fitzsimmons Invitational, then backed up the adjective with the assessment by an anonymous "awed" Teamsters official that he had "never seen anything like it." If he hadn't, he had never seen many of the other homes at La Costa or, in fact, any other luxurious but not spectacular split-level with a good view of a golf course.

A real issue concerning Fitzsimmons' place at La Costa, other than whether he ought to have paid the $250,000 he reportedly had spent for the unpalatial home, is that a check with the construction company that built it would have revealed that some, if not most, of the construction work had been done with nonunion labor.

To Fitzsimmons the idea that you couldn't represent "your people" if you're at La Costa while they're at McDonald's was absurd. Why should someone with a job as important as his, he would argue in an interview the following year, be paid a truck driver's salary? On this score, Harold Gibbons agreed with Fitzsimmons. "If you're gonna go by the norms of the society we live in, then it's [Fitzsimmons salary and benefits] shit," he said in an interview. "General Motors' head will get 800,000 dollars this year. Plus some bonus of maybe a million dollars. [Actually in 1976 the G.M. chief executive's earnings totaled $966,000.] Compared to that and put into the framework of the capitalist system, Fitz is underpaid."

This all made sense if, as Fitzsimmons had often told associates, you see union leadership as a business, not as a social movement. Fitzsimmons agreed basically with what Jimmy Hoffa had once told a reporter about union leading: "Everyone who writes about me seems amazed that I call it a business instead of a crusade or something." Hoffa had said. "Well it is a business. We are not labor statesmen. We are not humanitarians or longhairs."

Some union leaders, including some Teamsters who bore the scars of the early organizing campaigns of the '20s, '30s and '40s, would object to Hoffa's cynicism. But for years many of the men who made up the foursomes this morning at La Costa had taken the argument and run with it to extremes unmatched by any other labor organization. Times had changed since the first president of the International, Cornelius Shea, was paid $150 a month in 1903.

Jimmy Hoffa in New Jersey helps Tony Provenzano win the 1959 election as president of Joint Council 73. A year later, Provenzano's unsuccessful opponent was brutally beaten. Two years after that, a potential opponent in the next election was murdered. In May 1978 Provenzano went on trial for ordering the murder.

Jimmy Hoffa waves to 1961 Teamsters convention in Miami Beach. Robert Kennedy had recently become Attorney General and Hoffa would soon be in trouble.

Teamsters General President Frank Fitzsimmons testifies before Senate subcommittee in November 1978 on Central States Pension and Health and Welfare funds. He denied that Allen Dorfman had had any influence at the funds.

Teamsters Vice President Jackie Presser is interviewed by Cleveland *Plain Dealer* in February of 1977. His aggressive public relations efforts marked a radical departure from the Teamsters' past posture and placed him on a dangerous tightrope.

William "Big Bill" Presser, Jackie's father, waits to testify before Robert Kennedy and the Senate's McClellan Committee. He took the Fifth Amendment. Two years later he was convicted of obstruction of justice.

Jimmy Hoffa, Jr., talks to reporters the day after his father disappeared. Instinctively, the young lawyer assumed leadership of the family, screening the bogus ransom calls and pushing the FBI to do more.

Allen R. Glick. On May 29, 1974, the Central States Pension Fund approved a loan of $62,700,000 to Glick for the purchase of two Las Vegas hotel/casinos. He had applied for the loan nine days before without ever offering a personal financial statement.

Allen Dorfman appears before the McClellan Committee in 1958. The former gym teacher took the Fifth Amendment when asked about the millions of dollars in insurance he had sold to the Teamsters health and welfare funds.

C. Suspects Outside of Michigan

1. ANTHONY "TONY PRO" PROVENZANO **, age 58, known New Jersey La Cosa Nostra member and Teamster Local 560 Officer. Served time in Lewisburg Penitentiary with JRH and reportedly had a "falling out" with him while there.

2. STEPHEN ANDRETTA *, age 42, trusted associate of "TONY PRO", told Newark source RALPH PICARDO that he did not participate in HOFFA hit, but was left in Newark to provide alibi for "TONY PRO". (At the time of this writing ANDRETTA is to appear before Federal Grand Jury (FGJ) in Detroit after serving six weeks in Milan, Michigan, Prison for Contempt of Court.)

3. THOMAS ANDRETTA ***, age 38, brother of STEPHEN, trusted associate of "TONY PRO", reported by Newark source to be involved in actual disappearance of JRH.

4. SALVATORE "SAL" BRIGUGLIO ***, age 45, trusted associate of "TONY PRO", reported by Newark source to be involved in actual disappearance of JRH.

5. GABRIEL "GABE" BRIGUGLIO ***, age 36, brother of "SAL", trusted associate of "TONY PRO", reported by Newark source to be involved in actual disappearance of JRH.

6. FRANCIS JOSEPH "FRANK" SHEERAN, age 43, president Local 326, Wilmington, Delaware. Resides in Philadelphia and is known associate of RUSSEL BUFALINO, La Cosa Nostra Chief, Eastern Pennsylvania. His vehicle seen at meeting of La Cosa

-3-

Page three of the FBI's "Hoffex" memo, prepared for a Washington meeting of federal law enforcement officials involved in the Hoffa disappearance, lists the main suspects in the case outside of Michigan. "JRH" refers to James R. Hoffa.

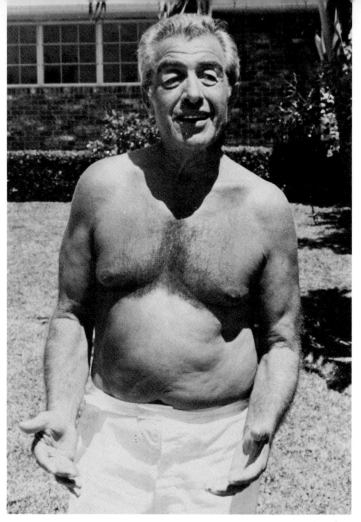

Tony Provenzano, in his backyard in Florida a week after Hoffa's disappearance, protests his innocence and tells reporters that he is only a truck driver.

Salvatore "Sammy Pro" Provenzano after his arrest for counterfeiting in 1971. The charges were soon dropped and he continued to run New Jersey Teamsters affairs for brother Tony.

Key Hoffa suspects: Left: Hoffa murder suspect Salvatore Briguglio on his way to appear in a December 1975 Detroit line-up. An eyewitness to Hoffa's departure from the restaurant parking lot where he was last seen identified Briguglio as having been in the car with Hoffa. In March 1978 he would be murdered on the street in New York's Little Italy. Right: Gabriel Briguglio, Salvatore's brother and another Hoffa case suspect, leaves a federal grand jury in Newark in December 1975.

A rare snapshot of crime boss Russell Bufalino in 1968. Though he escaped most headlines in the Hoffa case, all roads seemed to lead to him as the man with the clout and connections necessary to order Hoffa's elimination.

Ron Carey, president of Teamsters Local 804 in New York. A former United Parcel driver and an honest union boss, Carey was blocked in 1978 from moving up the Teamsters ladder in New York.

Teamsters Vice President Roy Williams, the Kansas City Teamsters leader who in 1978 allied with Allen Dorfman and other old-time forces in the union in an effort to be the one picked to replace Fitzsimmons.

Teamsters Vice President Harold Gibbons at a 1973 press conference after Fitzsimmons stripped him of his jobs for refusing to go along with the Teamsters' endorsement of Richard Nixon. Loyal to Jimmy Hoffa and to his socialist ideals at the same time, Gibbons built a model of progressive unionism in St. Louis. But he never challenged Hoffa or Fitzsimmons to reform the union nationwide.

Since the 1950s every general president of the International Brotherhood of Teamsters had been paid more than any other union leader in the country. By 1976 Frank Fitzsimmons' pay check was more than two thirds higher than George Meany's—$156,000 as against $90,000. Because lower-level Teamsters were allowed to occupy more than one payroll, there were many other Teamsters, including some gathered at La Costa for the Tournament, who also drew more than Meany in 1976. Jackie Presser was earning $35,800 a year from the International payroll, $800 from the Ohio Conference of Teamsters, $14,000 from Teamsters Joint Council 41 in Ohio, $117,000 from Local 507 in Cleveland, and $31,000 from two bakery unions affiliated with the Teamsters—a total of $198,600. Nineteen Teamsters drew $100,000 or more in 1976, 26 drew more than Meany's $90,000, 148 made $50,000 or more, and 324 made $40,000 or more.

Other unions had stayed somewhere in the middle between paying their bosses a salary in tune with the economic status of the workers they represented and paying them what the nature of the job might justify. In 1976, UAW President Leonard Woodcock drew $65,000, including expenses. At least seventy-five Teamsters were paid more. Unlike the Teamsters, the UAW never allowed its officials to be on more than one payroll.

The Teamsters argument that high salaries were justified by the importance of the jobs and the need to attract competent, honest, hard-working people to fill them would have been more persuasive had the forty-, fifty- and sixty-thousand-dollar slots been filled with that kind of talent. Roland McMaster, who earned $46,215 in 1976 as a Fitzsimmons-appointed "general organizer," had a conviction ten years earlier for accepting a payoff to guarantee labor peace to an Ohio cartage company. He had played a cameo role the decade before that in the McClellan Committee Report, in which he was charged with taking fifty-five head of registered black-angus cattle from a trucking company and making $56,000 in sideline trucking deals between 1953 and 1957. More recently, the Detroit *Free Press* had reported, just three months before the 1976 Fitzsimmons tournament, that from 1972 to 1974 McMaster had spent $1.3 million on a nationwide organizing drive that had netted the union only "about 750 drivers" and had "served as a smokescreen to get trucking companies to pay for labor peace." The method used by one "organizer" under McMaster's direction, the *Free Press* reported, included telling a driver that he knew where the driver's eight-year-old daughter went to school. When I asked Fitzsimmons about McMaster, he called him a "good trade-unionist who did a hell of a job in more ways than one."

Many more Teamsters on local, joint council, and International payrolls had similarly questionable backgrounds of criminal activity. But what pervaded Fitzsimmons' union more was a generally low level of competence in the top-paying spots. Much of it was the result of nepotism. Vincent Trerotola had no apparent ability or background, only his parentage, to justify his $84,000 a year. Teamsters payrolls were filled with sons and brothers and nephews of similar nondistinction, including Fitzsimmons' own sons. Donald, who would be cited by that Senate committee for helping to promote the insurance fraud for which his brother was indicted, drew his $47,000 from the International as a "general auditor." In an August 1977 interview, Fitzsimmons defended the hiring of his two sons, telling me that "What I'm doing with my sons is no different than what that goddamn Carter is doing with his sons and relatives in the White House." *

In 1976, among Fitzsimmons, Secretary-Treasurer Schoessling, and the sixteen International vice-presidents, there were seven sons, one daughter, one father, four brothers, one brother-in-law, and one niece on various union payrolls.

Under the constitution, general auditors held key jobs. They were supposed to audit the books of local unions to root out corruption. Although Donald Fitzsimmons and the other eleven International general auditors all were paid at least $47,000 including allowances in 1976, and averaged $52,000 each, none, according to Fitzsimmons, was a certified public accountant. Three were sons of other top Teamsters. The remainder seemed to come from locals or areas powerful enough to deserve the kind of patronage appointment for one of their own. The auditing they were assigned to do by headquarters usually involved the locals they had come from.

The auditors were only the most obvious example of the gulf between compensation and competence that Fitzsimmons had left behind in Washington the morning of the La Costa tournament. College degrees, job experience, and other credentials would have helped the top Teamsters in their argument that they should be paid as well as

---

* In 1977, two of President Carter's married sons were living at the White House with their families. However, the White House reported that no public money was paying for their food or lodging, and neither family member was on a public payroll.

the business leaders they met on the other side of the table. Still, among the senior ranks the absence of such credentials could be excused by the economic circumstances from which all early trade-union leaders in America had come. What was harder to dismiss was the fact that from Fitzsimmons on down, none of the top two dozen Teamsters, except perhaps Jackie Presser, Harold Gibbons and Alaskan Teamsters leader Jesse Carr was respected as an intelligent, sharp executive; and Gibbons was largely powerless, and Carr was content to be off by himself in his Alaska kingdom. The outlook for the next generation of Teamsters leaders was worse. Fitzsimmons may have wanted to be compared to business leaders in terms of compensation, but he certainly wouldn't have liked the comparison when the subject changed to performance in training middle managers for future leadership. There was no core of rising young talent in the Teamsters. The Vincent Trerotolas and the Donald Fitzsimmonses simply don't have what it would take to lead the world's largest labor union two decades from now.

By the middle 1970s, union work involved more than putting the picket lines in the right place. Professional economists were needed to analyze cost of living and other trends, and to evaluate complex wage, hours, and fringe-benefit formulas proposed at the bargaining table. Skilled attorneys were required to guide the union through laws and regulations having to do with occupational safety, equal opportunity, pensions, and union financial and organizing activities. As the largest and most diverse union in the world, the Teamsters needed these professionals the most. Under Fitzsimmons they lagged badly. On the day of the 1976 La Costa tournament the research department that analyzed the economy and contract packages had five people: two professionals, two paraprofessionals and a trainee. One of the professionals had some graduate training in economics. The law department had three lawyers, none with the top credentials Teamsters money could have bought. At the other extreme, the United Auto Workers had fourteen professional research people, twelve with graduate training, plus a second research staff of twenty professionals handling social security and other pension-related matters. There were nine full-time lawyers at the UAW.

This kind of thin professional back-up, together with the nepotism and union politics that limited the quality of the union's middle managers, auditors, negotiators and recruiters had, by 1976, put the Teamsters in danger of drifting into the next decade unprepared to meet the complex challenges of modern unionism. The union seemed to be moving forward only on its raw strength and past momentum.

On October 13, 1976, Fitzsimmons could point accurately to a record that overshadowed these subtle future problems. He had increased Teamsters membership by 500,000 since 1967.* He had successfully merged the brewery-workers union into the Teamsters. He had started the Health and Safety Department. Not hesitating in early 1976 to use the ultimate weapon, a strike, he had increased the truck drivers' basic hourly wage by $3.55 during his nine years in charge, as compared to a 97-cent increase during Hoffa's last nine years. Fitzsimmons took great comfort in these bread-and-butter accomplishments. These were the Teamsters issues he loved to talk about, not intangibles like the quality of management and the professional staff or the prospects for the union's leadership one or two decades from now.

This did not mean he wasn't concerned about the future. But his worries were much more personal. That morning at La Costa he was haunted by the fear that for him the great days of the early '70s were over.

The final confirmation that Teamsters power had shifted from Jimmy Hoffa to Frank Fitzsimmons had come in a tense confrontation between the two four years after Hoffa's imprisonment. In April 1971 Hoffa obtained a brief release from jail to visit his wife who was hospitalized in San Francisco. Despite orders from prison officials not to do so, when Hoffa got to San Francisco he convened a meeting of top Teamsters, minus Fitzsimmons, to discuss union business. Fitzsimmons later told me, in an account confirmed by others who were there, that when he heard what was happening he flew to San Francisco, went to Hoffa's hotel suite, and ordered the Teamsters to leave the meeting. Despite Hoffa's protest, they left.

The condominium salesman who conducts tours of La Costa tells you that on a clear day you can see Richard Nixon's estate in San Clemente from Frank Fitzsimmons' home that overlooks the La Costa fairways thirty miles south. Beginning with Fitzsimmons' election in his own right three months after the San Francisco confrontation, at the Teamsters convention in 1971, Nixon began a courtship of the Teamsters General President that erased the thirty-mile gap. The President paid a surprise visit to the executive-board meeting

* For more discussion on Teamster organizing see Chapter VII, pages 279–282.

held just before the '71 convention and praised Fitzsimmons as "my kind of labor leader." He sent his labor secretary, James D. Hodgson, to the convention to offer his own effusive tribute. There followed a series of San Clemente and White House invitations and other favors that seduced Fitzsimmons. Nixon appointed him to the Pay Board, his labor-management committee empowered to control wage increases, to which Fitzsimmons responded: "We intend to do what we can to implement the problem that is at hand today. As far as our position is concerned, the Teamsters' is the same as outlined here, that once we determine we will stand back of our decision."

Nixon made sure that his cabinet officials and top aides were accessible to Fitzsimmons. One Teamsters reception in 1972 drew six members of the Nixon cabinet, including the Attorney General. Fitzsimmons returned the favors. On July 17, 1972, he called the sixteen vice-presidents and three trustees together for an executive-board meeting at La Costa to approve his resolution that Nixon be endorsed for reelection. This made the Teamsters the only major union to support the Republican President. The only dissenter on the board was Harold Gibbons. Fitzsimmons soon showed the President the depth of his loyalty by stripping Gibbons of all his appointed power and salaries. He asked all the vice-presidents, except Gibbons, and all the organizers to kick in a thousand dollars to the campaign, and federal election reports revealed that he contributed $4,000 of his own.

A year later Fitzsimmons was one of Nixon's diehard boosters as Watergate began to close in, and in June 1974, the Los Angeles *Times* reported that the largest single gift, $25,000, to an anti-impeachment group organized by a rabbi named Baruch Korff had come from the Teamsters union. The same year Fitzsimmons took Teamsters legal business amounting to $100,000 a year away from Edward Bennett Williams, whose firm was representing the Democratic Party in its suit against the Watergate burglars, and gave it to the firm that Charles Colson had joined. Colson, who had resigned as White House Counsel, had been Nixon's liaison with Fitzsimmons.

It had all been more than worth it. "Those times at the White House . . . the parties . . . and the dinners are our most cherished memories," Mrs. Patricia Fitzsimmons recalled in a 1977 interview. "I can't tell you how much Fitz and I loved it, or how much we miss it now that those Carter people are there." "I remember seeing Colson leading him [Fitzsimmons] around like a new prize puppy," former Nixon aide John Dean recalled. "Fitzsimmons seemed thrilled just to be at the White House." "We don't have to do much," another Nixon staffer told *The New York Times* in 1972. "We bring Fitzsimmons in, give him a few minutes with the President, take him to lunch in the dining room and introduce him to Henry Kissinger." Outside the White House, Fitzsimmons showing off his latest golf putter or golf balls with the presidential seal became a source of mild amusement to friends and union cronies.

While Fitzsimmons collected presidential seals and other tokens of respectability in the early '70s, (according to his 1971 tax return, the tokens included two race horses purchased in Kentucky), he also took up a series of charitable causes that the press never appreciated. Like his claim of going to mass most Sundays, his charities were legitimate ones, and he developed for each an attachment. In 1970, he had started the tournament at La Costa. He explained seven years later that a picture-taking session in 1969 with some of the retarded and blind retarded children from the home for which the tournament was organized "moved me like nothing ever has before, and I decided to do something . . . I've always felt for handicapped children." His 1971 tax return revealed that in addition to sponsoring the tournament, he gave $5,300 of his own money to the home. During this time he also became a vice-president of the Muscular Dystrophy Association and raised money to buy special buses for crippled children and to build a drug-abuse center for young addicts.

But there was a darker side. On the night of February 12, 1973, according to reports later filed by an undercover agent for California law-enforcement authorities, Fitzsimmons, Allen Dorfman (then appealing a pension-fund kickback conviction) and Dorfman aide Alvin Baron met in the bar at La Costa with Lou Rosanova, a well-known organized-crime boss from Chicago. The undercover agent, who also sat in on the meeting, reported to his superiors that Rosanova, Fitzsimmons and the others had devised a new scheme to funnel Teamsters funds into organized-crime operations. The California authorities were interested, and they posted someone to follow Fitzsimmons the next day to see whom else he might meet with during his stay. The following morning a state lawman followed Fitzsimmons to San Clemente, where he watched the union president board Air Force One with Richard Nixon for the trip back to Washington.

Fitzsimmons had also been observed in Palm Springs on February 8 and 9 meeting at the Mission Hills Country Club and the Ambassador Hotel with aging Chicago crime-family boss Anthony Accardo. Also at the meetings were Accardo underling Anthony Spilotro, Dorfman, Rosanova and Peter Milano, identified by the FBI as a California organized-crime operative.

Cecil Hicks, the Orange County, California, District Attorney who supervised the undercover agent who covered the La Costa meeting, later explained to me that the Palm Springs and La Costa discussions involved a scheme to enroll Teamsters in California, Michigan and Illinois in a fraudulent prepaid health plan. Monthly payments on behalf of the members were to be made to a Los Angeles physician who would set up a health clinic to operate the plan. The clinic's monthly fee would come from money paid by employers into the union's health and welfare funds. The physician running the clinic was to kick back roughly 7 percent of these fees to a company called People's Industrial Consultants (PIC), which was a front set up to channel the money back to the organized-crime people behind the scheme. The top Teamsters officials involved were also to receive a portion of money kicked back to PIC. In short, John Doe, a trucker in California on whose behalf his employer regularly paid $10.50 a week into a health and welfare fund, would be enrolled in a prepaid medical plan with a clinic from which he would receive his regular medical care. The clinic would get a monthly fee from the health and welfare fund, of which some would be kicked back to organized-crime bosses and some to Teamsters leaders.

It turned out that D.A. Hicks wasn't the only one investigating the new scheme. Soon, he discovered that the FBI, pursuing a separate investigation of Rosanova, Accardo, Milano, and others had come across the plan and in January had begun tapping PIC's phones. The wiretaps were to end on March 6, unless extended by court order. To get the Justice Department to apply to the court for an extension of the taps, the FBI submitted an affidavit supporting a need for their continuance. The affidavit, which used information picked up by Hicks's informant as well as from FBI sources, made it clear that the FBI was on to a Teamsters–organized-crime case involving the general president of the union. In addition to describing the Fitzsimmons meetings reported by Hicks's man, it cited a number of phone conversations already tapped. In one, the physician who was to run the clinic was told that "the deal with the Teamsters is all set" and that Fitzsimmons had shaken hands with Milano and "made a deal with him."

The investigation never went further. In March, then-Attorney General Richard Kleindienst, a man not previously known for his reluctance to use wiretaps, turned down the FBI request to submit the affidavit to the court for approval to extend the taps. Through aides, Kleindienst explained that the investigation appeared to be turning up nothing. The FBI agents were amazed. Four years later it was revealed that Kleindienst, by then a private lawyer and convicted of testifying falsely before Congress,* had received a $125,000 legal fee for what he described as "a few hours work" in helping a client win a multimillion-dollar insurance-premium award from the Teamsters Central States Health and Welfare Fund. In an early 1977 interview, Hicks attributed Kleindienst's unusual turnoff of the investigation to the "love affair between Fitzsimmons and Nixon." He also showed me a memo circulated among California law-enforcement agencies after the federal investigation was quashed saying that federal agents had told Hicks's deputies that "any information pertaining to the investigation of either the misuse of Teamsters funds or illegal activities of Teamsters officials is frowned on by Washington."

The health-care plan and a dental-care plan that had also been talked about never went forward. This may have been because FBI agents, infuriated by Kleindienst's action, leaked the story of the aborted investigation to *The New York Times*. Having been spotted at the 1973 meeting caused some bad publicity for Fitzsimmons, but no lasting damage.

It was not until 1974 that the more ominous threats began to take shape—most importantly, the return of Jimmy Hoffa.

From the day when Hoffa went off to jail, Fitzsimmons had lobbied for his release, first trying to get Congress to investigate the tactics used by Robert Kennedy's Justice Department to put him there and then, with the coming of the Nixon presidency, trying to obtain parole or presidential clemency. As he had settled into Hoffa's seat, Fitzsimmons' ardor for the task of freeing Hoffa had cooled. Still, he had kept trying, partly because he felt obligated, and partly because he knew Hoffa's supporters expected it. By 1971, he and his close advisers had arrived at a happy compromise: get Hoffa a pardon but make it conditional on his not returning to the union. At the same

---

* Actually, Kleindienst was convicted of refusing to testify fully before a Congressional committee. This was a plea bargain negotiated after it was learned that he had lied under oath about the Nixon administration's handling of the International Telephone and Telegraph antitrust case.

time, the Nixon Justice Department, through presidential counsel Charles Colson, had sent similar signals that it would like to please the nation's Teamsters, to whom Hoffa was still a hero, before the 1972 election, yet not allow a convicted jury-tamperer and pension-fund embezzler to resume control of the union.

There may have been one more factor in the Nixon administration's thinking: money. By 1977 two sources, one intimately connected with Allen Dorfman, the other just as close to Tony Provenzano, would assert in interviews that, in addition to the thousand-dollar contributions to the Nixon campaign from Teamsters officials that were reported to election officials, Dorfman and Provenzano had each collected about $500,000 in cash and arranged to have it delivered to Colson in early 1973. The money was siphoned off from Las Vegas casinos, where cash is easy to come by, and from other mob fronts. It was a payoff for the restrictions on Hoffa's release, the sources claimed, although a third source said that a letup on any pending or future investigations of Fitzsimmons and other top Teamsters was also part of the deal. The same sources, as well as a federal prosecutor close to the Hoffa murder case, all added that the deal had been arranged by Fitzsimmons and Colson. In fact, Colson had pushed it first, they claimed, telling Fitzsimmons in 1971 about the pressure the Nixon administration was getting to release Hoffa and explaining that failing to do so might hurt the President's 1972 campaign. The payments were approved and arranged, the same sources explained, by the organized-crime leaders who wanted to prevent Hoffa's return to power. The site for one of the cash deliveries, one source reported, was the Circus Circus Casino.

On December 21, 1971, Nixon released Hoffa, approving a plea for clemency just two weeks after it had been submitted. The clemency application had been handled personally by Colson and then-Attorney General John Mitchell, who short-circuited the customary procedures, including consultation with the Justice Department's Criminal Division. This was just four months after the Federal Parole Board had turned down Hoffa's parole request for a third time.

A bitter dispute then set Fitzsimmons and Hoffa on a collision course, as the former claimed that Hoffa had agreed that he wouldn't return to union business when he was freed. Hoffa replied that he had never known that a written condition of his freedom was that he not participate in union business until 1980. Both men were telling the truth.

The truth—according to what lawyers, family friends, and other sources close to Hoffa later conceded in return for promises of anonymity—was that Hoffa had indeed agreed, orally, that he would not try to return to the union. As one source put it, "It was the kind of thing he just said 'Yeah, yeah' to, whenever someone mentioned it." But, the same source confirmed, Hoffa never expected he would have to keep the commitment. In fact, he had no idea prior to his release that such a stipulation had been written into his commutation document.

The reason Hoffa hadn't known about it being put in writing was that the draft of the commutation document he read before leaving jail hadn't included the no-union-activity clause. White House Counsel John Dean, who routinely handled criminal pardons and commutations, explained the confusion six years later: "I heard about the Hoffa commutation at the last minute. . . . Mitchell ordered me to draw up the papers, and he casually mentioned that Hoffa had agreed not to get back involved in the union. So, I said, 'why not put that into the President's declaration?' He agreed, so I researched whether we could do it, decided we could, and wrote it in. The whole thing was an afterthought added by us at the very last minute. I simply had the brains to put in writing what we thought everyone had agreed to."

That there had been an oral agreement, put in writing only as an afterthought at the last minute even after Hoffa had read a draft that didn't include it, would explain why Hoffa gave up the Michigan union posts that he had hung on to while in prison a few months before his release; since he wasn't yet out of prison he had to honor *that* part of the oral agreement. Dean's recollection also explains why, when Hoffa was released and learned about the written condition, he hadn't immediately protested it, as he might have done had the restriction caught him totally by surprise. In fact, when first released and made aware of the written restriction, he announced his intention to "do some writing and lecturing" but not to get involved in the union.

Five years later, Fitzsimmons knew that if anyone had been duplicitous, it had been Hoffa. He had sent messages to Hoffa ("this is what the feds are demanding") that he would have to promise to stay out of the union. He was aware that Colson had made Hoffa's lawyers agree. Hoffa agreed, even if he expected to renege.

Which is what happened. Hoffa's friends recalled that once he was out for a few weeks he received legal opinions that the condition was unconstitutional, and he decided to fight it. However, he had to keep quiet for a while. He would be under regular parole supervision until March 1973, and any move he made toward union activity might result in his being yanked back to Lewisburg on a probation officer's say-so.

It was not until spring of 1973 that Fitzsimmons heard the footsteps behind him. At a Washington dinner in his honor in April, Hoffa announced that he planned to get the courts to overturn the restriction on his union activities in time to run against Fitzsimmons in 1976.

From that moment until the Seventh Annual Fitzsimmons Invitational, more than three years later, nothing had gone right for Fitzsimmons. From the summer of 1973 through the summer of '75 it seemed that every time he picked up the phone somebody at some local somewhere in the country mentioned that Hoffa had been there shaking hands and getting support. Every week or two a newspaper or magazine carried an article about Hoffa's comeback. In 1974, the trucking magazine *Overdrive* reported that in a random poll 83 percent of the truckers questioned had said they would support Hoffa over Fitzsimmons in an election. In January 1975, Fitzsimmons read a news article in which Hoffa told a reporter that golf was for fat, older men and that twenty push-ups that took thirty seconds a day was all the exercise a busy union leader should have time for.

In late 1974 Hoffa had lost his first attempt to overthrow the commutation restriction in federal district court, but the decision was being appealed in 1975, and Fitzsimmons' lawyer told him that there was a good chance that Hoffa would win. It's not possible to know how the Court of Appeals or, ultimately, the Supreme Court might have decided. But a source in the Justice Department later revealed that a memo prepared there in early 1975 dealing with Hoffa's lawyer's argument—that a President was banned by the Constitution's separation-of-powers clause from attaching such restrictions to a judge-imposed jail sentence—had concluded that his position looked very strong.

During this time, mid-1973 through 1975, Fitzsimmons lost his friend at the White House; a Teamsters dissident group, PROD (Professional Drivers Council for Safety and Health) began getting public attention; and a reporter, Jim Drinkhall, who worked for *Overdrive*, began to make a splash with his monthly stories about how Fitzsimmons had been giving Dorfman and the underworld free reign on Central States Pension Fund loans. As a result, law-enforcement officials and other reporters began to focus on the Fund.

This was also the period when Fitzsimmons had begun, unhappily, to recognize the stake that the mobsters involved in the Teamsters had in him, and in keeping him there. Hoffa had been top man, usually the instigator in all their deals. Fitzsimmons had either stayed out completely, timidly approved the plans Dorfman or Presser proposed at the pension fund, or gone along as a slow follower, as in the proposed Rosanova-Accardo-Milano health-plan scheme. Fitzsimmons' problem was that by 1975 he had begun to see that if some of the more daring deals weren't halted it was *his* neck the feds—now minus his favorite commander in chief—would come after. He was satisfied, even eager, to live on his salary and expense account and forget about the old deals. The problem was that he didn't imagine they would let him. As one of his vice-presidents later put it, "Fitz just wasn't a free citizen."

In the spring and summer of that year, Local 299 in Detroit—the original home base of Hoffa and Fitzsimmons—had become the main out-of-court arena of Hoffa's comeback fight. To be eligible to be elected president at the '76 convention, Hoffa first had to get there by being an officer of some local union or a delegate appointed by a local. Throughout 1974 Hoffa and Fitzsimmons battled for control of 299. In the fall election that year, Hoffa ally Dave Johnson was kept on as president of the union, while Fitzsimmons' son Richard stayed on as vice-president.

This seemed to open the door for Hoffa. Johnson could resign as local president whenever the courts cleared Hoffa's return to union activity, allowing Hoffa to run in a special election before the convention; or Johnson could appoint Hoffa as a delegate to the convention. In March of 1975, Fitzsimmons fought back, sending a committee from Washington to Detroit to examine the local's books. In May, a federal grand jury—working on tips supplied by people at Teamsters headquarters in Washington, a government attorney in Michigan would later concede—also began investigating the local's books. Fitzsimmons was setting the scene for the International to seize control of 299 by trusteeship, if necessary, to block Hoffa.

Violence punctuated these and other maneuvers. Hoffa ally Ralph Proctor was assaulted outside a Detroit restaurant. A shotgun blast cost a local union trustee an eye. The aging Dave Johnson was savagely beaten, and his pleasure boat was dynamited. For Fitzsimmons these incidents were somewhat abstract. He had had nothing to do with them, and they didn't affect him directly. The next violent event hit very close. On July 10 a bomb exploded in Detroit under Richard Fitzsimmons' car as he walked toward it. He was far enough away from the remote-controlled explosion so that he wasn't hurt. But the point was made: the blast blew the car's hubcaps and other parts as far as the fence at Tiger Stadium a block away.

Twenty-one days after Frank Fitzsimmons got that reminder of the world he was caught in, he received another, stronger one. On the morning of July 31, 1975, the news broke that Jimmy Hoffa had been missing since the day before.

If the three and a half years from Hoffa's release to the day he disappeared had been bad for Fitzsimmons, the fourteen and a half months following the disappearance until the October 1976 Fitzsimmons Invitational was a nightmare.

First, Fitzsimmons' closest friends recalled, there was the shock of seeing this happen to someone who had recently become an adversary but on whom, Fitzsimmons said to one vice-president, he had "been hooked for thirty years." Fitzsimmons may have known in advance about the Hoffa murder, but it was nonetheless difficult to take. At the least, it spelled out what could happen to him.

Then came the blizzard of publicity and investigations. The press taunted him with speculation that Hoffa could have easily overthrown him had he not vanished. There were almost daily articles about the Central States Pension Fund. Prosecutors followed the cue, intensifying or opening all kinds of investigations.

Through the summer, the fall, and then the winter, the barrage continued. The press even deprived him of a temporary retreat to the better old days when it seized upon Nixon's appearance at the La Costa golf tournament of 1975, the former President's first public outing since leaving the presidency. They didn't write it up as a sign of a former President's respect for a union and its leader, but as a sinister clue to the link between the underworld and a disgraced politician. In the fall of 1975, Senator Robert Griffin of Michigan, ignoring a telephone plea from Fitzsimmons, circulated a resolution calling for a new McClellan-type investigation of the Teamsters. Before the year was out, this led to a Senate subcommittee investigation that wasn't on the scale of McClellan's but did find, by 1976, the insurance scheme that Fitzsimmons and his sons were involved in.

In March 1976, NBC aired a five-part investigative report on the Teamsters during its nightly news. The show brought Fitzsimmons to the point of near-hysteria, according to other top Teamsters. His ulcer flaring, his wife urging him to quit, and daughter Carol coming home each night from college with stories about her classmates' remarks, Fitzsimmons began showing a temper unknown at headquarters since the Hoffa days. He ordered the lawyers to figure out a way to sue NBC—a frivolous exercise that ended in a feeble letter to the Federal Communications Commission demanding that NBC give him equal time for a rebuttal. The Commission had no trouble rejecting the demand; NBC had asked Fitzsimmons to present his side in an interview on the shows, and he had refused.

While the lawyers were pursuing the attack, Fitzsimmons, according to two people who were present, walked into a negotiating session with the group representing the nation's trucking companies and accused them of having gotten NBC to do the series in order to embarrass and weaken him and the union on the eve of the new national Master Freight contract talks. Several people who sat on either side in these 1976 negotiations recalled that the NBC show and other bad publicity ended up getting the nation's truck drivers more money. As a top industry negotiator put it, "It hurt Fitz's pride so much that he decided he was going to get the best contract in history and no one, including us, was going to stop him."

And no one did stop him. Beginning in 1964, when Jimmy Hoffa had negotiated the first nationwide agreement between 400,000 truck drivers and warehousemen and their trucking companies, the Teamsters' technique had been to divide and conquer. Their successes in delivering for their members, under Hoffa or Fitzsimmons, were based more on the special structure of the trucking industry than on the talents of the union's leaders. Unlike the automobile or other industries where a few companies stand together against the union, there are some twelve thousand trucking companies, and no two or three or even twenty of them dominate. One big, powerful union negotiates against twelve thousand mostly under-capitalized, barely-out-of-the-red companies eager to get an edge by operating while their competitors are out on strike. Assisted by vice-president Roy Williams (the Central Conference area chairman and the man thought by many to be next in line for the presidency), Fitzsimmons, even in his fury in 1976, or perhaps because of it, played this advantage perfectly.

On Thursday, April 1, he called a strike, the first nationwide trucking strike in history. By Friday night, the major industry negotiators, Trucking Employers Incorporated (TEI), hadn't budged. But a smaller industry group broke ranks that night, making an agreement on Fitzsimmons' terms. Labor Secretary W. J. Usery, Jr., did Fitzsimmons the favor of announcing their agreement and calling on TEI to join in it. "In that situation," William McIntyre, then the president of TEI, recalled, "the industry's main bargaining unit [TEI] was terribly vulnerable. They [the union] had unity and we didn't. Fitzsimmons could go elsewhere to bargain, but where could I go?" TEI announced its agreement to the terms on Saturday.

McIntyre and others in the industry later called the 1976 settlement "a suicide pact," because its hefty 34.4-percent increase in wages, pensions and benefits over three years would drive companies out of business and Teamsters out of work. More surprising, many in the union would agree with his prognosis. More than a hundred trucking companies closed down or were merged in the first eighteen months of the contract (including two major bankruptcies on the East Coast). Noting this, Teamsters leader, Nicholas Kisburg, of Joint Council 16 in New York agreed that, "Yes it was a suicide pact. Fitz went crazy trying to show off. As a result, the industry and us are going to go down together. Everybody knows that."

The jury was still out the morning in 1976 that Fitzsimmons teed off at La Costa on whether the new contract covering 400,000 of Fitzsimmons' Teamsters actually helped or hurt them in the long run. But something else was already clear—the new contract would not quiet PROD, the press, the government investigators and the other critics.

Nor did the International convention that convened two months after the contract agreement in June. Fitzsimmons had planned to make the convention at Las Vegas his perfect comeback party—from the opening, as the band struck up "When The Saints Come Marching In" and Fitzsimmons and his vice-presidents came to the podium, to the last gavel that marked his reelection by acclamation. He invited Labor Secretary Usery, whose own department was reportedly investigating the pension fund, to come and express his support for Fitzsimmons. "I belong to this club because I believe in it," Usery gushed.

Chicago Mayor Richard Daly was there to express his affection for Fitzsimmons and his pride in carrying an honorary Teamsters membership card. "Spontaneous" floor demonstrations celebrated Fitzsimmons' renomination, while guards were posted to keep out PROD dissidents. Fitzsimmons also made a deal with Harold Gibbons that, according to Gibbons, eliminated the possibility that Gibbons would challenge him. He had given Gibbons some of the responsibility and salary he had been stripped of in 1972 in return for Gibbons' promise of support at the convention.

Fitzsimmons' speech expressed his struggle to beat back the critics and salvage his pride. He startled his audience by spending most of his time bitterly, at times incoherently, attacking PROD.

None of it had worked. The press gave as much coverage to the handful of PROD people parading outside as they did to the enthusiastic harmony within. And Usery's speech, instead of putting the lie to reports that the Labor Department was closing in on the pension fund, became a lightning rod for Congressional and press speculation that the Labor Department was dragging its feet. In response, the Department intensified its investigation after the convention. Seven weeks later Hoffa disappeared.

As the Fitzsimmons Invitational opened on October 13, 1976, even more difficult times were in store for its sponsor. The grand jury in Detroit and the Senate investigation subcommittee, convened in the wake of the Hoffa disappearance, were zeroing in on that insurance deal his sons were involved in. The scheme dated back to the better days of the early '70s. In 1971, Donald Fitzsimmons had agreed to go to work for Louis Ostrer of New York to help him sell a drastically overpriced life-insurance and severance-pay plan to local Teamsters unions. The Senate subcommittee later reported that Ostrer's plan allowed him to draw as much as 90 percent for commissions and fees and pass part of it on to the younger Fitzsimmons. In the case of one insurance policy this allowed him to draw $800,000 in commissions. The General Accounting Office told the Senate committee that the proper commission should have been $10,000. Ostrer had been stripped of his own insurance license in 1967 by the New York State Insurance Department for improperly diverting $700,000 from an insurance company and had since been convicted of two felonies for grand larceny and stock manipulation.

The Senate subcommittee reported in March 1977 that, although Fitzsimmons acknowledged knowing of Ostrer's criminal record, he had arranged for Ostrer and his son to present the plan to members of the International executive board in April 1972, so that the board members might recommend it to their locals.

Six days after they teed off at La Costa, Frank Fitzsimmons and his son Donald testified behind closed doors before the Senate subcommittee staff. Both knew that the staff was interested in how much the father had helped his son in the bogus plan, and in how much he had known about it generally. Subcommittee transcripts later revealed that the two Fitzsimmons told different stories.

Donald Fitzsimmons testified that when on Christmas day, 1971, he told his father about his intention to work for Ostrer selling the insurance plan, Frank Fitzsimmons had said, "Donald, this is the best thing you could do." He described how he had later asked his father to let Ostrer make a pitch to the executive board at the April, 1972 meeting and how he had been there at the board meeting helping Ostrer distribute the plan's literature to his father's vice-presidents. Finally, Donald Fitzsimmons told the subcommittee investigators that his father had indeed supported adoption of the Ostrer plan for business agents and officers of Detroit Local 299, where, at the time, the elder Fitzsimmons was still the vice-president of the local.

Frank Fitzsimmons didn't remember it that way. Sources close to the family recalled that Fitzsimmons was afraid that his son might try to avoid blame by attributing the scheme to his father, and therefore, he had stressed his own noninvolvement. He had not supported the Ostrer plan in any way, he told the committee, including supporting his own Local 299's adoption of it for business agents and officers.

In November 1976, when a federal grand jury called Frank Fitzsimmons to testify on the same questions, the split became more pronounced, a lawyer involved in the investigation recalled. In the course of casting their net out for leads in the Hoffa disappearance case the federal prosecutors had come across information about an Ostrer-sponsored insurance plan that Local 299 had purchased. They were particularly interested in evidence that indicated a new twist in the Detroit version of the Ostrer plan—that Richard Fitzsimmons, Donald's brother and recording secretary of the local in 1972, had in that year embezzled $5,000 from an Ostrer-type severance fund established for the benefit of the union members in order to buy life-insurance policies for himself and other Local 299 officers and business agents.

Frank Fitzsimmons reportedly began his grand jury testimony by pleading ignorance on most things concerning the Ostrer insurance policies. He danced around the opening hour of questions, dampening the prosecutors' hopes that they would be dealing with the helpless dummy the press had made Fitzsimmons out to be. During one break, he even told one of the government interrogators to "Say hello to my old friend Freddy Kaess,'' hoping to daunt the young attorney by his claimed friendship with then District Court Chief Judge Fred W. Kaess. But by the end of the session, he had run out of evasive maneuvers and was forced, in one prosecutor's words, "to put a lot of distance between himself and his kids. . . . He hurt his kids terribly by saying it was all their doing. . . . It was almost as if he was worried that one of them was going to try to nail him, so he decided to strike first. It was quite something. . . .''

Three months after Frank Fitzsimmons' grand jury appearance, Richard was indicted on the scheme to embezzle funds from the severance plan, and Donald Fitzsimmons was named as allegedly arranging the sale of the life insurance to Richard and the others in return for a hidden commmission. Still, the investigation of his sons and the insurance scheme was the lesser of Fitzsimmons' two major problems that morning of the 1976 Tournament.

The real hailstorm had started four months earlier, in June. Out of the blue, the Internal Revenue Service, reacting to all the press stories about the Central States Pension Fund, sent the Fund a letter at its Chicago headquarters revoking its tax-exempt status, retroactive to 1965. The IRS gave eleven reasons—different alleged acts of negligence, corruption and mismanagement—for its action. Panic set in in Chicago and among the 18,000 trucking company employers in thirty-three states. If the IRS action proceeded, all the Fund's interest and other earnings would be taxable back to 1965; and all of the employers' contribution to the Fund in the name of their employees would have been retroactively nondeductible. The IRS soon saw that its move would have penalized the pensioners by destroying the Fund in the name of cleaning it up. A few days before the revocation was to take effect, they postponed it.

The Labor Department quickly realized that IRS had stolen the show. Under the Employee Retirement Income Security Act (ERISA) passed in 1974, the Department of Labor was supposed to regulate the performance of pension-fund trustees in caring for the fund's assets. Now, with the IRS holding this club over the Central States Pension Fund, the Labor Department moved in to investigate past Fund loan practices. They intended to win reforms by using the IRS threat, and their own threat of a civil-damage lawsuit against the trustees under ERISA for alleged mismanagement.

In January 1976 a team of Labor Department investigators took over a large conference room in the Fund's Chicago offices, bringing their own secretaries, telephone lines, adding machines, even photo copiers, to help them pore through carton after carton of Fund records. Their names were the first entered every morning in the sign-in register at the Fund's reception desk.

Although the Teamsters union and the Central States Pension Fund are not synonymous—this particular fund is the pension bank for only about 400,000 of the 2.3 million Teamsters—the union's general president, along with seven other union leaders and eight representatives of the employers, have always been on the Fund's board of trustees. This arrangement became the focus of the Labor Department's reform activity: they wanted some or all of these trustees removed because they had been so negligent or corrupt.

What angered Fitzsimmons about the feds pushing him and the Fund this way was that since 1975 the Fund had been relatively clean. Daniel Shannon—the young, clean-cut, straight administrator that he and Bill Presser had hired in 1973—had been given full authority to manage the investments in 1975. As a result the loans to the mob fronts had ended. Even before, beginning in 1973, Shannon and his people had cleaned up the sloppy record keeping.

Fitzsimmons' lawyers had warned him that he had to negotiate anyway. He couldn't listen to Dorfman, who, as Dorfman recalled in an interview, advised him to "Tell the government to go fuck itself." ERISA was civil, not criminal law. And the government didn't have to prove guilt beyond a reasonable doubt. With just a preponderance of the evidence, they could nail Fitzsimmons and the others for all kinds of personal money damages for bad loans.

In July 1976, Fitzsimmons had agreed to negotiate. It would be the most difficult, pride-wrenching experience of his life. The government would keep coming back for more. And he would always have to give. Just five days before the 1976 Tournament and after months of negotiations, Fitzsimmons had reluctantly agreed to get rid of eleven of the Fund's sixteen directors and appoint five new "clean" ones, to a restructured board. He and vice-president Roy Williams would be the union leaders who remained.

At least one of the sources of his discomfort at La Costa on October 13 was that one or more of the allegedly "unclean" trustees didn't want to give up their seats. One vice-president recalled that "Fitz seemed scared that there would be some retaliation against him from the mob" for negotiating the resignations with the government.

Two weeks later Fitzsimmons finally obtained all eleven resignations and announced them on October 26.

A month later, in late November, Fitzsimmons was forced to make a new concession. In return for another extension of the IRS tax-exemption revocation and a forestalling of ERISA action by the Labor Department, he agreed to open negotiation on the question of reform in the Fund's management. For Fitzsimmons, this didn't seem terribly troubling. Fund administrator Shannon had already initiated such reforms, including limiting the percentage of investments risked in real-estate loans. In fact, Fitzsimmons' lawyer told him that the vaguely worded announcement was a face-saving way for the government to extend the suspension of the IRS revocation until a formal end to the investigation could be worked out. Then the Fund, with Fitzsimmons still sitting as a trustee, would be left alone. This was one of a series of assurances that Fitzsimmons and other top Teamsters would get from the lawyers that, as one high official later put it, "reminded me of the trainer in a fighter's corner who keeps telling the fighter he's fine after each round that he gets blasted."

In December 1976, the talks with the government stopped. With a new administration just elected in Washington, middle-level Labor Department officials insisted on waiting for their new bosses before coming to an agreement.

In Washington, the following January, incoming Labor Secretary F. Ray Marshall promised at his Senate confirmation hearings that he would make a cleanup of the Central States Pension Fund a high priority. Soon thereafter he hired Eamon Kelly, a Ford Foundation investment-management expert and an old friend, as a temporary consultant to be his personal representative in the Labor Department–Central States Fund negotiation.

In February the IRS and the Labor Department people, now led by Kelly, had their first meeting of the year with attorneys for the Fund's trustees, led by Colson law partner Charles Morin. The news that Morin took back to Fitzsimmons was shocking. The new team in Washington had changed signals. Kelly had presented new demands. They were simple, taking less than one page to spell out. But they were extreme. They wanted Fitzsimmons and vice-president Williams to resign from the Fund's board, and they wanted all the Fund's assets turned over to an independent bank or other outside money manager. And they wanted the agreement by March 15 or they would go into court. Thus began more than ten weeks of "I will, I won't" agonizing for Fitzsimmons.

At first blush, the government's sudden new demand was too much for Fitzsimmons to take. "More than anything else," a source close to the investigation later explained, "this was a matter of pride. Fitzsimmons couldn't let the government simply take the Fund away from him. He knew Hoffa wouldn't have done that. And remember, he was obsessed with living in Hoffa's shadow." Morin, on the other hand, warned Fitzsimmons that he would have to agree. Under ERISA, he explained, the Labor Department could go into court and get all the trustees removed and put in their own board if they could show that these trustees, including Fitzsimmons, had a record of irresponsibility. The Fund's over-all rate of return or record of paying pensions didn't matter. They would just have to show some substantial loans that were crooked or foolish. Also, Morin warned Fitzsimmons, the Labor Department could sue him and the other trustees personally to get back the millions of dollars lost on these loans. The Justice Department could bring criminal prosecutions, too, if fraud or kickbacks had been involved. The government was making no promises that they would *not* sue or prosecute if Fitzsimmons resigned, Morin told him, but it was less likely they would pull out all the stops if the agreement was reached.

Morin was never able to tell Fitzsimmons exactly what the government knew. Kelly never told him any of that. Instead, Kelly relied on Fitzsimmons, himself, to remember the Fund deals that did make him vulnerable and to assume the worst about what the government knew about them. "Morin and the others kept asking us what we had," one Labor Department investigator recalled. "And we'd say, 'Listen fellas, we've been using *your* records. *You* know better than we do what *you* did. . . .' But they kept pressing. One lawyer even cursed us out pretty badly. But we never told. You know the old adage: The guilty flee where no one pursueth."

In fact, the Labor Department investigators, notoriously among the most incompetent government sleuths, had found only a minuscule portion of the crooked loans arranged by Dorfman and company and approved by Fitzsimmons and the other trustees. Still, they had found, and they had reported to Kelly, several loans that were vulnerable under ERISA's standard that required trustees to be reasonably prudent. For one loan the collateral accepted had been nearly five million dollars in unpaid gambler's chits. Another loan involved property hip-deep in water. There were also clear miscalculations of interest on other loans that ran into millions of dollars in losses for the Fund.

Against this background, an odd, tragicomic period followed the government's February 16 demands, in which Fitzsimmons vacillated between resigning and staying on to fight. One day, he would meet with Morin, who would warn him not only of the dangers of fighting but also of the embarrassment that would come if the government got to present those horrible cases of loan mismanagement in a trial and in written briefs, all of which would be public. It wouldn't be worth it, especially given the probable outcome that the government would win. Especially embarrassing, Morin reminded Fitzsimmons, would be the deposition that he had given to Labor investigators and in which he claimed almost total ignorance of Fund transactions—which he, as a trustee, was supposed to have been watching over. Fitzsimmons would leave a meeting like this telling Morin it was OK to tell the feds he would resign and let a bank take over the Fund.

Then he would go back to the Fund trustees or the union's executive board, and they would talk him out of it. It would never be clear how much fear of some kind of mob retaliation played a role in his yielding to their arguments, but pride also played a major role. "Hoffa wouldn't have walked away from a fight," they would tell him. "Why should you?"

"It was bizarre," a top Labor Department official involved in the negotiation recalled. "We'd get a call from Charlie Morin telling us Fitzsimmons had agreed to resign. Then the next day he'd call back and say the trustees had passed some crazy resolution saying there was to be no agreement and no more negotiation." Morin was, of course, embarrassed. He described one such reversal to a Labor Department aide as "the worst day of my life." But he kept trying, and the Ping-Pong game would start over again.

Finally, on March 10, 1977, Fitzsimmons gave in. He met with Secretary Marshall and agreed to resign, to have Williams resign, and to give control of the assets to an outside, independent manager. The session in which he threw in the towel was a tough one for him; he spent most of it talking with Marshall about all kinds of other things before shifting the subject to the Fund and then getting on with the surrender. Marshall and the Labor Department people remembered the conversation before the capitulation vividly. Fitzsimmons had given what one labor aide called "the most sophisticated discussion analyzing the impact of economic conditions on labor unions that I've ever heard a layman give. . . . And he's supposed to be so stupid."

On March 13, 1977, the Fund and the Labor Department announced that Fitzsimmons and Williams had agreed to resign by May 1.

Immediately there came a new press attack that wounded Fitzsimmons' pride still more—not only had Fitzsimmons resigned from the Fund to avoid prosecution, they wrote, but he was also about to resign as president of the union. "You see," the hard-liners around him, including Williams and Dorfman argued, "they think you're weak because you didn't fight."

This was too much. Three weeks later, on his own, Fitzsimmons called representatives from all 742 locals to a sudden meeting. About two thousand delegates gathered at the Washington Hilton on April 6. Tall, broad International "auditors" like William Evans ($51,675 in salary and allowances in 1976) and business agents from the Pressers' Cleveland Joint Council 41 (one of whom told a reporter to "come to Cleveland so I can kick your ass, motherfucker") lined the entrance to the ballroom to keep the press out. Not that there was much news inside. The meeting, which cost $400,000 to $600,000 in travel expenses, was a pointless pep rally of speakers praising Fitzsimmons, attacking the press, and declaring Fitzsimmons' intention not to resign the union presidency and to run again in 1981.

Such was Fitzsimmons' apparent delirium that he offered the meeting a new explanation of why he had resigned as a trustee of the pension fund. It was simply because he needed to devote all his time to union duties, he explained—a claim that no one believed and that one union official told me was "the ultimate expression of his contempt for the membership" and "an insult to the intelligence and dignity of every one of us." The press that night showed the PROD demonstration outside the meeting and the reporters being held back by the auditors and business agents. The rumors about his resignation as president now seemed to intensify following his denials.

Soon, he actually started to reconsider his decision to resign from the Fund. If this was the way it was going to be, he told Dorfman and close union friends, maybe he should stay on as a trustee and fight the government rather than look weak. Late in the day on Friday, April 29, Eamon Kelly received a call from Morin saying that the trustees had reneged again and that Fitzsimmons and Williams were not going to resign on the May 1 deadline or at any other time. Kelly, who had thought that with May 1 two days away his job was over, was stunned. He responded only with a cool promise that the government's court papers would be filed Monday morning. Then, on Saturday, Morin again talked Fitzsimmons back into it; and using a State Police car to track down Williams in Missouri, he managed to secure the trustee resignations by Saturday night.

Things were still not totally settled. Through the remainder of the spring, Fitzsimmons and the others pressed the Fund's lawyers to try to keep some control over investments rather than pass it all on, as had been agreed, to an outside financial institution. The final surrender was not signed until June 30, when, with the Labor Department's approval, the Equitable Life Assurance Society was given control of the Fund's assets.

On July 21, the government's caution in not allowing the new "clean" Fund trustees to keep control of the investments was proved justified on another front. In addition to controlling the pension fund, the Central States trustees controlled the health and welfare fund, which collected money from employers and paid it to union members entitled to reimbursements for health-care expenses, severance pay, and other claims.

For years one of Allen Dorfman's companies had held the contract to manage the payment of these medical-care and other claims. According to Fund executive director Daniel Shannon, Dorfman's management of these claims had left much to be desired. Among other failings Dorfman's people had never been able to provide Shannon's staff with data necessary to plan the Fund's future financial needs. Beyond that, there was the problem of Dorfman's reputation as the mob's man at Central States and as a convicted Fund kickback receiver that logically dictated that someone else should get the contract when it came up for renewal. However, on July 21 the new trustees voted over Shannon's protest to extend Dorfman's contract another ten years. According to one trustee willing to talk about it, the men who had lobbied hardest for the renewal, other than Dorfman, were "former trustees" Fitzsimmons and Williams.

Even this ended as a humiliating setback for Fitzsimmons. Four days later, after the press got wind of it, the Labor Department threatened action. The trustees met and rescinded their vote.*

Also in the summer, a PROD group won an election against an incumbent executive board of Fitzsimmons supporters at Local 639, just a few blocks from headquarters in Washington. The press seized on this, too, playing up the local election as a mini-referendum on Fitzsimmons' rule. Back in Detroit, another Teamsters reform group, Teamsters for a Democratic Union, had been so successful on Fitzsimmons' own turf that Richard Fitzsimmons dropped his plans to

---

* Later they did renew his contract, but only for an additional year, to which he was probably entitled under an option clause in the old contract.

run for reelection as Local 299 vice-president, because he feared losing to a reform opponent.*

Rumors of his impending resignation dogged Fitzsimmons throughout the summer of '77. At sixty-nine, with his health unsteady and his arthritis and his ulcer bothering him more regularly now, the rumors were harder to take and resignation became more tempting. To make things worse, Fitzsimmons continued to receive signals that the agonizing pension-fund capitulation had not gotten the government off his back. The Justice Department, eager to make sure that the Labor Department not steal the show—as the Labor Department had been anxious that IRS should not—was looking into Teamsters affairs more aggressively than at any time since the Robert Kennedy dragnet days. One Justice Department lawyer reported that grand juries in at least seven different cities were investigating Fitzsimmons' involvement in the pension-fund loans, in his sons' insurance schemes and in the Hoffa disappearance. As the asset managers from Equitable began the job of assessing the pension-fund's real-estate loans, they discovered more irregularities, which they routinely passed on to the Labor Department, which in turn often sent the information to the Justice Department for possible prosecution. Meanwhile, the Labor Department was rumored to be preparing a massive civil suit under ERISA charging the Central States Pension Fund trustees with making imprudent loans, and they were giving the Central States Health and Welfare Fund the same going-over. It seemed likely that they would soon try to take away the trustees' control of this fund, too.

Fitzsimmons was also the target of charges that PROD had filed back in April with the executive board on behalf of rank-and-file members. They had asked the board to remove him for associating with, and employing, organized-crime figures, for nepotism, and for dereliction of duty. The board wasn't going to agree with PROD, but the union's lawyers had warned Fitzsimmons that the charges had to be given at least a semblance of an impartial board hearing. Otherwise PROD could successfully seek relief in court. The board's hearing would have to be set for sometime in 1978. This guaranteed more bad press, more embarrassment, and legal expenses that the law said Fitzsimmons personally had to pay. If PROD decided to appeal after the board exonerated Fitzsimmons, it would also mean a court fight with an uncertain outcome.

---

* He had replaced his father as the local's vice-president in 1971.

Toward the end of 1977, some vice-presidents and members of his family began to urge Fitzsimmons to avoid all the pressures and risks, take the hundred thousand dollars in severance already set aside for him, and get out while he could. Some, like Jackie Presser, were hinting more and more that only a new Teamsters image and a full break with the past would satisfy the critics. Presser never said it in so many words, but Fitzsimmons was starting to get the message.

As the Eighth Annual Frank Fitzsimmons Invitational Golf Tournament opened in the morning of October 12, 1977, close friends and family members reported that its sponsor was more troubled than he had been the year before. It was an open question whether there would ever be a Ninth Annual Invitational.

As 1978 came, it got even worse. His son's trial, in May, on the insurance scheme resulted in an acquittal. But by Fitzsimmons' own account (during one of our many early 1978 telephone interviews), FBI agents had begun visiting Fitzsimmons regularly, showing up every few weeks at the Washington office with no appointment, to ask again and again about his relations with Provenzano, with the Briguglio brothers, and with others thought to be involved in the Hoffa murder. Meanwhile, the Justice Department expanded its Teamsters dragnet, pulling together Organized Crime Strike Force prosecutors from around the country in a unit working exclusively on Teamsters corruption. One new possibility they were looking at involved whether Fitzsimmons had perjured himself in testimony that he gave before a Senate subcommittee in October 1977; in it he had denied anything improper about that $125,000 fee Kleindienst had received for delivering a premium from the Central States Health and Welfare Fund to an insurance-company client that embezzled the funds. He had also denied that Dorfman had influence at the pension fund. Rumors in the press about his resignation began to appear regularly, some of them leaked by his vice-presidents.

On February 1, 1978, the Labor Department filed a civil suit charging Fitzsimmons and sixteen other present or former trustees of the Central States Pension Fund with squandering away the Fund's money on fifteen different imprudent loans. This suit, the first of its kind under the 1974 ERISA pension law, would take years to be resolved in the courts, but in the short term it generated renewed bad publicity and posed the threat that Fitzsimmons would be subject to substantial legal fees and money damages. Some in the Labor Department conceded that though the civil suit was wholly unrelated to the management of the union (it concerned the pension fund's 1975–1977 management) they were using it, at least tacitly, as another way to force Fitzsimmons to resign his union post by holding out the possibility of an acceptable out-of-court settlement of the suit if he did.

Outsiders might be cynical about the ability of the government or the press to reform the Teamsters, since both had failed consistently for twenty years. But Fitzsimmons saw things more personally. He knew that people in the union, the government, and the press would be joining forces to take away the power, the private planes, and the top spots on the dais that the coffee gopher from CCC Trucking had learned to love. Even if the Teamsters were just going to lie low and look clean for a while to ease the pressure, he was in trouble. He was hardly the kind of figurehead to project the illusion of a break with the past. The more the union came under attack from outside, the more direct the pressure would be from inside. He was never going to get his chance to be a labor statesman. Maybe he would hang on in the top spot for a while. But it would be just that, hanging on.

CHAPTER IV

Provenzano

Union City, New Jersey, a city of 55,000 with many Cubans, is often called Havana on the Hudson. The name would not please Havana civic boosters. Union City is a grimy town, stuck in the Palisades across the Hudson River from Manhattan like an afterthought.

The Shop-Rite across the street from 707 Summit Avenue was a modern supermarket sometime in the early '50s. By the morning of the Seventh Annual Frank Fitzsimmons Invitational Golf Tournament, 25 degrees warmer and 2,500 miles away, its paint was cracking and the cash registers looked as clumsy and out of date as the peeling, tangled city compared to the shiny façades and the sleek digital boxes that make change in the shopping malls that line the nearby highways.

Bowlers at the upstairs alley next door are allowed to park in the Shop-Rite's small lot after 10 P.M., but a stern black guard, with a big brown gun strapped to his belt, stops noncustomers from parking there during the day. Across the street and just over to the right is the strip—a row of flickering neons wrapped around bold signs that advertise "go-go girls" and "live dancers." The half-dozen-or-so bars are uniformly sleezy and undistinguishable. How could one choose from among The Band Box, Izzy's Redwood Go Go Girls, Divers Inn, The Hustler, The Silver Slipper, The Oak Bar, and the New Hub Bar?

Around the block, the strip fades into a row of a dozen dingy shingle houses. People live in most of them, although a dry cleaner cleans in one, and a dentist drills in another. Around the block, just up the street from the Shop-Rite, there is Mary's Texas Wiener, a stand-up coffee-and-hero place where FBI agents assigned to watch the comings and goings across the street at number 707 have probably been pleasantly surprised by the home-made soup and the sausage sandwiches.

Number 707 Summit Avenue was once a bank. As the centerpiece in the triangle in the middle of town, the five-story building with its big clock carved into the façade over the front archway had been the hub of Union City. But by the time Sammy Provenzano teed off at La Costa, Union City was hubless. The bank was a discount dinette mart. The clock was stopped at 12:32.

Still, the FBI agents kept watch on the door around on the side marked *Teamsters Building—Dedicated to Service of the Nation.* Through that door pass people with business at 707 Summit other than dinette shopping. These were the offices of men who ran a powerful complex of Teamsters locals and were soldiers in an organized-crime family. It was here that the details of the Hoffa murder had been settled. Here one crossed the threshold of the Tony Provenzano labor empire.

The elevator operator at 707 Summit, a small frail man, had reportedly vouched for the presence of the Andretta and Briguglio brothers, and Tony Provenzano in the building on the day of the Hoffa disappearance. At 10 A.M. on March 3, 1977, he left his radio blaring in the small hallway as he took a visitor with no appointment to the fourth floor.

"Yup," he replied, those pigeons Tony Pro raises as a hobby were still on the roof.

The elevator whined and rattled open to a hard-floor hall lined by several old-fashioned doors with opaque glass running up from the middle. One listed a lawyer's name, another a dentist's.

There was no answer to three knocks on the door of Joint Council 73, the Teamsters Northern New Jersey umbrella organization that oversees most of the state's locals. The lights appeared to be out. Then, some slow, even footsteps from the other side. A light went on.

A smallish well-tanned bespectacled man opened the door about six inches.

"I was looking for Mr. Provenzano, Sir."

"I'm Mr. Provenzano." Salvatore "Sammy" Provenzano, Tony's forty-nine year-old brother.

In the last few years Sammy and brothers Tony and Nunzio had played musical chairs with Teamsters offices in New Jersey, depending for the most part on whether Tony's status with the law allowed him to hold a post. From January to December of 1974, when Tony Pro had finished the federal law's five-year period during which a convicted labor racketeer released from prison cannot go back to a union job,* Sammy Provenzano had gone from president of Local 560, the original Provenzano power base, to vice-president, but stayed on as president of Joint Council 73; Nunzio had moved from secretary-treasurer of Local 560 to president; and the newly liberated Tony Pro had become Local 560's secretary-treasurer. This is the way things stood as Sammy Provenzano answered the door that morning.

Joint Council 73 represented about 90,000 Teamsters in thirty-five locals that morning. Though they included garbagemen in Newark, and butchers in Perth Amboy, the majority were truckers and warehousemen who hauled factory parts and consumer goods. Northern New Jersey is the pivot of the transportation corridor stretching from Boston to Washington. With sprawling manufacturer and department-store warehouses and distribution centers built in the New Jersey swamps in the shadow of Manhattan's skyscrapers, the area is a giant loading dock for the New York metropolitan region.

"Yes, I'll talk to you, I guess," Sammy Pro answered, taking no pains to conceal his lack of enthusiasm. He was being polite, it seemed, simply because someone had come to see him and he had answered the door. Had I called first for an appointment he could have ducked the calls as he had the month before. Now, he couldn't turn me away without seeming rude and confirming everything the press always said about the Provenzanos.

---

* The Labor-Management Reporting and Disclosure Act of 1959, commonly known as the Landrum-Griffin Act, banned those convicted of certain union-related crimes, including extortion, from holding union office for the five years following a conviction or imprisonment (whichever is later). The reason that Jimmy Hoffa's post-prison activities had not come under this restriction, making necessary the controversial special pardon restrictions imposed on him was that the crimes for which he had been convicted, jury tampering and mail-fraud conspiracy, were not mentioned in the Landrum-Griffin Act.

He opened the door, a short, nondescript man in a colorful open sports shirt, a blue sports jacket with an intricately patterned plaid silk lining, and black double-knit bell bottoms over thin black socks and shining white shoes. He led the way through a small waiting room, sprinkled with bowling trophies and old copies of the Teamsters monthly magazine, into a brown room where a dozen and a half high-backed chairs lined a black rectangular table. "This is the board room, where our Joint Council meets," he motioned stiffly, looking and sounding like a rookie tour guide at the Vatican.

It was then that the odd resemblance hit home. The big somber color picture on the wall was Frank Fitzsimmons. But to the reporter who had been in and out of FBI field offices as well as Teamsters offices around the country, it looked like the FBI Director, Clarence Kelley.

We walked into his office. He took his seat, a handsome black-leather swivel chair, behind a wide, light-brown desk and alongside a table bearing two separate push-button phones. At the front left corner of his desk the "Salvatore Provenzano" on a wooden name plate was decorated with a sketch of a truck. I sat on a couch perpendicular to the desk. Though darkened by the drawn windowshade it was a comfortable room, thickly carpeted in a bright-tan color and full of mementos. A gold plaque on the wall from the 1976 Teamster Las Vegas convention, where he had been unanimously reelected an International vice-president, proclaimed Sammy Pro's "highest standard of leadership, character, and action on behalf of others." A Giants football helmet on the desk commemorated the role he and his members have played in building and staffing the New Jersey Meadowlands Sports Complex. Across the room there was a framed picture with two crippled kids: "Thanks to Salvatore Provenzano for helping make our 25th Silver Anniversary Telethon for Cerebral Palsy a great success," the inscription said.

He began by describing his work. "I try to mind my own business. . . . I don't want no trouble. . . . I'm just here to get the job done." The voice was polite, even, friendly. Also defensive.

Could a reporter spend a day with him on the job?

"I'll tell you what I do all day. But I'm not gonna let you tail me like some kinda cop. . . . I answer mail. I talk to my organizers. I go to negotiating meetings. What do you think I do all day, murder people?"

What were his toughest problems?

"I find nothing difficult. I'm well aware of the jobs I'm supposed to do. . . . My biggest problem? It's that I wear three hats. I'm down here as the Joint Council President. I'm upstairs [on the fifth floor] where I'm Local 560 vice-president—I just put Nunzie up there as president to take some of the load—and I'm International vice-president. You think that's easy? . . . And everyone says we get so much money. I only get $25,000 from the local [records he filed December 31, 1976, say it was $30,000, with expense allowances], $15,000 from the Joint Council [December 31, 1976, records say it was $20,000, with allowances] and the rest [$42,000 in the 1976 filing] from the International. But they figure because we're Provenzanos we've got to be robbing something."

As for other problems, "the biggest one we have here is the economy of the region. At one time 560 was the largest freight [trucking industry] local in the country. Eighty-five hundred members out of fourteen thousand were in freight. Now we're down to nine thousand to ninety-five hundred members *total* in the whole local. . . ." Another problem beyond the flight of industry to the South and Midwest, was competition from nonunion independent truckers—"These guys go to training schools for drivers, and get promised jobs as soon as they get out. Well, it's not true. So they borrow some money, buy a truck, and go into business for themselves and then undercut our people."

He stopped to take a phone call from Walter Shea, Frank Fitzsimmons' executive assistant in Washington, about a news article that reported that a trucking company was trying to contract out to independent truckers.

"Hello Walter. . . . I seen that." As he listened he licked a stamp onto an envelope of the water bill he had brought from home to mail that morning. "I seen him down there. . . . [Another trucking company] has tried it with their jobs, too. . . . We'll strike them. . . . Fitz is aware of everything, right? . . . O.K., Walter."

Our discussion resumed, shifting to another news article. He reached for it in his "in" box; it had been sent with a terse "Sammy For Your Information" note from Frank Fitzsimmons. It was from a New Jersey newspaper quoting PROD, accusing Provenzano of selling out his workers with "sweetheart" contracts—contracts that pay the workers less than they deserve, usually because the union boss has been paid off in some way. Provenzano bristled. "You see this shit? I've already talked to my lawyers about this. We're gonna sue

PROD and this paper.'' (A year later no suit had been filed.) ''They don't know the real story and they don't care . . . the fact is, you sometimes have to make concessions or a company will go out of business. . . . PROD says we're supposed to stop the world. They think we tell the boss to shit, and he shits. Well, that's not how it works. These guys will go out of business.''

As for a *Wall Street Journal* article published fifteen months earlier detailing such alleged ''sweetheart'' deals in which companies were paying Provenzano-union men wages below those stipulated in the National Motor Freight agreement: ''That guy [the *Journal* reporter] didn't know a fuckin' thing. He didn't know the difference between freight that would be covered by the Master Freight Agreement and goods that wouldn't be. I sat right here explaining it to him, but the fuckin' guy didn't want to hear.''

Two more phone calls came in rapid succession. Both were wrong numbers dialed by the same caller. Even the second time Provenzano explained the mix-up politely.

How do the members feel about the union, he was asked. Is there any dissension? ''Our meetings are very peaceful . . . that wasn't so fifteen years ago. But now the members realize which way the wind is blowing. In fact, it's too peaceful. We have nine thousand in the local, but if I can get three hundred to come to a meeting I jump up and down and shout with joy. . . .''

A bald, short barrel-chested man (later identified as a business agent) burst through the door. His sports shirt was wide open to his stomach. ''Sammy, I've got to talk to you for a minute. I almost got thrown in jail for murder today,'' be began, facetiously. ''A guy offered me twenty-five cents [in wage increases per hour] over a three-year contract and I almost killed him.'' They stepped into a lime-carpeted anteroom off to the left of the couch and shut the door. Five minutes later Provenzano was back behind the desk and the business agent left with a parting, ''I really appreciate it, Sam.''

Now, Provenzano answered questions about politics. He was a Democrat, but ''I supported Nixon in '72 because it was the only decent thing to do.'' Locally, New Jersey Governor Brendan Byrne was ''a close friend who'll have my support [in the November 1977 election] because he has guts.'' As for his union becoming more involved in the public sector, as in organizing police the way other Teamsters were doing around the country, ''I won't touch the public sector . . . because you're talking about taking tax dollars and you can never win . . . you can never get tax dollars away from politicians as fast as your membership would expect you to. . . ."

Finally, he talked about brother Tony. "He's been a truck driver or a union leader all his life since we moved from Monroe Street [on New York's Lower East Side]. . . . We all started as drivers. The men love him. He's active now as secretary-treasurer [of Local 560] and he wants to be more active. . . . He was framed the time he got convicted [for extorting a payoff from a trucking company executive]. Bobby Kennedy fixed it with the judge. . . ."

Mention of the Hoffa case sat him straight up in his leather swivel chair. A long indignant monologue followed. It was not a smirking indignation like that of a gangster going through the motions, knowing, and knowing the listener knows, that it's a game. It seemed real. He had either talked himself into it or he was telling the truth. The keynote lines went something like this:

"The day Jimmy was—uh, disappeared—we were all upstairs [in the local 560 office] playing cards the way we always do. . . . The idea that Jimmy and Tony were enemies is bullshit. They were best friends. . . . I'm the one who told Tony there could be nothing done about his pension, not Jimmy. . . . We loved Jimmy. . . . But because we're Provenzanos the cops come after us. We're used to it by now. But think of what it does to our families. . . ."

As we walked toward the elevator, he seemed exhilarated, eager to talk more, whereas an hour ago he had been so tentative. He volunteered breezily that this was the elevator shaft Tony had fallen down one Sunday morning in 1962, and how he really did fall down accidentally, and wasn't pushed by some mobster the way the cops said. He answered a compliment about his tan, explaining, "Fitz and I were just out at Harold Gibbons' wedding in Palm Springs. Quite a party." He promised he'd be available again if necessary although "Tony won't talk, because he hates the press for what they've done to him." His voice was bouncier than at the beginning but still soft— not at all spiced with the snarls one expected from a Provenzano. He was persuasive.

No less impressive was the postcard on his desk that day with a foreign stamp: "I did not forget you Tony, Nunzio, Sammy," it said in awkward, choppy ink. "My mother said a Hail Mary for you."

Jimmy Hoffa, Jr., is not the only one who would decline to join that postcard writer's mother in saying Hail Marys for the Provenzanos. There's the widow who went into shrieks of rage, friends recall, the day in December 1973 that she got a Christmas card from Tony Provenzano. She knew that Tony Pro was responsible for her husband's disappearance and murder. On the morning Sammy Provenzano entertained me, federal and New Jersey law-enforcement officials believed they could trace at least three such disappearances and/or murders to his brother, and a slew of extortion and embezzlement schemes.

On the day of the Seventh Annual Fitzsimmons Invitational, Tony Provenzano was a captain in the Genovese organized-crime family. Frank Fitzsimmons might call him, as he did in 1975, "a wonderful man," but many others in the union would go out of their way in interviews to say they were ashamed of him. In most, if not all the crimes Tony Provenzano engineered, the diminutive, polite Sammy Provenzano was believed by federal and state law-enforcement official to have been a junior partner, an accomplice, a front man or at least a willing bystander. Now, in early 1977, one of those crimes, that 1961 abduction and murder that resembled the Hoffa case, was coming back to haunt Tony and his younger brother Sammy.

Tony Pro had hated and feared the four and a half years he spent in jail on his last felony indictment, for extortion. The press accounts written at the time agreed that Provenzano had been stunned by the 1963 conviction. Throughout the three-week trial he had swaggered from his limousine (the union leased seven of them that year for its top echelon) into the courtroom, in a sharkskin pin-stripe suit and a diamond pinky ring. He had swapped barbs with reporters, and given odds of six to one for acquittal. At the end of each day he would chat lightly with the prosecutors—"his way of showing he knew us, which he didn't, and that he had things under control," one of them later recalled. Perhaps his confidence has been buoyed by the way his defense lawyer had fired away in cross-examination at the trucking executive who had fingered him, or by the encouragement he got from the ten or twenty burly union aides who had sat watching the trial each day, pitching pennies in the halls with him during lunch recesses.

The trial had had its rough spots. For a while, during young Prosecutor Matthew Boylan's two-hour cross-examination, Provenzano had been reduced to sweaty, handkerchief-mopping refrains of "I don't recall" and "I can't remember." At lunch the day of Prosecutor Boylan's summation to the jury, a Provenzano friend would later recall that Provenzano had gulped down four double scotches—one or two more than his trial-time routine. But, when the jury went out, this trial on federal charges didn't seem much worse than the state trial on similar charges that he had won the year before. So he had been shocked when the twelve men and women came back the next night and faced Tony Provenzano and said he was guilty as charged of taking $17,000 from the Dorn Trucking Company to guarantee an end to the discipline problem the company had been having with its union workers.

Jimmy Breslin, then in his heyday as a New York *Herald Tribune* reporter, came over to Newark the next day and filed this description of Tony Pro at the dock waiting to receive his sentence. Provenzano's lawyer had just advanced the argument that to sentence Tony Pro to prison would do no good because people who go to prison usually end up committing more crimes.

> "Mr. Provenzano," the judge said, "if you have anything to say at this time I will listen to it."
>
> Tony got up and walked to the lectern in front of the judge . . . He is a short heavy-set guy who has the puffed eyelids of one who used to fight. Drops of sweat sat on his upper lip . . .
>
> "All I want to say is that I told the truth on the stand and I stand on the truth I told with my hand on the Bible. . . ."
>
> He sat down after talking and the judge looked down at notes he had in front of him.
>
> "This sentence is to assure respect for the law. You stand convicted of using your position as a union official to extort money from private industry. . . . The time has come to serve notice on those who show no respect for the right of others . . ."
>
> Tony Pro was standing, his hands behind his back. He clutched one finger of his left hand with his right hand. Then, as the judge got rougher, he grabbed two fingers of the left hand and squeezed them. . . . The sweat formed all over Tony's face. . . .

The sentence: seven years in prison and a $10,000 fine.

"We were lucky," prosecutor Matthew Boylan recalled fifteen years later. As he explained it, his luck involved "a judge [U.S. District Court Judge Robert Shaw] who looked out from the bench and saw nothing . . . he was impervious to position or influence or pressure"; a prosecution witness, Dorn, who "cooperated more than he might otherwise have because he thought we knew more than we did"; and a defense lawyer who hammered away too hard for two full days at one of the prosecution's other witnesses who had only one arm, a fact that won the jury's sympathy for the witness.

Luck or no, the evidence Boylan presented was impressive. Most of it had been gathered initially in McClellan Committee hearings back in 1959. Provenzano had taken the Fifth forty-four times in front of Chief Counsel Robert Kennedy one morning that year. When Kennedy became Attorney General in 1961, he and the "get-Hoffa" squad had reopened their case file. Two years later it became the Kennedy Justice Department's best extortion prosecution.

It was a classic plot. The president of the trucking company, Walter Dorn, told the jury that back in 1952 he was having terrible problems with his union drivers. They seemed, for some unknown reason, to be engaged in a work slowdown, refusing, for example, to park the trucks in the garage in an orderly way that allowed them to be moved freely. Dorn had a series of luncheons with Provenzano, who was the a business agent for Local 560, to discuss the problem. At one lunch, he testified, he slipped Provenzano $1,500. At another, Provenzano had "suggested" he hire a certain lawyer to help with his labor problems. Provenzano wrote the lawyer's name down on a slip of paper. Beginning that year, and for seven years thereafter, the lawyer, Michael Communale received a two-hundred-dollar check every month from Dorn.

At the time of these payments, Communale was not a private lawyer but a prosecutor in the Hudson County, New Jersey, prosecutor's office. It was never clear whether Provenzano was using this payoff to him to pay off Communale or someone else in the local prosecutor's office for a past favor without the money having to pass through him, whether he was setting up a credit account in the then notoriously corrupt office for future favors, or whether he was simply laundering the money through Communale and taking the two hundred dollars, or part of it, back in cash from him each month. What was clear was that Communale did no work for the money; he had admitted that to the jury. In fact, he had never spoken to anyone in the trucking company during the seven years he received their checks.

Provenzano for his part denied ever taking "five cents . . . The only time I ever received money from an employer was when I was a truck driver." He also denied knowing Communale other than as an acquaintance. Fourteen years later, brother Sammy would stick to the same defense.

The jury of six men and six women hadn't bought it. The evidence aside, it was a gutsy verdict. Throughout the trial, ten or twenty Provenzano heavies had stared out at the jury from the spectator seats. And a few days before the trial ended the jury had been routed from their Newark hotel at 2 A.M. by a suspicious fire. Newark police and fire department reports indicate that the fire had apparently been started in two places and that someone had disconnected a fire alarm.

"Yeah, they were going for a mistrial with the fire," one Provenzano aide asserted fourteen years later, admitting the fire had been set. "Or at least, we figured it would scare the shit out of them." The effect of the fire and the men staring out at them wasn't lost on the jurors. One recalled, fourteen years later, that, "Yes, we was scared. I didn't sleep well for weeks. . . . It was the worst experience of my life . . . I still have dreams about it. But the judge told us we had to do our duty. . . . Don't use my name."

The judge had sequestered the jury in the hotel in the first place to keep them from finding out from newspapers, TV, or gossip about another incident that might have prejudiced them against Provenzano or scared them even more about finding him guilty. Two days into the trial an insurgent member of Local 560 named Walter Glockner had been gunned down outside his house with three shots in his back. The night before, Glockner had announced, following a tumultuous shop stewards' meeting (chaired by Sammy Provenzano), that he was going to "fight Tony Pro until they put me in a pine box." Provenzano told courtroom reporters the next day that Glockner was "accident-prone," and he arranged for the union to rule the death an accident so Glockner's widow could receive a $10,000 accidental-death benefit. He also promised college scholarships for Glockner's two children to be paid by the Josephine Provenzano Scholarship Fund named for his late mother. (Years later, the Glockner children turned the money down.)

The Glockner case was never solved; according to a New Jersey investigator who handled it, the one eyewitness, a drunken sailor, "disappeared off the face of the earth." Glockner, an ex-AWOL marine with a long jail record, was not exactly the hero or the "leader" of the anti-Provenzano movement that the press quickly made him out to be; but, as an anti-Provenzano shop steward at the Dorn Trucking Company, he had been a potential witness in Provenzano's Dorn payoff trial. His murder did indeed scare off other witnesses, and no doubt it shook up the heavily guarded key witness,

Walter Dorn. The only suspects ever developed in the Glockner murder case were a Provenzano brother-in-law and a known Provenzano
enforcer.

Other news kept from the jury involved Anthony Castellito. Dorn
had testified that Castellito, then the secretary-treasurer of the Tony
Pro Local 560, had been at the 1952 lunch meeting when he handed
over the $1,500 payment. Why hadn't Castellito testified, a juror
asked the judge at the end of the trial. "Not available," the judge
answered tersely, unwilling to explain that Castellito had disappeared
and presumably been murdered, in 1961.

Another event that was kept from the jury (which had already left
the courtroom, as had the judge) occurred during a recess near the
end of the trial. Provenzano stepped to the front of the room and
praised the judge and prosecutors for their "fair" handling of the
case. This was the same man who a few weeks earlier had denounced
Robert Kennedy at a press conference in terms so obscene that TV
newsmen had been unable to use any of their film, and reporters had
been unable to find any portion of the statement that was printable.

Fourteen years later, one of the prosecutors explained to me that
Tony Pro's gratitude was based on "a personal matter about him that
we didn't bring up that would have really hurt him." The personal
matter was that Provenzano had left his home in New Jersey in 1956
to live in another house with another woman. This was more than
just a matter of womanizing.* What made the liaison relevant was
that government investigators had found that another trucking company owner had purchased the second house for Provenzano. Provenzano had been indicted for this payoff six months earlier. Although the case was later dropped when the benevolent trucking
company owner died (of natural causes), the prosecutors in this Dorn
case could have introduced the matter into the record after Provenzano had introduced a letter from a pastor testifying to his moral
character. "Tony was really grateful to us about that," a prosecutor
recalled. "He didn't want to embarrass his kids by the first marriage,
or the pastor. . . . The FBI thought we should use it, but we decided
not to."

Following the trial, Provenzano spent some three and a half years
and tens of thousands of dollars in union money (from a special

* Provenzano once explained to a reporter that he always took the standard deduction on his
tax return rather than itemize expenses, so that he could spend all he wanted to "on the girls"
without having to keep records.

"defense fund") before finally going to Lewisburg Penitentiary on May 5, 1967. While out on bail during the appeals he was reelected president of Local 560 on December 4, 1965, by a 2–1 margin.

The four-and-a-half year stay at Lewisburg came at the height of his rags-to-pinky-ring career. Tony Pro had been born fifty years before, in 1917, the fourth of six children of Italian immigrants, on New York's Lower East Side. At fifteen he quit P.S. 114 and went to work as a ten-dollar-a-week helper at the H.P. Welch Trucking Company. Three years later he became a full-fledged driver. At the time he had also entertained dreams of becoming a prize fighter. Though this never panned out, his two-fisted view of things had not gone unnoticed by Anthony Strollo, a mobster who lived next door on Monroe Street and was by then a boss of the New York waterfront and some Teamsters locals. Strollo, who was also known as Tony Bender (and who disappeared in 1962), installed Provenzano as a shop steward at Welch's in 1945. Provenzano was known then, and would be thirty years later, as a hard-driving, hot-tempered man given to acts of impulsive violence.

In 1950, when Strollo decided to extend his reign to New Jersey, Provenzano was appointed to the post of organizer for Local 560. Soon afterward he was elected to the job. For the next ten years, he was appointed and then elected to a series of higher posts: business agent at 560, then president of 560, then president of the Joint Council. Beginning in the middle '50s, Provenzano, by now a member of the Genovese crime family, became instrumental in solidifying Jimmy Hoffa's power in the East. Among other things, he helped the fast-rising Detroit Teamsters to put together a series of gangster-run "paper locals" in New York—locals that had little or no real members but could nevertheless vote equally with legitimate locals in elections that determined who controlled the critically important New York joint council.

In return, Hoffa sent troops in to help Provenzano stave off a reform effort to block Tony Pro's election as Local 560 president in 1959.

The Hoffa-Provenzano alliance was typical of the bargains Hoffa struck with gangsters around the country: they helped push him to the top, and he helped them use their union posts for a series of money-making schemes: extortion from employers, loan-sharking, pension-fund frauds, and anything else that control of union muscle and money offered. The least that could be said about Hoffa's role in these alliances was that ultimately he too became their victim; his murder was carried out by one of the gangsters he had used.

Hoffa expressed his gratitude to Provenzano in 1959 by defying an order to remove him from his New Jersey posts, an order that had been issued by a Board of Monitors appointed by a federal judge to oversee the union because of all the corruption charges. (It was the first in a series of Hoffa challenges to the board that ultimately embarrassed it right out of business when it was denied the power to enforce its orders.) The next year, when a vacancy opened among the International vice-presidents Hoffa appointed Provenzano. In ten years, Provenzano had risen from local-union organizer to International vice-president.

From 1960 to the day on which he went to prison in 1965, Provenzano enjoyed the trappings of power and wealth. He lived happily with the woman who became his second wife in 1961, in the house in Clifton that had been purchased for him by the trucking company president and rode to work in a telephone-equipped chauffeured limousine provided by the union. Brothers Sammy and Nunzio were already on the union payroll, "Nunzie" had gotten into trouble in 1962 when, as vice-president of another Teamsters local in Newark, he was convicted of trying to extort $10,000 from a trucking company for a "sweetheart contract."

The only real trouble for Tony had come not from the law but from the other side. In 1962 he apparently did something that did not please his crime-family bosses. On Sunday morning, June 24 of that year, he was found semi-conscious by a floor waxer at the bottom of the elevator shaft at the 707 Summit Avenue Union building that Sammy Pro showed to me. He told police he had come in to do some paperwork and tend the racing pigeons he kept up on the roof. He had opened the elevator door on the first floor and, not noticing the elevator wasn't there, he had stepped in and fallen twelve feet to the basement. The police believed that he had been pushed.

Fifteen years later, one of the Provenzano's long-time organized-crime associates admitted in an interview that he had been involved in the accident, offering with no elaboration that it had something to do with "a heroin deal Tony was working on." (Several FBI informants had, over the years, asserted that Anthony Strollo, Tony Pro's original sponsor, had been involved in procuring longshoremen to help in smuggling heroin and that Provenzano had been involved in this with him.) Whatever the truth about the accident, Provenzano suffered six broken ribs. Nearly six years later, the union's records showed a $17,000 "workmen's compensation" payout for the fall. Provenzano had successfully claimed an on-the-job accident.

Other than that, things ran smoothly until Tony's surprise conviction in June of 1963.

In February 1963 Provenzano's biggest problem seemed to be finding ways of explaining to the press why he should have a higher salary than Jimmy Hoffa or President John F. Kennedy. At two union meetings, three months apart, both attended by fewer than 2 percent of Local 560's then-13,000 members, he had been voted salary raises of $25,000 and $50,000 respectively. Counting his Joint Council 73 salary and his International vice-president's salary this brought him up to $113,000 a year, making him the highest-paid union leader in the world, $23,000 a year better off than Jimmy Hoffa in legal income. When the press took notice of the indicted union leader's fortunes, Provenzano was backed into announcing that he was not going to accept the raises—although he appreciated the "vote of confidence" they symbolized. George Phillips, a Local 560 dissident whose objections to the raises at the union meetings had been overruled by Provenzano, wasn't convinced; he asserted that Provenzano would take the money one way or another, perhaps by accepting it in back payments if he went to jail.

Records later filed by Local 560 reveal that this is exactly what occurred. In the union's 1967 accounting of its finances to the Labor Department, filed on March 12, 1968, there appeared a contingent liability for "salary due former president Anthony Provenzano." In the 1970 accounting, filed in March 1971, this was listed as a $223,785 liability, and a first partial payment toward it of $22,850 was listed. The reports filed in the next seven years would show that Provenzano received $25,000 each year, through the end of 1977.

George Phillips, the man who had predicted these retroactive payments of the "rejected" salary increases, was the number-one thorn in Provenzano's side in the late '50s and early '60s. In 1958, Phillips, a blond-haired six-foot, 190-pound truck driver, led a group of Local 560 members to the union's quarterly meeting. Provenzano and his men had just returned from the International convention, where they had given all of Local 560's votes for president to Jimmy Hoffa. Phillips and a dozen or so friends wanted to know why the members hadn't been consulted before the vote. Fists started flying, and from then until 1965 Phillips led a group of dissidents in a losing battle against Provenzano.

In 1959, Phillips managed the "Green Ticket," a challenge slate mounted against Provenzano for control of 560 in the first contested election in the local union's history. Provenzano was aided by Hoffa-supplied campaign workers from New York and elsewhere. The shotgun blasts fired into the home where a Green Ticket meeting was being held and a bomb that exploded at Phillips' headquarters, must have discouraged the less hardy members of Local 560. Only about 50 percent of the members voted, and Provenzano won by a 2½–1 margin. However solid his victory, Tony Pro had not appreciated the campaign that Phillips' forces waged, and he was less than sanguine about the possibility that the fledgling opposition might be more successful the next time out.

In 1960, Phillips was severely beaten by three men who were waiting for him in a men's room. One gouged his eyes as the other two hit him. Phillips recalled seventeen years later that they "kept yelling 'Get off the ticket. Get off the ticket,' as they beat me." Temporarily blinded and suffering from a broken nose, he spent three weeks in the hospital. The "ticket" was the Green Ticket which had already announced its plans to go after Provenzano again in 1962. In 1961, as he made a delivery in Brooklyn, Phillips was attacked again, this time by three men carrying claw hammers. As he remembered later, "They thought they were going to get me behind the truck, but I was able to dive under and run out the other side. They finally caught up with me on the street and got me down on the ground. But I just kept kicking up at them from the ground so they couldn't hit me in the head. Then a couple of guys came out of a junk yard and scared them off." Phillips spent two weeks in the hospital after this beating.

It was also in 1961 that Anthony Castellito, the secretary-treasurer of Local 560 who hadn't been able to testify at Provenzano's trial, disappeared. This is the murder for which Provenzano would be indicted in 1976. Castellito was a long-time official of Local 560 and allegedly had participated in many of Provenzano's illegal payoff schemes—including the Dorn Trucking Company extortion about which he too had taken the Fifth Amendment at the McClellan Committee hearings. However, in 1959 he infuriated Provenzano by running for reelection as secretary-treasurer independently of the "Pro" ticket. He had refused to take sides in the Green Ticket fight against Provenzano. When the ballots were counted that year, he had run ahead of Provenzano. Now, in 1961, there were rumors that Castellito was going to go against Tony Pro in 1962, heading a Castellito-Phillips opposition ticket. In June of 1961 Castellito attended a union meeting at 707 Summit Avenue, had a cup of coffee at Mary's Texas Wiener across the street, then drove off in his brown, union-purchased Cadillac. He was never heard from again. In 1977 one of the men who claimed that he had helped plan the murder conceded his role in it and told me, "Tony ordered it. He's demented. It was pure vanity. 'Cass' ran ahead of him in '59. So he had him killed."

According to the 1976 indictment Provenzano had directed two men to plan the killing of Castellito: Harold Konigsberg, a long-time Genovese mob associate and convicted loan shark, and Salvatore Briguglio, the Local 560 business agent who would hit the headlines for his alleged role in the Hoffa killing fourteen years later, and who ended up dead of assassins' bullets on a New York sidewalk on March 21, 1978. The indictment charged that for their work on the hit Konigsberg was given $15,000 and Briguglio got a job as a business agent for Local 560.

Provenzano, the indictment states, first gave the two an office at 707 Summit to plan the event. Their plans are strikingly similar to what is believed to have happened to Hoffa: Castellito was lured that night to a meeting. (The meeting was to be at Castellito's summer home in upstate New York.) There he was knocked unconscious, then strangled with a rope. His body was disposed of so that it could never be found. Castellito, like Hoffa, had been a Provenzano ally who now threatened Provenzano's position. Provenzano had a solid alibi: on the day of the Castellito murder he had been in Florida getting married.

The Phillips beatings and the Castellito murder were not the only provisions Provenzano made to protect himself from the 1962 elections. He made sure that Phillips wouldn't run on the opposition ticket; he had him suspended from union affairs for a year in 1961, for starting a fight at a union meeting. As one long-time Provenzano associate remembered it, Provenzano arranged for someone to throw a punch at Phillips and for the local police to happen by the union hall as Phillips began to fight back. Phillips had some trouble denying the charges. The first forum where they were heard was Local 560's executive board—chaired by President Anthony Provenzano. From there, an appeal had to be taken to the Joint Council executive board, chaired by Joint Council President Anthony Provenzano. And from there, the final appeal was to the International's executive board, which was chaired by Jimmy Hoffa and whose New Jersey area member was International Vice-President Anthony Provenzano.

Provenzano took further precautions against a possibly resilient or stubborn opposition. Acting under his authority as Joint Council President, and with Hoffa's approval, he set up a new local, number 84. He put it in Local 560's building and gave it five hundred men. This way, even if he lost the 560 election, he would still have a union to run, thus making it possible to hold on to his Joint Council presidency and his International vice-presidency. And, using those two higher posts, he could switch men from 560 to the new Local 84 at will. Then, moving on another front, Provenzano offered to get Phillips and his people a charter for a new local if they would drop their Local 560 fight. The deal would have allowed Phillips to take a thousand or so of his strongest supporters—men who hauled new cars from New Jersey Ford and General Motors plants—into his own new local. Phillips turned him down.

So, with Provenzano under two different labor extortion indictments (the Dorn case and the case against him for accepting the gift of the Clifton house from the trucking company executive), the election went on as scheduled on December 14, 1962.

To win, Provenzano relied on more than the "Vote Pro" messages stenciled onto the rocks of the Jersey Palisades over the Hudson, or the "Grow and Grow With Tony Pro" ads that he placed in local newspapers. Although Local 560 stretches from deep into New Jersey to upstate Monroe County, New York, Provenzano set up only one polling place, and that was in Provenzano's stronghold of Hoboken. (By contrast, Ron Carey's Local 804 in New York designates three or four polling places at various locations of the Local's jurisdiction.)

The Hoboken polling place was a restaurant owned by Harold Konigsberg. Phillips and two of his supporters later recalled that, as known dissidents drove up the single-lane driveway to the restaurant parking lot, Provenzano's men made them run a gauntlet—rocking their cars, throwing things at them and shoving them around when they got out of the cars. Word of these confrontations spread quickly to potential voters, and far fewer than expected turned out to vote. Phillips also claimed that three thousand members hadn't been informed of the time and place of the election in the first place. Whatever the reasons, only 4,500 of the members came out to vote. Phillips claimed that Provenzano men from other unions were allowed to vote. When the ballots were counted Provenzano had won. The margin was a slim 577 votes.

The Labor Department moved immediately to investigate charges of vote fraud and intimidation. A few days later they found that the room they had been given at 707 Summit Avenue for their examination of membership records had been bugged by private detectives hired by Local 560. In the end, none of the major charges could be proved, and the vote was allowed to stand. After that Tony Pro moved quickly to have those two salary raises totaling $75,000 voted to him.

The 1962 election was the last big push for the insurgent forces. Three years later, even with Provenzano convicted in the Dorn case and quickly exhausting his appeals, the opposition was split into two slates and not nearly as effective. Provenzano, campaigning for the first time with personal appearances at truck terminals, won the 1965 election by a 2-1 margin. By 1977 Phillips had retired to the New Jersey shore, and election contests were history. Since 1965 no one has run against the Provenzanos.

When Tony Pro went to prison in May 1966, the executive board of Local 560, all Provenzano loyalists, met and appointed Sammy Provenzano to replace him. During Tony's 4½ years at Lewisburg Federal Penitentiary, where he worked as an assistant librarian in the honor unit, things seemed to run smoothly back home. According to the FBI and the New Jersey State Police, Nunzio, just returned from a six-month jail stay for an extortion conviction and on the payroll as a business agent, ran a lucrative loan-shark business, while Sammy administered the union contracts as Tony had done.

In March 1971, Sammy Pro was indicted for masterminding a counterfeiting operation. According to the indictment, Sammy Provenzano and Armand "Cookie" Faugno, a long-time Provenzano ally, had financed a counterfeiting ring operated by Faugno and two other defendants—Stephen Angelo and future Hoffa murder suspect Thomas Andretta. In July, the government abruptly dropped its case against Sammy Provenzano, announcing that there had been a mistake and that he had provided information showing that Salvatore Briguglio—a suspect in both the Castellito and Hoffa murders—and not Sammy Provenzano had been the counterfeiters' financial angel and supervisor.

Two years later, Briguglio was allowed to plead guilty. He served ten months of a fourteen-month term on the counterfeiting charge. When he got out of jail in 1974, Sammy Provenzano—the man who had turned him in to the feds—gave him back his old business agent's job at a bigger salary and appointed him a trustee of a twenty-million-dollar union pension fund. A year later, asked if he thought Sammy Provenzano had made a deal with Briguglio to get him to take the rap, a federal prosecutor who had worked on the case said, "It's possible, but we could never prove that. What's more likely, though, is that Sammy Pro knew about the scheme [the counterfeiting] but really hadn't been involved directly the way Briguglio was." As to why he gave Briguglio his old job plus a new one after turning him in, Provenzano later explained to me, "If you believe in our system then you have to give people a chance to be rehabilitated once they've paid their debt to society."

Briguglio's sudden involvement and his guilty pleas weren't the only odd developments in the case. On July 1, 1971, defendant Stephen Angelo disappeared forever. On the night of December 8, 1972, defendant Armand Faugno, out on bail and awaiting trial, left his home in Englewood Cliffs, New Jersey, and was never heard from again. It isn't known what happened to either man; but police were later told by an informant that Faugno's body had been destroyed by a tree-shredder and buried in a New Jersey dump. The two disappearances before the beginning of the trial cleared the remaining obstacles to Briguglio's 1973 guilty plea and eliminated the possibility that one of the two defendants could be pressured into cooperating with the prosecution. It also made it unnecessary for Sammy Pro to testify against Briguglio. Mrs. Faugno was the woman who received a Christmas card from Tony Pro three weeks after her husband's disappearance.

At the time, Faugno had also been facing pressure from the government on a loan-sharking charge against him and Thomas Andretta. In 1967 Mr. and Mrs. Arnold Henderson * had gone to the Middlesex County prosecutor's office to relate how Faugno and Andretta—henchmen in a loan-sharking operation run by Nunzio Provenzano—had terrorized them and their family. According to records in the prosecutor's office, Henderson explained that in 1961 he had needed money to pay off gambling debts and had been told by his bookie to see a runner for Nunzio Provenzano at a New Jersey restaurant. There he received a $1,000 cash loan to be repaid to Faugno in twelve weekly payments of $100 each—20 percent interest for a three-month loan. He wasn't able to make the payments, and by the end of 1962

* The name has been changed.

Henderson's debt, with interest, had climbed to $6,000. In March, Andretta followed him as he dropped off his children at school, and according to what Henderson told the prosecutors, Andretta warned him that he had better "make arrangements to see Armand [Faugno]." A week later Andretta came to Henderson's office and broke two of his ribs. It was then that Henderson went to the prosecutors. The prosecutor wired Henderson's phone so that there would be tapes of Faugno and Andretta threatening him.

Faugno and Andretta were indicted in 1967, but the case dragged on after Henderson developed cold feet about testifying against them. In December 1972 a New Jersey judge ordered Faugno and Andretta to appear for a "voice print" examination; the prosecutors thought they could at least try for a conviction with the wiretaps of the calls to Henderson. Nine days after the voice printing Faugno disappeared. The prints, which confirmed that the voices threatening Henderson were those of Faugno and Andretta, were later ruled admissible as evidence, and Andretta ultimately pleaded guilty to this charge and to the counterfeiting charge. He drew 2½ years for the loan-sharking and fourteen months for the counterfeiting; he was paroled in 1975, just in time, allegedly, to help out in the Hoffa murder.

Two years later, Local 560 business agent Michael Sciarra was indicted on another loan-sharking charge. This one involved a feudal system in which non-Teamsters debtors were given jobs in New Jersey trucking companies for a day or two at a time and then forced to sign over their earnings to the loan-shark collectors. The evidence in this case included the testimony of a victim's girl friend that she had been beaten and then told by one of the other defendants that he had used a lime-filled sock that time rather than a blackjack so that her face, while badly bruised, would not be scarred. Sciarra was acquitted, but a Provenzano-appointed shop steward was found guilty.

On Sunday night, November 9, 1975, business affairs were put aside. It was a night for celebration—the night of Tony Pro's coming-out party. Since he had left Lewisburg in late 1970 (and recovered from a near-fatal stomach illness he had suffered there), Tony Pro had on paper complied with the law requiring that he not have anything to do with running a labor union for five years. He had left the titular direction of Local 560 and the New Jersey Joint Council to Sammy and Nunzio. But he had stayed active, and had become a frequent companion of Frank Fitzsimmons, advising Fitzsimmons on union affairs, including the naming of Sammy as an International vice-president in 1971.

Connecticut State police later found that he had picked up some spending money during this time in the form of a $100,000 finder's fee for arranging that a Connecticut Jai Alai fronton would get a Teamsters pension fund loan to build its facilities. He had also arranged for a New Jersey Teamsters pension fund to lend $4.6 million to someone named Thomas Romano to start a land development and condominium in Florida. Federal investigators later discovered that in return Romano had sold Provenzano his home on the Intercoastal waterway in Hallandale, Florida, at a price $35,000 below its real value, while buying some Provenzano-owned land at a price above its value ($24,000 as against $5,000 assessed valuation). For the five years from 1971 through 1975, Provenzano spent most of his time at his Hallandale home, keeping in touch with Sammy and Nunzio by phone, and meeting friends and associates for lunch or dinner at Joe Sonken's Gold Coast Restaurant in nearby Hollywood. It was during this time that he reportedly helped to arrange the half-million-dollar "contribution" to Nixon's campaign in return for the imposition of restrictions on Hoffa's postprison activities.

Now the exile was over, and an Anthony Provenzano testimonial dinner at New York's Americana Hotel was arranged to mark the event. The proceeds of the $100-a-plate affair attended by sixteen hundred guests were directed to the Josephine Provenzano Scholarship Fund. Among the paying guests were Teamsters lieutenants from around the country and executives from New Jersey's largest trucking firms. "You might say it's sort of a command performance," one company vice-president told a newspaper reporter. "Every trucking outfit in New Jersey has someone here."

As the diners sat down in the huge candlelit room to "French Fruit Lucullus," tomato bisque, and "Filet Mignon Henri V" with truffle sauce, the band played "Hey Look Me Over" as Frank Fitzsimmons and about half the International vice-presidents entered and mounted the dais. The women sat together around the back of the ballroom. Closer to the front, their men, in costume ranging from denim leisure suits to silk tuxedos, poured scotch and bourbon from the bottles set up on their tables. The national anthem was played. A priest asked a blessing for Anthony Provenzano and his family. A few mild speeches from some of the vice-presidents followed. Then Fitzsimmons took the podium. First, he attacked the press for printing only baseless allegations about union corruption and never stories about the charities like this one that the Teamsters supported. "I realize that some of the publicity has to do with the unfortunate disappearance [then three months old] of Jimmy Hoffa. I want to say that I have no more idea what happened to Jimmy Hoffa than anyone in this room does." There was some nervous laughter.

Next came the guest of honor, who was introduced by the master of ceremonies as a man who is deeply devoted to charitable causes and to the fight for America's working men and women. Provenzano thanked everyone. Then he mentioned his mother's devotion to education and concluded with his thoughts on the women in the room that night. They were all "so beautiful" that "if I wasn't married I'd come around and propose to each and every one of you . . . Let's give them all a big round of applause."

In the days before the testimonial and even during the evening, there were rumors that Fitzsimmons was going to use the occasion to name Tony Pro an International organizer, which would signal his return to national prominence. As Fitzsimmons left that night he told a reporter, "I think Tony is a wonderful man, and if I decide I need an organizer, or I need him, I'll appoint him. That's all."

It didn't happen.

Provenzano had shrugged off the Hoffa accusations with the same smugness as that with which he had initially dismissed the Dorn case. The day after the disappearance he had told FBI agents that "you guys have five minutes," then flew to Florida. There he held a cheerful press conference in a bathing suit on his front lawn. Grinning, he told reporters "I'm just down here with my family. You guys make me look like a mobster. I'm not. I'm just a truck driver." Soon afterward he invited a *People* magazine reporter and photographer for a tour of his house. The three-page spread resembled a feature on a new movie star: readers were offered a description of the "concrete cherubs," the "star burst mirrors," and an "oil painting of Tony's mother which he surrounds with fresh flowers every day." Next, there was a stop in the kitchen, where he made spaghetti and hugged his wife. At poolside, he "sipped a vodka tonic, flicked an unlit Havana," explained that "we Sicilians like the hot climate," remembered that "I never read a book in my life," yearned for the days as a "Hoboken truck driver," claimed a "love" for Hoffa, and asked "to be left alone. I don't do anything abnormal. I'm not a faggot. My great joy is my family."

Nevertheless, by the time of the testimonial, the FBI was all over him and his associates, searching for evidence of involvement in the Hoffa case or of any wrongdoing that might put pressure on any of them to provide information about Hoffa's disappearance.

The dragnet had not prevented Provenzano from resuming power in fact if not by title. Tony Provenzano directed the operations of Local 560, as well as other Provenzano-controlled locals in the New Jersey Joint Council. More than that, the Hoffa murder had given him a kind of added stature in the International union: he had killed the man who so many of the other top Teamsters had thought was superhuman. This, plus his connections with the mob and his alliance with Fitzsimmons had made Provenzano, by 1976, in the words of one International vice-president interviewed just after the Seventh Annual Fitzsimmons Invitational that year, "one of the real bosses of the Union. . . . Fitz is afraid of him because of the Hoffa thing. I'd say he's much more powerful than most people believe."

That was the way things stood in April 1977, when Tony Pro flew out to the International executive board meeting in Las Vegas even though he was only technically a local secretary-treasurer. There he was observed by undercover police as he met with veteran mobster Joe Bonnano; and *Overdrive* reporter Jim Drinkhall spotted him merrily playing the slot machines at the Dunes Hotel and Casino, owned by former Hoffa lawyer Morris Shenker. A few minutes later, Drinkhall heard Provenzano telling two friends to go get dinner "because anything in this place I get for free." When Drinkhall later asked Shenker why he "comped" Provenzano (gave him everything free), Shenker explained that "Tony's a good player, why shouldn't I comp him. I've known him for twenty years. . . . He's out here for the board meeting."

"What does Tony need a title for," William Aronwald, then a federal organized-crime prosecutor in New York would explain the same week Provenzano was in Las Vegas. "He's not looking to make *Who's Who in America*. He just wants power and money."

On the legal front, however, Provenzano was again coming rapidly closer to making Who's Who at Lewisburg Prison. The government was getting nowhere on the Hoffa case, but they were finding other areas of Provenzano vulnerability. In December 1975 he had been indicted by a federal grand jury for allegedly having plotted to arrange a $300,000 kickback for an upstate Teamsters leader in return for the upstater's giving the Woodstock Hotel in New York a $2.3 million New York State Teamsters pension fund loan. On June 24, 1976, the feds indicted him for Castellito's 1961 abduction and murder. In the course of the Hoffa investigation, the federal Organized Crime Task Force had come across information linking someone named Salvatore Sinno to the Castellito murder. Sinno apparently had been one of the men who had done the actual killing with Briguglio and Konigsberg. The task force prosecutors pressured him to cooperate in return for not being prosecuted. He did, naming Provenzano, Konigsberg and Briguglio as the higher-ups in the plot. The same day of the federal government's indictment, prosecutors in upstate New York indicted Provenzano for conspiring to commit murder in the same case.

At the time of the 1976 Fitzsimmons Tournament at La Costa, Provenzano had reason to worry about the murder charge. Sinno was now being guarded by federal marshals at a secret location. There were also indications that Harold Konigsberg might also be turning. Sometime before 1969 Konigsberg and Provenzano had had a falling out, and in that year he sued the Provenzano brothers for money he said they owed him. His suit also charged that Tony Pro had passed word through the prison system when Provenzano was at Lewisburg and Konigsberg was at the Danbury, Connecticut, federal prison that Konigsberg would be killed and his wife and children blown up if he pressed his suit. In 1976 Konigsberg, in prison for loan-sharking convictions, was holding firm, though his case had been dismissed repeatedly. Konigsberg, "the king of the loan sharks," as he was known, was serving a forty-four-year prison term. Would he take revenge by turning against Tony Pro in the murder case? "There are some problems with Harold, but he's starting to come around," one prosecutor involved in the case stated in mid-1977. "The FBI has a signed confession from him that also implicates Tony and Briguglio, but we still don't know if he'll testify."

The week after the 1976 golf tournament at La Costa—which he hadn't attended because of bail-bond restrictions—Tony Provenzano won a major victory in the murder case. A federal judge decided that the statute of limitations prohibited federal prosecution of Provenzano for the 1961 murder. The ruling was controversial,* but an Appeals Court upheld it in March 1977. The government decided not to appeal to the Supreme Court. Appeals to the highest court, one prosecutor explained, are made "only if we want to establish a general principle of law that will cover many cases. Since we don't have

---

* The judge held that only capital crimes were exempt from the statute of limitations and that since there was *now* no longer a death penalty for the alleged crime it was not a capital crime.

a lot of sixteen-year-old murder cases lying around, the Solicitor General [the federal government's top litigator] decided not to go ahead.'' However, the New York State murder conspiracy charge in the same case was not barred by any statute of limitations. After a series of delays by Provenzano's lawyers, Provenzano, Briguglio and Konigsberg were due to stand trial in Ulster County, New York, in the spring of 1978.*

This was the case that was bothering Tony Pro as the Eighth Annual Fitzsimmons Invitational approached in October 1977. An unsophisticated upstate prosecutor was in charge, and the case, with all the evidence, would indeed be seventeen years old. Also, by the end of 1977 there were reports that Sinno was growing nervous about testifying against Provenzano. The delays that Provenzano's lawyer had won seemed to chip away at his resolve. Still, the prosecutor would probably hold onto Sinno and might possibly get a second participant in the plot, Konigsberg, to testify. They might also try to use this case, since Salvatore Briguglio was charged, to pressure Briguglio into talking about the Hoffa case. Provenzano was sixty years old. Either murder case, Castellito or Hoffa, could send him away for what would be a life sentence.

The other outstanding federal charge—the loan kickback conspiracy—didn't seem to be much of a problem. The kickback had never gone through, and Provenzano, though his name had been mentioned as facilitating the loan, had himself had no contact with the government's undercover informant. On November 11, 1977, a dapper, smug Anthony Provenzano would walk into a federal courtroom in lower Manhattan to hear the case dismissed because the government's key witness had recanted. A month later he would be reindicted; but without the cooperation of the key witness, the case seemed to be no threat. It was probably another government long shot to pressure Provenzano on the Hoffa disappearance. Yet, in March 1978 two young prosecutors presented the government's case with extraordinary skill, while Provenzano's lawyer made the mistake of acknowledging to the jury his client's notoriety. Provenzano suffered a setback even more surprising than his 1963 conviction. The jury found him guilty.

Meanwhile, Teamsters affairs back at 707 Summit Avenue in Union City were going well. Interviews conducted with rank-and-file members in New Jersey in 1977 and 1978 yielded stories of loan-

* On May 17, Provenzano's lawyer suffered a heart attack, and the trial was again postponed.

shark, numbers, and bookie operations being run by union shop stewards and business agents. These were the services the Provenzano union performed for their people. And a member who couldn't meet his shylock payments often found that the union people he "elected" became enforcers against him, rather than against the company he worked for. Members also reported that workers had been recruited to help in systematic pilferage of goods being trucked through the state. One union member talked about being involved in furs and jewelry; another about stealing electric appliances. "Everything you can imagine goes on here," one truck-driver member of Local 560 explained in a July 1977 interview. "I started stealing for them [the Provenzanos] after I got tied up owing one of their loan sharks several thousand. Now it's OK. Even with their cut, I've been able to finance a new house."

A random survey of union pay checks in 1971 suggested that as many as 60 percent of the truckers and warehousemen under Joint Council 73's umbrella were working at wages below those specified in the National Master Freight Agreement. Although trucking company executives conceded that they regularly gave cash "Christmas" presents of "a few hundred dollars, maybe a little more," as one put it, to Provenzano-controlled business agents, there was no new concrete evidence of larger payoffs. Nor was there solid proof that these lower wages were not often legitimate concessions to companies in trouble, as Sammy Provenzano had claimed. However, two top national trucking company executives—both of whom bargained for the industry in the National Master Freight negotiation—readily volunteered that New Jersey was the one place in the country where the Master Agreement was ignored at least as often as it was respected.

The Provenzano unions also continued in grievance procedures and supplemental bargaining to make concessions that hurt their men. "Every grievance [a dispute between the company and an employee over some work rule or disciplinary action the company tries to enforce] is like a new negotiation," one trucking company explained. "And these guys in New Jersey just don't get much help from their union on these things. That's where the deals are made that you can never prove."

In addition to these concessions, in the middle 1970s there was the new scheme, reportedly masterminded by the Provenzanos in concert with mob boss Russell Bufalino, in which labor-leasing companies would be allowed to hire truck drivers at below-scale wages and then contract out to companies needing drivers. Provenzano's New Jersey was one of the main areas of the country where the labor leasers were making inroads.

Beyond corruption there was the question of simple services that other Teamsters locals as strong as Provenzano's were able to provide. Neither Local 560 nor any of the Provenzano-dominated New Jersey locals under the Joint Council 73 umbrella had any of the health or recreation facilities that Harold Gibbons' local in St. Louis had provided its members for more than a decade. And unlike their counterparts in most Teamsters locals, business agents for Local 560 and other New Jersey locals controlled by the Provenzanos were, according to their own members, rarely seen in a shop, unless they were making loan-shark collections.

Ten years earlier, Local 560 members had had good fringe benefits compared to other Teamsters. By the middle '70s the benefits the New Jersey truckers got were among the lowest for medical coverage (only $10,000 maximum compared to $20,000 for Central States members), for life insurance (only $10,000 compared to $16,000 for Central States members) and for hospital coverage (only 70 days compared to 365 days for Central States members).

Perhaps one reason for the lowered benefits was that the health, welfare and pension funds of most of the Provenzano-controlled locals—totaling some $125 million—were administered by a man who had been hand-picked by the Provenzanos, and had been convicted of embezzling union funds in the past.

Another practice that didn't help the members involved the management of the union finances, as distinct from the management of its pension and health and welfare money. By 1975—because of the economic depression of the Northeast region and also because organizers and business agents weren't doing the job of recruiting new members—membership in Local 560 had fallen to 8,500 from a high of 14,000 in the '60s. But expenses hadn't been trimmed to meet this cutback in dues income. The local's 1975 and 1976 books showed $79,988 in loans to cover operating expenses. Over the same two years the local union laid out $151,918 for new cars for its bosses. Other Provenzano-controlled locals that did have money seemed to have used it as badly. By 1977, there was strong evidence that some of these locals were depositing money through certificates of deposit in some small New Jersey banks in return for loans from the banks to organized-crime-connected businesses.

Another example of questionable union leadership involved the Eastern Freightways and Associated Transport Companies, once two of the larger trucking companies in the area. In 1975 when Eastern merged with Associated, 150 drivers for Associated were laid off, while Eastern drivers with less seniority were kept on. Keeping men with less seniority meant that the merged company could pay lower wages and pension benefits. An assistant vice-president for the merged company was Angelo Provenzano, another brother, who later said in a deposition that his duties at the company for $31,850 a year were "a little bit of everything." The union-management committee that had approved the arrangement to keep the men with less seniority had been chaired by Sammy Provenzano. A year later it was discovered that the company, claiming financial hardship, had not kept up with the pension and welfare contributions that it was supposed to be making for its workers. The year after that, the company went bankrupt, leaving these pension- and welfare-fund debts to the union unpaid.

Situations like these had aroused some renewed dissent in the ranks in the middle '70s. But by 1977 it was limited to pockets of protest, often in the form of surreptitious support for PROD and other reform efforts. At Local 560, after the violence against Phillips and others, there had been no organized opposition since the 1965 election. "Why should your average rank-and-file guy oppose them?" one law-enforcement official who had prosecuted Tony Pro would explain in 1977. "The average guy makes a good living, even if in some cases it's lower than the master contract wage. He figures he'll do his twenty years and get out. Why risk getting his legs broken or losing his job by fighting?"

The Glockner and Castellito murders and the assaults on Phillips were not forgotten by Teamsters a decade later. Of four dozen New Jersey Teamsters I interviewed in 1977, more than half referred to the possibility of being a victim of violence if they were to complain about the union. Even some men who said that they thought on the whole that the Provenzanos had done well for them were fearful of talking about them. It was not clear whether the possibility of violence now is real or merely perceived; there haven't been any serious cases reported in recent years. But there hasn't been any serious opposition either.

Also, those who had tried more recently to organize sputtering opposition movements in other locals had been penalized nonviolently. One man who had planned to run in 1977 on an opposition slate in Local 641 had been fired for taking too long on a coffee break. It was clear that the union leadership had instigated his dismissal, and under the contract the union had had to approve it through the grievance procedure. Such retaliation was not uncommon. What was unusual in this case was that the man was eventually allowed to rejoin the union and was rehired. His former insurgent allies later charged that the reinstatement was made only after he had agreed to "go over to the other side" and keep the Provenzano forces informed about what the dissidents were planning. At Eastern Freightways, another firing had involved a member who had decided to run for shop steward against the Provenzano forces. He was dismissed for thievery. The witness against him at the grievance hearing was company assistant vice-president Angelo Provenzano.

As the publicity in the Hoffa case and other charges heated up in the middle '70s, the Provenzanos' apparent popular support would be used by many national Teamsters leaders to defend their continued reign: "Why should we interfere with the will of the men in New Jersey," the argument from the International's Washington headquarters went. "Who are we to say a guy is no good. Don't you believe in democracy?" The International constitution does, in fact, require the International general president, general secretary-treasurer and executive board to interfere in such ways as auditing union books to look for wrongdoing, monitoring elections, policing the rights allowed potential dissenters, and barring local people with questionable records, like Sam Provenzano, to such higher posts as International vice-president. From 1975 through 1977, the books of both Joint Council 73 and Local 560 were audited once by the International—by an auditor who was not an accountant and had been recommended for his job by the Provenzanos.

As the 1977 La Costa tournament approached, the Provenzanos seemed to have union affairs well under control. Frank Fitzsimmons was a firm supporter; and at home in Local 560 there was no opposition in the election held later that month. At the end of July on the day of an NBC television report that alluded to Tony Pro's role in collecting money to be paid to Nixon for the restrictions on Hoffa's parole, every New Jersey local president received a "Dear Sir and Brother" letter from Tony Pro announcing his appointment as "director of organizing" for Joint Council 73. Sammy would go to the tournament and, as he had been the year before, he would be an unabashedly public personality there. Sammy had always been the clean brother up front; the one who had his picture taken at the San

Clemente White House with President Nixon in 1971; who had golfed with Nixon at the La Costa tournament in 1974. In 1973 he had been the chairman of the Teamsters political organization that gave $2,500 to Brendan Byrne's gubernatorial campaign. In 1976 he had been given the key to Atlantic City. That year he had also begun trying to use the key to set up a phony local union of security guards that he planned to have in place to organize workers at Atlantic City's coming casinos. The press would get wind of the scheme and he would have to drop it. But throughout 1977 he pushed so hard to get jurisdiction over Atlantic City that the Teamsters International vice-president from eastern Pennsylvania, who thought he had jurisdiction, decided to resign his union posts rather than fight the Provenzanos.

As in 1976, Tony Pro was still out on bail on the Castellito murder charge, and he did not attend the 1977 Tournament. This in many ways summed up the Provenzanos' uneasiness. True, the family had accumulated wealth and power beyond their dreams. By 1977 Tony, Sammy, Nunzio, two daughters and a brother-in-law together were drawing $240,000 in Teamsters salaries, including $54,000 for Tony in the form of $25,000 for that "back pay" and $29,000 as secretary-treasurer. They were set for life with lavish pensions worth hundreds of thousands of dollars. This was their reported legal income.

Yet sources close to the family agreed that not all was well in the Provenzano world. There were clouds—a list of maybes and might-have-beens that gnawed at them. Tony's appeal prospects on the loan kickback plot did not look good. The Castellito murder charge also hung over him, and there was a chance that that too might be trouble. The conviction and four-year sentence that his boss and buddy, Russell Bufalino, would receive on a simple extortion charge a week after the Tournament would be an unwelcome omen.

Even if he survived the murder trial and won an appeal on the kickback verdict, avoiding the horror of a long prison sentence at age sixty, not all would be well. The publicity from the trial would be as bad as in the weeks after the Hoffa disappearance. At Tony's age he had hoped to give his wife and three kids, especially the youngest daughter, who was seventeen, quieter times in his last years. And he feared for his health.

For years he had been so troubled by a grave stomach ailment and a heart condition, that he had become a physical-fitness fanatic. One bug the FBI had planted in July 1974 overheard him telling a friend that he walked three to five miles a day to exercise his heart and improve his circulation and that he ate "ten times a day a morsel at a time [because] that's one thing you [do] with a heart attack [so as not to] overtax your heart.''

The next year guaranteed a continuing investigation of how Tony Pro had set up all the New Jersey pension funds under one questionably managed fund, and how he had been involved with Carmine Galente and Russell Bufalino in using union funds as a way of steering loans from local banks to organized crime. The labor-leasing sweetheart deals that he had helped Bufalino and the others with were also coming under scrutiny. In fact, a week after the Tournament the *Wall Street Journal* would run its long article exposing the whole mess and spurring the government on to produce indictments. Indeed, with the pressure generated from the Hoffa case still coming from the Labor and Justice Departments, it was hard to imagine any scheme, old or new, that would *not* be in trouble.

It was true that Tony Pro still controlled New Jersey from 707 Summit Avenue, but New Jersey's trucking industry had been slowly dying, and his legal problems or the bad publicity might even threaten his control there sometime soon. It was clear that dreams he had entertained as he planned the Hoffa disappearance, of becoming the number-one power in the International—perhaps by pulling the strings through Fitzsimmons or through brother Sammy—were now impossible. He had more influence over Fitzsimmons than most realized, but Fitzsimmons himself was now under pressure from the law and from the Jackie Presser faction in the union to bow out. If he did, there was no way Tony or even Sammy Provenzano, was going to be able to replace him.

A few months before the 1977 Fitzsimmons Tournament I rang the elaborate chimes of Tony Provenzano's doorbell at his fourteen-room house in Florida. Mrs. Provenzano, an imposing, handsome woman answered the door. Her husband had been indicted for setting up Castellito's murder the day they were married in 1961. Politely, but nervously, she asked the caller what he wanted.

"No," her husband wasn't home, she answered in an accent that reflected her French-Canadian birth. "Yes," a note could be left for him. She closed the door on me to get a paper and pencil. When she opened it, a tall wide-eyed teen-ager, a son or nephew perhaps, peered out from behind a living-room wall. As she took the note (which was never answered) and nodded to the apology for bothering her at home, there was a burning stare in her eyes. At first it looked like a kind of quiet indignation. It seemed to harden into anger.

CHAPTER V

Ron Carey

On October 13,1976, Ronald R. Carey got up at six-thirty, but not to play golf. Six months later, when I asked him what La Costa was, he replied that he thought it was the name of Frank Fitzsimmons' mansion out in California.

Carey wanted to be at the United Parcel Service "hub" in West-chester County by eight so that he could see the men before they went out with the day's deliveries. It is about a forty-minute drive from Queens up through the Bronx to the Mount Vernon UPS package center. He could probably have slept a little later, but most of the mornings since he became president of Teamsters Local 804, Carey arose earlier than he had to, without an alarm clock.

It wasn't that Carey had to be so intense about his job. By October 1976, at forty-one, he was nearing his ninth anniversary as the Local's president. He was so popular among the members that he could easily have missed many of the stops that he made each morn-ing. There was no chance they would not reelect him in December.

Carey made his rounds that morning before a ten-o'clock negotia-tion involving the Westinghouse appliance repairmen he also repre-sented. "Taking the pulse and looking for problems" was part of the job. He had done it just about every day since 1968, whether there was an election in the offing or not.

Carey didn't take chances. He hadn't forgotten how tough the first victory in 1967 had been or that the incumbent he had unseated "had become too remote . . . too invisible."

Carey had become a United Parcel delivery man when he was twenty, following three years in the Marines after high school. His father, Joseph Carey, had had the same job; in fact, he had just retired in January 1976 after forty-five years at UPS in the Bronx. Two years after coming on the job, the younger Carey had become a shop steward. Soon he enrolled in college labor-relations courses at night school. By 1963, at twenty-eight and after eight years at UPS, Carey "became concerned about the way things were being handled." That year he ran for business agent, "something that I had always dreamt about." He lost. Two years later, he lost again. In 1967 he put together a well-organized campaign. He was the campaign manager, and he ran at the top of the "Security and Future" ticket for union president.

Several months before the election, he had had word from a friend in UPS management that the company was happy with the people who were then running Local 804, and that they were going to try to get Carey out of his UPS job so he wouldn't be eligible to run. A few days later he had a message to report to his delivery manager. He expected the worst, and was determined not to take it without a fight. Carey went to the meeting clutching a briefcase, which contained a tape recorder.

"Ron," the UPS man began. "I'm afraid we're going to have to ask for your resignation."

Carey inquired why he would want to resign.

"Because we have evidence, Ron, that you've been having an affair with another woman. And, if you don't resign, we're going to have to turn that evidence over to your wife."

Carey asked him to repeat what he'd said, and to please speak a little louder. Then the wiry, intense thirty-two-year-old delivery man got up, opened the briefcase, showed his boss the running tape recorder and walked out. He did not resign, nor was he ever asked to. He won a lot of votes that year by playing the tape at meetings during the campaign.*

* Through spokesman Dan Buckley, the United Parcel Service declined to be interviewed or comment on this or any other aspect of its relationship over the years with Carey or the Teamsters union.

Nine years later Carey had solid loyalty and respect from the 5,500 men and women, mostly men, in Local 804. In December 1976 an opponent would get about 100 votes to Carey's 1,700.

Carey's 5,500 membership roll was down in 1976 from a high of 7,000 in past years, when the New York area's retail and trucking industries were healthier. A year later the number would still be about the same 5,500. The 5,500 members worked at jobs in Nassau and Suffolk Counties on Long Island, in the five boroughs of New York City, in Westchester and parts of other counties north of the City, and in parts of New Jersey. Officially, Local 804 is chartered as the "Delivery and Warehouse Employees of New York." Most of the members are deliverers or warehouse sorters and truck loaders for department stores such as Macy's, Gimbels, and Lord and Taylor. About 4,000 sort packages or deliver them for United Parcel Service, working at shipping terminals, or "hubs," in Queens, Nassau County, Westchester and Manhattan. Nonetheless, as with all Teamsters locals, the official name is broad: Carey's local does not even come close to including all the Teamsters in New York who are deliverers or warehousemen for retail-oriented companies; nor is Carey's local limited to workers with these kinds of jobs. He has clerical employees in factories and retail chains, some factory workers, and was then weighing an organization drive that involved restaurant workers.

Essentially, a Teamsters local charter, granted in 804's case by the International in the 1930s, is a license to hunt. Carey and his business agents try to hold on to the workers they have as they organize new ones wherever they can find them. The only limits are that they are not supposed to raid other Teamsters locals, although sometimes— though never in Carey's case—the Joint Council would wink at it if done indirectly and if they preferred the raider to the victim of the raid. Also, a local might be prevented by the International from raiding another non-Teamsters union if the International didn't want to engage in a fight with that union. Other than that and always in the case of organizing previously unorganized workers, Ron Carey and the other 741 Teamsters local presidents are in business for themselves. The more men he organizes, the more dues money he receives. The more dues he collects the more people he is able to hire for the union's staff and the more he is able to pay them and himself.

A few weeks before Carey made his rounds at the Mt. Vernon UPS hub, in October 1976, Local 804 trustee Pat Pagnanella had heard about a "shop" that might be ripe for such organizing. Part of Pagnanella's job, like that of the other ten union officers, business agents and trustees, was keeping alert to possible job sites where the employees might be persuaded to join Local 804. Through a friend, he had received a call from a clerk at the Consolidated Millinery Company on 34th Street in Manhattan, saying that she and the approximately thirty other clerical employees there, almost all women, might want to join a union. After some follow-up conversations Pagnanella had gone to the Consolidated management and asked to have Local 804 recognized as the clerks' bargaining agent. As expected, they had refused, which meant that under federal labor law Pagnanella would have to get a majority of the clerks to vote for the union in an election.

This week of the 1976 La Costa Tournament he was distributing 804's literature, emphasizing the benefits of unionization and urging the women not to be afraid of employer reprisals. Meanwhile, Consolidated had hired a New York law firm that specializes in fighting unions in such elections. Soon Pagnanella, Carey and the other Local 804 officers watched their hopes of winning the election reduced to nothing. First, posters and news articles showing Frank Fitzsimmons and describing his $156,000 salary, his private jet, and the house at La Costa were put up in the employees' gathering places and over their time clocks. Attached were messages asking the women if they wanted their hard-earned money to go for these kinds of expenditure. Other articles posted about the Central States Pension Fund loans to Las Vegas "gangsters" (Local 804 was not part of the Central States Fund) were posted. By the time the votes were counted on December 15, what had looked like an easy organizing drive was a shambles. The women voted 21 to 13 against joining the Teamsters.

A year later, Carey and his people still fumed over this reminder of how the name Teamsters could hurt them. This had not been a typical Teamsters organizing election; the women had seemed especially unsure about taking the bold step of unionizing, and the publicity campaign was perfectly suited to take advantage of their uncertainty. Still, Carey's experience must be duplicated elsewhere; federal records show that in 1976 Teamsters locals around the country received 30,000 "yes" votes and 36,000 "no" votes in representation elections involving a choice of Teamsters or no union. Since the AFL-CIO's record was slightly worse that year, it can not be clear that the Teamsters-Fitzsimmons reputation was at fault. But it obviously provided a convenient avenue for antiunion campaigns.

Nearly five months after Carey's trip to Westchester on the day of the La Costa tournament, he allowed me to follow him as he made his morning rounds to three other Local 804 job sites.

His first stop at 7 A.M. the morning of March 7, 1977, was at Local 804's office in Long Island City, Queens. As Tony Provenzano's Union City stares at Manhattan from across the Hudson, Ron Carey's Long Island City is over the Queensboro Bridge and across the East River from it. It is part of New York City's manufacturing gut that was being abandoned in the '60s and '70s, factory by factory, in favor of the more open pastures of Nassau and Suffolk counties. Long Island City is the kind of place where the subway runs above ground, screeching and rocking on an old elevated track, because it hadn't been worth the trouble to hide it underground. Ron Carey and Barbara Carey had grown up in Long Island City's residential area. They met at the high school a few blocks away from the Local 804 office and were married in a church near there when both were eighteen and Ron had finished one year of service. Until the Marines, Carey's only regular excursion out of the neighborhood was during high school, when he attended Manhattan's Haaren High because they had a swimming team. He and two of his five brothers had swum on the team; and Ron's breast stroke was good enough to earn him a scholarship to St. John's University, also in Queens. He had turned it down in favor of the Marines.

The Careys now lived in a modest house farther out in Queens in a neighborhood called Kew Gardens. He and his father had chipped in $18,000 for the house in the '50s then had it moved to Kew Gardens from near a Kennedy Airport expressway. His father had now gone back to school at age sixty-six. He still shared the house with the Careys and their five children, three girls and two boys, the oldest of whom worked for Macy's department store and hoped to become an accountant. Carey still tried to stay in shape swimming, though the round plastic aboveground pool in the backyard was never big enough to make him feel he was really pushing the old breast-stroke muscles.

Local 804's headquarters at 2420 Jackson Avenue, the "union hall," is a small orange brick building three stories high. The only advertisement of the union's occupancy of the store-front floor is some small lettering in the window, with American-flag decals on either side. On the second floor a sign says, "Prestige air-conditioned

Offices for Rent,'' although the prestige was in being next store to ''Rosemarie de Paris'' discounts, across from the City Fastener Company, and down the street from a gum factory. Carey stopped here first thing this morning so that ''the girls'' could begin work as soon as they arrived on some of the paper work he had taken home over the weekend.

Then we drove to the UPS package center in nearby Maspeth, Queens. It is one of the largest United Parcel package-sorting hubs in the country, Carey explained. The greeting sign on the door leading to the employee's cafeteria reads, ''Welcome to Maspeth, Where Every Package is a Guest of Honor.''

In the cafeteria, coffee, tea and trays of big, gooey thirty-cent pastries were on sale with the coffee to men who would burn off the calories lugging packages from their trucks for the next eight hours. About thirty drivers, most paired off in booths along a window overlooking a vacant lot, sat with their coffee and rolls. They talked quietly or not at all. All wore the brown open-collared shirt and brown pants of the United Parcel uniform.

Although Carey's double-knit gray suit, white shirt and black tie didn't match, it didn't out-do the uniforms either. Carey looked like one of the deliverymen dressed up. Which is what he was.

Carey moved that way too. He didn't glad-hand his men or overdo it with a wide smile that would have intruded gratingly on their dull winter Monday morning. He gave each of them a subdued hello, a quiet nod, or a wink of recognition. He was one of them. He didn't have to make his appearance there a big, forced event. As he sat nursing his coffee in a booth with his visitor, about a half dozen of the men approached, one by one, as they got up to check out their trucks. Each wanted to know what was going on with ''the next contract.'' Each time ''Ron'' (no one ever called him Mr. Carey or Ronald) explained that he had just received a letter ''from the company asking us if we're willing to begin negotiating early.'' Local 804's contract with UPS was due to expire the last day of May. It had been signed three years before, after a long strike—the longest and bitterest of the strikes that had come with each new UPS contract Carey had negotiated since taking over in 1968. It was no surprise that the men were already getting edgy; if 1977 turned out like 1974 they would be out on picket lines for thirteen weeks this spring and summer instead of bringing home the $300 a week or more that they now earned.

Carey continued his explanation. The letter from UPS had raised the possibility that if an agreement was reached before the May 1 deadline, the company was even willing to consider making any pay increases retroactive to last December. That sounded good, Carey told each of the men, but the danger was that in making the contract retroactive the company was probably also going to insist that it only run for two years, instead of the usual three. The catch here was that this way the contract would coincide with the contract that all the other UPS workers in the Teamsters Eastern Conference (stretching from Maine to Georgia) had negotiated. And the International Constitution had a rule that if more than two thirds of the local unions in an area conference (unions, not members) wanted to negotiate as a unit, any other local with a contract with the same company for the same time period had to join that unit and negotiate as part of it. Since 1968 Carey had been fiercely independent. He had avoided any negotiating alignments with the Teamsters hierarchy, winning instead what he thought were better contracts on his own. Now it seemed that he might be trapped. His men shared his independent streak, supporting his determination to go it alone.

On the other hand, Carey explained, no one wanted another long strike—in terms of money you can never really "win" a strike that lasts more than a week, he reminded each of the questioners. Besides, there were some terrible disadvantages in negotiating alone: in the last strike, in '74, UPS had done pretty well in diverting packages to nonstriking Teamsters in Connecticut and New Jersey who had refused to help Local 804. "So," he concluded, "we should at least sit down and talk." However, although he had the authority to begin such negotiation on his own say-so, he was going to send the members a letter next week suggesting that negotiation begin but asking them to vote by mail ballot to approve his suggestion.

The seventh man who came up to Carey wasn't wearing the delivery uniform. Al, a short, red-faced, white-haired man wearing a heavy plaid shirt and denim pants, was a yard shifter—he moved the big trailers that convey thousands of packages between the Maspeth Center and hubs throughout the country. His job was to get the trailers backed up to the right bays for loading and unloading. Al listened to Carey's report and agreed that "we ought to at least see what they have to say." Then he complained about the "Mondayitis" that had "taken over my shop. . . . Seven guys are out today. So I'm really movin'." Finally, he registered a complaint that Carey jotted down on a scrap of paper. The roadway and yard where Al had to shift his trailers around had become filled with "giant potholes that really make it ridiculous." Carey promised to talk to someone in the company about it.

His coffee finished, Carey led his visitor down a metal stairway through a heavy door into a truck garage about the size of two airplane hangars. Most weekday mornings about three hundred delivery drivers fanned out from here, one to a truck. Their jobs are distinct from those of the men who take the huge tractor trailers over the interstate to other faraway hubs, or from the sorters who route packages to all over the country as they came into the hub from local shippers or from arriving tractor trailers. Theirs are strictly neighborhood jobs, not unlike that of the local mailmen. They are assigned steady routes small enough in area so that in some parts of Manhattan a UPS delivery man may work the same three or four blocks every day. They are supposed to learn their turf well enough to make about eighty or ninety deliveries a day, as well as ten or twenty pickups of merchandise that are shipped or being returned by retail customers. This makes about fifteen stops an hour. As Carey, who had the job for twelve years explained it, "The company won't tolerate poor production. If you don't deliver as many as the day before they're all over you."

By the late 1970s retail deliveries—packages that customers buy at department stores and ship home—were far outnumbered by UPS's wholesale business of transporting supplies of parts and other products between manufacturers, distributors and retailers. In 1977 Carey's local drivers here and at the other hubs in the New York area delivered 100,000 packages a day.

The men about to go out from the giant garage were divided into groups depending on the areas of the city they covered. Carey walked a few hundred yards past several groups to one of about fifty that he knew hadn't yet heard anything about the letter from the company. The men were milling around in a semicircle, some playing with a stray dog that they had adopted the week before as a mascot, others sipping coffee from paper cups. They half-surrounded a crew-cut, stiff young man in a tie but no jacket. He was their supervisor. Carey greeted the future executive by his first name and asked to address the group when he had finished giving what looked to be the morning pep talk. This was the "shape-up" Carey explained. What it turned out to be was an upbeat discourse on the increasing problem of "BA's." "BA's," Carey whispered, stood for "bad addresses." It seemed that drivers were increasingly giving up on packages that had a wrong address, rather than trying on their own, by using a phone book or asking a building superintendent, to correct what probably was a minor misnumbering of the street address so that the delivery could be made. As an enticement, the supervisor declared, "We're now offering 25¢ for every corrected address. So, please help us out."

As the "shape-up" continued with other minor announcements, several men approached Carey with questions about "the New Jersey contract [actually, it was the Eastern Conference contract, which included the neighboring New Jersey UPS drivers] and how it compares to ours." The Eastern Conference contract had recently been concluded and, as Carey explained, it did provide slightly more than the $7.37 an hour the men were receiving that March morning. However, he assured the men, it was certain that in the new contract to be negotiated this spring the Local 804 people would leapfrog over the Eastern Conference again. (They would: the new contract would give the men an extra 94 cents an hour by June 1 and another 85¢ an hour by June 1978. The Eastern Conference would enjoy its advantage for only a few months before sinking below Local 804 again.)

The shape-up over, Carey addressed the men and explained for the eighth time that morning the UPS letter, its dangers and possibilities, and the ballot they would be getting in the mail. When he finished, almost half the men formed a smaller circle around him. "What should we do, Ron? What do you want us to do?" Again, he went through the pro's and con's, concluding that he thought, "We should sit down and talk, but I want you guys to think about it and make the decision." Nothing about the reply was condescending. Carey talked to his men as one of them. This was a special kind of leader. The men he led looked up to him and, somehow, he managed not to look down.

Later, Carey expressed what he considered to be "wrong with so many people in the Teamsters leadership. . . . They see themselves as different once they get elected. They start wearing pinky rings and talking out of the sides of their mouths. If they ever do visit a shop they stand off in a corner as if to say, 'I'm calling the shots here.' Well, I don't call the shots . . . I work for these guys. These drivers' dues pay my salary."

The International constitution passed at the convention in June 1976 mandated that, beginning that October, the dues paid by these men shaping up this morning at Maspeth and by Carey's other Local 804 members would be raised from $13 a month to $15, with about a thousand part-time workers (mostly UPS package sorters here and at the other hubs) paying $13. Out of these monthly dues the shop steward, who typically represents twenty or thirty of his co-workers at a job site, would be paid one dollar a month for each member he or she represented. Here at Maspeth there were about thirty shop stewards.

Another $2.65 of each $15 dues payment per month would have to be sent to the International in Washington. This "per capita tax," which would rise to $3.15 by the time of the 1977 La Costa Fitzsimmons Invitational, was the primary source of the International's income, providing $33.30 in 1977 from each of the International's approximately 2.3 million members. The fifty men surrounding Carey this morning would, therefore, be sending about $1,600 to Fitzsimmons and his people this year. Together, Carey's 5,500 dues payers would be sending $183,000 in 1977—payments which Carey would make with increasing frustration and bitterness as he mulled other events like the Consolidated Millinery organizing debacle.

Another 60 cents per month of the $15 in dues had to be paid to Local 804's Joint Council. Joint Council 16, run by Joseph Trerotola, would collect some $39,000 from Carey's local in 1977—about 3 percent of the giant Joint Council's budget—for doing Teamsters lobbying in the state legislature, resolving jurisdictional disputes among locals, resolving grievances that were appealed from the locals, serving as a general buffer between the local and the International, and employing Trerotola's son, Vincent, as perhaps the nation's highest paid clerk. The 1976 constitution mandated that Carey also pay 20 cents a month per member to the Eastern Conference, also run by Trerotola. This would amount to about $13,000 in the next twelve months. Thus, of the $15 per month that Carey would collect over the next twelve months from each of his members, Local 804 would keep only $10.55.

With overlapping payments from members coming on or off jobs in the same month, with the $13 a month dues in effect until October 1, 1976, and with the lower dues schedule for the 1,000 part-timers, this payment structure gave Carey $717,913 in dues for the year ending December 31, 1976. Of that, he had paid $189,466 in per capita taxes. He had collected another $101,736 in initiation fees of $200 each from new members who were replacing those who had retired or left.

The basics of Carey's 1976 budget, then, looked like this:

Income:		Expenses:	
A. Dues	$718,000	A. Salaries, benefits and allowances for officers and employees:	$446,000
B. Initiation Fees	102,000	B. Office expenses:	52,000
		C. Taxes:	13,000
Total	$820,000	D. Professional Fees (almost all legal fees):	37,000
		E. Purchase of office equipment:	10,000
		F. Per Capita Taxes:	189,000
		G. Miscellaneous:	22,000
		Total	$769,000

Not to be found in Carey's budget were any purchases of automobiles. In the year that Tony Provenzano's Local 560 in New Jersey, with eight thousand members, bought $96,000 worth of cars, Carey's local provided him with a $250-a-month allowance for his full-time use of his own Ford Maverick. With that $250 he bought gas and insurance, and paid for repairs. The other Local 804 officers and business agents who used cars got the same allowance. Counting these and other reimbursed expenses Carey received $34,134 in salary and allowances from the union in 1976. Nunzio Provenzano, president of Local 560, received $40,000. Carey's secretary-treasurer, who had higher expenses than Carey, received $35,000. Local 560 secretary-treasurer, Anthony Provenzano got $52,000. Carey's vice-president received $39,000. Local 560's vice-president, Salvatore Provenzano, received $30,000, plus another $59,000 from the Joint Council and the International.

In 1971, the members of Local 804 had authorized Carey and the other officers to give themselves salary increases that matched the percentage increases won in new United Parcel contracts. Carey and his people had never used the authority, because they felt the union couldn't afford to pay them more and maintain a large enough staff of professionals—officers and business agents—to allow them to visit all their shops regularly and give them adequate attention. In 1977, Carey had the same number of officers and business agents—ten, all up from the ranks, no relatives and no ex-cons—as Local 560 did, even though Local 560 had 45 percent more members. In early 1975, when layoffs had cut badly into Local 804's membership and, therefore, its union dues income, Carey and the other officers had all cut their salaries $100 a week for nine months rather than reduce staff.

Although Local 560 in New Jersey owned its building and, therefore, paid no rent, it had listed $145,000 in office expenses in 1976, compared to Carey's $52,000. This was largely because Local 560 officers and business agents had the free use of union credit cards for travel and entertainment. Carey abolished all union credit cards when he took over Local 804. Any meals had to come out of the officers' allowance, and all travel had to be authorized beforehand and be related unquestionably to absolutely necessary business. Carey's trustees, in fact, did what the International constitution said trustees were supposed to do. They made Carey and the other officers account for all expenses, including even long-distance phone calls. If Carey's phone bill went over $50 in a month he was required to explain how and why, call by call.

In addition to playing the UPS blackmail tape recording, Carey had made a big campaign issue in 1967 of the Local 804 President Thomas Sincox's use of credit cards. Records on file ten years later at the Labor Department showed that he had charged $3,000 in a week on entertainment just on the union's Diners Club Card. The incumbent president had had a reputation with the men here at Maspeth and elsewhere as "a big spender and playboy," one union trustee later recalled. "Ron hit hard on all those expenses, and it really hit home to the members."

Whatever it did for the members, Carey's campaign did not impress the people at the International. "They thought I was some kind of a joke," he remembered. "Even after I won the election I think they thought it was a fluke. They didn't take me seriously."

When Carey took office in 1968, then acting International General President Frank Fitzsimmons arranged for the departing Sincox to have a new job with the Joint Council, a cushion for the rejected incumbent that did not sit well with the members who had voted him out or with the insurgents who had replaced him. More than that, Fitzsimmons and Joint Council 16 President Joe Trerotola apparently decided that Carey could be treated the way the old president had been—that Carey would be willing to play second fiddle while they and their people negotiated his contracts.

When Carey had arrived for his first day of UPS negotiation in 1968 the United Parcel drivers were being paid $3.37 an hour. By March 1977 he had raised their hourly wages 119 percent, to $7.37, compared to a rise in the cost of living of 72 percent.) In addition, in June 1977 he would win another increase retroactive to December 1976. He had come to the UPS talks that day in 1968, a thirty-three-year-old package driver who had hardly had time to get used to not wearing brown all day. He was eager to deliver on the campaign promises his "Security and Future" ticket had made for tough but reasonable negotiating that would produce better wages and benefits with fewer strikes. But when he got to the bargaining table he found other Teamsters there to "help" him—higher ups from the Joint Council and the International—headed by International organizer Fleming Campbell and a man named Schmidt, whose first name, Moran, Carey habitually mispronounced Moron.

At first Carey said nothing. Then, after a few bargaining sessions, when Campbell and the others urged him in front of the company representative to take a softer line, he asked them to leave. They didn't. As the contract deadline passed, the bargaining was going nowhere, in part because the company hoped that Carey would be talked out of his position by the other Teamsters. In May, Carey's men went out on strike. Soon, the Joint Council representative quit the talks, storming out of the negotiations calling Carey a psycho. What really infuriated him, he told Carey outside the bargaining room, was Carey's insistence that Local 804 men get the right to retire with pensions after twenty-five years. The other UPS unions he represented, he told Carey, had a thirty-year retirement clause and he wasn't going to make a fool of himself by helping a green thirty-three-year-old kid win a twenty-five-year clause.

The International people also didn't like the idea that Carey was trying to do better than the other UPS contracts around the country. They urged him to settle, telling him that Fitzsimmons himself, wanted him to. The strike continued.

One night in July, nine weeks into the strike, Carey got a phone call at home. "You think you're so smart, wise guy," the voice said. "Go pick up the New York *Daily News*." The phone went dead. Carey went to a local newsstand. At first he didn't see it. If anything, he was looking for a small article buried somewhere in the back. Finally, almost as an afterthought he looked at the headline pages and found it, an article on page 3 announcing that "reliable sources" had informed the *News* that a probe was underway to see if the prolonged UPS strike was part of a "mob dominated conspiracy" that was being investigated by the U.S. Attorney Robert Morgenthau. The article suggested that Carey had kept the strike going in order to allow mob-owned trucking companies to pick up the business UPS was losing. The next morning a sleepless Ron Carey told any reporter who would listen that he would cooperate in any such probe and that he would welcome any investigation. Later that day, Fitzsimmons, acting, he said, because he was worried about the *News'* reports of the scandal, ordered Local 804 to vote on UPS's latest offer. (He had the authority to do this under the International constitution.) Carey put the offer up for a vote, although he told the members it was the International's idea, not his. The members rejected it overwhelmingly. The next day Carey won a new pact, which included the twenty-five-year pension and two other work-rule clauses that he had been fighting for and were not in UPS's prior offer. The men went back to work.

Nine years later Morgenthau stated that, "Local 804 was never a Teamster local that we investigated. I don't know where that story came from."

During the strike, Carey also got another variety of nighttime phone call. A voice urged him to check his car before he started it in the morning, or to watch out for his family. "I could tell when these calls started," one of Carey's business agents would later recall, "because Ron looked all shook up when he came in in the morning. He never volunteered the information, but we got him to tell us after a while."

By his own standard, expressed this morning nine years after the '68 strike—that you can never win a strike after you're out a week—he hadn't "won" in 1968 by staying out for nine weeks. And the people at the International could justifiably call him a "hothead" or "too militant," whatever their real motives and jealousies. But he had built a base for future gains that these men here in March 1977 would enjoy. And, somehow, he had come out of the long, grueling '68 strike with his men more strongly behind him than they had been before.

As the men left Maspeth that morning in their brown trucks, Carey made his way back up through the cafeteria and out to the parking lot to go to his next stop. The last door he passed through was by one of those "frisk-em" archways they use at airports to keep guns off the planes. An aging, disheveled guard—also an 804 member—kept a half-watch on the machine's indicator. This, Carey explained, was one of the company's ways of preventing pilfering. Other theft-prevention measures included allowing FBI agents to work undercover among the employees who sorted packages. (A favorite thieves' trick among the sorters was slipping address labels with their own addresses on to packages over the correct labels.)

Just to the other side of the archway, a half dozen young black men were milling around. "They're looking for part-time work," Carey said. This, he explained, was one of his toughest UPS problems. Throughout the country, since the '60s, United Parcel had rearranged its routine so that all the work stacked up during a few hours each day. This had allowed the company to replace full-time men—in package-sorting positions only, not as drivers—with part-timers. Part-timers usually worked only four hours a day from 4 P.M. to 8 P.M. They were paid a little less than full-timers and, more significantly, did not receive fringe benefits such as health coverage, vacation pay or pensions. In every negotiation Carey's biggest fight with UPS had involved holding back the move for more part-time workers in sorting. He had been far more successful than other UPS locals throughout the country, in part because in many areas where UPS had only recently begun operations it had always used part-time help. In his 1977 contract Carey would still hold on with a clause forbidding new part-time hiring except to replace full-time sorters who retired or quit. But even that did not bode well for the future. Attrition ultimately spelled the elimination of the jobs of the nearly two thousand full-time sorters he now represented; and no union could be strong if the core of its membership consisted of part-time workers with unstable jobs. What made matters worse was that he also now represented some one thousand part-time sorters, who paid $13 a month dues. The conflict here was obvious: how could he faithfully represent the interests of the two competing job categories?

The next stop was a small trucking company set off among warehouses and a few vacant lots several blocks away. This place, the Eastern Parcel Company,* was in Carey's words, "totally different from UPS. This is a real shit hole." About thirty trucks, all "straight jobs" (that is, one-unit vehicles rather than tractors pulling trailers) were backed against a ramshackle warehouse about 60 feet long and

* Actually, it has a different name, but Carey asked that it not be published because of the company's precarious financial situation.

30 feet wide, full of haphazardly stacked cartons and crates. There was no heat inside nor did there seem to be any ventilation to disperse the truck fumes. "This company is in terrible shape," Carey explained. "They've been on the brink of bankruptcy for years. If UPS's license didn't limit them to packages weighing less than 100 pounds, places like this would be out of business. Frankly I think it's because they have too many bosses, but whatever it is I know they're in bad shape because we've checked their books."

"As a result," Carey continued, "they literally cry when you go in to negotiate a contract." Crying helps: the men that morning were earning $5.50 an hour, as compared to the $8.60 being paid city drivers under the National Master Freight Agreement. Also, according to Carey, Eastern Parcel was six months behind in its payments to the union's health and welfare fund, and even a month behind in sending Carey the $15 union dues it deducted from the men's paychecks. "They're always behind," Carey commented. "We could come in here right now probably and take the warehouse and their trucks. But they're honorable people. Besides, if we closed them down eighty or ninety of our members would lose their jobs. So, we carry them."

This, of course, was the rationale that the Provenzanos used in New Jersey to grant contract concessions to their employers. The analogy isn't exact, since the Provenzano unions usually negotiated as part of the National Master Freight group and *then* granted exemptions, whereas Carey shunned the national agreement altogether in favor of negotiating on his own. But the situations were similar in the sense that like the Provenzanos—whose brother was on the payroll of one company that received a "hardship" concession—Carey's benevolence toward Eastern Parcel could easily have been encouraged by corruption. This discretionary power tests the honesty of union leaders the way few other jobs so consistently test men and women of Carey's relatively modest economic means. By all accounts—and these were gathered in a long series of interviews with employers, union members, and Local 804 officers—it was a test that Carey had always passed in circumstances that ranged from offers of free meals to free vacations to briefcases full of cash.

Carey moved through the cold, cluttered Eastern Parcel warehouse into a tiny windowless room with a coffee machine. The bulletin board announced a forthcoming union meeting. It was the employee rest room. Here, Carey exchanged routine union gossip with the shop steward. He then asked one of the bosses, a cheerful heavy-set man named Mike, about a change in work schedules. Soon a black man in his middle thirties peered through the half-open door. He was wearing a green corduroy hat and a heavy wool plaid jacket.

"Ron, can I talk to you a minute?" he began tentatively.

"Sure, Al, what's the problem?"

Al Lassiter, a driver for Eastern Parcel, explained to Carey about the problem he was having getting reimbursed for the money he had spent on doctors for his wife's recent illness. Also, just a week earlier his son had broken his arm and Al had had to take him to a hospital emergency room. He was worried about getting back the money that he had laid out for that, too. The shop steward, who already knew about the problem added some details, explaining to Carey that the snafu involved the union's recent switch to a health plan under which the Local 804 health and welfare fund paid the claims directly.

Carey pulled out the scrap of paper that he had used at the UPS cafeteria to record the yardman's complaint about potholes and wrote down Lassiter's name and problem. "Either me or someone else will be back to you in a few days about this," Carey promised.

Carey couldn't know that Lassiter would be interviewed at his Newark, New Jersey, home four months later and asked if Carey had delivered on his promise. "Oh yes, I got a letter two days later from the union explaining the problem and promising me the money," Lassiter recalled happily. "And very soon after that I got the money." As for Carey, he was "One of the greatest guys I've ever met. He's the best."

Lassiter's previous union experience was bound to make him appreciate Carey. He had started in trucking in the middle '60s at a company in New Jersey, where he was a member of the Provenzano-controlled Local 863. "In those days, me and my friends just didn't know what a union could be," he recalled. "The difference between Local 804 and 863 is like night and day. I don't want to get too specific, you know, but 863 wasn't anything like [804]. There the business agent, who we never knew, would come into the shop, pick two men and they'd go into the boss's office and negotiate a contract. When they came out, that was it. We didn't get anything to say about it. . . . Until I came here, that's the way I thought a union worked."

At about a quarter to nine, Carey left Lassiter and Eastern Parcel for the next shop.

Macy's warehouse on nearby Metropolitan Avenue looked bigger than an indoor stadium. It seems as if all of New York's furniture could be piled in here like a Noah's ark. In fact, the warehouse stores all the furniture and large bulk household goods for the New York City Macy stores, including the largest retail outlet in the world, in Manhattan.

Outside, trucks bearing the names of furniture makers from places like Hickory, North Carolina, and Martindale, Virginia, were lined up to deposit their goods. Carey explained, as we left the Ford dwarfed alongside one of the giant trucks at the front of the line, that these were probably independent drivers who owned their own trucks and drove here overnight from the South. "This waiting time kills them. It's all money down the drain. . . . Sometimes these guys work 120 hours a week. . . ."

Inside the warehouse it is like looking through a telescope at a toy store that stocks doll's-house furniture. Giant shelves—seven layers, in some places extending four or five stories high and blocks long— held hundreds of mattresses, box springs, couches, chairs, and tables. As Carey moved through the first of a dozen or more such aisles he nodded to a man operating a forklift that was picking a couch mounted on a wooden pallet off one of the top shelves. Elsewhere on the aisles, carts holding other goods moved along unmanned on automatic tracks, pulled by an electrical pulley system that guided them up and down and around the various aisles to the correct loading area. "Those used to be jobs," Carey mumbled, motioning to the robot carts.

The jobs Carey now represented here included all of the nonsupervisory personnel plus the men who delivered the furniture. (The deliverers were off today; they worked Saturdays but not Mondays.) About 250 men and women worked here, ranging from $231-a-week stock clerks in the shipping and receiving department, to $236-a-week forklift operators to $270-a-week drivers' helpers, to $280-a-week drivers. They all get thirteen paid holidays and paid vacations of as much as four weeks and three days depending on seniority. When Carey negotiated their first contract in 1968 the department-store contracts were said to be the Local 804 pacts most tainted by past corruption. Since 1969 Carey had won for the Macy's employees contracts that raised these wages an average of more than 100 percent (compared to a cost-of-living increase of less than 70 percent over that period) while raising the basic pension more than 200 percent.

Carey's first stop was at the warehouse repair shops, where the forklifts and other equipment are maintained. The shop steward, Artie, a man in his forties, got right up from a work table and approached him with a complaint: Yesterday, two repair jobs had been "farmed out" to outside contractors rather than "letting us do it." "Those bastards," Carey replied, although he seemed more resigned to the "farming out" problem than Artie was. "I'll talk to them about it," he added, jotting down another note on the scrap of paper. Artie then told Ron how his son, Steve, who drove a Macy's delivery truck, had been stranded last evening when the truck broke down in the Bronx near the end of his run. When no one from the Macy's garage would go pick him up—"even after I called them myself"—Artie had had to dispatch his other son, who also drove a Macy's truck, to get Steve.

Next, Carey remembered that Al, in the carpentry shop, had called him about a problem. On the way there he stopped to say hello to a warehouse cabinet finisher, a man who repairs furniture that has been damaged in transit. This was a craftsman among Teamsters. A stooped, smiling Italian who spoke little English, he had carved out, with stacked cartons and discarded cabinets, an office of sorts within the cavernous warehouse. Here he worked alone under a calendar from Nunzy's Liquor Store, coaxing the tables, chairs and cabinets back to what they had been before they were shoved around by his less nimble co-workers.

Al's complaint was that the warehouse manager had offered to give the carpenters vests to wear on cold days. The shop was close to the open truck loading area and the carpenters had very little protection from the winter temperatures.

"We don't want vests, Ron," Al said, slapping the top of his work table. "We have our own clothes. We don't want any uniforms. What we want is for them to build a protective wall. We want it warm." Carey nodded his agreement. "We're gonna be talking to them in the negotiations about building some kind of sliding wall. That's what they should do."

As he moved out down the aisle on his way up to the shop stewards' meeting he had called for 10:15, Carey ran into Bill, a man apparently in his early twenties. In a deep ghetto accent, Bill told him he had been "written up" for lateness. It was the third time, he wanted to know what to do. "Talk to Bob [the shop steward]," Carey answered. "They'll probably not hassle you too much. But you've got to watch the clock, man. They can be real bastards."

The stewards' meeting was in the warehouse's lunchroom. It was a small, grimy room with several dozen tables and, around the walls, a mix of vending machines and a microwave reheater that prepared various cans and plastic packages of pre-cooked food.

As Carey waited for all of the ten stewards to assemble he and those who were there listened to some tales by a gawky, balding black-haired man named Bert, who had once been a steward. The first was about "how crazy I went" when I went to pick up my son at the airport two weeks ago. He was coming in from California. . . . Well I get to the gate and he walks off the plane with no shoes on and hair down to here." That led to how the son, long unemployed, had gotten the money to go to California, in the first place. He had bought a van for $2,200 last summer. But one night "he was with some broad and tried to pull off toward the water off Cross Bay Boulevard [in Queens]. Well he ran the goddamn thing right into the water. . . . So he called the insurance company the next day and said it had been stolen. . . . They gave him twenty-eight hundred bucks for it. Can you believe that?" Next, an account of how Bert's girl friend was "mad at me for not introducing her to my daughter the other day" at a neighborhood gathering. "Can you imagine that?"

Bert finished his coffee and got up to go back to the cartons of houseware products he tended. He motioned Carey aside. "Ron, would you mind calling tonight so I can tell you we're going out for drinks Thursday night so the wife can hear?" Carey agreed. "Bert fools around a lot and uses me as an excuse," he explained later. "This way his wife will think he's with me. . . . He's a good friend."

The meeting had been called so that the stewards, nine men and one woman, could finish a tentative list of twenty-nine proposals that included working conditions, seniority rights, and other nonwage matters that they wanted to present at the negotiation for a new contract to replace the contract that expired eight weeks later. There was nothing extraordinary about any of the twenty-nine proposals—unless you happened to be the cold worker in the carpentry shop who wanted the wall built; or the man or woman in "binning" (sorting of merchandise for loading) who felt put upon by having to work a few minutes overtime with no option to refuse it, or the mechanic's "helper" who wanted to be trained to be a full mechanic.

Carey, who was now joined by Local 804 vice-president Gene Dugan, a veteran of past Macy's negotiation, went through the proposals painstakingly, trying to get the stewards' sense of which ones were most important and why. Several times he suggested a language change and once even a deletion. But in each case he relied on the consensus.

Eight weeks later, on April 28, 1977, Carey and the same stewards assembled in a small inelegant conference room on the second floor of Manhattan's Biltmore Hotel for one of the many negotiating sessions with Macy's.

G.G. Michelson led the Macy's team. A smartly dressed woman who looked to be in her early forties, Michelson was Macy's New York vice-president for labor relations. Carey had a curious relationship with her. On one occasion when he had been a guest speaker at a college seminar, Carey had gotten into trouble with the women in the class by referring to women as "broads." He routinely calls his secretaries "girls" and holds to the old male-female division of work and worlds at home. His wife, Barbara, is rarely kept posted on his work (she doesn't even know his salary) and he rarely aids in the household chores reserved for "the woman." Yet, he seemed to have no trouble at all dealing with Michelson's role as his counterpart in these negotiations. Their relationship across the table was professional and cordial. In later interviews both separately went out of their way to express their respect for the other's ability and integrity.

Michelson and Carey would bargain that day across four rectangular tables arranged to form a square almost the size of the room itself. They needed room. Carey brought his shop stewards to such sessions, and Michelson backed herself with four lawyers, two on either side.

As this session began, Michelson announced that since this was pay day the stewards' pay checks were on their way over to the Biltmore by messenger, "so that should put everyone at ease." The men chuckled, and one joked that he hoped the messenger "didn't get lost on the way." There were three hours of detailed discussion of changes in work rules, seniority rights, and the like, as outlined in the stewards' twenty-nine proposals and in Macy's counterproposals. There would be few formal agreements on anything. The most frequent last word on any question was Michelson's, "I'll get back to you on that, Ron." Everything was on first names, even between Michelson and the stewards. Nowhere was there evidence of urgency on either side, even though there were only three days left before the end of the contract. Michelson and her lawyers eventually left the room for Carey and his stewards to caucus, but not before both sides had agreed orally to work under the current contract for at least a week beyond May 1, with any changes in the new contract retroactive to May 1. They also agreed to convene at the same place Monday morning with the company arranging (and paying for) the room that time.

Three weeks later, and without a strike, the two sides agreed on a contract that raised wages an average of about thirty-two cents an hour, and incorporated about half of the stewards' proposed working conditions and rule changes. They included the building of a movable plastic wall to protect the men from the cold.

That morning in early March as he left the stewards' meeting at Macy's with me, Carey predicted the result. "I know we won't have a strike here. We haven't had one here in my memory. This is a relatively easy contract to handle."

Before he left the warehouse Carey stopped to talk to three men working the rows of Belgian carpets. A tall Irish-looking man with three top teeth at least a half inch apart announced to Carey that he was getting the bridge work for his mouth in about three weeks and asked when the contract was ever going to provide money to help him pay for it. "I know, we keep bringing that up," Carey replied. "But right now it's just more than they're willing to pay."

Making his way from the carpets to the warehouse door, Carey pointed to a section in a back row of carpets. "At Christmas time, they'll block off a few rows there and serve booze and potato chips," he remarked. "And one guy will stand here as a lookout for management." Carey is no year-round Santa Claus when it came to men not working, however. "If a member is wrong, we tell him," one of Carey's business agents explained. "We won't support him at a grievance hearing with some bullshit story. . . . Ron doesn't think people should get paid for nothing." Veteran shop steward Sam Begleiter recalled that on one occasion "The union insisted that a supervisor be added to the repair shop because men weren't performing and, as a result, Macy's was contracting the work out."

On the ride back to his office, Carey talked about the problems he had had organizing other department stores in the New York area. "You go into a place like Bloomingdale's, where the warehouse and delivery workers aren't unionized and try to organize them. Well, the company puts out literature about Fitzsimmons' salary or about the loans those other pension funds have made to Las Vegas. Plus, they pay almost what our people get anyway. So it's very difficult."

As for his own job, "Over-all, the key thing is using your time well. Even if you're locked in negotiations you have to use the early morning to get around to some shops. Otherwise the guys will think you're on the golf course or something, even if you were up until four the morning before, negotiating for them."

After two hours at the office occupied by paperwork, phone calls, a quick bite and a short conference with a business agent who wanted to make sure that a shop steward could be present when the Lord and Taylor security people questioned a member about pilfering that afternoon, Carey went back to the UPS Maspeth center. The delivery drivers were long gone, but at one-thirty the sorting area of the hub hummed. The work here begins at 1 P.M. and goes through the night; 600 or more workers sort about 180,000 packages each night shift.

Carey entered the sorting area through the door that leads to a grated metal parapet, where supervisors had scattered to watch the goings-on below. The place was about five blocks long and two hundred yards wide. Thousands of packages moved in front of men lined up assembly-line style. They plucked packages from the conveyors, read the addresses, then turned and tossed them behind into color-coded bins. On the other side of these bins, other workers removed the packages and distributed them into other bins geared to a more precise color code that divided the country into several hundred areas.

The sorters, Carey explained, who come on in shifts beginning at 1 P.M. and earn a 10 percent "night differential" above their basic wage, which he said, was "only fair because of what night work does to your family life." By March 1977, this had brought the full-time sorters' base pay up to about $330 a week. The sorters, Carey noted, were a "different breed of cat" from the drivers. They weren't uniformed; their jobs weren't nearly as interesting or as independent; they were usually younger, because there was a higher turnover; and here at Maspeth they were about 75 percent black or Puerto Rican.

Carey moved through the sorting line saying hello to the men. (There were no women.) A group of four blacks and one Puerto Rican—all young, wearing jeans, sneakers and plaid work shirts—stopped him in front of some orange crates that were bound from Florida to Plainfield, New Jersey. The youngest-looking told Carey that the supervisor had asked him if he would mind a transfer to a different terminal. "Do I have to go, Ron?"

"No you don't," Carey assured him. "The contract says you can stay here. If you don't want to go, just refuse him nicely. Say it's too much of a hassle to get there. Don't be rude or get into a fight, OK?" The young Puerto Rican had a question about his medical insurance, a third sorter asked about getting his hours changed, a fourth inquired about getting his brother a job.

Carey jotted notes on his increasingly cluttered piece of paper. For these and other members, he was the modern version of the political ward heeler. He must have said, "I'll see what I can do," every ten minutes during this and the other stops. Like the old neighborhood politicians, with their connections to the machine, Carey was the link between these men and the forces that controlled much of their lives.

While Carey met briefly with a supervisor, trying informally to resolve a work-rule dispute, Fred Holmes, a black shop steward and a thirteen-year veteran of the sorting area, discussed Carey and the Teamsters over a cup of coffee in the cafeteria with me and three of his fellow workers, who were also black. All praised Carey, expressed pride in Local 804's independence, and criticized Fitzsimmons for corruption and personal extravagance. Holmes added, "You can quote me as saying that that man [Fitzsimmons] stinks." The four agreed that, as one put it, "a minority of more politically militant blacks don't like Ron, because he's, you know, so straight."

It was not surprising that the "more politically militant blacks" at UPS saw Ron Carey, the white, blue-collar Long Island City native, as someone who did not exactly march to their beat. Labor issues aside, Carey considers himself a political conservative. He voted for Ford in '76, and Nixon in '72. His union newsletter a few years back had had this to say about the American political scene:

> If you want your father to take care of you, that's paternalism. If you want your mother to take care of you, that's maternalism. If you want Uncle Sam to take care of you, that's Socialism. If you want Comrades to take care of you, that's Communism. But—if you want to take care of yourself, that's Americanism.

That more of the young blacks didn't feel uncomfortable with their president was due in large part to what might best be called the debacle of 1970. That year Carey led a militant wildcat strike over a symbolic issue that united Carey's "Americanism" with the blacks' militancy: the wearing of American-flag lapel buttons and black-power emblems on the UPS deliverers' uniforms.

It had started innocently enough. Some of Carey's deliverers, heeding President Nixon's call to the "Great Silent Majority," began wearing lapel flags to show their support for the Vietnam War. Although a work-rule clause stated clearly that only the union button may be worn on the delivery uniforms, the company didn't dispute the wearing of the flag. Then many of the black delivery men began wearing black-power buttons. Then, "Irish power," "Italian power," and other buttons began to appear, including one in pseudo-Chinese that spelled out an obscenity when read backward. When the company received some customer complaints, it sought and obtained an arbitration ruling that said no pins or buttons could be worn.

Carey called a strike, and all four thousand of his UPS members walked. The strike lasted eleven days, during which Carey made an emotional speech at a City Hall rally, saying that "we are striking for the American flag and the pride of a man in his country or his race." He ignored a federal judge's $25,000-a-day fine against the union and $2,500-a-day fine against him, and vowed to go to jail "to defend the flag." In the end it was settled by an agreement that the men could wear the flag, but no other button or pin, and that Carey would pay a $500 fine, with no reimbursement permitted from the union.

Carey, just two years into his job, had been led rather than leading. Seven years later he conceded the point. "It never should have happened. Things got out of control. . . . a shop steward, a black guy, at UPS had told the men they could wear the black-power emblem and I felt I couldn't afford not to back him." As a result, the men lost about eight days' pay, with no supplemental benefits sent to them from the International because the strike was illegal.

If the 1970 UPS strike was the most unnecessary, the 1974 walkout was the bitterest. It lasted eighty-seven days and resulted in the killing by a New Jersey Teamster of a Local 804 trustee who had been one of Carey's closest personal friends.

Negotiation with UPS had begun on May 10, 1974, on the contract to replace the one expiring July 1. The major issue involved the use of part-time sorters. UPS was anxious to lay off full-timers, especially in their New York suburban package centers, where all the packages could be sorted in a few hours a day. After nearly four months of negotiation and two months of deadline extensions, Carey took his men out on August 28. That night Carey got word that the company had dispatched supervisors from the Manhattan and Maspeth hubs to drive the trucks over to the hub in Secaucus, New Jersey. The workers at Secaucus were members of Local 177, a local in the Provenzanos' Joint Council 73. New Jersey Teamsters were helping to break a New York Teamsters strike.

In response Carey sent pickets over to Secaucus to encourage their New Jersey brothers to stop processing the New York packages. As Carey explained, "Sammy Pro would have been the man to make the final decision. If you're a local president and other pickets show up at your place the first thing you do is call your Joint Council." Under federal labor law, the New Jersey Teamsters could not, in theory, have done anything to help Carey's people. But unlawful work slowdowns in support of striking by others, thereby eliminating the shop's capacity to handle the extra work sent over from the striking shop, are not unheard of. Also, Carey was especially incensed because the New Jersey Teamsters leaders had announced that they would not handle any Local 804 work, and that they were not now doing so.

As the work at Secaucus continued, Carey's men picketing on the scene became restless. Some started halfhearted efforts to block trucks arriving at the hub. Soon, a human wall of about six men formed in front of the entrance. In the middle was Ed "Doc" Dougherty, a union trustee who had run on the Carey slate in 1968 and had since become one of Carey's closest personal friends. At nine-fifteen, just as darkness had fallen, two high, wide headlights turned quickly into the UPS driveway. The truck sped wildly toward the gate, with the picketers in full view. Dougherty was the only one who didn't have a chance to get out of the way. He was killed instantly as his head was crushed under one of the tires.

That night, a nearly hysterical Ron Carey was cursed by his men for the first time. Many called him a coward because he had then ordered the pickets withdrawn from New Jersey to prevent more violence. Then he drove to Mrs. Dougherty's home to tell her what had happened and stay with her for a while. Still sleepless, he returned to Secaucus to make sure the pickets had left. There, he got into a screaming match with a driver near the entrance, calling him a strikebreaker, then hitting the brakes on the car he had borrowed so the truck would drive into him from the rear. Police cars drove up from all sides. He was pushed around, then handcuffed and arrested for drunk driving. He had had one beer with a sandwich that night and easily passed the breath analyzer test before they arrested him. He spent the rest of the night in jail crying for Doc Dougherty.

The Secaucus police who had arrested Carey had not arrested, or even detained, the driver of the truck that had killed Dougherty. This, despite the fact that Local 804 members claimed they had heard him making threats earlier in the evening to "run down" anyone who tried to get in his way. Three years later the Secaucus police chief hung up on me when I asked why; and a lawsuit was still pending by Dougherty's widow and children against UPS and the driver.

A few days after Dougherty's death, Carey swallowed the rage that not a single Teamsters official from the International union had come to Dougherty's wake and called Fitzsimmons to ask for help to prevent New Jersey from undermining his strike. Fitzsimmons' executive assistant, Walter Shea, replied that he had to be able to prove that the New Jersey locals were doing New York's work. Otherwise there was nothing that could be done. Carey got his proof. He sent packages to points that he knew would normally cause them to go through New York, and received them on the other end with labels indicating they had gone through New Jersey.

One day in the fall he brought this and other evidence to Washington for a meeting with Fitzsimmons. At the meeting, Fitzsimmons had swiveled around in his chair and had gazed out the window almost the entire time, saying nothing as Shea and Carey talked. Then, Provenzano came in and denied everything. "He looked at me as if to say, 'Who the hell are you coming down here and accusing me?' " Carey would later recall. Carey could not help but suspect that the limit on part-timers that he was going for and that the other locals hadn't won, was part of the reason he was getting no help. When I asked him, Provenzano denied it, telling me that he had tried to help Carey.

The strike continued on through the fall. The men lived off the $35 a week in strike benefits they got from the International union, the $95 in unemployment insurance they got from the state, and whatever they could earn at part-time jobs before or after picket-line duty without the union hearing about it. (The constitution prohibited taking a job during a strike.) Meanwhile, Carey challenged the company's claim of an $8,000,000 annual operating loss by hiring a national CPA firm, which did an audit suggesting that the loss might have been artificially created in part by "management fees" and other charges by the parent UPS company to the New York UPS company.

Finally, on November 21, with the heavy-volume Christmas delivery season approaching, the union and UPS agreed to a compromise settlement proposed by the Federal Mediation and Conciliation Service. The company won the right to replace full-timers with part-timers through attrition. But the union won a slowing down of the replacement to a limit of 180 new part-timers a year. The union also won wage increases averaging $58 a week, plus a cost-of-living escalator clause.

After meeting with the UPS supervisor on the day that we spent together, Carey drove back to the office on Jackson Avenue. As he did, he described "how horrible I felt about Doc [Dougherty] and the whole affair. It was the worst few months I ever had." Nevertheless, Carey volunteered a few minutes later, that "UPS is a very, very tough company, but they're also straight and good to deal with in many ways. They don't try to nickel-and-dime you, and they do use good, safe equipment." The conversation shifted to opportunities for corruption. No one had ever offered him a bribe straight out, Carey explained, but in his first year or two there had been blatant overtures. He refused to elaborate.

Later, others in Local 804 would not be as bashful. One trustee recalled that "in 1968 or 1969, before people knew how we operated," one employer negotiator "mentioned that Ron and I should be his guests for a Florida vacation 'if this contract gets settled quickly,' " while a department-store representative had passed word through an intermediary that "there would be cash in a suitcase for us if things worked out." Another business agent remembered that the owner of one small company had offered him and Carey some money to allow his company to go out of business, and reopen under his son's name, without a union contract.

Such opportunities for corruption in contract negotiation or in questions involving contract concessions such as those allowed by Carey at that run-down Eastern Parcel Company were nearly limitless. As Harold Gibbons remarked in an interview early in 1977, "That the labor movement has maintained its integrity to the extent that it has always amazed me. . . . Somebody is always trying to make a deal with you. . . . That more guys haven't succumbed is beyond my comprehension."

Two months after Carey's reticent discussions of corruption, two other stories by Local 804 officials described the lengths to which he was willing to go in order not to succumb to those opportunities. Sam

Begleiter, the Macy's shop steward, said that in 1970 when Carey looked as if he might have been in trouble with the courts over the UPS lapel-flag strike and the resulting fines, Macy's G. G. Michelson had told him during a break in their negotiation how bad she felt for him and asked if there was anything she could do to help. It was an innocent gesture, more a matter of polite commiseration than a specific offer of help. But as Begleiter remembers, "When the meeting began again, Ron immediately told the shop stewards what G.G. had said—'so,' as he explained it to us, 'it would be all out in the open' and we'd know that he told G.G. he couldn't accept any help.''

Another Carey associate told an unhappier story about one of Carey's close relatives who had been a maintenance foreman at a trucking company that had moved into Carey's jurisdiction. Because his relative now supervised Local 804 members, the two men decided that the foreman should quit his job to avoid the conflict of interest.

Carey was surrounded by Teamsters corruption. Interviews with executives of trucking and moving companies in New York revealed that cash Christmas gifts to business agents and officers of other locals were a way of life. Further out in Queens, airport freight Local 295 dominated by mobster Harry Davidoff was notoriously corrupt. His specialty, according to police, was running theft operations at the airport, as well as a loan-shark and numbers operation for his members. A Labor Department memo said that the only thing that kept Davidoff from officially being a captain in the Mafia was his "ethnic limitations." Manhattan Local 27's leadership had no such problems. The "Paper Products and Miscellaneous Drivers, Warehousemen, and Helpers" was run by convicted extortionist Patsy Crapanzano, who, the FBI claimed, was, like Tony Provenzano, a member of the Genovese crime family. He had gone to jail in the late '60s for forcing an employer to put his brother-in-law on the payroll for a no-show job. Local 813, the private sanitation workers, was similarly controlled by organized-crime forces, even though its boss, Bernard Adelstein, also had Davidoff's ethnic limitations. At Local 806 on Long Island, the union president would be indicted in 1977 for taking 80 percent of his local's pension fund income as compensation for himself for managing the fund.

How exceptional was a Teamsters leader like Carey in 1977? Although the question is impossible to answer with certainty, the best guess from a series of interviews with rank-and-file members, union leaders at the Local and Joint Council level, employers, and police officials was that of 53 Teamsters locals operating in the Joint Council 16 New York area, perhaps no more than ten were like Provenzano's New Jersey locals in terms of brazen corruption. Even these, it should be pointed out, had negotiated many good union contracts; it takes only a few sweethearts" to line the union boss's pockets. Another dozen or so were probably a little less extreme in their dishonesty—on the whole, representing their workers well, but usually taking something extra out for themselves in the process. At least another dozen, including John J. DeLury's city sanitationmen were, by all accounts, as clean as Carey's 804. The remaining two dozen or so were probably somewhere in the middle—usually representing their members faithfully but not above taking some liberties with union funds or accepting a Christmas gift or other favors in return for small specific concessions or for generally smooth employer-union relations. It was not a terrific box score—and certainly not equal to what would likely be found at the United Auto Workers locals. But perhaps it is no worse than the record of American businessmen in handling their expense accounts, in filling out their tax returns, or in other activities with comparably open opportunities for corruption.

What had to be more frustrating to people like Carey, though, was that Davidoff-style unionism was tolerated, often encouraged, in the Teamsters by the higher-ups. Outside of Washington, the best example was Carey's own Joint Council and Eastern Conference president, Joseph Trerotola. Trerotola was a former milk-wagon driver. He'd never been indicted for anything, and to many he had a reputation for having worked his way up the union ranks without ever taking so much as a cigar. Yet he had been supported all along the way by the most corrupt elements in the union and had set up his son, Vincent, to sell insurance to the corrupt locals in his Joint Council. At a luncheon interview in April 1977, after telling me about the 91 he had golfed at the La Costa Tournament in 1975 as foursome partner Richard Nixon scored a 95, he conceded that he would "never" go to the police or district attorney if he found out "for sure" that one of his local leaders was stealing from the union or extorting from employees. "You have to keep it in the family" he explained. "That's how you work it out."

By 1977 Trerotola's way of working it out had allowed Davidoff, Crapanzano, and other mobsters to thrive in his Joint Council. Crapanzano was the Joint Council vice-president and Trerotola's most likely successor. He, Adelstein, and another Teamsters racketeer—

Abe Gordon, who for twenty years had made a specialty of sapping Teamsters pension funds—virtually ran the Joint Council. He never made a move against them or any of the others, just as in early 1977 he hadn't moved to investigate or suspend the Local 806 leader on Long Island who had been indicted for embezzling union funds. Trerotola was known by his people, as one Joint Council organizer put it, as "Joe Shrugs . . . He just shrugs and says he can't get involved." "That's because Joe T.'s not a free citizen," one of Trerotola's fellow International vice-presidents would explain. "He's terrified of those people."

Carey is not by any means the only honest Teamsters leader. There are probably hundreds more like him around the country. He isn't a freak. But, as a man who would turn away all bribe offers, would take a salary cut when the union treasury was low, and would go out of his way to avoid even the appearance of a conflict of interest at his own relative's expense, he is not part of the "club" either. It was perhaps for this reason, and also as a result of the way he tried to stay independent of the International, that the word one got on Carey at Teamsters headquarters in Washington or at the Joint Council offices was that he was a "screwball," a "weirdo," a "strange guy," or, as four different people put it, "a naïve kid."

In 1971 Carey had had his first exposure to the Teamsters bigwigs who would come to feel this way about him. He had gone to the International convention at Miami. It was a trip that he and Barbara had looked forward to for a long time, his planned emergence in national Teamsters affairs at age thirty-five.

Barbara and Ron Carey left two days before the convention ended. Close friends explained that Carey had been outraged when the podium cut off his microphone as he rose to speak against a dues increase. Beyond that, he was disgusted, he told several associates, as one remembered it, "with the general attitude of the people. . . . Ron couldn't believe these were elected union leaders." In 1976, when the next convention was held, Carey stayed home.

However strong Carey's feelings were about the International, even in 1977 they were muted. He was not a vocal Teamsters dissident. He had allowed a kind of tacit détente to set in between Local 804 and the International. When Trerotola's son came to him to sell insurance to his local, he politely refused, but didn't blow the whistle on this obvious conflict of interest. He would send delegates to the convention and per capita taxes to Washington and they would send strike benefits if he had a strike. Nothing was ever mentioned in the *International Teamster* magazine about Local 804; and, as one 804 business agent said, "The fliers they send us go right into the garbage can." On April 6, 1977, when Frank Fitzsimmons called on all the local leaders to convene in Washington to hear him denounce the press and vow not to resign, Carey sent two delegates instead.

The most logical alternative to such quiet toleration would seem to have been for Carey to withdraw his Local 804 from the Teamsters altogether, eliminating the per capita taxes and the stigma that hurt organizing efforts. Under the Teamsters International constitution this is virtually impossible. Article XX of the International constitution provides that "No Local Union can dissolve, secede, or disaffiliate without the approval of the General Executive Board [Fitzsimmons and the International secretary-treasurer, the vice-presidents and the trustees] while there are seven dissenting [local union] members." Thus, the International or Joint Council would need to find only seven of Carey's 5,500 members against secession. Members who did not send the International notarized statements that they did want to secede would be considered, under the constitution, as against secession. Finally, under another article of the constitution, if Carey were to try to secede and fail he could be brought up on charges and run out of the union for "fostering secession."

Carey's choices were to get along quietly as best he could or to fight from within. It was not until early in 1977 that friends would say he had begun, slowly, to get into more of a fighting mood. A lot of things had been building up. There was Doc Dougherty's killing. There were the organizing defeats that now came more consistently when the bad Teamsters image was turned against him. There were the news stories that had contributed to that bad image, stories that he seemed to see each day since the Hoffa killing, and that reminded him that others were getting rich from the same job he was doing for a salary that barely kept his family in the middle class. It was all building up. Still, as he drove with me back to the office from the UPS center that afternoon of March 7, 1977, Carey talked guardedly about these things. He was not ready to do or say anything drastic.

He had not, for example, reached the point that Florida Teamster Travis Dumas had reached. On June 11, 1972, Dumas's best friend had announced that he was going to run as an insurgent for president of Teamsters Local 390 in Miami. Three days later he was killed, gangland style. So Dumas ran in his place and won. When he took over he wasn't quiet about his honesty or his opposition to the International and his area conference the way Carey was. Nor was he shy about his opposition to corruption. When a trucking company executive offered him a bribe, he called the police, had himself wired, then accepted it. When he was solicited for a phony insurance plan for his members—one of those plans that the Fitzsimmons sons were involved in—he told the police about it. As a result, he carried a shotgun with him at all times to defend against the "contract" he said publicly, had been put out on his life. When mobster Harry Davidoff tried to muscle in on Dumas's Miami airport territory, Dumas—a strapping 6'3", no-nonsense guy—flew to New York, warned Davidoff to stay out of Florida, and then told the press about it. This was the same Harry Davidoff who ran the Kennedy Airport local in Carey's borough of Queens and who had reportedly forced some companies to move their contracts from Carey's local to his. Unlike Dumas, Carey had suffered him silently. Unlike Carey, Dumas continually and publicly accused his joint council and area leaders of corruption and collusion with employers.

Also unlike Carey, Dumas did not win reelection. In 1975 the joint council, the area conference and the International put up a candidate and pumped money into his campaign. He beat Dumas with an argument that the Local could not afford to be "an island," cast off on its own.

This was a good point, given the way Dumas kept losing grievances for his members when they were appealed to the joint council or the Southern Conference. With all the time he spent fighting bigger battles he hadn't tended to his members in their shops. By the end of 1976, Dumas wasn't even a Teamster, let alone a Local 390 officer; he had been suspended for three years by the International executive board on the dubious charge of having obtained a mortgage for the union building without proper membership authorization. In March 1977, the same month that Carey took me on his rounds to UPS and Macy's, Dumas was in his Miami living room sitting under a plaque on the wall reading "Love One Another"—a silver hand-gun at his side, his right leg propped up and held together by twenty-six stitches he'd gotten after an accident the week before on the part-time, low-paying, nonunion warehouse job that he had been forced to take. There, he showed me a letter he had written, unsuccessfully trying to get attorney F. Lee Bailey to help him in a class-action suit against the Teamsters. The letter concluded with a statement charging that

Fitzsimmons had declared "war against dissident union members in a country started by dissidents."

In March 1977 Ron Carey was still staying out of that war.

Carey ended his day on March 7 by returning from UPS for more phone calls and paper work at the office. The Local's headquarters at 2420 Jackson Avenue had been rented soon after Carey took over in 1968. "The place before was a shithole," Carey explained, as he searched for a coin for the parking meter. "It was across the street over there, two flights up. It really looked like what you'd expect a Teamsters hall to look like in the movies—you know, a few chairs falling apart in a dark, dirty room."

Carey's substitute was a modest ground-floor complex of five linoleum-floored rooms. There was also an anteroom lined with black and gray filing cabinets, where three clerks and a secretary worked, and a small veneer-paneled room called the "Ed Dougherty Memorial Conference Room." Carey's office was the only private one, and the only one with a carpet. It was decorated with union bowling trophies and all kinds of certificates, including several for the local Parkinson's Disease Association, a charity that Carey had become involved in when one of his workers contracted the disease and "We all felt terrible because we couldn't do anything to help him." Carey dialed his own calls, placing one to hire a hall for an upcoming meeting and another to a business agent who had called from a negotiation to get some advice.

On a wall outside Carey's office was a "night duty" chart that listed the names of all ten union officers, trustees and business agents. "Each of us has a period when we're on call at nights," trustee Pat Pagnanella explained. "Even Ronnie. If a member calls anytime after hours the answering service gets the call, then calls the guy on duty. The same goes for weekends. . . . If you're on call you have to stay near the phone." The chart indicated that Carey had had night duty for two weeks in December and two weeks in April. As for what kinds of call come in, Pagnanella, a husky but low-key former truck driver, again pointed out the social-worker, ward-heeler nature of the union's work: "It could be anything, ranging from a shop steward who's just been involved in some kind of dispute on a night shift to a member who's upset because he's just found out his wife's been fooling around."

"You'd be surprised at the calls we get about family problems,"

Carey added, walking over from a desk where he had just set up a mini-assembly line to mail out the letters asking the UPS members to decide on early negotiation. "I got one recently from a guy who was in tears because his kid was 'a little retarded' and he didn't know what to do. They come over to us in the shops with these problems or they call us. Sometimes they talk for fifteen minutes about nothing before they break down and tell us what's wrong. Sometimes we can only offer advice or sympathy, but a lot of the time we have programs we can refer them to."

Behind Carey's desk there was another chart indicating the vacation time each union officer had taken and the time he was entitled to. (Each officer was allowed the same vacation time given UPS members.) Carey's listing indicated that he was theoretically entitled to 26 weeks and 85 hours in unused vacations. From 1972 through 1974 he had taken no vacations. In 1975 and 1976 he had taken one week each, both times at his father's bungalow in northern New Jersey. ("Where else could I afford to go with five kids," he said, smiling.)

At five o'clock Carey was still in the office when his visitor departed. An hour later and at six o'clock on eight of eleven subsequent occasions later that year when I checked, Carey was still there, often by himself, answering "Local 804" when the phone rang.

At least nine occasions a year, not counting negotiating sessions, Carey also worked weekends; conferences or division meetings were held about once every other month on a Saturday or Sunday and general-membership meetings were held on Sundays three times a year.

In April 1977 one such membership meeting was held in the auditorium of the National Maritime Union building in the Chelsea section of Manhattan. Outside, a vendor monopolized the coffee and donut business from the back of a truck while a group of five or six Young Socialists distributed anti-Teamsters, anti-UPS literature urging militant worker action. A hundred-or-so men milled around. Most were young, about half were black, and many had their wives and children with them. When the meeting started, a fast count indicated that about 350 to 400 members (out of 5,500) had assembled. Local 804 meetings were often better attended (especially when controversial issues were on the agenda), but even this was better than most Teamsters locals.

Secretary-Treasurer John Long, a burly man with a deep voice, began from the podium with a report on the union's finances. He droned on for ten minutes or so under a heavy undercurrent of chatter. Smoke began to cloud the half-filled two-tiered auditorium. He summed up his report, "So we done pretty good."

Next Carey walked across the stage and took the microphone. He was wearing the same gray suit he had had on that day in March when we made the rounds at UPS and Macy's. He spoke loudly, with his mouth almost against the mike. His audience seemed as accustomed to his being up there as he did. The "g" at the end of "going," "planning," and "negotiating" seemed to drop off more consistently than usual, as if to remind his audience who he was. His cadence was three beats faster than it was in more private talks, as if given an extra charge by the amplifier, the podium and the sight of an audience.

He began with a report on the coming contract talks to be held with W. & J. Sloane, Lord and Taylor, Macy's and UPS. With Macy's and Sloane he predicted "tough bargaining," but "hopefully no strike." As for Lord and Taylor, "they've offered seventy proposals to our fifty. . . . We're headin' for a strike." With UPS, he also wasn't optimistic. "I don't think you can ever trust them," he said. Since the other UPS Teamsters unions did not have an attrition-only clause for the replacing of full-timers with part-timers, Local 804's clause would be subject to attack—"they're not going to want to embarrass that man in Washington by giving us better than he got; and I don't have to tell you who he is." He promised to keep reporting on the negotiation as it progressed, and he added that "at least the company knows we're determined"—and they must have known it, given the fact that there had been a strike over every UPS contract in the last twenty years, including the one that had lasted three months in 1974. Then he asked for questions from the floor. There was one from a young Oriental who wanted to know what Carey was doing for part-timers. Carey pointed out that he was trying to win some fringe benefits for part-timers in the next contract; in fact, he would end up winning them pension rights, some paid days off, and health-care coverage.

Next, a black shop steward was introduced to talk about the "Doc" Dougherty memorial trust fund. The fund had been started to build a union building in his memory out of member contributions. A pamphlet distributed to the members entitled, "Let's Keep the Promise," and including a poem about Dougherty by trustee Pagnanella's wife, said that there was now about $30,000 in the fund, most of it raised from a car raffle. A big fund-raising effort was being kicked off, the steward said. "Don't let anyone fool you. It would be a grave injustice not to participate. So please send a check for five or ten dollars. I know how things are, but send whatever you can afford." He was followed by a stout Italian-American man, who related the story of Dougherty's death. Then, to put things in the hushed room back on the upbeat, he exclaimed, "Look at this building. [The huge National Maritime Union complex]. It has a swimming pool . . . health facilities, meeting rooms. This is what *we* want!" The cheers were followed by a parade of shop stewards bringing up checks for money they had raised the week before from their members. Each of about a dozen announced his company and check—"Richie Vicaro, W. & J. Sloane, fifty dollars"—telethon style. Next, there was a brief report by the chairman of the summer-camp committee, who told the members there was still time to apply for their kids to go to the summer camp upstate that the local sponsored in conjunction with a group of New York unions. Members' children could spend a few weeks out of the city there at low rates based on the family's ability to pay.

Then Carey inducted two new business agents. They repeated after him the following oath: "I solemnly swear to uphold the International union constitution and, moreso, to uphold the Local 804 constitution."

The last order of business was a speech by trustee Howard Redmond, a tall young man in a loud plaid suit who walked to the microphone with a nervous grin. "I know you guys always laugh about this," he began, "but I want to remind you of our alcoholism program." There were roars of laughter. His face reddened. "Seriously, for many of us it's a problem." More laughter. "But it can be cured if we just face it as a sickness. So far we've done well with the people who've come to us. . . . Please, let us know. Call me or Ron or talk to your steward and we'll refer you to a program we're involved with. Everything will be kept confidential. Remember, it's nothing to be ashamed of." Redmond got a standing, laughing ovation. Carey added a note about there also being a drug-abuse referral program, then closed the meeting.

Later that month, Howard Redmond talked about his alcoholism program, his job at Local 804 and Ron Carey. Redmond had run for trustee on his own in 1974 against the Carey-supported candidate. "Yet Ron welcomed me in and gave me more responsibility than I ever expected," Redmond recalled. "He's been fantastic. He's allowed me to do the job. He lets me make my own decisions and mistakes, and then helps me out of them." For Redmond, becoming a trustee at age thirty-two was a dream. "I all of a sudden really had an important job."

At the same time, Redmond was not proud of the national organization his job was connected with. "If I go socialize at a party or something, I'm reluctant to say I'm a Teamster," he conceded. "We have a lousy reputation. . . . And in trying to organize new people that reputation had already gotten me thrown out of two shops this year." When Redmond took the job in 1975 he worked so hard at it that "I lost my wife. I was working eighteen hours a day, and the old lady wanted me to quit. But I told her it's the first time I've ever had a position." For ten years prior to the union job, Redmond had been a truck loader and then a tractor-trailer driver for UPS. Before that he had been in the Army since high school. "I think I was an alcoholic in the Army," he recalled. He was also certain that his father, a brewery-truck driver, was an alcoholic: "That's what killed him. I didn't realize it till I grew up. But then I thought about it. He always had to have a shot and then a beer, even in the morning." In 1975, as a business agent, for the most part handling the feeder (interstate tractor-trailer) drivers and sorters at UPS, Redmond's interest in alcohol problems was renewed. "It was just something I picked up," he remembered. "I ran into a guy, a good worker, who had to be carried out of the building ten or twenty times. So I tried to get him into a program, which I did. . . . He's back at UPS now."

The big step in starting the program, Redmond explained, was "convincing UPS that they couldn't just fire people—that it's a sickness." By 1976 he had instituted a referral system whereby workers could be placed by the union in alcoholism therapy at a Long Island hospital. If they required in-patient detoxification the company would hold their jobs open for them, and while they were hospitalized, they would receive disability payments. They would pay $160 for the therapy for all twenty-six weeks, no matter how much of that time was spent in the hospital. The union's key role, he explained, was "being a place they can approach for help, plus the fact that we make arrangements with UPS." (Thus far, only the 4,000 UPS employees out of the 5,500 members of Local 804 were included.) These arrangements, in addition to holding a job open for the patients who enter the hospital for detoxification, included arranging nondriver jobs for the participants who were in good enough shape to get the program's therapy without being hospitalized.

Redmond reported that after about a year in operation the program had referred twenty-five patients, "most of whom have been rehabilitated or are well on the way." The small number, he said, "in no way means it's a small problem. There are hundreds of men out there who need the help. I know, because you can see it in the absentee records. The next thing is getting people to admit that they're sick and to see that if they don't do this they'll destroy their lives."

In May 1977 Carey was again at a podium looking out at his members. But this wasn't a routine meeting. He was in a large room at the Waldorf Astoria Hotel this time, to present an agreement he had worked out with UPS for the new contract to take effect July 1. If the members approved, it would be the first time in recent memory that Local 804 had settled with UPS without a strike.

The contract that Carey presented contained the one major concession he had warned them of in March and in his prenegotiation letter. He had agreed to make it retroactive and therefore to let it run out on April 30, 1979—the same expiration date as that of the Eastern Conference contract. Thus, the next time he would have to negotiate as one of the seventy-five locals in the fourteen-state area represented by the Conference. However, he had inserted in the new contract a clause providing that Local 804's protection against part-timers replacing full-timers, which he had again won, would be continued as a Local 804 supplement to any new contract worked out in 1979 in which 804 was part of an area-wide agreement. He also planned, he told the members, to insert other supplements to any area-wide UPS contract that would be worked out in 1979.

In return for allowing Local 804, with these supplementary protections, to fall into place with the area-wide contract schedule the next time around, Carey had won a number of major concessions from UPS. He was successful because his past record left no doubt that he would strike and because UPS was anxious to have Local 804's contract cover the same time period as the others so that negotiation could be more unified, even if there were going to have to be some Local 804 supplements. Counting a pay increase of 20 cents an hour retroactive to December 1976 that UPS used to sweeten the pot,

Carey won wage increases of $1.79 an hour—or $71.60 a week—across the board. This again put him just ahead of the other UPS locals. With all the raises, including one geared to cost-of-living increases, a Local 804 sorter working a 40-hour week on night differential plus one hour a day overtime (which was normal) would make $464.07 a week by June 1978; and a daytime delivery driver would make $445.55. Carey also won $2.68 an hour in increases for part-time workers.

Whereas the old contract provided pensions of $475 a month for those who had twenty-five years' service and had reached age fifty-five, then dropping down to $235 when Social Security payments began at age sixty-five, the new contract provided $500 a month for life, with no drop-off at sixty-five. Major medical insurance coverage, disability benefits and allowances for surgical and dental work were raised. Three days off with pay were added to the five weeks' paid vacation (depending on years of service) already provided. Regular part-timers won pensions, and were given the same health coverage as the full-timers. Finally, Local 804 became the first Teamsters local in the New York area to get a prepaid legal services program. UPS full-time employees were given free use of a lawyer to perform certain kinds of services. (A month later, when Carey tried to find out which legal services were most important to his members, he would get a shocking lesson in Local 804 sociology: the members overwhelmingly listed divorce actions as their highest priority.)

The May meeting was the most relaxed UPS contract meeting Carey had ever run. His audience was mostly young sorters and deliverers who were used to striking. As if by habit, there were still a number of calls to battle from the audience, but they turned to cheers as Carey laid out the package.

By June the members had approved the contract overwhelmingly after Carey had sent them their ballot and the proposed new contract with a letter in which he pointed out that "We know what happened to the seventy-four other [Eastern Conference] teamster locals who decided to go on strike [in late 1976] and remained on strike for approximately fifteen weeks. . . . We have won better results without being on strike for a single day. . . ."

Also in June, Carey settled a brief strike of warehouse people at Lord and Taylor. A month before, he had expected it to be a long one; he had spent a whole weekend negotiating day and night with a company that, as he put it, "was trying to get me to walk out . . .

they were pounding the table, screaming and yelling . . . they were trying to force us out on the street. I knew it, so I just had to sit there. I did everything but eat shit.'' (Lord and Taylor spokesmen later declined to comment on the negotiation.) The issue, again, was the introduction of part-timers. Carey was worried not just about the jobs of full-time people at Lord and Taylor but also about other department-store warehouses if the part-time precedent was established here.

"Lord and Taylor had clearly decided that the issue was important enough to have a long strike over,'' Carey recalled later. "They were prepared to sit us out.'' In June, Carey partially turned things around. When he went out on strike he had well-dressed members picket Lord and Taylor's suburban stores—a move that surprised the company. The strike was settled within a few days, with Carey getting a compromise that none of his members would be laid off to be replaced by part-timers.

By the summer of 1977 Ron Carey's career had clearly reached a new high. He had settled good contracts with UPS, Macy's, Lord and Taylor, and other employers. With UPS he had given up some of his independence, but he was going to be on the new area-wide bargaining committee, and he had obtained Local 804's right to have supplements to the area agreement. His members, with a few exceptions, supported him enthusiastically: only about a hundred votes had been cast against him in the election that previous December. In an interview that summer he looked back happily at what he had done for his members in the nearly ten years since his first election: solid, unquestionably honest and well-managed pension and health and welfare funds that provided excellent benefits; good wages; decent severance pay; safe equipment; the alcoholism referral program; a drug-abuse referral program; a program that arranged for union members to buy cars through the union at one hundred dollars above wholesale cost. Most of all there was the personal service Carey and his people provided: all ten union officers and staff, from president to business agent, had a set of rounds they made each morning, and every night one of them was on duty to take calls. As a Macy's warehouseman put it, "Over-all, the difference between what we have now with Ron Carey and what we had before is the difference between night and day.''

But for Ron Carey, reflecting as he did on where he was that summer, where he had been and where he wanted to go, the past few years had not brought the night-and-day differences in his life that he had hoped for. "In terms of power and money and the other things you'd expect I'd have after ten years," Carey explained, "this job really hasn't brought that. I love the job, but it hasn't brought exactly what you, or even I before I got it, would expect."

"Our life styles haven't changed a bit, since Ron took office," wife Barbara said in the same interview, with an amused half-smile. "He's the big union leader, right? Even the mail man asks him to get his son a job. But he doesn't have any power like that. . . . The only change in the last ten years is that Ron seems to keep looking more and more tense when he comes home at night." Carey's salary from the union was about $5,000 more than he had made as a driver (with about the same pension). Since 1968, increases in it had not kept pace with cost of living.

Nor had the years brought him new opportunities to move ahead in his career. Carey is ambitious. For several years he had been thinking about how to move up in the Teamsters power structure. But he always saw the same obstacles. His détente with the outside Teamsters world had given him peace, but it had also boxed him in. There was no way the crooked local leaders, the half-crooked local leaders, or the local leaders who winked at other people's corruption were going to elect him to run the joint council. Sure, they had asked him to take a second-level spot on the joint council's executive board in 1975 but he would have been, in his words, "just a puppet, not someone with real power—so I turned it down." If anything happened to joint council president Trerotola tomorrow, Carey now speculated, "They'd either let Crapanzano move up or give it to one of the other guys from the old school. I wouldn't have a chance."

Later in the summer of 1977 Carey summed up his situation this way: "Ten years ago, I was going to change the world. Now I'm stuck."

Adding to Carey's frustration was the fact that for all his negotiating success in 1977 he had continued to suffer setbacks from forces he couldn't control. Some were to be expected, like the failure to organize workers in a New York restaurant chain because to be recognized the union had to sign up 51 percent of all the workers in the chain rather than just 51 percent of the workers in the two or three largest restaurants who had come to Local 804 for help. But most of the setbacks were directly attributable to the forces higher up in the union. "It's getting ridiculous," trustee Howard Redmond complained. "Every time we go into a shop there's another story in the paper about some Teamster being brought up on charges. It kills us." One organizing effort in the spring of 1977 that had looked as if it would succeed had been ordered stopped by the International because Washington decided that this time they didn't want to raid the mechanics union. Carey had to obey the order; otherwise they could put him in trusteeship.

Worse than that, Carey explained, was the "low balling" that, in 1977, continued to eat away at his membership rolls. "Low balling" is a procedure whereby one trucking company takes away business from another company where Carey's members work by underbidding that company for the work. This forces layoffs of Carey's people. The underbidding is possible either because the underbidding company has a sweetheart deal with another Teamsters local (allowing it to pay substandard wages), or because the company has arranged an even better deal with the other local to employ one or two union members (so it can call itself a union shop) and then, with the tacit agreement of the union, staff the rest of its jobs with lower-paid nonunion help.

According to Carey, by 1977 he had lost hundreds of jobs that way, including many to "reputable department stores who use the lowballers for deliveries. . . . It's ridiculous. The truckers have one or two union members on the payroll and the rest work for $150 a week." One major culprit union, Carey said, was Teamsters Local 814, a union that law-enforcement officials had long suspected of corruption. (Throughout 1977, the president of Local 814 did not return twelve phone calls asking about their contracts, and the joint council refused a request to provide copies of his contracts, which the International constitution requires be filed with the council.) "I've screamed at the joint council," Carey recalled, "that we need a rule that at no time can one Teamsters local underbid another Teamsters local. The way it is now, I told them, some guy in another local gets taken care of and he underbids me and my guys. But they refused to do anything."

Some people closest to Carey observe that there is something more subtle about the way the Teamsters hierarchy treat him that infuriates him at least as much as anything specific. As one friend in the union put it, "They still treat Ron like a kid, and that really gets to him." A decade after Carey's first election, joint council and International

Teamsters officials routinely referred to the forty-two-year-old veteran of dozens of strikes as "a good kid," "a nice kid," "a tough kid," or "a naïve kid." But always "a kid."

"Yes, that bothers me," Carey said uncomfortably. "Yes, I can't even begin to tell you how much that bothers me. It's all part of the attitude up there."

"Do you think they think of you as a sucker?"

"Yes, probably," he replied, quickly, as if he had gone over the same question with himself or with Barbara many times. "And that's what I hate. Because I've never been a sucker. I can't tell you how much that gets to me."

By the day in October 1977 that *they* teed off at La Costa for the Eighth Annual Fitzsimmons Invitational, it was clear from talks with Carey and those close to him that it was all starting to "get to" him more and more: the failing organizing drives, the low-balling, and the "attitude" from the big shots who looked at him as if he were a kid or, worse, a sucker. Just as bad were the news stories that sometimes, with Barbara's lighthearted prodding, made him feel like a sucker—articles about crooks in his job getting rich and enjoying places like La Costa, while he swam minilaps in his plastic pool and his wife wore costume jewelry. Ron Carey is fiercely honest, but the scrappy "kid" from Long Island City is also fiercely competitive—and it killed him to see others in his profession making out so well while he struggled.

The worst frustration of all, that summer, was that Carey could see nothing better ahead. What else could he do but hold onto détente? He couldn't take over the joint council. Screaming publicly about the "attitude" and the corruption and joining an insurgent movement, which was his only other alternative, were also out. That might let off some steam, but at this point he still wasn't convinced, he said, that it would change anything. It might make things worse by triggering new harassment, perhaps even violence.

The tenth anniversary of Ron Carey's first election should have been a happy one. He had mastered the job, and he should have been looking forward to bigger and better things.

He wasn't.

CHAPTER VI

Dorfman

Allen Dorfman was among the best golfers at the Seventh Annual Frank Fitzsimmons Invitational. In this as in other things he is more polished than his Teamsters friends. He dresses more stylishly, speaks better and prefers Rolls-Royces and Mercedes to Cadillacs and Lincolns. He's better built, better kept, better groomed and much younger-looking than fifty-four. Much of his look came from the steam baths, herbal wraps, and massages he took at La Costa's plush spa, and the tennis, handball, paddle ball and golf that he played at a country club he had cofounded just outside Chicago. He also carried himself with more confidence than the others—as a respected business executive among admiring friends, a rung or two down the ladder. There was no hint that this was a man who had been subjected to the indignities of prison life three years earlier.

In the La Costa group Dorfman was a star. He was cosponsor of the Tournament, which he had won the first year it was held, and he and his father had founded the Little City Home for blind retarded children for whom the Tournament was being played. The following May he would be the Little City's "man of the year" at a $200-a-plate Chicago fund-raising testimonial. By Dorfman's own morning-after account, it would be attended by "six hundred of Chicago's top business and civic leaders—executives, judges, the mayor, you name 'em, they were there."

Dorfman was richer than the other players. In 1948, all that his good looks, athletic ability, college degree, war medals, and driving ambition had gotten him was a $4,000-a-year job teaching Phys Ed at the University of Illinois after graduation. Five years later the gym teacher was a millionaire one-man insurance conglomerate. And by the time of the 1976 Fitzsimmons Invitational, according to one Internal Revenue Service source, he was worth ten to twelve million dollars.

How Dorfman moved so far so fast is the story of the looting of one of the nation's largest private pension funds. It was accomplished by schemes that funneled hundreds of millions of dollars in investment capital to organized crime and set off a time bomb. By 1976 the bomb had perhaps ten more years to tick before it might explode the dreams of hundreds of thousands of Teamsters who had reason to think they had solid pensions.

Since the middle 1960s most of the accusations about the Teamsters union actually involved Dorfman and the Central States Pension Fund, not the union itself. The fund—the Central States, Southeast and Southwest Areas Pension Fund—is the fund in which Teamsters members' pensions are kept. Only a minority of Teamsters members, about 350,000 out of 2,300,000, have their pensions in this fund. The pensions of the other Teamsters, mostly in the East or the West, are held in 230 separate, unrelated funds. Eight of them had assets of greater than $100 million by 1977, but all but one, the Western States fund, are far smaller than the Central States fund, and most have never been touched by scandal.

The events that put Allen Dorfman in de facto charge of the Teamsters Central States Pension Fund, as it became the mob's bank, began by accident. In 1949 Jimmy Hoffa, the main force behind the Michigan Teamsters and the Central States Drivers Council (composed of Teamsters locals throughout the Midwest and parts of the South), was looking for ways to expand his power. Also in 1949, the unions he controlled started taking in money that new contracts dictated had to be set aside by employers for members' health and welfare insurance.

During this time, Paul "Red" Dorfman, Allen's father, was a kingpin in the Chicago mob. According to old FBI memos, he was one of the five or six people in Chicago closest to Tony Accardo, the man who had seized power over organized crime there after the death of Al Capone. The elder Dorfman was head of the Chicago Waste Handler's Union. He had taken over that union in 1940 after its founder and secretary-treasurer was murdered. The case was never solved.

Red Dorfman's sudden rise in the Waste Handlers Union had prompted the chief investigator for the Illinois State's Attorney to protest to the AFL-CIO, calling Dorfman a "discredit to legitimate labor," and noting that the elder Dorfman had "never been a member of the union or worked at the craft" and had made his first appearance at a union meeting and had paid his first dues the night he was made the secretary-treasurer. "Red was a real tough guy, a hood's hood," one top former Teamster who met him back in the '40s recalled. "He was a small, thin, red-haired guy and talked kind of low. But he was the kind of guy who'd walk in and throw two bullets on a guy's desk and tell him, 'The next one goes in your fuckin' head.' " Dorfman had been a featherweight prize fighter in the ten-and-twenty-dollar-a-night class in the '20s. In 1928 he had been indicted for rigging primary ballots and using "terrorist tactics" in a local Illinois election. (Forty-six years later there was no record of the disposition of the case.)

In 1942 he was indicted again. He had calmly ended a phone conversation with the chairman of a waste handlers employers' association when the two couldn't agree on the wages to be paid the men in Dorfman's union, then walked a few blocks to the man's office and beat him. It wasn't a simple fist fight. The police report stated that the former prize fighter used brass knuckles concealed in a glove. The employers' association chairman, according to contemporary news stories, appeared at the police station with black eyes and a battered face. But the case was later dropped, because the victim refused to testify.

In 1949, according to several Teamsters sources, Red Dorfman met Jimmy Hoffa, and they worked out a deal. "I was at one of their first meetings," one former top Teamster recalled. "Jimmy and Red got to talking, and they realized they were made for each other. Plus, they liked each other." The deal called for Hoffa to get an in from Dorfman with the Chicago mob. With this help Hoffa could solidify and expand his power base by using underworld "muscle" to back up new organizing drives and to gain the loyalty of other Teamsters locals. Ultimately Dorfman's introduction was to give him the credentials to work with organized-crime groups throughout the country. In return, Hoffa offered Dorfman's twenty-three-year-old son, Allen, actually his wife's son from a previous marriage, a new career by giving him the multimillion-dollar Central States health and welfare business. There weren't yet any pensions to invest.

Records on file in the state of Illinois show that in 1949 Allen Dorfman formed a company called Union Insurance Agency with his mother, Rose. Early in 1950 Union submitted its bid for the Central States health and welfare insurance as an agency representing a small Mount Vernon, New York, insurance company that proposed to carry the policy. (Union was bidding—that is, providing a cost estimate—on life-insurance policies for the Teamsters within the Central States health and welfare fund.) At the time, Dorfman's agency had no office and he hadn't yet gotten an insurance license. Another highly reputable life-insurance company, with assets five hundred times greater than the Mount Vernon company also submitted a bid through an agent, asking for premiums lower than those set by Dorfman's company. Yet the contract was given to Dorfman.

Under federal law a board of trustees made up of an equal number of representatives of the union and the employers made the decisions on such contracts. In practice, the employer (trucking company) trustees agreed to Hoffa's demands, a capitulation of their fiduciary duty that would be duplicated with more damaging results several years later when similar trustee boards were convened to decide Central States Pension Fund loans. The dynamics here were simple and reveal a naïveté in the federal Taft-Hartley law—why should a trucking company executive risk Hoffa's wrath (and "labor problems" at his company) to oppose Hoffa's decisions on where Hoffa's union's insurance money should go. As one employer summarized it, "If Hoffa's choice was bad and things went wrong, that was the members' problem, not mine. It wasn't my money. Why should I go against him on this?"

So, beginning in 1950, Allen Dorfman and his mother, Rose, got the life-insurance business from the Central States health and welfare funds, by then officially known as the Central States, Southeast, Southwest Health and Welfare Fund. The Dorfmans' contracts soon expanded to sickness and accident insurance, and in 1951 Allen Dorfman reported income to the government of over $75,000. In 1954 he declared $166,000, and his mother declared $156,000.

Meanwhile, Red Dorfman continued to hold up his end of the deal. In 1951 he sent his close friend John Dioguardi, a convicted labor racketeer, better known as Johnny Dio, to work for Hoffa setting up "paper locals" in New York that would help Hoffa take over the New York City Joint Council. (Dio later became famous for being the mobster who allegedly ordered the acid-throwing attack that blinded labor columnist Victor Riesel.)

New York State records show that by 1953 the State Insurance Department was investigating Allen Dorfman and the money his Union Insurance Agency was drawing from the Mount Vernon company for delivering the Teamsters business. A department report criticized the Mount Vernon company for paying the Dorfman agency $26,000 for "expenses," above and beyond handsome commissions, without obtaining adequate expense vouchers. When Dorfman refused the insurance department investigators' request for access to his accounting records to verify these "expenses," the department canceled his New York agents' license. His company nevertheless continued to draw its commissions from the Mount Vernon company, a practice that prompted the Insurance Department to censure the company but did not end the company's arrangement with Dorfman.

In 1959 Robert Kennedy and the McClellan Committee focused on Red and Allen Dorfman. Nearly a year before, Kennedy had sent two committee staffers to Chicago to dig out what they could on the Dorfmans' affairs. Now, in 1959, one of the investigators, Martin Uhlmann, a graying veteran General Services Administration accountant, took the witness stand. He presented evidence of damage done to union members by awarding the insurance business to the Dorfmans. Uhlmann established that of the $3,000,000 in commissions and fees that Allen and Rose Dorfman's company had received from the Teamsters from 1950 to 1958, $1,650,000 had been excessive by the standards set by the National Association of Insurance Commissioners and the New York State Insurance Department. There was also testimony as to how these excessive fees and commissions had affected the union members; in 1954 and again in 1956, benefits paid to the members participating in the plans had been cut while the premiums were increased.

Uhlmann produced checks and records showing that Dorfman had personally received $182,000 from the Mount Vernon company between 1953 and 1957 in payments for travel and entertainment "expenses," not counting another $158,000 paid to his agency for such "expenses." The fees were over and above the millions of dollars in commissions the Mount Vernon company paid the Dorfmans. Of the $182,000 in supposed reimbursements, the records showed that Dorfman had submitted vouchers covering only $78,000. Most of the vouchers for the $78,000 were, the investigators testified, "totally unsupported" by receipts and other documents. And in at least one case the Committee heard testimony that some vouchers that had seemed solid were false: a Chicago furniture dealer told the Senators that in 1956 and 1957 he had given Allen Dorfman fake invoices so that he could charge $7,300 worth of furniture for his home and his mother's as business expenses for office furniture.

The Committee was also told that Dorfman's agency payrolls were filled with relatives—eight aunts, uncles and cousins as well as his wife (listed under her maiden name). None of them had any experience in the insurance business and one worked full time managing the camps and other properties that Dorfman owned in Wisconsin.

What seemed to fascinate Kennedy and the Committee members most, however, were investigators' accounts of the money Dorfman had withdrawn, sometimes in cash, from his companies. (By 1957 he had spun off Union Insurance into twenty-three different corporate entities.) Between 1949 and 1957 he had withdrawn a total of $332,427. The spring seemed to be the most active period; on April 22, 1957, he had withdrawn $44,000 from his companies' bank accounts. When the Committee was unable to trace what he had done with all of it, it prompted speculation that he had been sharing the moneys with Hoffa and others in cash payoffs. Five years before, in 1954, a House committee chaired by Representative Clare Hoffman, had suspected that Dorfman had diverted $100,000 from his companies to Jimmy Hoffa. Red and Allen Dorfman had taken the Fifth Amendment when asked, and Hoffa had angrily denied it. Now, as the McClellan Committee raised the same suspicion, Hoffa again denied taking payoffs from anyone, and the Dorfmans took the Fifth Amendment on every question.

Allen Dorfman continued to expand his insurance operations following the 1959 hearings, relying almost completely on the Teamsters health-and-welfare-fund businesses diverted to him by Hoffa. By 1963, according to an Internal Revenue Service source, his companies were earning nearly $5,000,000 a year in premiums and fees. Meantime, Dorfman grew personally close to Hoffa. In 1963 Dorfman was indicted as one of the confidantes who allegedly had helped Hoffa fix the Chattanooga, Tennessee, jury.

Hoffa was convicted, but Dorfman was acquitted. By 1964, the two owned several businesses together.

The bond building between Dorfman and Hoffa was a marriage, after decades of a deal-by-deal courtship, between the Teamsters union and organized crime. The real payoff for both sides came a few years later through another, fatter money source: pension funds.

Hoffa and the Teamsters had been surprisingly late in recognizing pensions as a prize to be won in collective bargaining. Several other unions had begun winning pensions for their members at the close of World War II, with the biggest breakthrough in 1946, when John L. Lewis won pensions for his mineworkers in a bitter battle that precipitated government seizure of the mines. Next came the steelworkers and other major unions. Hoffa, the heir apparent in 1955 to Dave Beck's presidency, negotiated his first pension in January 1955. Under the plan, which covered some 100,000 truckers and warehousemen in the Midwest and South, each employer paid two dollars per worker into a pension fund each week. This meant that about $800,000 a month flowed into the fund so that in the first year almost ten million dollars had accumulated. By 1965 the monthly cash flow had increased to six million, the result of a doubling of the number of workers covered and a series of boosts in the employer contribution that brought it up to seven dollars per worker each week.

Several decisions that were made in these first ten years of what has become known as the Central States Pension Fund affected the fortunes both of the workers who depended on it and the mobsters who fed off it. First was the decision, in 1955, as to how the Fund's board of trustees would be constituted. The Taft-Hartley law required only that there not be *more* union leaders than industry representatives on the board. But Hoffa insisted that the board have *as many* union people as employers. He demanded not only parity but that there be at least six members on the board from each side of the bargaining table. The latter demand, for a large board, was based on his confidence that the more employer members there were, the more likely it was that he could split them and win a majority on any vote. The industry leaders were worried about giving in to Hoffa. They wanted a small board with a clear majority so that they could avoid such scandals as the award in 1949 of health and welfare insurance contracts to Dorfman's company. According to a biography of Hoffa by Ralph and Estelle James,* the issue of the composition of the

* *Hoffa and the Teamsters*, Princeton, N.J.: Van Nostrand, 1965.

board came to a head at a March 1955 union-industry meeting. According to a transcript quoted by the Jameses, Hoffa left the meeting saying, "Representing the union, we will file a grievance against every carrier . . . and we will take you out on strike, God damn it, until you do agree to draw up the proper kind of trust that we can live under. I can tell you that much, and I will, God damn it. Take that home and see how you like it." As the Jameses noted, "Hoffa's thrust carried its point. The employers knew full well the tremendous latent force inherent in the open-end grievance procedure; the image of selective shutdowns, dictated by Hoffa over hastily manufactured grievances, came immediately to mind." The employers capitulated, and Hoffa had a twelve-man board with equal union-employer representation.

The employers soon gave in on another key point. They agreed that a simple majority could decide all questions. Most other pension fund boards required that decisions be made by a majority of both the union representatives and the employer representatives.

Several months later, there was a decision about how the investment of the fund's money would be handled. There were two options. The first was to make it an "insured plan," whereby all the money was turned over to an insurance company to invest in return for payment of stipulated, guaranteed pension benefits. The second was to make it a "trusteed plan," under which the trustees would make the investment decisions themselves either directly or indirectly through a bank. The insured plan would later be chosen by the Western Conference of Teamsters, whose fund would ultimately become the largest private union pension fund in the country and remain clear of scandal. It would also be the choice of several other Teamsters groups and funds in other unions. Hoffa wanted nothing to do with the insurance companies. He claimed that the union shouldn't trust any company with that power and that the trustees could make better decisions. He won the argument.

Still, Hoffa did not immediately plunge the Central States Pension Fund into the loans that would win such notoriety in the next two decades. Over the first four years of the pension fund, through 1959, Hoffa let banks invest most of the money for him. But even in those early years Hoffa began to realize that his mushrooming millions offered potential leverage far beyond the general good will (and in some cases, influence on bank decisions to lend his friends money) that would come by giving the money to strategically favored banks for them to use for loans and other investments that they decided on.

Instead, he wondered why the Fund should not be its own bank, lending directly to persons and businesses willing to do something in return for Hoffa or the Teamsters. By all accounts Hoffa felt that becoming its own bank offered the union another advantage. He sincerely believed that real-estate investments were the gold mines of the future and that the Fund couldn't go wrong by making its own real-estate loans. As one government investigator later remembered, "Jimmy once told me that real estate, any real estate, was a good long-term investment. And, he especially believed that hotels, resorts, and other leisure-type properties were the best things to buy into, because Americans were going to have lots of spare time in the future."

Central States Pension Fund records show that the first Fund loan, in 1956, was a $1,000,000 ten-year mortgage at 6 percent a year to Cleveland Raceways. As with many of the early loans, Dorfman was not involved directly. The loan had been encouraged by Ohio Teamsters boss and Hoffa ally Bill Presser, for a friend of his. In 1958, when Robert Kennedy raised questions about the prudence of the racetrack loans, Hoffa apparently got nervous; the loan was immediately repaid to the fund. It may have been the last case of Hoffa or Dorfman backing away from a bad loan.

In 1957 Hoffa authorized five loans totaling $3,705,000, including one to build the Castaways Motel in Miami. All five loans were at 6 percent interest. Another—$1,000,000 to a department store at a time when the store was being picketed in a bitter strike by another union—was typical of the connections and kickbacks involved in many of the loans. The owner of the store was Benjamin Dranow, a long-time Hoffa ally, who, the McClellan Committee later found, had given two $2,000 fur coats to the wives of two of Hoffa's closest friends.

By 1961 Dranow's department store was bankrupt; the pension fund was out $766,000 of its $1,000,000; and Dranow had been indicted and convicted on eighteen counts of bankruptcy fraud for personally siphoning off more than $100,000 of the store's cash before allowing it to go under. The next year he was convicted of tax evasion. Two years after that, Dranow and Hoffa were indicted and convicted for defrauding the pension fund through a conspiracy involving twenty-five million dollars in fourteen pension fund loans that were made so that Dranow and others could bail Hoffa out of a bad Florida land investment.

In 1958 the Fund's loan activity continued to expand rapidly; there were ten loans totaling $16,022,000, none at more than 6 percent. The loans included $800,000, at 5 percent, to a trucking company owned by a member of the Fund's board of trustees; $735,000 for a building in Buffalo, New York, owned by a business partner of Ben Dranow; and $250,000 for a golf course to be built by Hank Greenspun, the editor of the Las Vegas *Sun* and a Nevada political power. Another loan in the 1958 package involved $1,800,000 to build the Atlanta Cabana Motel, the first in a chain of motels owned by a company run by Jay Sarno. Sarno later got fund loans for the Circus Circus and Caesar's Palace hotels and casinos in Las Vegas. In 1959, he got another Fund loan, $3,600,000 at 6½ percent for a Dallas Cabana Motel. As the Jameses reported in their book, the transcript of the board meeting in which that mortgage commitment was made indicates that Sarno had offered to pay a higher rate than was ultimately stipulated by Hoffa and the board.

According to a source close to Dorfman at the Fund, Sarno's was probably the first loan that Dorfman had a direct hand in arranging. Later Sarno was identified by federal and local police as a "front man" for Dorfman's Chicago mob associates in the ownership of the Circus Circus in Las Vegas.

The floodgates opened at the Fund during 1959, 1960 and 1961. Dorfman arranged several mob-connected loans, and Hoffa continued a general policy of using his bank to reward friends and influence others. The Fund's records show that sixty loans totaling $91,600,000 were made. Most went to mortgages on shopping centers, hotels and motels, and land development. Generally such properties are by far the riskiest loans imaginable. The slightest change in a highway location or a local tax law, for example, can ruin most such investments.

Most of the loans, according to sources at the fund and to the results of subsequent investigations, involved a cash payoff, a mob connection, a friendship, or all three. The Eastgate Coliseum in Cleveland got $850,000. The president of Eastgate was Jackie Presser, and the loan, according to Presser himself, was arranged by his father, Bill, and by Allen Dorfman. Soon the loans there would reach $1.6 million, and by 1964 Eastgate, unable to meet its payment, would go out of business. (The Coliseum and the loans were then taken over by Sam Klein of the Bally Corporation, a close friend of the Pressers, at a bargain price of $1,000,000.) Other loans totaling

$6,000,000 in 1959 and 1960 went to the Hyatt Hotel Corporation. The Fund's counsel at the time was a former law partner of the Hyatt chief executive. Ultimately, another $44,000,000, some in the form of debenture purchases, was advanced to Hyatt.

Indirectly another hotel chain was built partly with Fund loans during this time. In 1961 the Jupiter Company, which was constructing Ramada Inns, received the first $4,000,000 on what was to amount to $25,000,000 in loans. According to the Jameses' book, the construction company had been borrowing money for its projects at 10 percent; it paid the pension fund 6¼ percent.

Other loans during this time included those made to two New York restaurants, Chandler's and Toots Shor's, to the Crystal Towers Apartments in Miami, to the Washington Motor Hotel in Maryland, and to the De Soto Hotel in Hot Springs, Arkansas. A hotel that was almost built with Teamsters money was Washington's plush Madison. A loan for $7,000,000 was arranged by I. Irving Davidson, a Washington wheeler-dealer and close Hoffa friend, who told friends about the finder's fee that he was to receive from the group that was building the hotel. However, according to Davidson, "At the last minute the hotel people decided to go elsewhere for their money."

Also during the years 1959–1961 the Fund took the plunge into Las Vegas. The major loan recipient was a group headed by Morris "Moe" Dalitz, a well-known former bootlegger who had led a mostly Jewish organized-crime group in Cleveland before moving to Las Vegas in the middle '50s. Eventually, Dalitz and three partners swung another large series of Fund loans, through Dorfman, to build La Costa. But in 1959 their first loan was to build the Sunrise Hospital in Las Vegas. Then beginning in 1960 Dalitz borrowed money to finance the Stardust Hotel and Country Club, the Fremont Hotel, and the Desert Inn, all in Las Vegas. These investments were followed later by loans to finance the Dunes Hotel and Country Club (controlled by Hoffa's lawyer, Morris Shenker), the Landmark Hotel (with loans arranged by Teamsters vice-president Roy Williams), the Four Queens, the Aladdin, the Circus Circus, and Caesar's Palace, all in Las Vegas.

Pension fund records show that from 1965 to 1972, $20,400,000 was lent to Caesar's Palace. Later, FBI memos asserted, Jay Sarno, the ostensible boss at Caesar's Palace was a front; in 1965, it was alleged, a mob meeting was held in Palm Springs, California, to discuss the division of hidden ownership of Caesar's Palace between New England and Midwestern organized-crime forces. Suspicions about Caesar's Palace were rekindled in 1975 when, according to Nevada Gaming Control Board records, the Caesar's Palace parent company (called Caesar's World) entered into a deal with someone named Alvin Malnik to buy two resort hotels in Pennsylvania that Malnik had purchased with the proceeds of his own pension fund loans. The deal raised a suspicion about Caesar's World that still lingered in 1978, when the company moved to set up gambling operations in newly liberated Atlantic City. It appeared that Malnik was well known by law-enforcement officials as an associate of long-time mob financial wiz Meyer Lansky. The purchase-lease deal that Caesar's World had given him was highly advantageous to him and terrible for the stockholders of Caesar's World, a publicly held corporation.

In 1959 the pension fund made a loan to Mercury Records. Mercury was owned by Irving Green, who turned out to be an old Hoffa friend who gave Joe Louis a job in 1957 right after the prize fighter had appeared as a character witness in Hoffa's Washington, D.C., trial. Green was awarded a $2,170,000 mortgage, an amount that exceeded the Fund's stated limit of two-thirds of a property's value. Others who assisted in Hoffa's legal and public battles were similarly rewarded. A sympathetic news commentator in Miami received a $28,000 loan in 1961. A black public-relations man who helped Hoffa with newspapers in the black community got $96,000 to build an Ohio motel that went bankrupt almost immediately. William Loeb, the publisher of the Manchester, New Hampshire, *Union Leader*, received $2,000,000 in loans to refinance his paper's debts. Prior to the loan, Loeb had routinely criticized Hoffa as he had criticized other union leaders. He met Hoffa during a 1963 Teamsters contract dispute in New Hampshire, and the loan was negotiated soon afterward. Following the loan, during the 1964 presidential primary campaign (in which the *Union Leader* had always played a key role), Loeb published articles attacking his preferred candidate, Barry Goldwater, for having criticized Hoffa. Loeb later spearheaded publicity efforts to get Hoffa freed following his 1967 imprisonment, and he offered a $100,000 reward for information about illegal government wiretapping used against Hoffa by the prosecution.

Loans such as these that gave organized crime a huge slice of Las Vegas from which enormous amounts of cash could be skimmed, and gave Hoffa's friends a break elsewhere, produced a bizarre pension-fund investment portfolio. Most pension funds are decidedly conservative. They invest primarily in government bonds and might put perhaps 2 percent of their assets in real estate. By 1963, Central States had accumulated $213,000,000 and had placed 63 percent in real-estate loans and mortgages and only 3 percent into government bonds, with the remainder in bank accounts and corporate bonds.

As this pattern continued through the early '60s Allen Dorfman continued to concentrate on Central States health-and-welfare-insurance schemes, dabbling only occasionally in pension fund loans.

In 1964, a few months after he was acquitted in the Tennessee jury-tampering trial in which Hoffa was found guilty, Dorfman and his father were indicted for extortion. A San Francisco insurance man named Stuart Hoppes told federal prosecutors in San Francisco that both Dorfmans had threatened him in an attempt to extort $100,000 they said he owed them. Hoppes claimed that Allen Dorfman made several phone calls in which he threatened to kill Hoppes' family and put him in a "concrete overcoat." Allen and Red were acquitted of the charges. Thirteen years later, Hoppes was still claiming that the threats had been made and called Allen Dorfman "the most vicious, crooked scary guy you'll ever meet."

Hoffa and the other members of the board of trustees at the health and welfare fund (which is technically separate from the pension fund) didn't agree. In 1964 they voted to declare Dorfman's company, by then called Conference Insurance Consultants, Inc., "the sole and exclusive agent for the [health and welfare] fund for all its insurance needs" for a period of ten years. This gave Dorfman complete control to place all the Central States insurance.

Dorfman's role in the pension fund, however, was still minor. People who were close to the pension fund and to Hoffa or Dorfman at that time later recalled that Dorfman provided Hoffa with advice on many loans, including the Las Vegas loans in which Sarno reportedly fronted for the mob. But Hoffa made the primary contacts with people like Dalitz and Shenker in Las Vegas, and he alone made the decisions. Organized crime had input through Dorfman or people like Bill Presser in Cleveland, especially if a payoff to Hoffa was in the offing or a debt for a past "organizing" favor could be settled. But Hoffa was the boss.

Dorfman did use the pension fund to his personal advantage, with Hoffa's acquiescence. One of his most profitable pension fund deals began in 1963, when he arranged to use the pension fund to buy an insurance company. Before that, he had owned agencies that placed insurance for commission, not the company that did the insuring. Now he could make money two ways by having his insurance agency place life or health insurance with his insurance company. At the beginning he set up a man named Nemerov to own the company, Reliable Insurance of Ohio. Dorfman gave Nemerov application papers for a $4,000,000 loan from the pension fund to buy the company. Nemerov signed them and Dorfman submitted them for quick approval. Within three years, after Dorfman had funneled millions of dollars in premiums to Reliable and after a series of highly complicated paper shuffles, Allen and Rose Dorfman owned Reliable without having to put up a penny. A year later, after an even more complex series of transactions, which involved Dorfman selling Reliable's guaranteed insurance business to a larger company for just under a million dollars' worth of stock in the larger company, Dorfman had near-control of the larger company. By using the pension fund loans and the health-and-welfare-insurance profits he hadn't had to spend a cent of his own.

In 1966, Dorfman again used his influence at the Fund to turn a no-risk profit. Lou Poller, a frequent Fund borrower, was having trouble getting approval for a $2,000,000 loan for a Miami, Florida, property. Labor Department investigators found ten years later that Dorfman helped him get the loan, receiving 50 percent of the property as a payment for his help. As of the end of 1976, Poller still owed $1,580,162 on the 6½ percent loan.

At about the same time, with his protégé Alvin Baron, Dorfman used the pension fund to turn over $200,000 with no investment. Through a series of paper transactions he and Baron took over the failing Cove Inn in Naples, Florida, by assuming its Fund loan of $1,700,000. Then they sold the place for $1,900,000 by arranging for the buyer to get a $1,900,000 fund loan.

But the real action for Dorfman at the pension fund didn't come until March 1967, when Jimmy Hoffa was, as Harold Gibbons put it, "shipped off to the shit house." By that morning of March 7, 1967, when Hoffa went to prison, the Fund was taking in more than $14,000,000 a month and had assets of $400,000,000. The Fund had nearly doubled in assets since 1963. But it would more than triple again in the ten years following Hoffa's departure, making Dorfman's post-1967 impact on the Fund far more significant than Hoffa's earlier influence.

According to three eyewitnesses and just about anyone who was around at the time and could be asked about it ten years later, when Hoffa left for prison he told Frank Fitzsimmons and his other top aides at the union that, as one witness put it, "Allen speaks for me on all pension fund questions. He's the guy in charge while I'm gone." Fitzsimmons nominally replaced Hoffa as a member of the pension fund's board of trustees. But he obeyed Hoffa and left the loan decisions to Dorfman. He still respected and feared Hoffa, and he felt challenged enough by the union presidency without bothering with the pension fund. There was another reason: he was scared of Allen Dorfman and the forces Dorfman represented. "Fitz ran for his life from Dorfman," Jackie Presser recalled candidly, more than ten years later. "He was scared to death of Allen, and still is." Presser was in a good position to know, since it was his father, Bill, who, as an International vice-president, was the only pension fund board member to assert himself enough to share any of the power levers Dorfman soon seized. Fitzsimmons stayed out of these affairs as much as he could. As another vice-president recalled, "Fitz was scared of his shadow. And Dorfman and his crowd terrified him." The same vice-president recalled that Fitzsimmons, at least at the beginning of his tenure, "would come in to his office and see Allen using his office, sitting at his desk even, and never say a word."

Officially, Dorfman was never anything other than an employee of the pension fund board. On March 23, 1967, less than three weeks after Hoffa's jailing, the Fund's board passed a resolution naming Dorfman a "special consultant." Over the years there would be various versions, offered by Dorfman and the trustees, of what Dorfman's duties were: in one, his mandate was to use his insurance expertise to check the quality of the insurance coverage carried by potential borrowers; in a 1977 interview he told me he "managed assets" and did "general work." Whatever his purported title or duties, Allen Dorfman became the man to see for a pension fund loan.

On the afternoon of July 28, 1967, two hooded gunmen crouched behind the shrubbery at the end of a suburban Chicago driveway, their shotguns poised. Their target was Allen Dorfman, whose house was at the end of the drive. The ambushers saw Dorfman leave the house with Perry Franks, a friend and pension-fund-loan recipient. Both men got into Franks's Cadillac for the drive to the Hillcrest

Country Club golf course. As the car reached the street, the first shotgun blast hit Franks's front right fender. Franks jammed down the gas pedal. Dorfman ducked forward. Two more blasts hit the side of the car and a third hit the back as the caddy swerved off the road. Then the shooting stopped.

"That was Allen's warning," a Teamsters vice-president explained in 1976. "I think it was the New York guys, the mob in New York, who arranged for him to be shot at. Or maybe it was Detroit. Whoever it was, it was their warning to Allen that the Fund wasn't just his and it wasn't even just for the Chicago boys. With Jimmy gone, everyone wanted in on the action."

A loan-by-loan review of Fund records and an examination of analyses of Fund activities done over the years by the FBI, the IRS, and the Department of Labor, confirm that Dorfman got the message. He made more than enough deals for himself providing rich kickbacks on Fund loans, but he also serviced the various organized-crime groups who claimed their share of the pot. The result was that the Fund became a special bank where loans depended almost always on the right kickbacks or the right organized-crime connections.

By the time Dorfman lost direct or indirect control over the loans in 1974, the Central States Pension Fund had about a billion dollars in outstanding loans on real estate. This was only 20 percent less than the nonresidential real-estate loans held by Chase Manhattan Bank, the nation's second-largest bank. And it was about the same as Chase had on its Real Estate Investment Trust. In short, the mob had control of one of the nation's major financial institutions and one of the very largest private sources of real-estate investment capital in the world.

It would take a separate volume to describe all the fraudulent loans or all the loans made to organized-crime fronts during Dorfman's tenure as one of the nation's most powerful bankers. In 1977 the Labor Department reportedly needed an eighty-page memo just to summarize the seventy worst loans. The memo described not only loans that went to suspect borrowers but also loans in which interest was mysteriously undercalculated or never paid at all, thereby costing the Fund and its pensioners millions of dollars.

The loans to the Circus Circus Hotel and Casino in Las Vegas probably best illustrate the Fund-mob alliance that built so much of Las Vegas. Fund records show that in February of 1971 the Fund, on Special Consultant Dorfman's recommendation, purchased the land on which the complex was built for $2,600,000, but then leased it to the Circus Circus Corporation. Also in February, the Fund voted a loan to the same corporation for $15,500,000. In March of 1972 a loan of $2,600,000 more was approved. Four months later the Internal Revenue Service put a $1,191,000 tax lien on the casino/hotel for unpaid taxes. Three days later the taxes were paid.

Jim Drinkhall, the *Overdrive* reporter, found out that Circus Circus raised the money to pay IRS through a bank loan after the pension fund, again on Dorfman's say-so, promised to pay the loan back to the bank immediately and have Circus Circus sign another note to pay off this money. Then, in March of 1974 the Fund lent the Circus Circus another $7,600,000. By 1977 Circus Circus' loans had been restructured, and they owed the Fund more than $26,000,000. The loans had been arranged so that various payments of interest and principal were delayed or deferred under a repayment plan so complex that a pension fund spokesman in late 1977 called it "impossible to figure out"; he termed the entire history of Circus Circus loans "absolutely incredible."

Records at the Nevada Gaming Commission also show that back in 1968 Dorfman had been given an option by the Circus Circus owners to buy 6.8 percent of its stock for $75,000, an amazing bargain in itself, and that the entire $75,000 was to be paid by dividends from the stock. Asked eight years later how he got the deal, Dorfman denied that arranging of the Circus Circus loans had been involved, explaining that "they were my friends, that's all."

The controlling interest in Circus Circus on paper at the time the loans began in 1971 was owned by Jay Sarno. Sarno had begun with a loan for the Atlantic and Dallas Cabana motels and continued with a loan for Caesar's Palace, in which he later sold his interest. At most banks Sarno might not have been considered a model borrower. In the Las Vegas court that had handled Sarno's divorce, records showed that from 1969 to 1971 Sarno had single-handedly lost $2,600,000, gambling in three Las Vegas casinos. The same court records showed that he still owed $2,000,000 of the debt in markers at the Sands, Caesar's Palace and the Riviera.

To many Nevada gaming officials and federal investigators, Sarno and his debts weren't particularly relevant, because in their eyes he wasn't really the owner. The mob from Chicago was, and he was the front. One of the rare visible signs of this hidden control was discovered by Drinkhall when he noticed that when Dorfman came to Circus Circus he often conferred not with Sarno but with the owner of the small Circus Circus hotel gift shop—a man named Anthony Stewart. Going through a maze of county deeds and other records, Drinkhall found that Anthony Stewart was Anthony Spilotro.

In the "morgue" of one of Chicago's major newspapers, the envelope that in 1977 held all the old news clippings on Anthony Spilotro was labeled "Anthony Spilotro—Hoodlum." According to a small-time Chicago gangster who had known Spilotro since childhood, "Tony used to brag in high school that when he grew up he'd be head of the Mafia." By the time he reached his thirties Spilotro hadn't made it that far, but he was definitely high up in Chicago's organized-crime family. He looked the part. Every picture of Spilotro looked like a mug shot; he had dark wavy hair, a swagger, and the face of the neighborhood tough guy. By the time he moved from Chicago to Las Vegas in 1971 he had been arrested twenty-two times, mostly for gambling, robbery and burglary. Included also was an arrest in Antwerp, Belgium, for planning a giant jewelry heist. The police also suspected him of several underworld executions, but he had been convicted only of petty larceny, gambling, disorderly conduct, and filing a fake federal loan application, and he had never been penalized with more than a fine. In most of the major cases against him, the witnesses the prosecution needed for testimony had gotten cold feet. "Tony has the eyes of a killer," a top organized-crime prosecutor explained in 1977. "I mean he really is an old-fashioned cold-blooded murderer. I wouldn't want to testify against him."

Before he moved to Las Vegas to take over the Circus Circus gift shop in 1971, Spilotro was described by the executive director of the Illinois Crime Investigating Commission as "one of the most dangerous gang terrorists in the Chicago area." The Commission described him also as one of the major "juice men" in the country. "Juice" in police slang is loan-sharking, and FBI and local police files in the Chicago area are thick with stories of Spilotro's army of enforcers who put the squeeze on hard-pressed loan-shark victims, who often owed 20 percent interest per week. Spilotro worked for loan shark and gambling and bankruptcy-fraud specialist Felix "Milwaukee Phil" Alderisio, who worked for Joseph Auippa, who worked for Tony Accardo. This put Spilotro in 1971 about as high up on the crime totem pole as any thirty-three-year-old had a right to expect; by most accounts, Auippa was the day-to-day chief of the Chicago mob, while the aging Accardo was boss-emeritus.

Spilotro's 1971 transfer to Las Vegas had not been a demotion. According to one source close to Dorfman and to two federal prosecutors, Accardo and Auippa wanted someone high up and tough on the scene there.

The Nevada and federal investigators believed that Dorfman had served Accardo (his father's original benefactor) and the others well by providing them the loans, through Sarno's investor groups, to build and run Circus Circus. There they could "skim" hundreds of thousands of dollars a month—that is, siphon off a portion of the casino's receipts before taxes are calculated. Tony Spilotro, gift shop proprietor, was to be in charge of their investment. Things were made more urgent by their suspicion that Sarno might be taking out more than his share in order to pay his gambling debts.

Eventually, by 1973 the Nevada Gaming Control Board officials would gather enough evidence on Spilotro's involvement to force Circus Circus, to take back his gift shop lease. After that, he simply met the Circus Circus officials elsewhere and, according to these officials and to federal informants, stepped up his use of phone-booth-to-phone-booth business conferences.

Spilotro's brother, John, reportedly served as a courier for the operation; FBI memos written at the time indicate that they had an informant so close to Tony and John Spilotro that he traveled with John on flights between Las Vegas and Chicago when Spilotro was carrying briefcases full of cash.

The same FBI memos described various meetings between Dorfman and Tony Spilotro and noted that when Spilotro went to Chicago he frequently stayed at Dorfman's house. Also in the FBI files were records of Dorfman's phone calls from his La Costa condominium, records that revealed contacts between Dorfman and Spilotro and Spilotro's brother.

One of Tony Spilotro's stays at Dorfman's suburban Chicago home in Deerfield, Illinois, had been made necessary by his 1972 indictment for the murder in Chicago nine years earlier of a syndicate loan-shark collector who reportedly had been caught holding back on some money that belonged to the organization. At the trial, the state's star witness, one of the other two men who allegedly had participated in the murder, told of how he, Spilotro and the other alleged murderer took turns shooting and stabbing the victim and then finally cut chunks of flesh out of his arm after he had stopped quivering and moaning. The jury found the other accused murderer guilty but acquitted Spilotro.*

* The other defendant's jury conviction was overturned on appeal because of improper admission of evidence during the trial.

That the relationship between well-dressed, country-club-going Allen Dorfman and Spilotro, a true strong-arm gangster, was so close that Spilotro stayed in Dorfman's suburban home with Dorfman's wife and children says something about organized crime's metamorphosis during the '60s and '70s. As one federal prosecutor and veteran Dorfman-watcher in Chicago explained in 1977, "The mob now has to have people like Dorfman. With the stuff they're into now—paper stuff like pension frauds or bankruptcy fraud, as opposed to the old extortion or loan-shark rackets—they can't get by only having gorillas like Spilotro. How could you set up a guy like Spilotro at a pension fund? You need a guy like Dorfman who can talk, and who's sophisticated and seems respectable. It's a marriage of necessity."

Many government investigators who also knew Dorfman well suggested in interviews during 1976 and 1977 that the product of that marriage—sophisticated "paper" crime involving millions of dollars from the Central States Pension Fund—was best illustrated in a case the federal government brought in 1974 against Dorfman, Spilotro and six others for a crime they had allegedly committed from 1971 through 1973. The case also illustrates the problems of prosecuting such alleged crimes: all the defendants were acquitted. It was this alleged deal, involving a pail company in an obscure town in New Mexico, that reportedly was the topic of many of those meetings reporter Drinkhall had observed in 1972 between Dorfman and Spilotro.

The government stumbled onto the case. In 1971 the Internal Revenue Service had begun a tax-fraud investigation of Irwin Weiner, a Chicago bail bondsman who had long been suspected of having ties to organized crime. IRS files, obtained from a source six years later, indicate that in 1971 the Revenue Service recruited a uniquely placed informant named Harold Laurie to work on the Weiner investigation. Laurie, who would operate under the code name "Jackson" in his reports to the IRS, was a three-time convicted embezzler who had agreed to turn informant in return for no future prosecution for another scheme he had been involved in as a front for the Chicago mob. What made Laurie so important to the revenue agents was that he was still involved with Weiner in business deals. Also, the man Laurie really took his orders from was Felix "Milwaukee Phil" Alderisio, the long-time Chicago organized crime loan shark and bankruptcy-fraud expert who reportedly was Tony Spilotro's immediate boss.

In 1971 Alderisio was in prison, but the IRS knew from Laurie and other informants that he was having no trouble getting orders out to

Weiner, Spilotro and others. A memo in the IRS "Jackson" file says that on June 21, 1971, Laurie told the IRS agents that Weiner, Alderisio and, ostensibly, Laurie were planning to have Weiner take a $600,000 loan from the Central States Pension Fund to renovate and reopen a pail factory in Deming, New Mexico. The pension fund had lent $4,500,000 to the same company in the '50s and '60s only to have to foreclose on it in 1969, when the factory went bankrupt. Now, Laurie told the agents, Weiner and Alderisio planned to take as much of the $600,000 as they could for themselves and then let the company, named Gaylur Products, go bankrupt again. As Laurie put it, "Their [Alderisio and Weiner's] only concern is to get all the proceeds of the loan and operate the plant for a while and then stick the union with the loss."

The IRS was still bogged down in its investigation a year and a half later, when the FBI backed into the same caper. In January 1973 an FBI informant reported that Frank Fitzsimmons had met with Accardo, Dorfman, Spilotro and Weiner out in California and that one of the topics that had come up was a pension fund loan involving Weiner.

The major upshot of this series of Fitzsimmons West Coast meetings with suspected organized-crime figures was the ill-fated investigation into Fitzsimmons' possible involvement in the prepaid health-insurance-fraud scheme. But as an afterthought the FBI in California told the FBI in Chicago about the Dorfman-Spilotro-Accardo-Weiner pension fund conversations. The Chicago agents were quickly intrigued by what they found. Before long they bumped into IRS agents working the same beat. But there were none of the sparks that usually fly between two police agencies who find they're on the same trail. In a rare display of cooperation, encouraged by the prominence of the targets and facilitated by the caliber of the agents who happened to be involved, the IRS and FBI agreed to pool their efforts, working under Assistant U.S. Attorney Matthias Lydon.

U.S. Postal Service agents were also involved. The federal government often uses the open-ended crime of "mail fraud"—broadly interpreted as the sending of anything fraudulent or even just untrue through the mails—as a way of prosecuting white-collar crime. The men from the four agencies—IRS, Postal Service, FBI, and the U.S. Attorney's office—made an excellent team. They worked fifteen-hour days together and then retired to a local bar to trade theories of the case. "It's a wonder all our marriages held up," one of the investigators later recalled. "For more than a year during that time [1973 and 1974] the only two days I didn't work were Thanksgiving and Christmas."

Using Laurie's continuing information—a series of highly revealing almost daily memos about this and other Chicago mob operations—and with other leads, the investigators soon pieced together what they believed to be a conspiracy to defraud the pension fund. The scheme involved not only Alderisio and Weiner but allegedly four others.

Their alleged roles, as presented into evidence at the trial, are worth describing in some detail as a way of illustrating how these pension fund schemes worked:

1. *Allen Dorfman.* He was the one who arranged the 1971 loans to the Gaylur Company that ultimately grew from $600,000 to $1,400,000. In fact, he had personally delivered the loan checks to Weiner. Laurie reported, according to the "Jackson" file, that Dorfman's cut of the action included a $7,000 cash payment from a Gaylur company check that Weiner had cashed, plus several thousand dollars in merchandise purchased by Gaylur, but sent to Dorfman's home or to his mother's home in Florida. The merchandise included a television, a steam cleaner, a refrigerator freezer, and stereo tape player. Also, Weiner reportedly took $10,000 in cash out of the company to pay for the paving of Dorfman's driveway in Deerfield, Illinois. And, in what may have been a bankruptcy fraud within a bankruptcy fraud, Dorfman was also linked with a Chicago company found to be controlled by Weiner that received a $42,000 loan from the Deming company to market lunch stands called "Weenie Wagons." The company quickly went bankrupt. Other memos indicated that Dorfman had concocted false letters to be sent to Gaylur showing commitments by others to buy the company's products. The purpose of the letter was to give the pension fund trustees something for the record to justify their confidence in the company's ability to repay the loans. As a sidelight to the case, another Laurie memo about Dorfman alleged that Dorfman had arranged the Circus Circus loan and that he had a hidden interest in the hotel/casino.

2. *Tony Spilotro.* Spilotro was reportedly a key figure in arranging for Dorfman to submit the loan to the Fund. Weiner worked most directly with him. Perhaps as a measure of where Spilotro stood in the hierarchy compared to Dorfman—notwithstanding his lesser life style—he apparently received as his cut at least as much as, if not

more than, Dorfman did. Weiner gave Spilotro $33,000 of the company's money—$16,000 of it in cash in a briefcase that Laurie was dispatched to deliver—to open his gift shop at Circus Circus and get settled in Las Vegas. And he gave a friend of Spilotro's another $2,000 in cash the day the friend was released from prison. Weiner also arranged several thousands of dollars in cash payments to Spilotro's brother.

3. *Ronald De Angeles*. De Angeles was the man Weiner picked to manage the Gaylur factory. He was more than a plant foreman. He had long been known as the mob's electronics wizard. In 1970 the boat De Angeles was operating on Lake Michigan just off the Chicago shore was raided by Chicago police, who found it full of sensitive radio-electronic equipment. When they decided that they couldn't prove what they believed—that De Angeles was intercepting radio messages connected with the police surveillance of organized-crime figures—they gave him a summons for water pollution.

De Angeles had also been suspected of masterminding the killing of a syndicate informer with a radio bomb a few years before.

The "Jackson" file reported that for moving to New Mexico to set up the plant, De Angeles had been given—all by the Gaylur Company—a $33,000 home, a $35,000 private plane, $1,700 in "personal expenses" and a $500-a-week salary. In addition, De Angeles was probably the main conduit for funneling the big money from the pension fund loan to organized-crime bosses back in Chicago. Company records revealed that he had received a $150,000 contract for "services to be performed." De Angeles reportedly also used company money to buy $2,000 worth of wiretapping equipment (which was reportedly used to tap the phones of Weiner's children, whom Weiner suspected of narcotics involvement.) He used another $7,000 to pay a lawyer's fees for himself and mobster Sam Battaglia and to complete payments on a new car for Battaglia's son.

4. *Joseph "The Clown" Lombardo:* Lombardo, an alleged loan-shark racketeer, drew $19,000 from Gaylur. He was involved in a fiber-glass company in Chicago that helped launder money for the mob. A partner in that company, Daniel Seifert, would later agree to become a prosecution witness against Lombardo and the other alleged Gaylur pension fund fraud conspirators.

By January 1974 the operatives of IRS, FBI, Postal Service and Justice Department were sure they had put together a solid case.

They staged a long series of grand jury hearings—including one in which a tongue-tied Fitzsimmons testified that he knew very little about what went on at the pension fund even though he was a trustee. Finally, on February 19, they got the grand jury to indict Alderisio, Weiner, Dorfman, Spilotro, De Angeles, and Lombardo on twelve counts of embezzlement and mail fraud for milking the pension fund of the $1,400,000 in loans that had gone to the now-bankrupt Gaylur Products Company. Also indicted were two Fund trustees who, the government charged, had made trips to the Gaylur plant and had known about the fraudulent nature of the loans.

On the day of the indictment, the prosecution team got a good taste of what they were up against. Normally defendants on the day they are indicted are arrested or at least ordered to appear in court to be booked and post bail. But that was the day on which federal agents watched Dorfman play golf all day at La Costa with Fitzsimmons and mobster Lou Rosanova. While the other defendants flew in from around the country to plead innocent and post bail, Dorfman's lawyer, Jerris Leonard, a former assistant attorney general in the Nixon administration, had made the arrangement for Dorfman to appear two weeks later. The press reported that Leonard asked the U.S. Attorney in Chicago for the delay as "a courtesy" to himself, because he was involved in another case. However, Dorfman told me in a 1977 interview that he had asked Leonard to get the delay explaining, "I wanted to stay out on the coast because I was working on a prison reform program with Jimmy Hoffa."

The prosecution's top witnesses in the case were two insiders-turned-informants, Harold Laurie and Daniel Seifert (who had been involved in the Chicago fiber-glass business with Lombardo.) By the time the trial began nearly a year later only one witness was available.

On September 27, 1974, at about 8 A.M., Daniel Seifert, age twenty-nine, arrived at the small plastic-products company just outside of Chicago that he had taken over a few weeks before. His wife and his two-year-old son were with him. As they entered the office the Seiferts were confronted by two ski-masked gunmen. As his wife and son watched, the men pistol-whipped Seifert. Then one fired a shotgun at his head. Somehow, it only grazed his cheek. Seifert ran out the door and over into a small, nearby factory, shouting for someone to call the police. The gunmen followed him. One pointed a shotgun at Seifert from about ten feet across the factory floor. According to the autopsy, the blast ripped away the back of Seifert's head. Somehow he still kept running and made it out a second door. There a third gunman was waiting. His shotgun blasted through Seifert's chest. The three killers then piled into two cars, one driven by a fourth man.

The FBI speculated that the gunmen had intended only to scare Seifert, not to kill him, and that only an unexpected argument or panic caused by the presence of his wife and child had caused a change in plans. "You don't plan a 'hit' with four guys with shotguns driving two cars during rush hour," one investigator later explained. Whatever their plans, the gunmen executed the "hit" with something less than precision. The Seifert murder was followed by a chase scene that had elements of the "French Connection" and the Keystone Cops. First, the two cars speeding away were quickly spotted by a squad car from the suburban Elmhurst Police Department, which had received a radio report of the shooting. The police chased the two cars to a parking lot at a Pontiac dealership. There, the gunmen abandoned one of the cars, a Ford, and fled in the second, a Dodge. Somehow, the police didn't catch up with them there. A few blocks away the Dodge crashed into another car. Again the Elmhurst Police didn't get there in time, and the Dodge sped away. Then another cop in another car saw the Dodge and joined the chase. But two minutes later, the cops in both police cars somehow lost sight of the fleeing Dodge. The gunmen, apparently now in the clear, quickly dug a new hole for themselves. They crashed into a car that was stopped at a light. This one was owned by an off-duty policeman, who chased the Dodge. This cop also lost sight of the Dodge.

In the Ford that had been abandoned in the parking lot, the police found a police radio, a police siren, a ski mask, and a pair of handcuffs.

The FBI immediately entered the case on the grounds that Seifert had been killed to prevent testimony in a federal trial. They traced the police radio found in the Ford from the manufacturer to a store, which listed a phony security company as the purchaser. The signature on the purchase slip, however, belonged to the girl friend of one of Weiner and Spilotro's closest associates. The FBI agents also discovered that the same phony security company had bought a radio crystal capable of capturing the FBI's special radio frequency. "A wizard like [Ron] De Angeles could have figured out our frequency," one agent later speculated. "This gives you some idea of what these guys can do to us."

The FBI then traced the Ford itself and found that it was registered to the phony security company. Tracing it back from its place of original sale the agents found that the first title of the car had been registered to a man named Kemp, who, it turned out, didn't exist. But they were able to lift a fingerprint off the title, and they found that it belonged to defendant Joey Lombardo. Also, they found that the title and ownership papers had been notarized by a secretary in Irving Weiner's office. More important, a salesman at the Ford dealership picked Lombardo from a mug shot as the "Mr. Kemp" who had bought the car. Then, two days later the salesman insisted that he had made a mistake. "He was terrified," an agent explained. "Right after he spotted Joey [Lombardo] from the mug shots the first time, he read something about the case and that was it." As for the secretary who had notarized the title, she claimed a stranger had come in off the street to get some papers notarized, that she had no idea who it was, and that any connection with her boss's trial was simply a coincidence. Lombardo denied any knowledge of the car.

FBI files show that the Dodge getaway car had an even more interesting history. Two months after the murder, the FBI got a tip that a man named Arnold Smith * had provided his home garage as a place to hide the Dodge. The tip seemed promising. The home was located right where the last cop had lost sight of the car, and Smith was believed by the FBI to be an associate of people involved with the Lombardo and others suspected in the case. When the FBI checked with neighbors they were told that the Smith's driveway had always been filled with toys and used as a play area, but that on the day of the Seifert killing it was clear. Also, neighbors noticed the garage door closed that day for the first time in memory, with the windows blacked out with spray paint. "Our theory is that the car was hidden there and then cut up with torches and carted out," one agent explained.

The agents also said that the same informant also told the FBI that Smith's wife, Charlotte, had died mysteriously soon after the Danny Seifert murder. "The informant told us," the agent recalled two years later, "that early in December Charlotte and Arnie got into a fight, because she was worried about Arnie's bad friends. . . . Anyway, she went to a friend of Arnie's who she thought was straight and told him the story of the car. She used names and everything, and asked

---

* His name has been changed in this account.

him to talk to Arnie for her about straightening out. Well, instead this guy, the friend, spoke to the guys she named and told them she was talking. A few days later she was found asphyxiated in her car in the garage. . . . Her husband said it was suicide, that she had had too much to drink and had fallen asleep in the car with it running as she pulled into the garage. But the neighbor told us she never ever pulled the car into the garage [before]. And the tests done on her showed some alcohol but not that much. . . . It was also very unusual that there was no autopsy. Just a very quick burial. We tried to exhume the body when we heard the story, but Arnie of course, objected, and the State's Attorney's office, which rules on those things, ruled against us. Not enough evidence, they said.''

With these and other leads—including an account by a terrified ex-con who refused to testify but admitted to the police that he had had the bad luck to see the men leave the Ford and pile into the Dodge at the parking lot, and identified one of them as someone he had known in jail—the FBI was soon certain who three of the four murderers had been and almost sure of the fourth. All worked in Alderisio and Spilotro's organization doing mostly burglaries and robberies, and two worked there directly for Lombardo. Still the FBI had no witnesses who could identify the suspects, except for the two who refused to testify. In 1978 the four murderers, probably known to the FBI, were still free.

In 1978, Dorfman, Spilotro, Weiner, Lombardo and the others charged in the Gaylur Products pension fund fraud that Daniel Seifert had been going to testify about were also free. A jury had found them all not guilty in 1975.

Seifert's murder had been the first of many setbacks for the prosecution team. Seifert was so much the key witness in the case against Lombardo that soon after Seifert's death the government dropped the charges against Lombardo altogether. Seifert would also have provided some testimony damaging to Dorfman, Spilotro, and the others. His death had not gone unnoticed by Harold Laurie, the other informant witness. ''After Seifert was killed, old Harold was never the same,'' recalled one of the federal investigators. ''We protected him around the clock and all that shit, but it didn't matter. He had seen what could happen. Sure, he testified, and under the circumstances he was pretty good. But he seemed to hold back a little. Especially with Spilotro. Spilotro would stare at him on the witness stand and Harold would break into a sweat. He knew what Spilotro was capable of. He knew Spilotro was probably the guy who had ordered Danny [Seifert] hit or, at least, had approved it. I remember at one lunch break when Harold was testifying, he was a basket case because of Spilotro. A totally broken man, crying and whimpering.''

Reluctant witnesses were not the government's only problem. The Gaylur trial highlights the problems in prosecuting organized-crime cases, especially one that involves an allegation of a complicated white-collar fraud. First, there was the question of what the jury could be told about the defendants' past activities. Federal Court Judge William Bauer refused to allow the prosecution to discuss the defendants' criminal backgrounds. It was a routine decision, obviously justified. A jury should decide the specific facts alleged in an indictment without being prejudiced by a defendant's past misdeeds or reputation. This allowed the defense lawyers to present Spilotro, Weiner and De Angeles as independent businessmen who had simply tried, and failed, to make good on an investment in a small pail company in New Mexico.

Another judicial decision involved evidence about the final setback that had forced the company into bankruptcy in 1973, thereby losing the Fund's $1,400,000 loan. The real cause, according to evidence found by the government, was that a plastic-supply company had decided to stop doing business with Gaylur because of the criminal backgrounds of Weiner, De Angeles and the others. In a special, closed hearing, the judge refused to allow the government to present this information—though internal memos at the plastics company proved it—since it would introduce the subject of the defendants' bad reputations. This allowed Weiner's lawyer to make an impassioned argument to the jury that the oil embargo of 1973 had caused a plastics shortage and that that was what had caused Gaylur to lose its plastics supply.

Similarly, the jury could not be told that Seifert's murder was the reason there was only one knowledgeable witness.

The prosecutors were also hampered by the long time it had spent on the investigation before bringing the case. They claimed that this had allowed Spilotro, De Angeles and the others the additional time to change various records. The problem, the government agents later asserted, was compounded by the fact that since Deming, New Mexico, was so small, "those guys knew within ten minutes whenever one of us had arrived and who we were talking to.''

The money the government claimed went to Spilotro in payoffs was explained away by the defense lawyer: it was listed on the company's books as loans to De Angeles, which he in turn lent to his businessman friend, Mr. Spilotro. As for the Cadillac and the home De Angeles had received, he was "holding those items in trust" for the company, the company's books said, while the other money De Angeles got was for "repairs" at the factory.

The night the jury went out to deliberate the Gaylur case the men from the IRS, FBI, Postal Service and U.S. Attorney's Office went out for a few drinks. They were a little nervous about what the jury would decide, but certain that after weeks of extraordinarily complicated testimony they would need at least a day for deliberation. When they got a call at about 11 P.M. that the jury had reached a verdict that would be announced in the morning, their hearts sank. It was too fast. "When we got that call, we knew it was bad," one lawman remembered. "So we kept drinking. It was like a wake." Dorfman and all the defendants were declared not guilty on all counts. The jury had taken only 2½ hours to decide and had referred to only two of the hundreds of envelopes and files full of evidence.

Allen Dorfman had usually had the same good luck in court. But not always. During some of the time the alleged Gaylur fraud was reportedly taking place, he was serving time in a federal prison for conspiring to line his pockets with some of the proceeds from another pension fund loan.

That case was simpler. In 1972 Dorfman was convicted of conspiring to take a $55,000 cash kickback for arranging a $1,500,000 pension fund loan for a wheeler-dealer named George Horvath. Actually, according to the trial transcript, Horvath had already borrowed more than $15,000,000 in five different loans from the Fund since 1963. All those loans had gone unpaid when Horvath's various businesses—including a mohair company and the Montmartre Hotel in Miami Beach, had gone bad. The loan the government caught Dorfman on was Horvath's last one. It was approved in 1967 for a New York company called Neisco.

According to Horvath, Neisco, which later also went out of business, was created solely for the purpose of receiving this new loan. In 1971, the U.S. Attorney in New York authorized his staff to make a deal with Horvath, who was then in trouble with the government over some Swiss bank accounts, for leniency in return for testimony about his pension fund loans. Horvath testified that when he had asked Dorfman to arrange the last loan Dorfman had told him over breakfast that the Fund had lost so much money on him in the past that it was going to take $55,000 in cash to arrange the new $1,500,000 loan. Horvath agreed, and delivered the money (in twenty-, fifty- and one-hundred-dollar bills) to Dorfman's office in Chicago twelve weeks later. He said he gave it to Dorfman in a large manila envelope. Two days later his Neisco loan was approved.

Horvath's testimony was essential to Dorfman's conviction, but other factors were also important. First among them was the decision by Dorfman's lawyer to put Dorfman on the witness stand in his own defense. This allowed the Assistant U.S. Attorney handling the case, a twenty-nine-year-old lawyer named Richard Ben Veniste, to challenge Dorfman's credibility. Ben Veniste, who later made headlines as a Watergate prosecutor, put Dorfman in knots. He got him to contradict his tax returns, and to claim that his breakfast meeting with Horvath was a chance encounter. He also forced Dorfman to admit that on occasion he had pushed for pension fund loans for businesses in which he, Dorfman, was a part owner.

The trial also demonstrated how weak the pension fund trustees were in their relation to Dorfman. Four of the sixteen board members testified in Dorfman's defense. Each claimed that Dorfman had been against the Horvath loan. But Ben Veniste's cross-examination of them hurt Dorfman more than if they had never been called to testify. The young prosecutor got all four to admit that although they were the trustees and Dorfman was the employee of the board, they were hardly in control of Dorfman or the Fund. As Ben Veniste put it in his summation: "All this goes to the defendants' relationship with the other trustees who testified . . . on this defendant's behalf . . . These are not your kindly white-haired gentlemen from the four-o'clock movie who sit around protecting little Jennie's inheritance."

One of the trustees, Murray "Dusty" Miller, who was then an International vice-president, pleaded ignorance of Fund activities and performance this way:

BEN VENISTE: In 1967 did you know whether as a result of your investments you made money or lost money?
MILLER: Oh, I don't think the Fund has ever lost money.
BEN VENISTE: Do you know?
MILLER: No.
BEN VENISTE: Do you have any idea as to what the yield was?

MILLER: No. But I think the Fund made money.
BEN VENISTE: You think so?
MILLER: Yes, sir.
BEN VENISTE: Do you know how many loans were in default or
which moratoriums had been granted in the year 1967?
MILLER: No, sir.

By the time of his testimony Miller was no longer just a vice-president and a Fund trustee but the secretary-treasurer of the entire International union.

There are two other footnotes to Dorfman's 1972 trial. One involves a press report a year later, reconfirmed to me four years after that by an eyewitness who had supplied consistently reliable information to the government, that Dorfman was seen at the Barclay Hotel during his stay in New York for the trial, brandishing a receipt for a $100,000 cash contribution to the Nixon presidential campaign signed by John Mitchell. Dorfman showed the receipt to several friends as a way of assuring them, and presumably himself, that one way or another he had come out of the trial untouched. In 1977, a lawyer close to former Attorney General Mitchell would only say that "I've heard that story too, and it may very well be true and it may not."

During the trial, Ben Veniste asked another of the trustees about a private plane that the pension fund had leased from Allen Dorfman. Further checking revealed a more complicated story than a simple lease—and a far better deal for Dorfman. It turned out that in 1972 Dorfman, through one of his insurance agencies, had purchased a three-year-old, twelve-seat Grumman Gulfstream jet equipped with bar and bed from Frank Sinatra for $3,000,000. Then, Dorfman's insurance agency leased the jet to the pension fund for $30,000 a month. The Fund then allowed Dorfman the exclusive use of the jet. Ostensibly, Dorfman was to use the jet for his pension fund consultant activities; but in 1972 Jim Drinkhall spotted it twenty-five different times at the small airfield that services La Costa. By buying the jet himself through his insurance business and then having the Fund lease it from him—rather than simply having the Fund buy it in the first place—Dorfman was able to deduct the jet's depreciation from his insurance company's tax return. Since the lease (nine years at $360,000 a year) more than paid the $3,000,000 cost, Dorfman owned the jet without paying for it and earned money on it by using it as a tax deduction. Asked about the transaction in 1977, two years after public and government pressure had forced him to get rid of the plane, Dorfman had no problem admitting the tax-avoidance scheme. "There was nothing wrong with that deal," he explained. "We did it because the pension fund [as a tax-free entity] couldn't take the tax deduction and I could. What's wrong with that?"

Dorfman's good fortune on the Sinatra jet deal didn't end there. It turned out that he had floated loans to buy the jet in the first place. One of the loans he got was from the Amalgamated Trust and Savings Bank in Chicago. The two top executives of the bank were also partners in Chicago's ill-fated McCormick City Project, the venture that built a hotel and convention hall complex in Chicago. At the same time Dorfman was getting his loan from their bank, they were getting the first of their loans for $21,800,000 from Dorfman's bank (the Fund) to build the hotel at McCormick City.*

At Dorfman's sentencing hearing on the Neisco case, on April 26, 1972, his lawyer told Federal Court Judge Murray Gurfein about his client's war record, his charitable activities and the number of people who were dependent on Dorfman staying out of prison. Given Dorfman's pension-fund-loan activities the last point was probably closer to the truth than the lawyer wanted Judge Gurfein to believe.

The court record shows that the judge also received letters from two Chicago judges on Dorfman's behalf. Presiding Judge Joseph Power of the Criminal Division said that "Allen Dorfman is . . . a warm and generous person who gives much of himself to help others less fortunate." Judge Daniel Covelli, citing Dorfman's "substantial contributions" to "a multitude of charitable causes," called him "a fine family man who is respected and looked up to in his community. Hastening his return to society," Judge Covelli added, "would be of inestimable benefit to the community, the charitable institutions, and his family." Although the two judges and Dorfman's lawyer emphasized his contributions to charity, Dorfman's tax returns, obtained from a government source, showed that in 1971, with an adjusted gross income of $166,332, his only charitable contribution was $25 to the Crusade of Mercy. In 1970 with an income of $222,731, he gave nothing to any charity.

---

* The problems later associated with this pension fund loan—that it suffered as the whole McCormick City Project foundered—should not be confused with another Teamsters-related problem at McCormick Place that involved the corrupt Teamsters local that controlled who could work and what could be moved there.

Prosecutor Ben Veniste reminded Judge Gurfein that "the people most concerned with this case . . . were the members of the Central States Pension Fund, who were betrayed by Dorfman for his own personal profit." By 1977 Ben Veniste could have added in this regard, that less than $1,000,000 of the $16,000,000 of the members' money loaned to Horvath in various loans over the years had been paid back, with all the other debts in default. Judge Gurfein gave Dorfman a one-year prison sentence.

Following a series of appeals Dorfman entered the maximum-security federal prison at Marion, Illinois. He served ten months before being released for good behavior. "I learned to adjust there," Dorfman later recalled, reflecting on his prison time. "Just like I adjusted to fighting the Japs at Iwo Jima." On November 10, 1973, while at Marion, Dorfman received a letter from the IRS (addressed in matter-of-fact computer type to "Jail Number 00081-140, U.S. Penitentiary, Marion, Illinois, 62959) telling him that he had been assessed $34,926 in taxes and $17,463 as a "fraud penalty" for failing to report on his 1967 tax return the bribe he had taken from Horvath.

Though the Horvath payoff was Dorfman's only conviction, pension funds records, FBI files, Labor Department investigatory memos, and several other sources suggested literally dozens of other instances in which Dorfman had acted in his interest, in the mob's interest, or both, in doling out the pension fund money. There were, to list a few, an eleven-million-dollar loan to build the Connecticut jai alai facility, for which the borrowers paid Tony Provenzano a "finder's fee"; a loan to Bally, the slot-machine company, at a time when Dorfman, Frank Fitzsimmons, and the Presser family owned stock in the company; a loan to a car dealer in Illinois who ended up buying a condominium, called Canongate in Florida that Dorfman owned a piece of; and the loan to Meyer Lansky associate Alvin Malnik.

Then, of course, there were the loans—forty-six of them totaling more than $93,700,000—to build La Costa. These were given to the group headed by former Cleveland racketeer Moe Dalitz.

But the Dalitz-La Costa loans were not as large as another group of Las Vegas loans given in 1974 to a thirty-one-year-old real-estate salesman whom nobody had ever heard of.

On May 29, 1974, the Fund approved a loan of $62,700,000 to Allen R. Glick to purchase the Stardust and Fremont hotel-casinos in Las

Vegas. Eventually, with additional loans for these ventures and other loans for other ventures, the Fund would back Glick up to $160,000,000. Glick obtained that May 29 loan nine days after he applied for it and without ever filing a personal financial statement. Technically the money went to a corporation, Argent, that he owned. Had he filed a personal statement it would have shown that he had four and a half years of business experience and that he had been a $200-a-week real-estate salesman in 1970.

Why Dorfman and the pension fund trustees showed such confidence in the short, loudly dressed, balding thirty-one-year-old quickly became a popular guessing game among federal organized-crime prosecutors, Nevada gaming officials and reporters. By 1977 there was still lively speculation on the details, but near unanimity on a general theory: Allen Glick was a front for hidden organized-crime ownership of his Las Vegas properties. "I have this dream," one lawyer involved in a civil fraud case against Glick explained in 1977, "that the mob looks at high-school yearbooks and picks a hundred guys who look smart and clean like Allen. Then over a year or two they narrow it down to ten people, then two, and finally they select one guy out of college or law school and approach him and say, 'You're it. We're gonna set you up in business and you'll get a nice cut and give the rest to us.' Well, that's what I think happened with Allen."

Even without dreaming, others speculated that the emergence of Allen Glick—smart, intense-looking, with a spotlessly clean past—as an overnight Las Vegas tycoon second only to Howard Hughes, was the product of long planning for the incubation of the "perfect front." Further support for this incubation theory was that four years before the 1974 Fund loans, Glick had been able to acquire half a San Diego real-estate company that was reportedly worth millions of dollars for a $2,500 note. The acquisition had set him up as a credible businessman for the time when he would approach the Fund for the $62,700 loan.

After interviews with dozens of people who were close to Glick at the Fund or who had investigated him for various law-enforcement agencies, plus a check back through Glick's past (that included such far-flung searches as a review of his college yearbook to look for early connections) a more likely theory is that the front man's role for Glick was not as painstakingly orchestrated as it might have seemed.

Glick was born in Pittsburgh in 1942 into the middle-class family of a local scrap-iron dealer. In 1961 he went to Ohio State University and graduated with a B.A. in 1964. His grades were not terribly good, but he managed to get into Case Western Reserve Law School, from which he was graduated in 1967. He then entered the Army, where he compiled an impressive two-year record as a helicopter pilot in Vietnam. He left as a captain with a Bronze Star in 1969. In the fall of that year he, his wife, Kathleen, and their young children moved to San Diego.

Why the Glicks decided to settle in San Diego is unclear, although there is no reason not to believe Glick's often-repeated explanation that they had enjoyed vacations there and thought it was a good place to raise a family and for him to start a career. More confusing is the question of why he didn't practice law there, but instead took a $200 a week job as a real-estate salesman. Again, there is no reason not to believe Glick's explanation that he couldn't find a good law job and had cooled to the idea of being a lawyer anyway. Whatever the reason, a year later, according to Nevada Gaming Control Board records and to a deposition Glick gave in a lawsuit in 1975, Glick met a man named Dennis Wittman who owned another real-estate company. The company, called Saratoga, had been involved in several ventures with the realtors for whom Glick then was working for. When Wittman offered Glick the opportunity to move over to Saratoga at $500 a week, Glick took the job.

A year after that, Wittman gave Glick nearly half of Saratoga's stock for a $2,500 note. This was the transaction that later raised suspicions that even then Glick must have had some hidden (presumably mob-connected) guardian angel. Saratoga was worth millions of dollars on paper. However, a closer, retrospective look at Saratoga reveals that Wittman's apparent gift wasn't much of a gift at all. By 1977 Saratoga would be bankrupt and involved in a maze of lawsuits brought by angry investors who had put money into the company on Glick's or Wittman's say-so. The various lawsuits would allege different versions of the same scheme: Saratoga took money from investors—mostly doctors in the San Diego area—by offering them partnerships in a land venture. Glick and Wittman would buy the land with these investors' money. Then, using the land as collateral, they would borrow money from a bank and buy more land with the borrowed money. One lawyer summarized the process this way: "It was all a house of cards that was going to fall in sooner or later. They used Saratoga as a vehicle whereby other people's money would finance this monster. They convinced people that they had assets worth more than they had paid for. It had to collapse." The best theory, then, of why Wittman gave Glick so much of the company was not that Glick had underworld sponsors, but that he, like Wittman, was good at talking people into investing in Saratoga's land ventures and that the company then wasn't really worth much anyway, unless the two could continue to build up the house of cards.

In the summer of 1972 Glick was happily moving ahead with Saratoga when, according to Glick's own 1975 deposition, he was contacted by a Columbus, Ohio, man named Eugene Fresch. Fresch was a friend of a friend of Glick's from their Ohio school days and had just moved to San Diego. According to Glick, after several conversations, Fresch asked the rising young real-estate dealer if he'd be interested in joining him in a really exciting venture: the purchase of the financially troubled Hacienda Hotel and Casino in Las Vegas, which was then on the selling block. Glick was intrigued. They went ahead with the deal in late 1972, with Fresch arranging financing through a bank he knew back in Cleveland.

The application that Glick filed with the Nevada Gaming Control Board in 1972 to allow him to buy the Hacienda showed that even then he was living high. He listed the ownership of two cars: one a Lamborghini, license plate number ARG (for Allen R. Glick), and the second a Mercedes, plate number 2ARG. The application also showed that he had borrowed his share of the Hacienda purchase price, $2,300,000, from the soon-to-be-bankrupt Saratoga.

Although the Nevada records show that the Hacienda continued to lose money after Glick and Fresch bought it, the two started looking almost immediately for more Nevada investments. By early 1973 they had focused on the King's Castle Hotel and Casino near Lake Tahoe. (Later it became a Hyatt hotel.) Checks with several people involved with Dorfman and the pension fund four years later revealed that this was when the Glick-Central States Pension Fund link began. According to a reliable source close to the Presser family, Fresch, who was from Cleveland, knew someone who knew Bill Presser. Presser, also from Cleveland, was then the pension fund's most influential trustee. Fresch contacted Presser, this source claimed, and Presser told Fresch to meet with Dorfman and Alvin Baron, the Dorfman protégé who was going to mind things at the Fund when Dorfman went to prison in March.

According to a source who was there, in early March, Glick had a secret meeting with Dorfman and another Fund trustee at La Costa to discuss a loan for King's Castle. The intended setup was to have Glick make whatever he could on the hotel, while allowing Dorfman's organized-crime friends to take something off the top at the casino. Thus, Edward "Marty" Buccieri would run the gambling operation for Glick at King's Castle, a vantage point from which he presumably could "skim" off the mob's take there. Buccieri was well qualified for the job: since the '50s, according to law-enforcement records, he had been a courier for Meyer Lansky's people. In 1961 he was arrested and convicted for executing an infamous mob frame-up of a reform sheriff in Newport, Kentucky, by drugging him, throwing him into bed with a stripper and taking films. Since 1970 Buccieri had been working as a pit boss at Caesar's Palace, where he allegedly was involved in watching the mob's hidden investment. He was also a partner of Dorfman's in a real-estate business.

Buccieri's qualifications were so good that it ruined the King's Castle deal: just as Glick and Fresch were about to buy it, the Nevada Gaming Control Board informed Glick that if Buccieri was sent in to run the casino they would refuse to license it. As a result, Glick and Fresch backed away. Nevertheless, soon thereafter Glick got his first pension fund loan—sixteen million dollars to finance an Austin, Texas, real-estate venture in which three former pro football players were partners. Eventually one of Glick's tenants on the site in Austin would be the IRS—one of the agencies investigating him.

The big Glick loan of $62,700,000 was made in May 1974. The money would be used to buy out the Recrion Corporation—owner of the Stardust and the Fremont—from Delbert Coleman and the other stockholders through a tender offer. Originally, former Hoffa lawyer and frequent loan recipient Morris Shenker, who already owned the Dunes Hotel in Las Vegas, was going to make the deal with Coleman, also using a Dorfman-sponsored pension fund loan. But Shenker backed out at the last minute and Glick was allowed to come in.

The filing Glick made with the Securities Exchange Commission at the time of this loan and his purchase of Recrion showed that he was paying a $421,000 "finder's fee for the fund loan to someone named Todd Derlachter. It turned out that Derlachter was a Southern Californian whose name had come up in various organized-crime investigations. Why Shenker suddenly dropped out of the deal, and why Glick needed to pay anyone a finder's fee for the loan, when he had already borrowed from the Fund and from Dorfman in the past and therefore didn't need anyone to "find" the Fund for him, were two of the more perplexing questions associated with the deal.

Three years later a lawyer involved directly in the deal tied the two mysteries together and provided a plausible solution to both, based, he said, on firsthand knowledge. "Shenker had to get out," he explained "because Dorfman and the others at the Fund wanted him out. They were afraid of all the bad publicity because of all the other loans he had [more than $100,000,000] at the time for the Dunes and other properties] and because of his past reputation. Also, he had been Hoffa's lawyer, and with Hoffa trying to come back [this was 1974] they were worried about Shenker's loyalty. I heard Dorfman say this. . . . So Bill Presser remembered Glick and said how clean he was and everything. 'Let's give it to that nice kid, what's-his-name,' he probably said." The records show that Derlachter was made a $10,000 a month "consultant" to Glick in addition to getting the finder's fee. The same inside source explained that, "We told Shenker we wouldn't give it to him, but that he could deliver it to Glick and take something out for himself and his people. So Shenker had Derlachter contact Glick . . . I think Derlachter's payment [the finder's fee] went to Shenker and to the mob guys Shenker was involved with. That way Shenker didn't feel so bad." This last part of the explanation is made more plausible by the fact that Derlachter was known to be an associate of Shenker's.

Whatever the details of the arrangement—this version seems most logical, but could not be completely confirmed independently—by June 1974 Allen Glick was the owner of the Stardust and the Fremont. He had also agreed to take over another $12,000,000 in Fund loans previously made to the Stardust and Fremont, plus two more Fund-financed ventures in California that had failed—an additional $32,000,000 in loans. One was a shopping center in Oakland, the other the Beverly Ridge Estates near Los Angeles. Then, in December, the Fund lent Glick's Argent Corporation another $25,000,000.

Glick, installed in a luxurious office high atop the Stardust, commuted to his home in La Jolla, California, by private jet. He had consoles of telephones and batteries of secretaries. His desk was covered with memos having to do with the financing and the day-to-day operations of the Argent empire. But by 1977 it was clear, though not provable, to investigators at the Nevada Gaming Control Board that the real power was elsewhere.

When Glick took over he hired Frank "Lefty" Rosenthal to be chairman of the Argent executive committee and to take control of all the gambling operations on a ten-year $250,000-a-year contract. In an interview with *Business Week* a year later Rosenthal exuberantly explained, (perhaps too exuberantly for his own good) that he was the casino boss, and that "Glick is the financial end, but policy comes from me." Why, under normal circumstances, Rosenthal would get the job was difficult to imagine, since before Glick's takeover he was a baccarat dealer at the Stardust casino. The Gaming Board's records show that he had other qualifications. He had long been an organized-crime lower-echelon bookie. In 1960, he had pleaded no-contest to a charge of bribing a college basketball player to fix a game. More than that, Rosenthal was a close friend of Tony Spilotro's. This was the key to the front setup. "Think of it as a corporation," one Nevada FBI agent who had followed the Argent case explained. "Dorfman arranges the loans. Then there's Spilotro, who's the company's corporate vice-president from Chicago. Rosenthal is his manager of skim. And Glick—well, they let him run the hotels and be the front, but he stays away from the casinos." Also involved with Rosenthal and Spilotro was long-time mobster Jerome Zarowitz, who, FBI sources said, was there to make sure that New York organized-crime factions got some share of the cash out of Glick's casinos. Zarowitz, who had served twenty months in prison for trying to fix the 1946 National Football League championship game, was also believed to have been one of those watching over the hidden mob interest in Caesar's Palace. In 1970, federal agents conducting a raid at Caesar's Palace had found more than a million dollars in cash in two safe-deposit boxes leased to him.

A memo prepared in 1975 by a California police agency on Glick, summarized the Argent front-man skimming operation by explaining that the plan was for Rosenthal and the others to "skim the 'gub' out of the two casinos, driving them into bankruptcy, and [then] be unable to make his payments to the Teamsters [pension fund]. The Teamsters [pension fund] would then be forced to foreclose . . . leaving the Teamsters the owner of Recrion [actually renamed Argent]." Then, the memo writer might have added, they could let someone else take over the loan and start the process all over again.

"The way they do this," a Chicago prosecutor who had investigated the Dorfman-Spilotro aspect of the alleged arrangement explained, "is like you'd expect to read about in a novel. They set up a guy, a guy like Glick, while they fleece his place. And they let him live so well with cars, and planes, and good clothes, and secretaries, and everything else, that he looks like he's in control.''

There was no question that they let Glick live as if he were in control. In 1974 a Los Angeles *Times* gossip column ran this item about Glick:

> If you ask us we'd say that Mr. and Mrs. Allen R. Glick's new home in La Jolla has been royally housewarmed. . . . The Glicks (he's involved with the Stardust in Las Vegas, among other things) completely redid the 40-year-old house . . . It now has tennis courts, a pool, a sauna, cabanas, fountains, gazebos, separate guests' and servants' quarters—and other amenities. They really should be terribly comfy there. . . . For the housewarming party they invited some 400 guests, including nearby neighbors, friends from Las Vegas, and Mrs. Glick's hairdresser Felipe. . . . Mrs. Glick's mother and grandmother and her sister and brother-in-law from Atlanta, were there, too. And the Glick children in Little Lord Fauntleroy velvet suits helped their parents receive guests before retiring to their second-floor quarters, where they hosted a kiddies party of their own.

Glick, however, realized that there was another side of the life he had chosen. The plush home was guarded in a way that few other executives would find necessary—electric fences, guards, guard dogs, and a system of closed-circuit television cameras scanning the grounds. His children were also guarded, and they were not allowed out to play with other youngsters in the neighborhood.

If at the beginning, even with these precautions, Glick didn't fully appreciate the implications of his marriage to Dorfman and the pension fund, a murder on November 9, 1975, probably helped drive the point home.

At about four o'clock that afternoon, Mrs. Tamara Rand, the fifty-one-year-old wife of a prominent San Diego gynecologist, was sitting on a stool in her kitchen having a cup of tea. According to a report filed the next day by the coroner, the first bullet hit her in the back of the neck. The second went into her skull through her left ear and sent her sprawling onto the floor. Her right elbow hit an air conditioner as she landed on the linoleum. Then, the coroner noted, the gunman reached down, held the High Standard semiautomatic against Mrs. Rand's chin and fired three more shots. Not more than two hours later, Dr. Philip R. Rand came through the back door at 4021 Bandini Street, found his wife lying in a pool of blood and called the police.

The San Diego police never solved the Rand case. But after compiling several thick black loose-leaf books full of interviews and memos, they were certain that it had been a mob "hit." The 22-caliber High Standard (with a silencer, the ballistics tests showed) used in the murder was the same kind of weapon used in a more than a dozen suspected gangland hits throughout the country, including those earlier in the year of aging Chicago mobster Sam Giancana and of Marty Buccieri—the man who had been slated to run the King's Castle casino for Glick.

Before long the San Diego detectives came across Mrs. Rand's connection with Allen Glick. Mrs. Rand, an independent investor and deal maker, had met Glick in 1971 and made several investments with him. By 1972 she was heavily involved in Glick's Saratoga ventures, busily investing her money and her husband's with him. She had entered into a partnership with Saratoga on one venture and in 1974 supplied Glick with the cash that literally kept Saratoga afloat while he was negotiating the deal to take over the Stardust and the Fremont. But by early 1975, she was among the most outspoken of Glick's disillusioned investors. Bitterly disappointed, she claimed to her lawyer that Glick had misled her into believing that in return for her loan she was going to get a portion of the Las Vegas properties. In the spring of 1975, according to notes she had given her lawyer, she had gone to Glick in Las Vegas and threatened to report him to the SEC and other authorities.

The San Diego Police and others investigating the case, including the FBI, never suspected Glick of being involved in the murder. They surmised that Glick had mentioned his problems to Rosenthal or someone else behind the front, and that Glick's benefactors realized that Mrs. Rand might easily make trouble for Glick with accusations of fake SEC filings or fake filings with the Gaming Board concerning his and Saratoga's financial condition. As one detective who worked the Rand case put it, "Rosenthal or Spilotro or someone else, but not Glick, had Tamara killed. . . . Glick knew nothing about it. You see, that way it served two purposes. It saved Glick's reputation by getting rid of her. Plus it made an impression on Glick. This was those guys' way of showing Glick what could happen if you crossed them, even if, like Tamara, you crossed them without ever knowing you were even doing it. . . . Poor woman. She was just trying to get her money back from a young, soft-spoken guy who she had kind of loved in a way and who jilted her. She didn't want any trouble."

This theory of the Rand murder was backed in 1976 by an associate of Tony Spilotro's who claimed to have heard him talking about Rand just before her death and, in 1977, by a source at Argent who asserted that, "that's what a lot of us around here thought." Of course, as a San Diego detective concluded, "We'll never prove that or any other theory until someone involved talks, and that's not gonna happen."

Glick's shock was followed by a series of unsettling events in 1976. It was in January that the Gaming Control Board told Glick that Rosenthal's record was tainted and that he could not run Glick's casinos. Glick agreed to pay Rosenthal his $250,000 a year salary anyway; and soon law-enforcement officials in Nevada regularly observed Rosenthal with Spilotro at the Las Vegas Country Club, where, they believed, both men were meeting frequently with Stardust and Fremont casino executives. In May, Gaming Control Board agents staged a "raid" on the Stardust casino counting room; there, according to board sources, they found a skim in progress—the cash was being split, some to be counted for taxes and the rest to go to the skimmers. This was part of a larger investigation that eventually yielded a 600-page board report alleging a $7,000,000 skimming operation over a period of less than a year just from the slot machines in Glick's casinos. (The amounts skimmed from the gaming tables were not ascertained.) The man in charge of the slots swiftly and conveniently fled to Mexico to avoid prosecution, permitting Rosenthal and Glick to blame the whole thing on him and claim ignorance.

For Glick, the raid was a blessing of sorts—with the Nevada officials watching Argent's casinos so carefully, the skimming operation had to stop, at least for a time. In 1977 Glick was able to show a profit for Argent after showing consistent losses during the past years. However, the Gaming Control Board was still trying to prove that he knew about the skim; the IRS was suing him for $9,600,000 for tax deficiencies (for not declaring various income and for spending corporate money on his expensive cars and other high living without declaring it); the SEC was suing, claiming he had fraudulently overstated Argent's financial condition and had used Argent as "his private source of funds in flagrant disregard of his fiduciary duty for purposes of remodeling his home, paying off personal indebtedness and living expenses"; and he faced several fraud suits going back to his days at Saratoga. The murder, the investigations and perhaps some hindsight, had made him nervous about the whole arrangement. As one of the people in his office explained, Glick was "getting much more testy. Even scared. Wouldn't you be? What do you think happens when they don't need you anymore?"

Allen Dorfman wasn't frightened in 1977, but he too was of less use to the mob than he had been. Since the end of 1974, when he rushed through a flock of shaky loans, the pension fund had stopped all loans and continually yielded to government pressure to reform—a process that culminated in spring 1977, when Fitzsimmons resigned from the board, and an insurance company was appointed to manage the Fund's assets. Although most of the changes had been prompted by the passage of ERISA in 1974 and the government pressure that followed, the changes had started in 1973 when the trustees had hired Daniel Shannon—a former Notre Dame football star, an accountant, and then the head of the Chicago Parks Commission—to be the executive director of both the pension fund and the health and welfare fund.

The decision to hire Shannon had been prompted by an onslaught of negative news articles about the Fund, especially Drinkhall's almost-monthly *Overdrive* pieces, which had begun in June 1972 with a report entitled, "How Your Sweat Finances Crooks' Cadillacs." There was also concern among Fund lawyers and a few of the trustees, confirmed by an outside audit that they had commissioned—that pension applications were coming in so fast that the present management of the Fund couldn't keep up with the paper work.

At first Shannon's only job was to manage claims made to the pension and health and welfare funds and to direct the Fund's staff. Even in this capacity he quickly came up against the Dorfman forces. Dorfman went off to prison in March, but he left Alvin Baron behind to be "assets manager" of the pension fund. Baron, a gruff hulk of a man, was universally hated by the staff, especially by the secretaries who were often reduced to tears by his profanity and general abusiveness. (Once, to make sure a point registered on one of the Fund's borrowers he mashed his cigar out on the man's desk, spat on his rug, overturned a chair, and walked out.) Shannon and Baron clashed. A few weeks after he arrived, Shannon fired the Fund's comptroller, an old Dorfman crony. Baron quickly rehired him. Shannon fired an assets evaluator, another Dorfman hack, whose last job before coming to the Fund had been as a gas-station attendant; Baron hired him back. Several months later, Shannon was asked to approve the purchase of eight thousand pens stamped with the Fund's insignia. Shannon didn't think much of the idea; the Fund was not in public relations, he argued, and the pens were an odd size that made writing with them almost impossible. According to Shannon and some of his close aides, a few hours later Baron burst into his office, explaining between four-letter words that the pens had to be approved, because a friend owned the pen company. Shannon refused, and Baron threatened to "wipe the floor" with him. He backed down when the former football star got up from behind his desk to accept the challenge. Baron was infuriated when Bill Presser declined to overrule Shannon. About the same time Shannon started getting anonymous phone calls at home threatening his wife and children.

These clashes aside, Shannon's work in his first year was important but not terribly exciting. He had inherited an operation that was responsible for keeping employment and financial records for hundreds of thousands of workers and yet was not computerized nor adequately managed. He recruited a staff of Ivy League business-school graduates, which led to the firing or replacement of 28 of the 30 top people, while expanding the staff from 200 to 750. He also budgeted $8,000,000 for a computerized "history project" designed to collect accurate records of 400,000 employees' work histories. Soon, the pension and health and welfare funds divided into two camps: the old-line Dorfman-Baron forces versus the clean-cut, young Shannon people, who as late as 1977 could be heard whispering jokes about top Teamsters and their mob connections. (One wisecrack was that the Little City Home for blind retarded children, which Red Dorfman had founded and Fitzsimmons had supported with the golf tournaments, was occupied by retarded children who had been blinded by Teamsters goons for the extra publicity value of having them be blind.)

In early 1975 Baron left the Fund, and in March, following a board meeting a month earlier in which worried trustees discussed their possible liability under the new ERISA law, Shannon was given the job of managing the assets. Baron's departure was caused by a fast-breaking government investigation of a $200,000 kickback he reportedly took for arranging a loan of $1,300,000 to a cemetery in California. Shannon's staff had reported the payoff to federal authorities after a routine meeting in which the borrower showed records of the kickback in order to demonstrate how he was spending his money. In November 1976 Baron was indicted on the payoff charge.

As soon as he took over the assets, Shannon put whatever money wasn't involved in real estate into trust accounts in various banks for them to invest.* But whatever public pressure these changes relieved was restored when Hoffa disappeared. It was after that that the IRS revoked the Fund's tax-exempt status.

Then came the negotiation with the government and the agreement that Fitzsimmons and the other trustees would step down and turn the assets over to an outside insurance company. All during this negotiation Dorfman was urging Fitzsimmons not to yield. As he put it in an interview a year later, "I told Fitz to tell the government to go fuck itself. Why should we just give it up?"

When they did give up, all was not lost for Dorfman. He still had the contract from the health and welfare fund to process all its claims. That contract expired in 1978, and Shannon had long been urging that it not be renewed, because of Dorfman's reputation, the possibility of corruption in claims, and the poor data Dorfman's staff collected and provided to Shannon's budget planners. However, in July 1977 the Fund's new trustees voted Dorfman a ten-year extension of the contract. According to two of the trustees, this happened after intense pressure on the trustees from Teamsters Vice-President Roy Williams and Fitzsimmons, mostly from Williams, who was a close friend and ally. A few days later, after pressure from the government and the press, they rescinded the vote and postponed consideration of the renewal.† Nonetheless, for the clean, new trustees to have granted the renewal to the convicted felon in the first place was extraordinary. "You see that," commented another vice-president the week of the renewal. "You think these new trustees aren't scared shitless of crossing Dorfman. Look at that. Look at how they were going to give him all the health and welfare insurance for another ten years. What power that guy has."

The month before, Dorfman spent an hour with me discussing his power and what he had done with it. It was, he claimed, "my second interview ever, and the first guys totally fucked me."

---

* In 1976, just as it seemed that candidate Carter might do well enough in the Democratic primaries to become President Carter, the Atlanta bank run by Carter's good friend Bert Lance was chosen to get one of these trust accounts. This later raised eyebrows, when Lance's financial affairs came under fire and he had to resign as Carter's Budget Director. Indeed, Lance's bank was minor league compared to the other banks that got the accounts. But other than reports that the Fund reacted to a suggestion from one of its trustees who lived in Atlanta that depositing the money with Lance and the bank might be politically helpful, my investigation found no specific *quid pro quo* or anything inappropriate involved in the deposit.

† Later, it was renewed for one year.

The Amalgamated Insurance Company offices occupied two floors of a new office building next to Chicago's O'Hare Airport that was owned by the Central States pension and health and welfare funds. Two large, elegant gaslight-shaped lamps on the far side of an open room full of clerks busy at computer consoles marked the entrance to the anteroom of the boss's office. Dorfman, in a soft-brown well-tailored suit, matching tie and pinstripe shirt, greeted his visitor with a short smile, a strong handshake and then a gruff "I don't normally do this, but you called so often—" actually, it was twenty-seven times at home and at the office—"I hate the press."

There were plaques and testimonial pictures everywhere: one from the Little City Foundation; two from the Hillcrest Country Club (one for each of the two years he had been the club's president); a golden shield from the "Paul Dorfman Habitation Unit" at Little City; the 1976 "Affirmative Action" award from the Chicago Black Community Breadbasket Association; four golf trophies; and other awards and memorabilia. On the coffee table there were more trinkets and two more charity plaques, interspersed with handball and racketball magazines and a book about Napa Valley wines. Over to the side of the fruitwood desk above the phone console were three large color portraits mounted on easel frames, each with its own small spotlight. One was of Fitzsimmons, the other two of Teamsters vice-presidents Roy Williams and Robert Holmes. Farther down the wall, toward the fireplace that faced the desk at the other end of the room, hung a collage about four feet long with dozens of color pictures of Allen Dorfman in various settings and poses. Most showed him with his family or on a golf course.

Dorfman took his place in the high-backed brown leather chair behind the desk. He popped a few mints into his mouth, looked up and barked, "Let's get started." The first question, about whether he felt he had been maligned by the press, elicited a barrage of venom and protestations that in form and substance characterized the rest of the hour's conversation. The press were "a bunch of scumbag jerk-offs, whores who try to make a buck by destroying me, even though I give to more charities than any man I know of. . . . Why do I give to charity? Because I remember when I had nothing." He continued, pointing to the plaques, "If you don't believe me, look at that wall. . . . You never know what persecution is till you feel it. . . . You know what it does to your family? I've got the greatest wife in the world and four perfect kids. Three are college graduates with honors.

And they've had to read about how bad their father is ever since they were born." (In an earlier telephone interview Dorfman's wife had offered the same perspective of her husband's notoriety, saying that, "the press has made our lives miserable. But you get used to the persecution after a while if you believe in your husband like I do.")

"I remember the McClellan hearings," Dorfman continued. "It was all bullshit. You'd go and you'd testify—" actually, Dorfman only took the Fifth Amendment; he never testified—"and you'd go home and read about it in the papers. And you'd see what the scumbags write and you'd say to yourself, 'If that's what happened, where the fuck was I sitting all day?' It was all bullshit. Oh those hearings. You know why they were held, don't you? I mean, what the fuck else do you think generated all the publicity that made the Kennedys? The Kennedys ran it. That chairman, the great Senator John McClellan. He was a drunken alcoholic even then. We'd sit there and he'd have a glass full of booze, even in the morning. He told everyone it was . . . tea, but it was booze. You could smell it . . ." Dorfman was interrupted by a buzz from his secretary. He stopped, popped another mint, grabbed the receiver, punched a button on the console, listened to her for a minute, then punched another button.

"Hi, Morris, how are you? Listen, you out at the hotel? Good. Can I call you back later? O.K." After confirming that the call was from former Hoffa lawyer Morris Shenker, phoning from his pension-fund-financed Dunes Hotel, Dorfman answered a question about the union's and the pension fund's recent effort, led by Jackie Presser, to use advertising in an effort to change the Teamsters' image. This was a sore point. His face reddened as he began. "What the hell do they need public relations for? That's all bullshit. Who the fuck cares what the public thinks? The John Jerk-off in the street doesn't pay anything into the Fund. Fuck John Doe Jerk-off. The members, they're the ones who count, and they know they get paid their benefits. . . . That fund is the greatest fund in the world. Why don't you compare it to the Chase Manhattan Bank's REIT [Real Estate Investment Trust] or to the REIT of any other bank. I'll match our record against any of them. That pension reform law is the biggest fraud ever. Who needed it? . . . They should reform the banks."

"What about Allen Glick? Why did you give him all that money?"

"Allen was a nice kid. This is America. You see a smart young honest kid who has an idea and you give him a chance . . . He wasn't totally inexperienced the way the jerk-offs in the press say. He'd run the Hacienda for a year and been a successful real-estate guy. You tell me what's wrong with that. So far the loans have been paid."

Another buzz interrupted. This call was from "Frank." After exchanging hello's, Dorfman said, "Yes, . . . I agree. . . . and then, "I'll talk to you later . . ." before hanging up. "Yes," that was Fitzsimmons on the phone, he said. "I'd say I talk to him almost every day. . . . Why? He calls me for advice." He refused to say what the "advice" related to—a logical question, given the fact that Fitzsimmons had resigned as a trustee from the pension and health and welfare funds and had no business reason to be in contact with Dorfman. (Seven weeks later Fitzsimmons told me in a telephone interview that "the only contacts I have with Allen are once in a while if I run into him on a golf course.")

Asked about his alleged links to organized crime and his relations with Tony Spilotro, Dorfman's face again flushed. "If I'm such a bad guy why did six hundred people come to my [testimonial] dinner last week? The whole room was filled. There were federal judges, all the top bankers, everyone from the Mayor [of Chicago, Michael Bilandic] on down. They don't think I'm a hoodlum. Go ask them.* I'll show you records, facts on paper, that *prove* that all the cases against me were frame-ups and that all our loans were sound."

"What about Tony Spilotro?"

"Well I'll tell you about him. I never even met him until that bullshit trial [the Gaylur Products pension fraud case] in 1974." Before that I swear I never knew him." Dorfman's assertion here was contradicted by FBI reports that he and Spilotro were frequent companions and that Spilotro had been Dorfman's house guest in 1973. "But I'll tell you this about Spilotro. He's a nice guy. And if he's involved in the Mafia, then I'm the bishop of Chicago."

Dorfman continued on, denying the existence of organized crime, challenging the honesty and the heterosexuality of members of the press and questioning the patriotism of "antiunion" politicians like the Kennedys. Rapidly talking himself into higher levels of indignation, he concluded with a pronouncement on the state of the nation:

"I used to think this was a great country. I took shrapnel in the ass in the war from the Japs and got a medal handed to me by Roosevelt. I believed in all that. But it was . . . bullshit. My biggest mistake in

---

* On September 29, 1977, a spokeswoman for Mayor Bilandic confirmed that the Mayor attended the Dorfman dinner, which was a fund-raiser for the Little City Foundation, but the spokeswoman added, "Please understand, he went to honor Little City, not Allen Dorfman."

life has been having too much faith in the goodness of people and of the country. I used to think this was a democratic country. But it's not. It's all bullshit. Look what they've done to me. Look at what you've got a few miles from here. Slums. Slums, where people are getting fucked over. Well I'll tell you this. There's gonna be an uprising. You ain't gonna fuck people around forever and get away with it.''

Many government investigators who had watched Dorfman and the Teamsters' Central States Pension Fund over the years believed by 1977 that any real uprising that would be associated with Dorfman would involve Teamsters who, because of the way the Fund had been fleeced, wouldn't receive the pensions they had been promised.

Actually, as Dorfman and his friends assembled for the 1977 Fitzsimmons Invitational to raise money for the kids at Little City, the pension fund was not exactly on the verge of bankruptcy as Teamsters dissidents and some in the press had charged. But it wasn't as solid as Dorfman and his friends claimed.

The true picture—the real answer to the bottom-line question of just how much damage Dorfman and his friends had done the Fund—was by no means clear.

However, one aspect of the question was clear. There was no doubt that the fund's notorious loan policies had severely shaken the confidence of many of the 450,000 Teamsters and their families who were either counting on the Fund for future pensions or already receiving them. One of the great benefits of pension programs is supposed to be the psychological burden they lift from workers who are nearing old age and would otherwise fear the future. For many who were depending on the Central States Pension Fund and who read the news stories about the Fund's bad loans and crooked management, that worry must have been renewed. There was the added torment of knowing that the money had been set aside for their old age, but that someone had taken it from them.

On the other hand, much of that trauma had come not from the real damage Dorfman had done but from the way the press had misstated or exaggerated it. The most basic error involved reports that failed to distinguish between the Central States fund and other Teamsters pension funds, thereby implying that all Teamsters member pensions were in trouble when, in fact, most weren't. Other, smaller funds, such as those based in Philadelphia and New Jersey and another serving a Long Island local, were the victims of highly questionable financial practices, but they were a minority. The other big mistake invariably involved a news account of a Central States pension applicant being denied his pension unjustly—which may have been true—but which went on to imply that such denials were the gangsters' way of making up for all the money they had taken from the Fund—which was not at all true.

In fact, the Central States fund had a record of approving 92.5 percent of all applications—a rate of approval higher than that of the Social Security system. If anything the Fund may have been negligent in approving too many applications. Until 1976 their records of exactly how long individual Teamsters had worked (and had had employers pay into the Fund for them) were sorely lacking, and the applicant's own records that he might use to substantiate his claims were usually worse. More often than not when the records were bad the Fund had simply given such applicants the benefit of the doubt and approved the pension. Frequent press references to a "maze of lawsuits" by rejected pension applicants were thus exaggerated; from 1972 through 1977 there had been fewer than one hundred such suits, even though by 1977 there were some 12,000 applications filed each year.

Articles about one celebrated victim of the pension fund's alleged plot to deny pensions never mentioned that he was a twice-convicted robber whose claim against the Fund was dismissed by a federal court. Fund records show that by 1977 the pension fund had paid out $1.4 billion in benefits to 123,000 Teamsters and their families and was currently mailing $21,000,000 a month to 74,000 pensioners. Also, record-keeping had finally been modernized, with a new system developed for handling applications efficiently and quickly.

In months of interviews I didn't find one Teamster in the Central States who knew someone who had had a pension application denied. Yet many still were worried because of what they had read in news articles.

Dorfman and company hadn't needed to deny pension applications: through the mid '70s more than enough money had built up and was still coming in from employer payments to pay the pensions easily. Fund records show that in December 1976 some $50,439,000 was paid by employers to the pension fund and the health and welfare fund, while approximately $33,500,000 was paid out in benefits by the two funds. The real problem was where the Fund would get the money in the next decade when the bad loans and poor investment management would, according to several experts at the Labor Department, finally start to throw the cash-flow projections out of whack.

This raises the fundamental question of just how many "bad" loans the Fund had made, and at what cost to the pensioners and future pensioners. The answer depended, in part, on how one defined a "bad" loan. A review of all the Fund's loans since 1957 indicates that if all the loans that went to people connected with organized crime were added up they would probably total about $600,000,000 of the approximately 1.2 billion the Fund had given out over the years in real-estate and other such loans. The exact amount will depend on how far you reach to connect a borrower to "organized crime."

This is a shocking estimate, yet it isn't in the long run relevant to the question of how much damage Dorfman and the others did the pensioners. It is arguable that everyone, not just pensioners, paid a high social cost for the Fund having put more than a half billion dollars into the hands of organized-crime operatives or those connected with them.

Whatever these costs to society were, if any, the more relevant truth was that the Fund's organized-crime loans often didn't cost the pensioners anything. For example, the La Costa loans to the Moe Dalitz group—thirty-one different loans totaling 97 million dollars, covering the spa, the country club, the condominiums, the shopping center, and other facilities—had, as of the end of 1977, all been paid regularly with interest. With La Costa's business going well there was every reason to believe that when those loans matured in the 1980s and 1990s they would be paid back on time. If not, the property and facilities behind the loan were clearly worth the money owed. In the 1970s, business was booming in Las Vegas. From 1966 to 1976 the gross wagering revenues in Nevada's casinos had tripled. As Nevada officials at least temporarily scared the Chicago mob away from its plot to skim Allen Glick's casinos to death, it seems possible that a good portion of the $240,000,000 that the fund was owed by Glick's and other Las Vegas casinos in 1977—an incredible 24 percent of the Fund's total loan portfolio—will be repaid, although in many cases at interest rates well below what should have been charged. Organized-crime loans were not necessarily "bad" loans.

Nor were loans made to friends or associates of Dorfman's or of top Teamster leaders necessarily "bad." Hoffa had arranged early on for a loan to a small company run by his daughter's father-in-law in St. Louis. The loan was paid back on time and in full.

To review all the loan files to determine with certainty which loans came by way of borrowers not mob-connected but nonetheless having some kind of an "in" with Hoffa, Dorfman or someone else at the Fund would be impossible; the files on the Fund's 900 loans would be more than 240 feet high if stacked, and in most cases they would not mention the "in." But a random check of ten seemingly non-organized-crime loans found seven (accounting for 75 percent of the money involved in the ten loans) for which there seemed to be a fairly obvious connection between lender and borrower. (In two cases the borrowers were direct relatives of a Teamsters vice-president or a Fund trustee; in a third case the borrower *was* a trustee.) If this 75 percent "connection" rate were to hold true for other non-organized-crime Fund loans—and Labor Department auditors agreed that it might—then this would mean that some $450,000,000 would have been lent that way. This would leave only $150,000,000 of the $1.2 billion lent out over the years being given to non-organized-crime borrowers who were not related to anyone of influence at the Fund—or only 12.5 percent of the loans being made in totally arms-length transactions.

As Dorfman pointed out, conventional bankers regularly lend money to friends and associates. "It's natural," he explained, "David Rockefeller does it, doesn't he? You think the Chase Manhattan Bank doesn't do what we do—lend money to people they know. Those are the people you have confidence in." On the other hand, it is difficult to believe that however strong the "old-boy" network at such banks really is that only 12.5 percent of the Chase Bank's loans, or of those of any other large bank, were made in arms-length transactions, while half went to organized-crime friends and another 37.5 percent to other friends or associates.

But, again, while those percentages say something about Dorfman's banking standards, they don't answer the question of how much was really lost to the pensioners by Dorfman's special brand of banking.

"You have to look at two numbers to get that answer," a source intimately involved with the Labor Department's loan-by-loan investigation of the Fund from 1975 to 1977, explained in late 1977. "The first number," he continued, had to do with "the money they lost by giving the mobsters and their other friends loans at interest rates lower than they should have been. The Fund's files had many loans that were given to high-risk borrowers at interest rates below the market rate for such risky construction loans and, in some cases, even below the "prime rate" given to the best credit risks. Glick's Las Vegas loans were given at a time when he was far from being a candidate for a prime rate. Hotels and casinos are especially risky, and Glick himself was a man with no real business record except the fact that he had actually fallen behind on his first Fund loans for his Texas office-building venture. Glick's $63,000,000 for Las Vegas was lent at 9 percent at a time when the prime rate was 11½ percent. Logic would dictate that Glick pay at least 2 percent above this prime rate, or 13½ percent (assuming that logic in some way qualified him for a loan at any rate). Similarly, the January 1974 $12,000,000 to the Bally slot machine corporation was made at 6½ percent at a time when the prime rate was over 9 percent.* Bally's own filing with the SEC reveals that in the year prior to these loans they would have had to pay rates well above the prime rates for millions of dollars on loans made through conventional banks.

"If you lend someone ten million dollars at a rate 4 percent below what you should," the same Labor Department aide explained, "you're giving him a $400,000 gift. And if the loan is for ten years, that's four million bucks . . . We estimate that at least—and I stress the words 'at least'—one hundred million dollars have been lost that way, either through low interest rates or, in other cases, through miscalculation or underpayment of the interest when on paper an appropriate interest was charged. . . . That's money down the drain. And it has nothing to do with the bad loans that weren't paid back. This was $100,000,000 lost on 'good' loans."

In addition to this $100,000,000 in lost interest money, there were the loans that had gone "bad." This was where the really big money had been lost. By the end of 1977, even rough estimates of these losses were difficult, but all the Labor Department people and others who had looked carefully at the Fund seemed to agree that the damage was such that this represented a potential time bomb for the Fund and its participants.

Their gloomy calculations worked this way: In 1977 the Fund by

* Pension fund officials explained the loan by noting that, as part of the transaction, the Fund was given an option to buy 25,000 shares of Bally stock. However, a Fund spokesman also noted that the option price then and since had been above the market price of the stock, and the option had not been exercised.

its own public estimates was said to have assets of $1.4 billion. This was said to be broken down into three categories: $400,000,000 in stocks, bonds and other securities; $100,000,000 in real estate owned and operated by the Fund because loans on these real-estate parcels had defaulted; and $900,000,000 in outstanding real-estate loans. The problem was that the paper estimates of the value of the two real-estate categories—the $900,000,000 in real-estate loans and the $100,000,000 in loans already foreclosed on—were worth nothing close to the $900,000,000 and $100,000,000 the Fund said they were. It is true that many of the Fund's bad loans had already been written off by then and were not included in these estimates. For example, the loans to the New Mexico rubber company that Dorfman, Irving Weiner, Spilotro and the others had allegedly milked had been written off, as had the $16,000,000 loan given to Glick for the Texas property he had bought with some football players just before floating his gigantic Las Vegas loans.

But these write-offs were, according to Labor Department investigators who had examined the Fund, just the top of the iceberg. Dozens, if not more, of the loans were listed at face value when, in fact, there was little hope that they would be paid back in full or that the property behind them was worth that much if the Fund had to foreclose. In many cases the Fund had delayed the write-offs by throwing good money after bad: when a loan was hopelessly overdue they would seize the property and then loan more money to someone else so that the new borrowers could take over the property and the old loan. (Glick had been given still another loan to do this with Beverly Ridge Estates in California.) When this happened both the old debt and the new debt were listed on the books as assets. In other cases the Fund had simply sat by, doing nothing, while the loans were not paid. For example, when the Valley Die Cast Corporation, an allegedly mob-connected company in Detroit, defaulted on a half million dollars in loans, the Fund made no move to collect from Valley's parent corporation, which had guaranteed the loan.

By 1977 it was impossible to tell just how much less than the claimed $1.4 billion the Fund's assets were really worth. Executive Director Shannon, while only conceding "possible write-downs," said it would take $10,000,000 just to appraise all the properties involved in the loans. In October of that year, when the Equitable Life Assurance Society took over management of all the Fund's assets, they began an appraisal. Seven months later it was still going on, with final assessments on all properties not expected until the fall of 1978. All that one of the people at Equitable involved in the appraisal would say with certainty was that the Fund's records were so bad—there was never even a real list of all the assets—and some of the loans were so unusual that the job was "like starting from scratch to reconstruct a bank's books after there had been a fire."

One such problem of evaluating the assets is illustrated by the $2,000,000 owed by one mob-connected borrower. The property backing the $2,000,000 loan consisted of two vacant lots worth $60,000 at most. Yet the borrower himself seemed wealthy and had been making regular payments. "Was the loan worth $2,000,000, $60,000, or something in between?" an appraiser wondered aloud in 1977. "If he keeps paying, it's a good loan. But if he stops—and he did that on another loan they gave him—what have we got?"

By the end of 1977 the new government-pressured Fund policy of ending its emphasis on real estate and shifting into conservative investments dictated that the Fund act to arrange faster payment of some of those $900,000,000 worth of real-estate loans. Since many of these loans were shaky and even many of the stronger ones called for big "balloon" payments at the end, getting the Fund's money back quickly was going to require substantial concessions on the interest or even the principal owed—if it was going to be possible at all.

"That's when the problem will begin to show," an investigator at the Labor Department said in late 1977. Although just how big "the problem" is remained to be seen, sources scattered in various government agencies and at the Fund seemed to agree that as a result of Equitable's investigation many of the real-estate assets tied up in Fund loans would have to be "written down" to reflect lower values, so that the Fund's billion dollars' worth of real-estate holdings ($900,000,000 in loans and $100,000,000 in foreclosed properties) would probably actually be worth at least $200,000,000 less than that.

"You look at that billion dollars [in supposed real estate] and you know it's a joke," one of the top government investigators explained. "There are loans listed that haven't paid interest or paid back any of the principal in years, and they're backed by worthless property or property that may be worth something but not the paper value of the debt." Also, there had been an additional $85,000,000 to $100,000,000 in loans already written off.* This yielded an estimated total loss of

* No one at the Fund could provide an exact count on the dollar value of write-offs through 1977.

at least $285,000,000 ($200,000,000 + $85,000,000) in real-estate loans. Even this gap could widen still more if, as feared, the mob-connected borrowers—like the man with the two vacant lots and the $2,000,000 loan—walked away from their loans once they realized the Fund had dried up as a loan source and there would be no point in keeping up the pretense of being a good credit risk.

Dorfman and others at the pension fund were quick to defend these losses (although they denied they were anywhere near that high) by citing the failures of various real-estate investment trusts ("REITs") run by the big banks. The REITs had, indeed, suffered disastrous losses in the middle '70s, with Chase Manhattan's (Dorfman's favorite whipping boy), for example, recording $330,000,000 in losses in 1976. The bank's REIT losses were probably proportionately less than the Fund's, but that isn't the point. The comparison isn't fair. By definition REIT investments are supposed to be risky; that's one reason why the banks segregate these investment activities from others. Pension funds are supposed to be just the opposite. They are intended to be conservative investors, providing a steady flow of income to supply certain payoff requirements in future years. The only fair comparison is one that stands the Central States fund up against other pension funds. In that contest Dorfman and other Fund defenders were unable to find any other pension fund that had invested even moderately in risky real-estate loans as compared to stocks and bonds, or had given loans with such disregard for interest rates, collateral, or the credit-worthiness of the borrowers.

If the estimated $100,000,000 minimum of losses due to low interest were added to the $285,000,000 lost from bad loans (loans that went bad or would go bad and had insufficient collateral behind them to pay the Fund back), the total would come to $385,000,000. Still, in 1977 the pensioners weren't feeling it. That will come later. In the ten years following 1977 a greater and greater percentage of Teamsters are scheduled to start getting pensions; the retirement rate will exceed the death rate of Teamsters then on pensions at a pace of nearly 1,000 a month. Equally important, the newly retired Teamsters will be entitled to at least $550 a month, whereas the ones who would be leaving the pension rolls (because of death) had received pensions based on earlier contracts, some as low as $90 a month. Pension fund plans, of course, are supposed to anticipate such trends; that's what actuaries are for. In fact, actuaries in this and other pension funds hadn't predicted the high rate of relatively early retirements in the

'70s, nor had they fully anticipated the national increase in life expectancy. This is why so many pension funds face severe fiscal problems in the next decade.

But at Central States such general mistakes weren't the real problem. The crunch would come not just because the actuaries had been wrong but also because the actuaries and the Fund planners had based the rate they set for the pensions ($550 a month) and the rate they set for employer payments to cover these pensions, on the assumption that the Fund would be drawing income at a certain rate of return from assets that totaled $1.4 billion dollars. If the assets were really worth much less, then the income from the assets would be that much less.

When Equitable finally arrives at its estimate of the Fund's assets, the Fund will have to cut back on the pensions paid or increase employer contribution so much in new contracts that employers will limit wage increases or impose wage freezes. "When Equitable comes out with their estimates," a former top Labor Department official predicted in late 1977, "that's when everyone is going to have to sit down and say 'we can't keep paying $550 a month or we'll be broke in five years,' or six years, or whatever. Or they'll have to make the members themselves pay into the Fund or somehow get the employers to pay more just to keep the benefits at the same level. And remember, keeping the benefits at the same level isn't even that good because of inflation." If such adjustments in pension payments or money paid in aren't made to fill the gap between assets on paper and real assets yielding money, the fund will be broke by sometime in the late 1980s or early '90s.

This is Allen Dorfman's legacy to the Teamsters in the twenty-two states where the Central States fund is the primary pension fund: their money, a capital source that matched or exceeded the funding power of all but the very largest banks in the country, has been used as venture capital for organized crime. They have probably lost at least $100,000,000 in undercharges for interest and $285,000,000 in bad loans, and they face stagnation or cutbacks in their pensions or a bankrupt Fund.

In the latter half of 1977, when the people from Equitable began examining the Fund's real-estate loans, they noticed another Dorfman racket. It had never received government or press scrutiny, though it had probably netted Dorfman hundreds of thousands, if not millions, of dollars. Most of the time, whenever a property had a

Fund loan it also used a Dorfman insurance agency to obtain its liability and casualty insurance. "It looks like it was an unwritten rule," one of the Equitable assets managers explained in early 1978, "that when you got a loan from the Fund you bought insurance for your property from Allen Dorfman."

As Dorfman teed off for the Eighth Annual Fitzsimmons Invitational on October 12, 1977, lawyers at the Justice Department were poring over a Labor Department memo that listed, as one investigator put it, "the seventy-or-so most obviously crooked loans." They were trying to determine which of these loans might call for civil prosecution for violation of ERISA's requirement that the trustees act with "reasonable prudence" and which might call for criminal prosecution for fraud or embezzlement. They said that they had made no promises not to pursue such cases when they had gotten the old trustees to resign in 1977 and turn the assets over to Equitable, and that they were eager to go ahead. But their prospects for successfully prosecuting these cases were not good; the failure of the case against Dorfman, Spilotro, and the others for allegedly embezzling money from that loan to the New Mexico pail company had shown the pitfalls involved in these kinds of cases, especially if they were brought as criminal rather than civil charges. Some of the loans might make good ERISA prosecutions. However, since most of the bad loans had been made before ERISA was passed in 1974, it seemed unlikely that the law could be used to recover much of the losses from the trustees who had authorized the loans. Besides, it is difficult to imagine a court making the trustees personally pay back the millions of dollars lost on bad loans that might have been made after ERISA took effect. (ERISA provided for personal repayment either by the trustees or by whatever insurance company, if any, had insured them against such claims.)

Labor Department officials in interviews in late 1977 expressed satisfaction with the way they had been able to use ERISA, not because they expected to recover the Fund's massive losses but because they had used the new law to take control of the Fund's assets so that the pensioners wouldn't suffer more losses. "The real story here," explained Assistant Labor Secretary Francis Burkhardt in November 1977, "is not that we'll recover some money, though we may. It's that, rather than sit around and wait for criminal prosecutions to take some of the crooks out of the picture so new ones could take their place, we've taken the money away from all the crooks by taking control of the Fund away from them. That's what's important.''

Nonetheless, on February 1, 1978, the Labor Department did file a civil suit against those who had been trustees of the Fund since ERISA, charging them with failure to exercise their fiduciary responsibilities in making fifteen different post-ERISA loans. Among the imprudent loans alleged was the $30,000,000 debenture from a subsidiary of the Hyatt Corporation for the Four Queens Hotel-Casino in Las Vegas and the $2,200,000 loans to Meyer Lansky's associate Alvin Malnik. The suit charged that the Hyatt debenture was undersecured and that the Fund had agreed to modify Malnik's loan obligation after giving him the money. Other transactions listed included the failure to enforce the Valley Die Cast Corporation loans, failure to assure that a $25,000,000 construction loan to Glick's Argent Corporation was actually used for construction, and the payment to Baron of a ''large sum of money in the nature of a gratuity'' when he left the Fund. The suit was expected to take years to be decided and was not likely in any event to produce payment of substantial damages by the defendants. It was more probably part of a government effort to pressure Fitzsimmons into resigning, to make the Labor Department look diligent, and to pressure Shannon, who was named in the suit, to testify against the trustees in criminal prosecutions.

Dorfman was not named in the ERISA action since technically he hadn't been connected with the Fund's loan decisions after ERISA was passed. But he had been hurt when control of the Fund's assets was given over to Equitable. That meant his loan racket was over. Also, properties holding Fund loans would no longer be allowed to buy casualty and liability insurance from Dorfman's agencies if that insurance did not meet Equitable's standards of adequate coverage. As one observer privy to Equitable's dealings with the Fund predicted, ''You can bet that in most cases, if not all, Equitable's going to tell them [the Fund trustees] that Dorfman's coverage is no good and they have to go to a legitimate agent.''

A likely candidate to take the place of the loan and insurance incomes as profit centers for Dorfman and others is the Central States health and welfare fund and other Teamsters health and welfare funds. ''Managing health and welfare funds could be the new thing,'' a top Chicago organized-crime prosecutor predicted in 1977. ''It's not like a pension fund, where an actuary or the government under ERISA says 'the money is running out; there must be something wrong.' With health and welfare funds you just raise the rates and you make your payoffs through consultant's fees on fraudulent claims." With the Central States health and welfare fund paying out by 1977 more than $12,000,000 a month in health and welfare claims through a claim management agency owned by Dorfman, such opportunities were obviously there; a one-percent leakage would be $120,000 a month from that fund alone. Prepaid legal service programs, just beginning to become a Teamsters fringe benefit in some areas, are another equally possible growth area for Dorfman and others at the top of the Teamsters–organized-crime hierarchy.

By October 1977, Dorfman, for all his daily contacts with Fitzsimmons and Vice-President Roy Williams, thought to be Fitzsimmons' possible successor, hadn't yet been able to get his Central States health and welfare claims processing contract renewed, because of the pressure from the press and the government to keep him out. True, the trustees had voted to renew it in May. But then a few days later they backed down when the Labor Department, spurred by this new trustee embrace of Dorfman, began a massive investigation of the health and welfare fund and Dorfman's role in it. By February 1978 they had allowed Dorfman to exercise his option to keep the contract going for another year. (Legally, they probably had no choice under the terms of the old contract.) However, he was probably not going to get a new contract in 1979, and it seemed likely that if the Teamsters were going to pull off any new schemes with health-and-welfare or legal-service funds they would do it without the notorious Dorfman as their front.

The trustees' reversal on the health-and-welfare-fund contract was Dorfman's real distraction as he set out, that morning of October 14, 1977, at La Costa, to beat the others on the golf course the way he usually did. It so rankled him that in a telephone interview the week before the tournament he refused even to acknowledge the problem. In an uncharacteristically stammering voice he claimed, quietly, that the trustees "haven't backed down at all. They've given me the ten-year renewal [on the health and welfare contract], signed, sealed and delivered." It wasn't true. Dorfman's name was a lightning rod for bad press and government heat. The trustees, other top Teamsters, the mobsters, and Dorfman himself, all knew it. Dorfman, of course, was willing to take the heat the way he always had taken it. The others weren't. They didn't need the extra luggage his name now carried.

As 1978 began there was talk among highly placed Teamsters that the new trustees planned to renege on the agreement with the Labor Department and take control of the assets back from Equitable. Signaling their new, defiant attitude, in April they summarily fired Shannon, agreeing to pay him a year's severance on the written condition that during that time he would not talk to anyone in the press or to any government investigator unless he was subpoenaed. Soon thereafter the two actuarial companies that Shannon had hired to calculate new, honest cash-flow projections were dismissed, and a friend of old trustee Roy Williams was hired as a replacement for Shannon as Fund administrator. Dorfman, a close Williams ally, reportedly was behind these moves. Yet it was unlikely that he personally was going to be able to benefit from them, even assuming that the government would sit by idly while the Fund tried to shift back to the old days.

Dorfman was going to have to step aside, at least for a while, and maybe forever. He had enough money to survive it. A brief that his lawyers filed two weeks before the Tournament to protest the Labor Department's massive subpoena of his health-and-welfare-fund files conceded that 85 percent of the claims business of his Amalgamated Insurance Company was related to the Fund. But his other insurance agencies were still making generous commissions selling liability insurance to trucking companies, another profit center of the Dorfman-Teamsters partnership. How much of this and other income he had to share with organized-crime allies isn't clear, but his share definitely left him quite comfortable. Still, lying low just isn't his style. He likes to fight it out with loud, out-front protestations of innocence and, when necessary, with equally indignant courtroom defenses.

Besides, what would happen when he was no longer useful to the mob bosses he had served so well?

CHAPTER VII

Al Barkett

Records at the CCC Trucking Company in Cleveland, Ohio, show that on the October day in 1976 that former CCC driver Frank Fitzsimmons teed off at La Costa, Alfred Barkett * hauled ten tons of auto parts in a CCC tractor trailer between Cleveland and Cincinnati. He earned $115 for the 484-mile trip.

Barkett is not a typical Teamster. In a union of 2,300,000 men and women working at hundreds of different jobs, there isn't one. Nor could a reporter, after scores of interviews, identify the "typical trucker" among the 450,000 drivers and warehousemen. Some are politically conservative, others are liberal; some are happily married, others are divorced; some are loners, others never miss a union picnic or bowling night; some are CB-radio freaks, others, like Barkett, hate CB's; some are heavy drinkers, others are teetotalers. Most are white (about 90 percent) but they come from a variety of ethnic and religious backgrounds.

Barkett isn't exceptional either. His name was among those that

*Alfred Barkett's name and some minor family details have been changed to protect his privacy.

turned up when Jackie Presser, who had taken over public relations, asked several locals to supply a list of Teamsters who represented the life style, work, and attitude toward the union of the "average" truck driver. My conversations with hundreds of rank-and-filers confirmed the choice. Presser, as he had promised, seems not to have screened his selection on the basis of how he expected the candidate to answer questions.

Barkett's company was also as representative as any in an industry characterized by immense diversity. CCC, the Cleveland, Columbus and Cincinnati Highway Company, Inc., ranked 100th among the 17,000 trucking companies in the United States with gross revenues of $21,000,000 in 1976. It owned 17 terminals, more than 1,000 pieces of trucking equipment, and employed 600 people in Illinois, Indiana, Kentucky, Michigan, Ohio and West Virginia. It was a good solid company.

On June 7, 1977, Al Barkett drove a round-trip run between Cleveland and Columbus. The short trip, 250 miles compared to the 400 miles he and the other over-the-road drivers averaged daily was planned so that I could ride with him and be back by six the next morning to ride with a local delivery driver.

The CCC Cleveland terminal, where we started out that evening, was in an area of abandoned lots on the edge of the black ghetto. About twenty-five soot-covered trailers, some with tractors hooked on in front, were scattered around the parking lot inside a fence. Another twenty or thirty trailers were backed against the terminal building, in their own loading bays.

CCC Operations Vice-President Charles Hassing, a husky former driver who had started at CCC thirty-one years before, explained that CCC's major business was shipping auto parts—"Hang around here for twenty-four hours," he said, "and you could have all the parts you need, except the actual body frame, to assemble a car." Inside the terminal among cartons of mouth wash, loose-leaf binders, glue, bread stuffing and aspirin, were steering columns, transmissions, windshield-wiper motors, and just about everything it would take to put a car together.

Al Barkett wore narrow jeans, a blue shirt and heavy work shoes. He grinned easily and shook hands sturdily with his guest rider. He is a bigger-than-average man, though not eye-catching in width or length the way many other truckers are. He looked about 6 foot 2, and 200 pounds, with big hands, lean legs and medium-broad shoulders. A slight bulge over his belt made him look like a forty-year-old in excellent but now-softening shape. Only above the neck did he look his real age, fifty-seven. He had white hair and a gray-black mustache.

Barkett did not have a nice office. The inside of the tractor—the "cab"—was lined along the doors, the seats, and the dashboard in brown vinyl. It was thin, cheap, hard vinyl, and although the tractor was only three years old it had a dozen or so tears. Three years of Ohio highways had given it a smoky-gray dullness. The floor was just the floor. The 1974 assembly line hadn't bothered to put anything over the steel except a small rubber mat, where Barkett's feet were parked all night.

What the newcomer to Barkett's cockpit noticed more than anything else was the noise. At first you assumed it had to do with bringing the truck up to speed as it left the lot. But for the next eight hours it stayed about the same, except for a groan just before each upshift.

"Oh, you'll get used to that," Barkett predicted cheerfully, and inaccurately. Five minutes out of the CCC lot, he ground the gears upward in preparation for an entrance onto the interstate. In 4,000 pounds and 15 feet of car, this would have been just another city ramp. In Al Barkett's truck, this and every other stretch of road was something special. It had bumps, turns, inclines, a texture and character, which the truck faithfully reported. You felt the motor pull to make up for an incline so slight that a car would coast effortlessly over it. You noticed the winding paths of the ramp, because you could look out the window and see the tail end of the trailer folded up almost alongside you.

Barkett's was the best, most modern equipment around. Still, the rig was the size of an average studio apartment and often weighed as much as 80,000 pounds—or 25 medium-sized cars. No one has figured out how to build equipment to pull such a load without making every hill an event and every turn a maneuver. To qualify to pilot this cargo, Barkett explained, tractor-trailer drivers "needed four years' driving a straight job (a truck that's one vehicle, not a tractor and trailer) or had to go to a driver's school for four months learning how to move these things."

Some people, like Richard Nixon, speak in a tone that says they calculate every word. Others as if it's an obligation or a nuisance, like waiters at expensive French restaurants. Some talk as if it's fun to get the words out. Over the steel drone of the engine and later, when we left the truck, Barkett's voice was resonant. He sounded a bit like Jason Robards. But he wasn't stern, and the potential growl was smoothed with a happy lightness. It was as if talking put him in a good mood.

"I wish we had a better seat for you," he volunteered as we rode on to I-76. He coughed then spat out the window, just missing his oversized side-view mirror. "Mine, over here, is adjustable and it's an air-ride. That's required in the[union] contract. . . . My back has stayed pretty good over the years because of seats like this. Some pains once in a while, but, you know, nothing serious like a lot of guys get. And none of those sores on your ass, either. . . . Your seat, though, that's for shit. But, you know, you're usually not allowed to have anyone ride with you in the cab anyway. So the company figures, what the hell."

"These lading slips here will tell you what we're carrying," he explained, first reaching for an empty shirt pocket, then flipping through some papers off to his right in the dusty gap between the two seats. Tonight's load was twenty-five packages of "Host Favorite" bread stuffing, one carton of General Motors fender bolts, seven cartons of auto air-conditioning condensers, ninety-five cartons of copper tubing, eight cartons of steel screws, and a hundred packages of "Frosty Acres" bread stuffing. It weighed a total of 14,500 pounds. This was a light load; more often than not, Barkett and the other CCC over-the-road drivers carried 80,000 pounds, the maximum allowed on interstate highways.

Barkett's job tonight was to drive to the Columbus, Ohio, terminal, one of fourteen CCC way stations in Ohio.

"This is really a nothing trip," he explained. "I like the ones to Cincinnati or Chicago much better. On those, I make much more money. You see, you get paid by the mile, plus for the time you spend waiting at the terminal."

"But don't you get bored driving that far?"

"No. I mean, sure it's tedious. But you get used to it. It's better than sitting at an assembly line or in a freight yard. I like it. I like to get out of town and just go. At the end of the day at least I feel like I've done something. I mean, I'll know I moved all that shit back there from Cleveland down to Columbus. That's more than the dispatcher or some guy filing papers can tell himself."

What Barkett didn't like about the job was the schedule.

"The worst part is the hours. It's not that it's at night. I don't mind that. I've been driving at night since 1948. It's that I never know what time I'm going to have to start or what time I'll finish." As Barkett explained, fifteen years before there had been an arrangement by which the CCC drivers picked a particular "run" (say Cleveland to Cincinnati at 7 P.M.), and it was theirs every day as long as they wanted it. The choices were awarded in order of seniority. But in 1962 at the union's request, the setup was changed. Now the men get to pick, or "bid on," their runs each night. A majority of the men had wanted this because "they're greedy. This way they can pick the best run every night. Under the old system if, let's say, they had an extra run to Cincinnati but you were signed up for the run to Wheeling [West Virginia, a relatively short trip] you couldn't take it. The guys who had signed up to take all the extra runs would get it. Now, each night you can jockey around for the best runs out there based on your seniority. The greedy guys, and that's most of them, love it. The company loves it, too, because they get all that flexibility. I mean, they can assign runs day by day and pick the hours they want you to leave. . . . Before, it was like a regular job where you knew what your hours were. I used to go to work at nine every night. I knew when to get up and when to sleep. Now, it's for the bullshit. . . . Now, I have to start work usually anywhere from seven at night to two in the morning. I get one of the first picks because of my seniority, but I still have to get up and answer the phone anytime from four on, to pick a trip."

According to operations manager Hassing, at one time many companies, including his, had run "sleeper teams" of two drivers. One would drive for ten hours and then go into a small compartment in the back of the cab just behind the seats to sleep while his partner continued. Or, a driver driving alone would pull over after ten hours and go into the compartment or go to a motel that specialized in truck-driver layovers. Now, at CCC, Hassing had said, there were no two-driver teams and "95 percent of our drivers are back home every night. Our men really appreciate it." In other companies, which specialize in longer runs or coast-to-coast trips, it is still not unusual for men to be gone a week at a time. The Teamsters union contract has mandated that truck motels be radically improved over the barracks the companies used to pay for them to stay in. By 1977, most of the thousands of trucks out on the road with sleeping compartments—

you can tell them by the small window visible behind the driver's seat and the extra length of the cab—were used by independent truckers anxious to keep the costs of their one-man operations at a minimum by avoiding motel bills. Such independent drivers were known to make produce runs from California to New York in as little as seventy-two hours, a pace that gave them only a few hours in the sleeping compartment each night, and which should have given other drivers on the road more than enough reason to be afraid of a truck with a pilot asleep at the wheel plowing into them.

Although he liked to "get up and go" and didn't like local day work, Barkett was now eying a new assignment.

"I have to tell you, I've been thinking about moving into the warehouse. I've been debating between that and the road job. It pays the same, but there's no responsibility. I mean here you can have an accident or fall asleep or be late getting to your stop. Plus the hours are for shit. There you have none of that. Plus, now with the pallets and tow motors and the lifts, there's no lifting to be done. I mean, there isn't any job in America that's tough any more physically, including that one. No one in this country lifts more than fifty pounds of anything anymore." Pallets are the wooden trays under which any heavy cargo is loaded. They are made so that forklifts can slide into their grooves and lift the entire package. Since the trucks are backed against the docks at a warehouse, the forklift simply lifts the pallet, drives it onto the truck and lets it down.

The odometer on Barkett's tractor read 206,810 miles. "Oh don't go by that," he warned. "It doesn't register a lot." He guessed that he and the other CCC over-the-road drivers averaged 400 miles a day. Teamsters union Research Director Norman Weintraub also estimated that most drivers averaged 400 miles each work day and nearly 100,000 a year. A check of CCC's 1976 report filed with the Interstate Commerce Commission revealed that the company had logged 9,080,267 over-the-road miles that year using 98 drivers who drove an average 92,656 miles.

According to Barkett, "Before they had all those interstate highways and these good motors, I'll bet you we averaged half that mileage even though we worked longer hours." Based on that estimate, over fifteen years Barkett had driven the equivalent of around the world at the equator more than 84 times.

Over those miles, Barkett had two "chargeable" accidents and three "fender benders" that were not chargeable. A chargeable accident is one judged by the company to have been at least in part the driver's fault. The driver could be disciplined or dismissed for such an accident (following a hearing before a joint union-management grievance committee). Barkett's first chargeable accident had come fifteen years ago—"I came down into a curve on an icy road that hadn't been salted and went right into the guard rail. I was pretty badly banged up in my head and back. Had to stay out of work about two months." The second one had been seven years ago. "A car stopped short in front of me and I hit him pretty bad. No one was hurt, though."

Among Teamsters, Barkett's relatively spotless record for twenty-nine years of driving is not unusual. In fact, thousands of drivers had better safety records; every month the Teamsters' magazine shows a few of them getting awards for twenty-five years of driving with no chargeable accidents. On the other hand, executives at any trucking company, many of which, like CCC, were self-insured, could tell stories about the notoriously inept, or drunk or drugged drivers they had had to contend with. What they didn't mention was that many such driver problems, especially drug abuse, were caused by the companies pushing them to go too far or too many hours without a break.

Whatever the infrequency of Teamsters accidents compared to the mileage they drove, the toll adds up. Federal highway records showed that tractor-trailers in 1976 comprised less than 1 percent of all vehicles on the road, but accounted for 8.9 percent of all fatal accidents. The problem was getting worse: while all fatal accidents increased only 1.2 percent from 1975 to 1976, those involving tractor-trailers rose 16.8 percent.

"We used to have regular safety meetings at the company each year," Barkett recalled. "It was kind of a banquet where they'd give awards to the drivers who'd had no accidents that year. Not any more though. Now they just expect you to do it. . . . Times have changed. They don't have those kinds of functions any more. They just expect the men to go out and do the job, take their checks and go home."

He thought CCC "is a real good company. Their equipment is real good, and they don't cheat on tires or things like that. . . . We've all got shatter-proof glass now, and the air brakes are real good too," he added, pointing toward the dashboard and a gadget that served as a back-up to his conventional pedal brakes.

A later check revealed that although the shatter-proof glass and the air brakes were required by law, CCC's over-all equipment program is discretionary and is quite good. CCC trades in its trailers every six years and its tractors every four years, a refurbishing practice that is not wholly unique but also not universal.

CCC has never run in the red. However, the $826,000 profit recorded in 1976—less than 4 percent of operating revenue—showed that equipment-replacement decisions or any other expenditures in this business could not be made casually. Indeed, the close-to-the-line nature of the industry makes it as tough a business from behind an executive desk as it was from behind a steering wheel. By the end of 1976 new tractor-trailers like Barkett's cost an average of about $40,000. The price had increased more than 50 percent since 1972, a period during which new car prices had increased about 30 percent. To make matters worse, diesel-fuel bills (to the tune of four to five miles per gallon) had skyrocketed; and by 1976 the industry's labor costs under the new Teamsters National Master Freight Agreement exceeded 60 percent of all its expenditures.

CCC is a "common carrier." These are companies licensed by the Interstate Commerce Commission (ICC) to haul customers' freight at rates based on distance and weight and space taken up by the cargo. A second category of trucks out there with Barkett that night were "private carriers," trucks owned by companies that existed primarily for a purpose other than shipping merchandise. A Sears truck bringing goods from a Sears warehouse to a Sears store is a private carrier. Drivers for private carriers are often not Teamsters, but part of the union represents the company's other employees. A third group are the trucks driven by owner-operators. These are individual entrepreneurs—estimated at about 100,000 in 1976—who lease or own their own trucks and are not Teamsters. There are two kinds of owner-operators. The first, often called gypsies, carry goods, such as unprocessed food, vegetables, fruits, or lumber, whose shipment has never been regulated by the ICC. The other owner-operators are those who had leased themselves out to an ICC-licensed common carrier. These drivers are often found hauling steel and other heavy materials.

Common carriers like CCC are further divided according to the routes that the ICC has licensed them to cover or on whether they are specially licensed to haul commodities such as heavy machinery, new cars, oil or chemicals.

All licensed-carrier companies are required to submit their rates to the ICC for approval. Rates are normally the same among companies, unless a company files with the ICC for a special exception. Thus, competition comes not in costs but in the service each company offers, such as convenient location, pickups, fast delivery and dependability. It was for this reason that Barkett and all the other over-the-road drivers at CCC drove only at night; CCC's customers generally want overnight deliveries. Such service competition is so fierce that the five largest common-carrier companies together— United Parcel Service, Roadway Express, Consolidated Freight-ways, Yellow Freight System, and McClean Trucking—had less than 10 percent of the total industry revenues in 1976.

Though there were several hundred thousand Teamsters members working in 1977 for common carriers like CCC, only a small minority were "typical" long-distance over-the-road truck drivers like Barkett. Most worked in the terminals and warehouses loading freight, or drove the "city" trucks that picked up or delivered merchandise locally. Usually, the city trucks were "straight jobs," that is, trucks that were body on chassis, not detachable tractor and trailer. About 80,000 Teamsters working for common carriers drove big tractor-trailers "over the road" as Barkett did that night. There were probably another 100,000 Teamsters who drove over the road for private carriers or who drove automobile carriers or other special long-distance equipment.

"This company's very strict," Barkett continued. "They watch us carefully. I mean, you see lots of guys at the [truck] stops who've been drinking or taking pills. But not any CCC guys, or for that matter any U.S. Truck Lines guys. [CCC is a subsidiary of United States Truck Lines, which owns several trucking companies]. The company won't stand for that kind of shit.

"And [operations manager] Hassing is a good guy. I've seen him work his way up from the bottom, and all along the way, even where he is now—you know, the big boss and everything—he hasn't forgotten how to be a human being."

A minute later Barkett changed his tune. "But I'll tell you one thing, they've really put the pressure on us. I mean, they usually won't let us make a short run like this one [to Columbus from Cleveland], because they want to squeeze more out of us. You see, they'd rather have two guys doing three guys' work and pay them overtime in order to avoid paying the extra fifty dollars a week in pension benefits."

The Teamsters contract called for a payment, actually of $55, from the employer to the pension fund and the health and welfare fund for each full-time employee. The amount of the contribution was the same for each employee no matter how much mileage or overtime he logged.

"They just keep squeezing and squeezing. It's good for the greedy guys, I guess. But it's bad if you want to only work a certain amount each day. It's also a little dangerous, too. I mean, you can get tired out there if you're logging ten hours night after night.

"You see, that's the catch to all the equipment being better. Years ago I didn't have any windshield wipers, OK? But I didn't *need* them, because if it rained, I could pull over and park. Now you can't park. The name of the game today is hurry up, hurry up. It's the same thing with seats. The contract gives me an air ride seat. But years ago I didn't *need* that seat because I could pull over and get out and take a walk. Today it's hurry up. I guess I don't blame them with the equipment and gas costing so much. But it's lousy . . . Plus they expect you to go much further because of all the highways. So my job is tougher than it was in '55 or '65."

Other interviews revealed a difference in attitudes among Teamsters. Many drivers young and old, shared Barkett's resentment about the long hours and the hurry-up ethic. But others, probably a majority, seemed to welcome the action and the extra money. One issue of the Teamsters magazine reported in 1977 that Teamsters Safety and Health Department director R. V. Durham "acknowledged [that] driving ten-hour runs . . . the maximum time allowed by DOT [The U.S. Department of Transportation] on a single run—has taken its toll on the health of drivers. Durham said they have a higher-than-average incidence of hemorrhoids and prostate trouble. But, he added, although some guys say they want an eight-hour day and time-and-a-half after 40 hours, that's not the type of job in the trucking industry. Most drivers want to work 10 hours and I try to stay in tune with what the vast majority of our members want."

Durham noted in the same article that changing the ten-hour rule to eight hours would "cause mass relocations of terminals because all runs are geared to ten hours." He did, however, point to a work-hours problem not felt by Barkett but mentioned by many other Teamsters: "It's more important that there be more time off between trips . . . DOT rules now require a minimum of eight hours between trips. But . . . it can take a driver a couple of hours to check out of the yard before going home to get some rest." Another problem had to do with the concept of "on duty" time. A driver could be on duty for fifteen hours at a stretch under DOT rules and the union contract, although he could only be driving 10 of those hours—that is, he could be in the warehouse, waiting for a load or checking it in, for five hours. Moreover, any breaks he took during work, such as rest stops on the road, did not count as on-duty time. A driver taking frequent work breaks could be at work for more than fifteen hours at a stretch.

The International union's Safety and Health Department was established in 1973 to address such problems. According to several Teamsters vice-presidents and trucking-company executives, its creation was the result of the pressure PROD had put on the Teamsters by raising safety and health issues the union had ignored. The union's lapse was especially critical, since the government had taken no initiative to push their causes. Federal law provided that all safety and health rules regarding truck driving were the province of the Department of Transportation, and not the Labor Department's Occupational Safety and Health Administration (OSHA). Over the years, the DOT had proved to be drastically understaffed and underfunded, not to mention weak-willed.

Although by 1977 the Teamsters Safety and Health Department was still no model of effective advocacy in these areas, it had, in the words of one top trucking executive, become "fairly aggressive in raising these issues." Also in 1976, Fitzsimmons had won agreement in the contract for a standing union-management health and safety committee to consider those questions and resolve them through a grievance system. By 1977, the union's Safety and Health Department and this joint committee were involved in studies or negotiation having to do with noise, hemorrhoids, carbon-monoxide dangers, and the maneuverability and shock-absorption problems related to where axles and wheels on the tractors and trailers were mounted.

Barkett answered a question about safety by noting that "A lot of these safety issues are bullshit. Some guys complain too much. . . . The union does a pretty good job on this."

Our talk shifted to what he thought more generally about the union. He began tentatively: "I'm sitting here driving this truck for twenty-nine years and raising a family, and there are all kinds of forces out there in the union that I know nothing about. That much I know . . . I mean, there are probably gangsters involved and all kinds of things. With everything you read in the papers, some of it has to be true

. . . but the way I look at it, they [the union leaders] have a bad name with the public for a number of reasons. Some are valid and some aren't. I mean, they're no better or worse than the steelworkers or the stockholders at General Electric. You know, every president of every company steals. It's just a matter of the public's impressions. And I'll tell you something else. I'm a lot better off because of that union, and I know it. No number of news articles can change that. I know that nonunion drivers do a lot worse, and our grievance procedure is real fair. The leaders have been good to us. They've brought us a long way as far as benefits are concerned. . . . Sometimes I think the officials are shit. . . . But the PROD officials might be worse. Here, I know what I have."

Barkett spent the next fifty miles trying out different ways of expressing his attitude about his union and its leaders. They were rule-benders (or perhaps sometimes lawbreakers) in a rule-benders and lawbreakers' world; their misdeeds had perhaps been exaggerated but not invented by the press; and when all the plusses and minuses were added up, they had definitely helped the members more than they had hurt them. It was a view echoed by most other Teamsters whom I talked with in 1976 and 1977. Yet Barkett seemed self-conscious about it. Finally, after about an hour, he added an extra ingredient. It was a feeling that would be expressed in one form or another by most men I interviewed, and it suggested the trouble Frank Fitzsimmons would have had if he had been required to be elected directly by the rank and file instead of by delegates at a convention.

"I'll tell you my impression of Fitzsimmons and those guys and what they stand for. I don't like Fitzsimmons. I mean, he's for the bullshit. Playing golf with Nixon and living up there [at La Costa] in that big house with the plane and that car. He's gone too political. I mean he doesn't care a shit about me and the guys pushing these trucks. Sure we get good contracts. I mean the man himself really doesn't care. If he did we'd get better contracts and better hours. . . . I'll tell you this: I felt just the opposite about Jimmy Hoffa. I'd rather have Hoffa than the whole bunch of people they have now. They're all for the bullshit. Hoffa was for me. I met Hoffa once. He was tough-talking. And he was out there for the rank and file. But these guys, they've all gone too political."

"What does 'going political' mean?"

"Oh you know. Jockeying around for the best jobs. Looking to kiss asses and play up to people to get more money . . .

"When I heard Hoffa was missing, it didn't surprise me. It's part of what I said about all those forces out there that I don't know anything about. I figured he was trying to come back, and all those guys he used to deal with just didn't want him back. That's what the papers said . . . When I heard the news, I just figured that dirty S.O.B. at the top is tied to the Mafia something fierce. I'll tell you this: if it can happen to Hoffa, it can happen to anyone, so you have to be careful. That much even I know just sitting here in this truck for twenty-nine years."

Soon the topic shifted to the union leadership in Ohio and to Barkett's local union, Local 407:

"Well Jackie Presser [Ohio Teamsters leader and International vice-president] is trying to change the image of the union, and I think that's a real good thing to do." Barkett chuckled then grinned, his eyes lighting up as he turned to his passenger. "You know, everyone in this country thinks all our officials are crooks and that every one of us drivers has a bottle of booze and a whore up here in the cab and that we're going to go ninety miles an hour to run you off the road. So changing the image is OK with me. But Presser and the others are so goddamn political. They don't care about me. Fitzsimmons, Presser and the rest of them are so far removed as far as being one of us is concerned. Presser is so far removed from my backache here in this truck.

"And everything is dictated from Washington, anyway. Presser might be OK, but he takes his orders from Washington. There's no local freedom. I'm a shop steward, so I go to all the local meetings, OK? But if I get up at a meeting to say something, they don't want to hear me. They tell me to sit down. Everything is so political. It took us two years to get one sentence in the local by-laws changed about how often we hold elections. Every time one of us raised it from the floor, they [the officers of Local 407] said We'll check into it and we'll let you know. That's because they had to go back to their bosses, the Pressers [Jackie and his father, William], who had to go to their bosses in Washington. Isn't that something?"

"What about your pension? Do you worry about how they've handled your retirement money?" (Barkett's pension money is in the Central States Pension Fund.)

"Well, I have to admit I've worried a lot about it. It's like every day there's another article in the papers about how they've given money to some Las Vegas gangster or something. All of us see that stuff and talk about it. Yes, I worry about whether the money will be there when I need it. You know they put in $55.50 a week for me.'' Actually the employer's weekly payment for each employee was $28.00 for the pension, plus $27.50 for health and welfare benefits including health and life insurance. ''And you like to know it's all staying there.''

''Have any of your friends or other guys around the terminal who've retired recently had any trouble collecting?''

''Well, that's the thing. I know lots of guys who've retired and I've got friends who know lots more. And all of them have collected with no problems whatsoever. Really, no problems at all. Also, I got a brochure a few months back signed by that football star they hired to run the Pension Fund. What's his name, Shannon? Well, I wrote a letter to them asking six questions about the brochure. And I heard from them within two weeks and got a really satisfactory answer. So, that makes me feel better. I just hope the money holds out. That's all.''

A check of Central States Pension Fund records showed that retired members of Barkett's Local 407 had received 36 million dollars in pension payments since 1957, and that on the night in June that Barkett pulled his rig from Cleveland to Columbus and back there were 1,622 retired Local 407 members receiving pensions. No retired 407 member had had an application for pensions rejected in the previous six months.

Interstate 71 runs two lanes on each side. As we talked, Barkett spent just about all of his time in the southward right lane. He averaged about 55 m.p.h., often slowing to 35 when climbing a hill and never exceeding 65. When other trucks—lighter in load, more powerful under the hood, or pulled by a heavier foot on the accelerator—passed him, he'd belch the air horn. The passer would honk back, then put his right blinker on. Seconds later Barkett would flash his lights on. ''That's to tell him he's far enough ahead so that it's clear for him to come back into the right lane ahead of me.''

None of this happened when passenger cars passed. They seemed to be on a different track altogether. From high up in the cab, they were like mice scurrying past a helpless clumsy giant. To someone watching them from the right lane, their freedom of speed and maneuverability was something to envy.

Until the Teamsters became a force to be reckoned with, Al Barkett and his fellow truckers had lived in the right lane of the American economy. In the 1930s and '40s and into the '50s, truck driving was sweatshop labor on wheels. A 1938 contract found in the archives at the Teamsters' headquarters, an eight-page document (Barkett's 1977 version was 159 pages) covering eighteen trucking companies in Barkett's area, contained no mention of limits on hours worked or the type of equipment to be used. There were no paid vacation, no paid holidays, no paid sick days, no insurance, no pension. The basic wage rate was 60¢ an hour, or 2.75¢ per mile, compared to a 1977 rate for Barkett of 21¢ a mile on the road and $8.44 an hour in the terminal.

In 1977 Barkett earned $28,200. This was slightly more than the average of about $25,000 earned by CCC over-the-road drivers that year—but not unusual, given that many CCC drivers and thousands of drivers around the country, "the greedy ones," collected enough miles and overtime to earn more than $30,000. By any standard, this put the dark-blue-collar trade of Teamsters truck driving well up into the middle, or even upper-middle, class. In addition, that year Barkett's company paid benefits guaranteeing him $550 a month for life upon retirement plus his normal Social Security benefit at age sixty-five; the best over-all health insurance available, for him and his family and covering dental work and eyeglasses and full protection against the costs of any hospitalization up to $100,000; and a $16,000 life-insurance policy. He received five weeks' paid vacation each year (with the pay for each of those weeks based on his average weekly mileage), and got six days of paid sick leave and nine paid holidays.

In 1948, Barkett made $80 for a six-day week. According to the best cost-of-living indicators, this would have to be $235.00 in 1977 to match the inflation spiral—far below his average gross of $542.00. More recently, the cost of living, according to the U.S. Bureau of Labor Statistics, had increased 79.6 percent in the ten years from 1967 to 1977. The earnings of the average Teamsters driver under the National Master Freight Agreement had increased 148 percent.

"Yeah," Barkett said, responding to a question about his union contract. "There's no union stronger than the Teamsters. The pay is good, and the retirement thing is much better than other places. There are lots of other good benefits. You see this?"

Keeping his left hand on the wheel, Barkett put his right hand deep into his mouth. After some fumbling around it emerged, shining with saliva and holding a false tooth held in place by a set of thin wires.

"This fake tooth cost me a hundred and twenty dollars and the union paid a hundred dollars of it. (My wife doesn't like me to pull this out and show people. Says it's disgusting.) They pay for eyeglasses, too. I mean I have protection and security in this world that I never dreamed of. And some years, I even make more money than Hassing."

To which Hassing later replied, "Yes they do. A lot of guys on the trucks have made more than many of their bosses. It's a reverse of what it used to be in the old days, when the men were all mistreated. The fact is that management brought the unions in by the way they treated people. . . . They'd make guys sit for eighteen hours for eight hours' pay. They'd come and wait ten hours to be assigned eight hours to work. . . . Now, if a guy comes in and hits the clock he's guaranteed eight hours of pay and gets paid for waiting time."

In 1977, Barkett's gross of $28,200 exceeded the earnings of automobile assembly-line workers, other factory workers, mineworkers, steelworkers, and just about any other blue-collar workers, with the possible exception of some construction-trades jobs for which far more training is required. Auto assemblers, for example, averaged about $17,000 that year, including payments for overtime.

Barkett in 1977 could also look forward to a better pension than those in other lines of work. If Barkett were to retire from CCC on October 1, 1978, after thirty years of service, he'd receive $550 a month for life. Had he been an auto worker for thirty years, he'd be entitled to $451 a month; as a steelworker he would get about $400, the specific amount depending on his prior earnings. And these auto and steel pensions are the cream of the crop. A worker who had labored thirty years as a member of the National Upholsterers' Union would be entitled to about $150 a month.

Not every Teamsters trucker or freight handler in the United States has the same contract as Barkett's. Some, including many under the control of union bosses like Tony Provenzano, work under sweetheart contracts that pay them much less; and others worked in areas where economic hard times have forced the union to make legitimate concessions to employers. But in most areas a majority of the Teamsters involved in trucking or warehouse work were, as Barkett was, covered by the National Master Freight Agreement.

The Master Freight Agreement and other similar but separate agreements covering auto handlers or chemical drivers nationwide have dozens of so-called supplemental agreements tailored to the needs or circumstances of a particular region of the country or a particular type of job. However, these supplements usually contain only minor variations in wages, jobs rules, holidays, and other conditions. One of the great accomplishments of the Teamsters negotiators by 1977 had been their success in winning nearly uniform wage rates across the nation. As Harold Gibbons said, "We eliminated North-South and city-noncity wage differences in this union so that no one is a second-class citizen and so that no company can benefit by moving out of some city. You get the same pay in Meridian, Mississippi, in this union as you get in St. Louis."

"The other thing about the union that's important," Barkett told me, "is that they protect you. They make sure the senior man gets his choice and they make sure the company can't fire you without a reason." Under Barkett's contract, he cannot be fired or disciplined unless the joint union-management grievance committee determines after a hearing that there is just cause to take action against him. And, if a man with less seniority than Barkett gets offered, and accepts, overtime or a longer run before Barkett has a chance to turn it down, the company has to pay Barkett also for the same overtime or the longer run.

Sitting in Barkett's cab and listening to him explain them, I thought these protections seemed reasonable. Often they don't work out so reasonably. One owner of a medium-sized New York-based moving company put it this way: "I never even go to the grievance committee hearings any more. It's a joke. All the votes always split 50–50 with labor and management each voting its side. Then they decide to split the difference, either by letting one side win one and the other side the next one or by compromising on all of them. It's ridiculous. Suppose I see a guy stealing. I don't have the right to say 'Brother, I saw you steal; you're fired,'' or 'Brother, I saw you in a bar when you're supposed to be on a moving job; you're fired.' No. It goes to a hearing. And I either lose or they tell me to give him a warning. If I ever objected, they'd pull all the workers out, and I can't afford to keep my equipment tied up even a few days without going out of business."

As for seniority rules, another executive, this one based in Ohio, told of how his terminal manager had spent four hours one afternoon trying to find a senior man to offer him an overtime job. He dispatched another employee to a dock to try to find the senior man at the pleasure boat he owned, all to no avail. The next day the senior man claimed he hadn't been contacted, and that he had been home all day. The grievance committee awarded him the overtime pay.

These are, very likely, extreme cases. To dwell on them is to ignore the abuses that would probably be more common on the other side if the protection wasn't there—employees fired or skipped over for overtime on the whim of bosses. Union-imposed rules such as these, or those that rigidly classify job categories so that drivers are not allowed to lift anything at all and "helpers" are required in many categories for even the simplest work, are necessary in some form. But they have often been unreasonable and bureaucratic. And they have caused major or even fatal hardships to some companies operating at the fringe of solvency.

The Teamsters had won such rules, along with generous wages and fringe benefits because they had special leverage in negotiating with the trucking industry, an industry of thousands of companies, only loosely united even at bargaining time. The special economics of their trade—high capital investment in equipment, total dependence on mass labor to make the equipment produce revenues, and an inability to carry over, from one day to another, lost work or revenues or business opportunities—made strikes especially deadly weapons.

This special leverage is supplemented by the union's financial strength. The Teamsters have the resources to organize and support long strikes, a fact that cannot go unnoticed at the other side of the bargaining table. This is particularly important when Teamsters enter bargaining sessions with new groups of employers in industries they have recently organized.

Harold Gibbons explained it this way early in 1977, as he described negotiations with a recently organized soda-bottling company in Missouri: "You see, when you get to a bargaining table, all the fucking conversation that an articulate person can make to that employer means shit. The employer's looking right through him. In back of his mind, he's sitting in his office and planning the strategy of the negotiations. How strong is that union? How much damage can it do? How much is it gonna cost me if I make peace? And they weigh these things. Now, if you're a puny union with limited resources and no outside forces to help you . . . you're in trouble. When you deal with the Teamsters you're not getting a bunch of Sunday-school teachers. It's a tough, tough union. And it's got economic strength. Rich, with all the money in the fuckin' world. We literally run our union on the interest of the funds we now have."

Records show that in 1976 International Brotherhood's interest income of 8.5 million dollars did indeed cover office and administrative expenses, but not the approximately fifty million dollars that the International spent that year on other budget items.

"That's how rich we are," Gibbons said. "And they know that. They know we can pay our men who go out on strike forever . . ."

In 1977 Al Barkett received that strength and protection for $18 a month in dues—less than one percent of his earnings. By any standard it was a bargain. No wonder then, that the Teamsters had been able to sign up almost all the workers in the trucking industry plus hundreds of thousands of others eager to put this tough, rich union to work for them. From the early '60s to 1977 Teamsters membership of 450,000 in trucking and warehousing remained more or less stable, because they had already signed up most of the available workers in the industry. In most other areas of American labor, the Teamsters had outrecruited every other union. Thus, even with essentially no new truckers, Teamsters membership had grown from about 1,500,000 in 1960 to about 2,300,000 by 1977. Exact membership counts were impossible because they fluctuated daily.

According to the U.S. Labor Department from 1960 to 1973, overall union membership in the United States increased by 15 percent, while Teamsters union membership increased by 30 percent. From 1974 to 1977 union membership in the United States leveled off and perhaps even declined. Labor experts judge that this is because non-union employment conditions improved, while the appeal of unionism diminished, especially in the eyes of younger workers entering the labor force who had little appreciation of the unions' historic role and were sympathetic to criticism of unions as autocratic and remote from real worker needs. Nonetheless, the Teamsters managed to keep growing, except when fluctuations in the economic cycle forced periodic layoffs, which cut basic membership.

Through 1975, 1976 and 1977, every issue of the *Teamster* magazine brought Al Barkett and his fellow Teamsters reports of recruiting victories. During one month the Teamsters won organizing elections involving 44 meatcutters, drivers and warehousemen at a food-processing company in Biddeford, Maine; 118 workers at a silk-screen company in Onalaska, Wisconsin; 55 employees at a parts-and-body shop in Nashville, Tennessee; about 100 drivers, warehousemen and cutters at a poultry supplier in Pittsburgh; 30 lathe operators, machinists and welders in Chillicothe, Illinois; 7 enamel-company employees and 20 tree cutters in Chicago; several dozen clerical workers at a trucking company in Pennsylvania; 50 woodworkers in Richmond, Virginia, plus some 15 other groups of workers.

In the middle '70s the Teamsters were losing slightly more organizing elections than they were winning, and they were having special trouble with elections involving large groups of employees. In these, management geared for battle with the elaborate, modern antiunion campaigns that were now plaguing all unions. The Teamsters were especially vulnerable because of the corruption that management was able to hint at. But by dint of the number of recruiting drives they mounted, the Teamsters managed to gain members as other unions stood still or dropped.

Teamsters organizing director Norman Goldstein explained to *The New York Times* in 1977 the Teamsters' uniquely aggressive organizing ethic: "Let's say there's ten people [working for one employer]. We'll go after them. The AFL-CIO might not think ten people are worth the effort." The Teamsters have had the money and resources to go after these small groups. On the other hand, the AFL-CIO, as a federation, did no substantial organizing itself, and its member unions couldn't afford to undertake organizing campaigns that provided so small a payoff. The National Labor Relations Board's records for the twelve months ending in June 1976 showed that the Teamsters had participated in 2,543 organizing elections involving a union against an employer seeking to keep the union out—about fifty elections a week. During the same period, all the unions that were affiliated with the AFL-CIO were involved in 4,695 such elections, and non-AFL-CIO unions were involved in only 828. While the Teamsters accounted for about 10 percent of the nation's union membership, they participated in 31.5 percent of all the elections. And, while 50 percent of the AFL-CIO elections involved employee groups of less than twenty, 71 percent of the Teamsters elections involved groups that small. "We have so many small groups," explained Teamsters Research Director Weintraub, "that we have at least fifty thousand different contracts. Every month the NLRB [National Labor Relations Board] report shows us in elections involving two, three or four people. If people ask us to come in, we go in."

There was another factor. In 1957 the Teamsters were thrown out of the AFL-CIO, a move forced by AFL-CIO President George Meany, who said he was disgusted with Jimmy Hoffa's corruption.

(Hoffa was president-elect of the union and would become president in early 1958.) By making the Teamsters the outcasts of labor, Meany made them his main competitor. Until the United Auto Workers broke away from the AFL-CIO in 1968, and even thereafter, in most industries the Teamsters became the only real force for competition in the labor movement. Without the Teamsters, a worker was faced with a monopoly; the AFL-CIO-affiliated unions did not compete with each other. The Teamsters offered an alternative. The Teamsters had no hesitation about competing for members with an AFL-CIO union or any other union, nor, did they hesitate to try to raid a group already in an AFL-CIO union.

"If you look at unions as a consumer issue, I guess you have to say the Teamsters are a great thing," PROD's Arthur Fox, a Ralph Nader disciple, conceded in 1977. "Without them there'd be no competition. AFL-CIO unions won't raid other AFL-CIO unions, and they won't cross jurisdictions to sign up unorganized workers in another trade where there's another AFL-CIO union. But the Teamsters will go anywhere."

The Teamsters relished a good raid fight. They were, as one Labor Department official explained, a "warm body" union, ready and willing to sign up any "warm body," without regard to trade or jurisdiction—a point illustrated by the fact that when the Fairfax County, Virginia, police joined the Teamsters they were signed up by a Washington, D.C., local that had been originally chartered as a milk-wagon driver's union.

Jimmy Hoffa used to say, "it would take a Sears catalogue" to list all the varieties of jobs in which Teamsters members were employed. By 1977, it might have required the yellow pages. Al Barkett's Teamsters brothers and sisters are everywhere. One of every ten union members was a Teamster—nearly one of every hundred Americans. In addition to the 450,000 in the trucking or the freight industry, a small sampling of major Teamsters job categories included so many tens of thousands of factory workers that the Teamsters were the fourth-largest manufacturing-workers union in the nation; 60,000 brewery workers; 80,000 farm and cannery workers; 2,100 clerks and technicians at Blue Cross/Blue Shield; 2,000 workers at Allied Chemical; 10,000 Safeway Supermarket workers, and 4,000 at A & P; 1,500 in the factories of Columbia Records; thousands of sanitation men in cities throughout the country, including 10,000 in New York; 25,000 airlines employees; and cab drivers in major cities throughout the country, including Philadelphia, Cleveland and San Francisco. There were also the thousands of groups of ten or twenty or fifty or a hundred workers in a range of jobs around the country so far-flung that it would put the Sears catalogue to shame: hair stylists, tugboat captains, bailiffs, animators, rent-a-car clerks, egg farmers, X-ray technicians, teachers, armored-car drivers, even zoo keepers and animal trainers.

Teamsters organizing of clerical workers, computer programmers and other white-collar workers was especially energetic. Canada also presented a fruitful new area for Teamsters expansion. By 1976 Canadian Teamster membership had grown to 75,000 and a separate Canadian Conference had been established. A year later, the conference was eagerly preparing to organize the thousands of workers that would be hired to build the planned Trans-Canada oil pipeline.

In 1977 Teamsters were also organizing in a controversial area. They were recruiting police. About 20,000 police officers had been signed into local Teamsters unions from city cops in San Diego, to prison guards in Ohio, to airport and subway police in Washington, D.C. This number represented only 4 percent of the nation's 500,000 police. Even in Michigan, the state with the heaviest concentration of Teamster-cops, the numbers were negligible. There and in other states Teamsters efforts to organize police in major cities had failed. There had been alarm from civic leaders and the press that allowing the Teamsters to organize the police was tantamount to letting the fox into the chicken coop. Barkett didn't agree: "Hell, they [the police] are just trying to use some of our union's muscle to get a good wage. They're just looking out for number one. That's all. And there's no reason I see to think that the union leaders, even the really bad ones, will corrupt the police. Hell, I'm a Teamster and they haven't corrupted me. They don't have me stealing or anything."

There have been no reports, or even hints, that the Teamsters have tried to use their police recruits as partners or accessories in crime. There were, however, strong indications that the union was winning good contracts for their new law-officer members. In Flint, Michigan, the Teamsters boosted basic police pay from $14,800 a year to $18,200 in eighteen months. "It's no big deal" San Diego Police Chief Eugene Kollender remembered several months after his troops signed a representation contract with the Teamsters. "They [the Teamsters leaders] have been very professional. It's just like any other union."

The Teamster-cop relationship makes good copy but it may be less germane to the issue of law and order than the conduct of Teamsters pension or health-care plans, or Teamsters extortion plots, or numbers running and loan-sharking by corrupt Teamsters locals. The corrupt Teamsters locals have often been able to gain influence over law-enforcement officials through bribery or other means without getting union cards for police. Someone as far down the ranks as the cops on the beat would be of little use, anyway. Union membership could provide a ready avenue to approach low-level cops for tip-offs on pending investigations, but few police have that information. In fact, few police departments have ever investigated the Teamsters. More important, there was the possibility that the police would serve as a force for making their unions more honest, especially since most union corruption was directed against the union membership.

A sign on Route I–71 announced sixty miles left to Columbus, and Barkett concluded his assessment of police joining the Teamsters. "I'll tell you this, though. Those cops better be prepared to be a little embarrassed. I mean, if you go to a party or a gathering that's not with other Teamsters, you feel funny saying that's what you are, because of our reputation. . . . It's not such a great, proud thing, like they say it is in the *Teamster* magazine."

I asked Barkett what else he read at home. "Well, in my memory I don't think I've ever read a book. I don't have time to read books. But I've read the *Reader's Digest* every month cover to cover for twenty years. And I read *Newsweek* cover to cover every week. And our daughter brings us *The New Yorker* when she's finished with it, and I sometimes read that. The wife reads it too. . . . I do a lot of reading. I mean, I'm lucky if I get six or seven hours of sleep on a work day. When I get home I usually don't go to sleep until one in the afternoon, because I read first. Then I get up at five to eat and watch Walter Cronkite, then sleep from about seven to nine. The other thing I do a lot of is working with wood. And I've done work on most of the rooms in our house. . . . Most weekends, most of us drivers rest. I like to be with the grandkids or work with my wood. Or in the nice weather I work on the cars. I do all the work on our cars myself. . . ."

"What about holidays?"

"Well, last Christmas we spent at home with the family. . . . New Year's, we went to a church dance. We go to a few dances a year. We

went to one run by the church for retarded kids last weekend. . . .
We very rarely go out to dinner. Maybe four times a year. . . ."

I asked him how he spent his vacations.

"Well, you know, we get five weeks, and I like to split it up. You
just tell them at the beginning of the year what you're gonna do. I'm
taking two weeks starting next week. Then, I'll take a week in September and one in October, then one around Christmas time. . . . I'm
spending most of my time on the vacation next week helping my son
and his wife move into his new home in Indiana. They just got a new
house. We don't travel much on vacations. Elizabeth, the wife, hates
to fly. We're invited to a kind of family reunion out in Tulsa this
summer, but we can't go because of her fear of flying. . . . Usually
we just stay home or we drive somewhere. We drove to New York
City twice. The last time it was to take my son and his wife to the
airport there for their trip to Europe. . . . We stayed in town a few
nights at a place called the New Yorker [a midtown hotel since
closed], and I'll tell you it's some city. We saw a car accident right
there on the avenue that you wouldn't believe. Some guy's car went
out of control and went right up on the sidewalk and into all the store
windows. . . ."

"Would you like to do more traveling?"

"Well, we're gonna drive out to California sometime—you know,
San Francisco. I'd love to see San Francisco. I'd love to go to Europe
too, especially London. But I don't know about that."

About thirty miles out of Columbus, Barkett pulled the truck into
a gas station-snack bar for a coffee break. We sat across from each
other. His hands, clasped on the table, looked much larger than on
the big steering wheel. His features, hands, nose, eyes, seemed to
swell at the small formica booth table with the mini-juke box built
into the wall just above the salt and pepper shakers. He smiled at me.
He was enjoying the talk, and he looked forward to the opportunity
to continue without having to worry about the horn or the air brakes
or the curves in the road or whether he could be heard over the noise.
"I must drink about twenty cups of coffee a day. It's killing me. . . .
I've tried to stop, but I'm still at it. Honey, could you bring us each
a cup?"

"You see that guy over there," he asked in a near-whisper, as he
pointed to a thin, bleary-eyed man in a cowboy hat who looked about
twenty-one and was sitting at a table by himself puffing a cigarette.
"He's on pills. Lots of guys are. You can tell by looking in their eyes.

I see them at stops all the time. But not our guys. Our company is very strict." Trucking executives said in interviews that absenteeism and pilferage were the two biggest employee problems, but Barkett disagreed:; "No, I'd say it's pills and drinking, and also drivers who drive when they're too tired to. I mean, look at that guy. He's about to go out and drive a big rig like ours."

We talked about Barkett's early life, a topic on which he spent two cups of coffee and the walk back through the parking lot to the truck. "My dad came here from Lebanon when he was eight years old. My mom, too. They came through New York and just kept going till they got out to Iowa, where they knew some people from the old country. There were seven kids in our family, and until I was ten we lived in South Iowa. Then we moved to Des Moines. I still have relatives there. My dad owned a greenhouse all his life. He didn't make a lot from it. I mean, at Christmas you'd get a forty-nine-cent jackknife, and that was a big deal. But we never went on relief. . . . We lived in a good old regular bungalow-type house. As small as it was, I got my own room, because I was the only boy, with eight sisters. They had to build a room for me.

"When I was born if you had a job you were OK. That was what respectability was. But there were no jobs . . . I mean, you couldn't even marry a job. As a kid I'd walk the streets looking for work. In 1938 (at eighteen) I got a job unloading railroad cars full of produce. It paid $25 a week. That's when I first joined the Teamsters. I was green. A guy came up to me and told me I had to join the union. The initiation fee was $25, and dues were $2 a month. Shit, I'd have joined anything to keep my job. I still managed to go through high school, even with the job. . . . I came to Cleveland after service in '46." Barkett served in the Army during World War II, but never left the United States. His wife, whom he met at a Lebanese community dance, had some relatives in Cleveland, and they thought he could get work. There was no work in Iowa.

"After coming to Cleveland, I worked in a printing shop for about a year. I ran a press. But I didn't want to stay inside all my life. Also, the master printer was supposed to show me how to set everything up, you know, really learn the business. But he didn't want to show me too much. He was afraid I'd ask for a raise or go get a better job at another press. So I left, and after a while I took this job."

We reached the CCC terminal on the outskirts of Columbus. "Be alert," a sign warned us at the parking lot gate. "Be aware. You are professionals out there." Barkett pulled the truck into the lot, which was much smaller and no better paved than the one in Cleveland. There was one yardman, backing a tractor up under a trailer. He looked about Barkett's age. Barkett waved to him, lowered the window and exchanged gossip about a mutual friend's imminent retirement. Then he walked inside, punched a clock to record his waiting time and dropped his lading bills on the dispatcher's desk. The office—12 by 20 feet in area, a glass-enclosed room, just neon lights and gray-green metal desks—was nearly empty. The clock said nine-fifteen.

Two drivers in plaid shirts were talking to the dispatcher about a fellow driver who at age thirty-five still lived with his mother "and was waiting around to take all her money." The drivers and the dispatcher eyed Barkett's companion suspiciously, then kidded Barkett about the shortness of his run tonight. He accepted a cup of coffee and waited about fifteen minutes before taking some papers from the dispatcher. On our way out he took me through the repair shop. As in the yard, only one man was working the night shift, replacing some tail lights on a trailer. We walked out into the lot.

Barkett found the right number trailer among about a dozen, all without tractors. It was backed against a fence. "That's it. I'll be right back," Barkett said. He walked around the building to where he had left his truck. Moments later he pulled around and backed the rig against the fence. Then he jumped out, went behind the cab and cranked down a metal stand on which the trailer would rest when he pulled the tractor away. He disconnected some wires connecting the tractor and the trailer, ("They're for the lights and brakes") hopped back up into the cab and pulled away. He backed the newly liberated tractor up against the trailer he was to take back to Cleveland and slid it into place. He cranked up the trailer's metal stand, connected the wires, kicked the tires, went back in to punch out on the time clock. We were off.

"We have to drop this trailer off at a Chevy plant in Parma," he explained. "Parma's out near the airport on our way back. This trailer's only got a bunch of racks in it to hold some car parts. It's real light. You'll feel us bouncing a lot more now. You can tell when a truck's carrying a light load or no load at all by the way it bounces over a bump. You see that one there," pointing to a white truck speeding by in the left lane. "He's real heavy."

It was dark, and at 10 P.M. the traffic on Route I–71 had thinned considerably. The few headlights there were in either direction seemed to belong to trucks.

"It must get pretty cold at night on this road in the winter."

"Oh yeah, but we have great heaters." He flicked a switch on the dashboard to demonstrate the tractor's blower. "No. That's one thing that's no problem. We didn't even have trouble during that real bad month of cold weather [the great cold spell of January and February of 1977] last winter. And you know, Ohio got it the worst. We lost some work, though, because some factories shut down because they ran out of fuel. I'll tell you, that really pissed me off. You know those oil companies had the fuel. They were just saving it so they could raise prices."

The conversation stopped for a while. In a matter of minutes the noise, the darkness, the steady vibration that didn't let an inch of road slip by unrecorded had lulled me. This is the noisy silence Barkett faces eight to ten hours a night.

"Don't you get sleepy out here at night?"

"Yeah I do. But you fight it. And you get used to it. Also, I sometimes use a radio."

"A CB?"

"Oh no. I hate them. There's too much yackety-yack bullshit. No. I sometimes carry a little portable AM to pass the time. I listen to the late-night talk shows, or sometimes some music. Late at night you can pick up shows from all over. There's an all-night talk show out of Philadelphia. That's my favorite. They talk about politics, and books, and everything. And they get some really crazy people calling in to them."

Forty minutes from Columbus, Barkett turned the truck off the highway and onto a side road, "so I can buy you a decent dinner."

There were about twenty tractor-trailers in the vacant lot adjoining "The Best Diner." Inside, Barkett took an empty booth next to one that was occupied by a man and a woman who had emerged from a sleeper-cab next to where he had parked his rig. The woman, about thirty years old, had a nest of silver hair puffed about eight inches high and glistening in the diner's bright lights.

The menu listed vegetable soup, two kinds of fried chicken and pot roast as the night's specialties. "Now don't look at those prices, just order," Barkett warned. "You're my guest here.

"This is one of the few good places left, and even this one's not so good," he said as he ordered a hamburger. "It used to be, before the interstates, when there were only two-lane roads that lots of food places competed for our business. Now with only a few exits off the highway, there's no competition. And the food is no good. The days of the great truck stops are over.''

Over two cups of coffee he talked more about his union: "You know our local has seventy-three hundred members. Only about a thousand are [over-the-] road drivers, and the rest are city drivers or in the warehouse. But we do real good if we even get three thousand to vote in an election [for union officers].''

I asked him what kind of attendance they had at meetings.

"Oh God. I'd say maybe we get three hundred people. I go to all of them because I'm a CCC shop steward. But getting back to the elections, another problem as I see it, is that they don't screen business agents too well. I mean, anyone [in the union] can run for business agent. Anyone who pays his dues can. So they get guys running who really don't know anything. They know less than I do . . . And sometimes they win. So you get a guy getting a big salary and an expense account and, you know, a Lincoln or Mercury paid by the union, and he really doesn't know anything."

"What about the local now? Are the leaders honest?"

"Well, I told you my problem with them in that they take orders from Washington. But I think they're pretty honest, although I have to admit there have been all kinds of accusations in the press about how they spend their money. Still, the books are kept really strict and they're open to any one who wants to see them. . . . Eddie Lee, the secretary-treasurer, really seems to run things. You must of heard of him. He's the guy who always wears a cowboy hat and boots. . . . The president, [John] Tanski, is OK, I guess, but I'm backing the guy running against him next year."

Local 407 Secretary-Treasurer Thomas "Eddie" Lee was a long-time ally of the Presser family. A flamboyant, cigar-smoking Cleveland labor boss, he had never been accused of any wrongdoing by any law-enforcement agency. However, in 1971 a Labor Department memorandum described Local 407 as a union which "has a President . . . with a record of including murder and robbery. This over-the-road local is the largest Teamster local in the metropolitan area . . . [The] Vice-President has a record of strong-arm robbery."

Several months after the nighttime ride with Barkett, Lee—wearing high boots, ten-gallon hat and a silver Smith and Wesson magnum—conceded that the president who had preceded him had gotten into a little trouble over a death." He also described his union as 97 percent contented but said that "socialists had been sent in to stir up shit. They're the dissidents."

I asked Barkett if there would be reprisals against him if he backed an opposition candidate.

"Oh no. They don't do that. But sometimes if you vote a guy out and the guy was tight with the Pressers, the Pressers get him another job with the Joint Council or the statewide union. You know, he gets thrown upstairs. Other than that, the Pressers and the other big bosses don't interfere with our elections. . . . Once a guy gets in, though, they get him to go along with them."

"Have you ever had any contact with Bill or Jackie Presser?"

"I met the old man [Bill Presser] once . . . As a shop steward I made an appointment to see him with a driver who had lost his wife. You see, the city drivers had an insurance policy where they got a thousand dollars for a dead spouse. Well the road people didn't have that policy, but this guy—he was a road driver—just couldn't understand that. He wanted a thousand dollars for his wife's death. And he wanted to see Presser. Well, on a Monday I asked for an appointment. And, you know what? We got in on Thursday. Just like that, a meeting with the head of all the Ohio Teamsters. Presser was very nice. He told us how he got into the labor movement because his mother was beaten on picket lines in the garment center in New York. He heard us out and then explained to this guy why he couldn't get his thousand dollars. . . . You see, I'm really dissatisfied with the Pressers only because of how they let Fitzsimmons steer them around. . . . It's the Washington people that really runs this union. That's why it's a bad union."

"But the Pressers support Fitzsimmons, don't they?"

"Well, I guess you're right. But that's because they get all that money from him. Besides, who knows, maybe they're afraid not to."

"Have you ever thought about joining a Teamsters dissident group like PROD?"

"Well, I'll tell you. I've thought about it. They're pretty active around here. . . . But I really have no desire to be in an insurgent movement. This union's been good to me. A lot of other guys do have the desire. But they don't do it, because they figured it would be an exercise in futility. You know, you don't fight City Hall. . . . A lot of people feel what's the use. . . . There's fear involved too. I mean, you don't want to be found off a New Jersey pier, do you?"

Barkett paused, as if to play back what he had just said. He looked down into his coffee, and then around the diner, as if he were checking whether anyone was within earshot.

"Actually, I went to a PROD meeting over at Kent State [University in Kent, Ohio] last summer to see what was going on. And, I'll tell you, I was impressed. I think PROD's doing a lot of really good stuff. And I know a lot of guys who aren't members of PROD, like me, agree. And it's not just young guys. It's the older ones like me who've been around and are tired of all the bullshit."

"Then how come you don't join something like PROD? Are you afraid?"

"Well, I guess there's some fear. Also, the grass always looks greener, as they say, on the other side. Who knows if once I joined, that I'd like those guys? But, you know, there's something else too. I don't believe you should dance with two partners. So if I joined PROD, I feel like I'd have to quit the union—you know, that means give up my job. . . . I'd at least have to quit being a steward. . . . If you're in an organization, you shouldn't be supporting a group that's opposing it. And I want to be in this organization, because that's my livelihood.

"I'll tell you this: a lot of guys around here think exactly the way I do. I'll bet you not more than 30 percent of the members really support Fitzsimmons and the other bosses in the union. The other 70 percent all have mixed emotions like I do. But there's not much we're ready to do about it, because it wouldn't matter and it might mean no work." He took a last big gulp of the coffee.

"Are you proud to be a Teamster?"

The question seemed to bother him more than any other, perhaps because pride is so important to him yet at war among those mixed emotions. He would come back to it during the night and during interviews over nine months, but his first try at an answer seems the most instinctive.

"Yes, I'm proud of my work. And I'm proud to be in their union because it's got a great bunch of guys who are members and who work hard and honestly. But sometimes, I'm not proud of the people who speak for us. No, I'm not proud of them. I get so goddamn steamed up sometimes. Like when Fitzsimmons at the Las Vegas Convention [in 1976] told the dissidents [PROD] that they could go to hell. That's bullshit. What's the definition of a dissident? Dissidents founded our country. Who the hell is he to tell them to go to hell? For that, I'm not proud. But I am proud of being a Teamster, for making a good living and sending my kids through school and not owing any money on my house and driving a good car.''

It was darker and even emptier than before, when Barkett guided the trailer back onto the interstate. About twenty miles later, he interrupted more talk about radio stations and road fatigue, pointing to a sign for a place called Butler and announcing "that's where my daughter Florence lives, over in Butler. . . . I guess you could say she's my problem kid. . . . She's a real independent, stubborn kid. You know, she doesn't believe in the system and all that shit. Long hair, dirty clothes, everything like that.''

"A hippie?"

His face tightened. "Yeah. That's right. That's what she is. She's twenty-four years old and she's still bucking the system. She's so hard-nosed. Says the system is full of shit. I mean, I don't like the system either . . . what with all that shit and those payoffs going on in Congress. But I can't fight it, because I've got to feed a family. I'm not in Congress. I'm right here. . . . So she's over there in Butler doing nothing . . . working as a cook in some restaurant. . . .

"She's smart though; went through high school in three years and then to the state university. But then she left and opened a pottery store over there in Butler. Her mother lent her two thousand dollars for it and I fixed up her car. Well ten months later, about two years ago, she left the goddamn thing. Decided to go out to New Mexico. She left some kids there to run the store, and they were stealing her blind. She lucked out though, because the Urban Renewal people decided to do a project there and they came and bought her out. But she didn't get all her money back . . . including our two thousand. Her mother, she's never gonna write off that debt until it's paid . . . I guess we spoiled her when she was little.''

"What do you think she thinks of you?"

"Oh, I know what she thinks. She thinks I'm some kind of nut because I've worked all these years in these trucks, and for what?"

Barkett was happier talking about his other two children.

"Mary, the thirty-two-year-old, is terrific. She had a bad marriage and got divorced about four years ago. But she's over that. I've got three granddaughters from her, one five, one twelve, the other seven. . . . She works in an art shop in Cleveland, and she's getting married again next month. And my son, Bill, he's twenty-seven. He's an engineer in Michigan. With a Ph.D. He's married, and his wife is expecting another grandchild. You should see Bill play basketball.''

At Parma, Ohio, at about 1 A.M., Barkett pulled in to the Chevy factory to drop off the trailer. It was a giant complex of long, window-less buildings surrounded by floodlit fences. Barkett took about twenty minutes delivering his papers and unhooking the trailer, leaving it in a row of similarly headless boxes that were lined up in a dark lot behind a guard house. As we left, the guard at the gate made Barkett open the door of the cab for an inspection. "I guess they figure I'm gonna drive out of here with an extra transmission or something. Some guys do, probably."

From there it was only another half hour to the CCC terminal. We were bareback. With the trailer gone, all that was behind us were some wires dangling from the back of the cab and the big, greasy black disk that had hooked under the trailer. The tractor and its driver seemed now to enjoy new freedom. Barkett didn't agree. "We hate to ride without a trailer hooked on," he explained. "You'd think it would be better, but it's not. This way there's no stabilization. You hit a bump and the cab goes all over the place. It's terrible."

At the terminal Barkett punched in, dropped off his signed loading slips and bought another coffee from a vending machine. A driver who had pulled in just behind us approached him with a question about air-conditioning in the trucks. The 1976 contract mandated air-conditioning in all trucks by 1978 unless the drivers, through the union, agreed in a separate negotiation with the company to waive the requirements because air-conditioning wasn't necessary in a par-ticular region of the country. The week before, CCC had sent a letter to the union members saying they were going to ask the union-man-agement grievance committee to waive the requirement in Ohio. Bar-kett, as a CCC shop steward, was responsible for explaining such issues to the drivers he worked with. "It's nothing," he explained. "We don't need them [the air-conditioners] anyway" because we all drive at night and it's not hot here." The other driver nodded, then turned away.

Another man, who had been unloading one of the trucks, came over to say hello. A squat, graying Irishman of about fifty, with wire-rim glasses, he was introduced as Al Fay. Told that he was talking to a reporter, he too volunteered ambivalence about the union. "I've got no complaints really, except that the top guys like Presser should spread some of the money around. But I'll tell you this, Hoffa was much better than that jerk Fitzsimmons. Sure he stole, but everybody does. He did us good; that's what counts. . . . This is a great job," he continued after a pause. "I've been here twenty years, and it's the only job I ever had where I wasn't laid off."

As Fay got up to go back to the loading platform, he turned and added a special reason of his own for appreciating the union: "One other thing I should tell you. Without this union, I'd be broke, and my son would be dead. I have a kid, twenty-four years old, who was born sick. Been in and out of hospitals all his life. He was born without a spinal column. Then he had to have his bladder removed and replaced with a bag. Then there was an infection and they had to remove part of his hip bone. He's in a home now. It's been thirty-five thousand dollars in bills—all paid for by the union. [Actually, the union-run, but employer-paid, health and welfare fund paid the bills.] I've never had any trouble with getting any claim paid over all these years. Now, you tell me where else I would get thirty-five thousand? So I've got no complaint. Except for the guys on top."

Barkett offered to drive me to my motel. "It's out near the airport, and so's my house. In fact, why don't you stop off at the house first for a drink. The wife would love to meet you, and she'll be up. Hell, she stays up till three thirty or four every morning reading. I swear she does. She's one of those night people. Never understood how she does it since she has to get up to get to work at nine. [She worked four hours a day as a bookkeeper.] but don't worry. I'll get you out of there real fast . . . otherwise she'll talk your head off."

Al Barkett's 1973 Plymouth provided a vivid measure of just how noisy his truck had been. The day before the tail pipe and muffler had broken off. After eight hours of the tractor-trailer, the Plymouth's deep roar seemed like little more than an annoying tick.

There were lights on downstairs in the house on Elmhurst Avenue. It was a smallish house with a front lawn about 20 feet deep that sloped upward enough to require three steps to a walkway that led to the front stoop. Leaves rustled in the 3 A.M. June breeze as we walked from the driveway through the unlocked side door. Three women sat around a paper-tableclothed dining-room table in a room about twelve feet square. All the available table surfaces and the side walls were decorated with graduation pictures from one generation and baby pictures from another. One of the women was introduced as Elizabeth, the other two as Elizabeth's friends. "They're planning the party and making the favors for Mary's wedding," Barkett whispered as he guided his visitor quickly into the kitchen. "She's getting married again next week." Elizabeth, a dark-haired woman whose rounded figure reminded me that Barkett was fifty-seven, immediately followed. "I'm gonna drive them home soon, and I'll be right back," she said. She was also whispering. Barkett interrupted. "No, he's got to get up at six tomorrow. He doesn't have time. Why don't you go upstairs and pull out that scotch I got that time—he likes scotch—and we'll have one drink and then I'll take him to the hotel."

Elizabeth came back with the scotch after a ten-minute search that made her husband nervous, and then returned to the dining room. It was a pleasant kitchen, average in most ways. Except that there were plants everywhere—a dozen ceiling hooks and five shelves' worth. "Oh those are Florence's," Barkett explained with a frown. "When she went off to New Mexico two years ago, she asked us to take care of them. Even though she's back, she doesn't really have a place yet. So they're still here. I wish she'd come and take 'em."

"Oh, don't bring that up." Elizabeth had slipped back into the kitchen. "It's so crowded here with them. A few, I'd take. But this is too many."

"I told him about how we went to New York to drive Bill to the airport, and about the car accident we saw near the hotel. He's heard of the New Yorker hotel."

"That's quite a city," she began slowly. "How do you like it? I bet it's everything they say it is."

We talked for about twenty minutes. Then Barkett declared that it was time to go. "Let me show you the basement on the way out." Down the short flight of linoleum steps were three rooms filled with cartons. "That's Mary's stuff from the home she had during the first marriage, plus more of Florence's shit," Barkett said. One space, however, had been cleared in the center of the room. Standing there was as big a dollhouse as has ever been sold in the most elegant toystore—a mansion full of miniature rooms, the front wall cut away to reveal the furnishings and inhabitants. "That's my woodworking," he explained. "I did this all myself for the grandkids. All the furniture, too. Even the wallpaper on all the little walls."

As he guided his stunned visitor away from the hand-crafted dollhouse, Barkett added a last leg to the tour—a pantry closet under the stairs. "Isn't the wife something," he said, pointing inside to a walk-in closet nearly the size of his dining room. "She buys everything in bulk for us and for Mary. She gives it all to Mary." Inside was a food stockpile that could rival the White House's fallout shelter. A quick count of just one item, Campbell's soups, yielded forty-two cans.

"You'll have to come back," Barkett declared as he steered the Plymouth toward the motel, "so we can talk more." A month later, on one of the occasions that I accepted his invitation, Barkett led a tour of the areas we missed during my first early-morning visit. Outside was a backyard about twenty yards deep with a built-in barbecue pit and an apple tree. "Oh, it's got bad apples," he chuckled, "but the berries over there are great. The grandkids pick them and have them with cereal for breakfast." Off to the side was a garden full of tomatoes and peppers that Barkett explained he was "in charge of." The garage, though big enough to hold the Plymouth and the Ford, was filled with "more of Florence's stuff" and two mechanics-sized jacks that "I use to prop the cars up. I do all the work on them myself." Back inside the house, there were three bedrooms upstairs—small ones made smaller still by paneling and shelves that "I did all myself." The beige bedroom Al and Elizabeth shared was no bigger than the other two and had a crucifix over the small double bed. "We're Catholics, but we don't go to church much. My kids say people go to church to be seen in good clothes."

We spent the rest of the morning in the kitchen he and Elizabeth shared with Florence's plants, going over "my drawer full of union papers and things." First he pulled out a pamphlet for DRIVE— Democrat, Republican, Independent Voter Education—the Teamsters political-action organization. "I've never joined this. I mean, why should I send them money. The union dues are too high as it is without spending extra." *

"Do you vote the way they tell you?"

"Hell, no. I've never cared who they want me to vote for. I vote the way I want to. I mean, I'd never vote for an antilabor candidate, but I don't need them to tell me that."

"How'd you vote in the last election for President?"

"I voted for Ford. But I think I like Carter now. I'll tell you—I liked [Democratic Congressman Morris] Udall the best of all the guys who ran."

Barkett's description of his politics revealed a mixed bag: he had voted for McGovern in 1972, Humphrey in '68, Johnson in '64 and Kennedy in '60. He thought people should be licensed to own guns, but allowed to have them; he was against "any abortions at all," and he favored the Vietnam war. As for the role of unions in politics and the economy: "Hell, everyone says unions like the Teamsters are too

* Federal law requires that union political action be funded with separately solicited contributions, not with union dues.

powerful. Well, you show me a union that's more powerful than GM or Standard Oil.''

Next, from his drawer Barkett took the letter he had written to Central States Pension Fund, the one he had said he got such a good, prompt answer to. It revealed Al Barkett as an unusually careful man: among the six possibilities he had taken the trouble to ask the pension people about was: "If I commit suicide after I retire at any time, can my wife collect a pension for the rest of her life?"

"Why'd you ask them something like that?"

"Oh hell. I just figured I should think of all the possibilities. I'm not going to kill myself. But why not find out about everything?"

The letter was followed by another document that revealed that the man with the easygoing voice wasn't easygoing when his seniority rights and his wallet were involved. It was a carbon of a protest Barkett had penciled to the union in February:

> On the afternoon of the 16th of February a junior man . . . was called in to run a Cincinnati turn. I was not called. I went on a Dayton via Columbus. I am claiming paye for the difference in mileage, which is roughly 81 miles.

"Here's something that's not about the union but somehow it got mixed in with these papers," he said, offering a sheet of paper on which a poem entitled "New Babe" was handwritten. The first line extolled the "Joy of new daylight." "It's a copy of a poem I wrote for my new granddaughter that Bill and his wife had last month," he explained, his eyes lighting up. "You'll understand what it's like when you have a kid. . . . I've written poems for each of my children and each of the grandchildren. I do it the day they're born, then put it in their baby scrapbook. . . .

"This here's the stub from one of my last pay checks. It's not that typical, because it doesn't have overtime, and because it's for two weeks—you see, I was going on vacation for two weeks, and when you go on vacation they give you the two weeks in advance." The check stub, dated May 21, 1977, read that Barkett had grossed $1,122.36 for the two weeks. From that the withholdings were: Federal income tax of $295.60, social security tax of $65.66, state income tax of $23.26, and city income tax of $11.22, yielding a net payment of $726.62 for the two weeks. So far that year, he had earned $12,531.51 of which he had had $3,295.99 withheld for federal income tax. "The federal tax is a little higher than it should be," Barkett explained. "You see, I declare no dependents, so when tax time comes I get something back instead of owing money. It's a way of forced saving. Last April I got six hundred dollars."

The last papers he pulled from the kitchen drawer were copies of his local union's spring newsletter and the International's monthly magazine. The Local 407 newsletter featured glowing reports on the Central States Pension Fund's records-modernization program, the Teamsters blood-donation drive, a recent stewards' seminar, and an announcement of the annual family picnic to be held July 11 at Chippewa Lake. "That was yesterday," Barkett said. "We had a great time. The wife baked some cakes and some chicken. . . . We went with a whole group. You bring your own drinks and food and you play softball or swim on the lake. We didn't get home till eight."

The copy of the monthly *International Teamster* included articles describing how the Teamsters were helping flood victims in South America and children stricken with muscular dystrophy, how the Central States Pension Fund was "Tops in the Field," and how the airline industry was being targeted for a recruiting drive. Mixed in with the articles were pictures of Teamsters sons and daughters who had received college scholarships from a local or from the International. (Dozens of such scholarships are awarded each year.) Also scattered throughout were pictures of Teamsters who had won back-pay awards after the union had gone to bat for them to protest their dismissal from their jobs. (One showed three truckers from Worcester, Massachusetts, who had won a total of $20,000 in back pay from a grocery chain that had fired them.)

Finally, there were about a dozen letters from rank-and-filers extolling the union's virtues and, in most cases, expressing affection for Frank Fitzsimmons. (A random check of these letters in four issues of the magazine later revealed that many of them had been solicited by union officials from shop stewards. Some had actually been drafted by union officials.)

Having emptied the drawer, Barkett leaned back in the chair and answered a question about his retirement, "No, I'm not gonna retire for a few years yet. Maybe I'll move to a cushy job in the warehouse, but I'll stay with the company. . . . Even if I do retire—in a few years—I'm not just gonna sit. I couldn't just sit here inside. I'd take a job outside, maybe as a mechanic. I can't be inside."

"Looking back, are you satisfied with what you've done over the years?"

"I've been thinking about that. . . . On the one hand, I've got this house all paid for. We bought it for seventeen thousand dollars back in '34, and I know I could get sixty-five thousand dollars for it. But remember, I did all that work on it, including adding this room here onto the kitchen. And I've got my cars, and the kids are through school. Bill's got his Ph.D., Mary just got remarried, and Florence, well she's starting to get straightened out. But she asked us for two thousand dollars yesterday to buy a Quonset hut to live in. I've never been sick—never called in sick even—and the whole family's healthy. So that's good. You asked the first time in the truck if I was proud of being a Teamster and I am proud of all that."

"So you're satisfied."

"Well, that's what I was going to say. The wife says I could have done better, and I know I could have. We could have saved up a lot more money than we have."

"How much do you have?"

"Well, we've got the house, and then the bank accounts have about twenty thousand dollars."

"Twenty thousand is a lot to have saved."

"Yeah you think so. But it's not. If I retire, and if inflation keeps going, I'm not gonna have shit from shinola. You see, we could have done better if we'd saved. Maybe I should have been in charge of the money. The wife's a big spender. I mean, just recently we got her a new mounting for a wedding ring. And last October we ordered a new dining room set for twenty-nine hundred dollars. You know, real good stuff. Not that shit that falls apart. In fact, it's supposed to be delivered today."

As if on cue, the phone rang. It was the trucking company confirming the furniture delivery. Barkett's voice toughened; he'd paid $2,900 for the set, he told the caller, and waited eight months. So they had "better carry it in just right and set it up the way the wife wants it—and not until she gets home from work, so she can be here to inspect it." He hung up and sat down again.

"As I was saying—" his face returning quickly to its normal grin— "we spend a lot. I don't regret it, I guess, but I have to admit to you that I'm ashamed to be sitting here right now after all the money I've made over the years and tell you that I only have twenty thousand dollars in the bank. . . ."

Barkett came back to how he felt about the union, first delighting in the "truckers hall of fame they're building out in Iowa," then settling down to a more general assessment:

"The original union idea was beautiful. You know, the mineworkers song—"Sixteen tons and you're deeper in debt." Well, John L. Lewis said that was bullshit, and he was right. . . . I'd say the Teamsters-union idea peaked about twelve or fifteen years ago. Then it was great. But now those guys have too much money and they've gone too political. Still, for me the union has been good. You have to remember the Depression. When we were kids, anybody who had a job was supposed to be really great. That's what life was. It's an idea that really sticks with you. And, with the Teamsters, I've had a good secure job. I've made more money than I ever dreamed of. If I get sick, they'll pay for it, and if I die the wife will get something.

"These are things you can't laugh at. The Teamsters have given this to me."

CHAPTER VIII

Charlie McGuire

Roughly, when Frank Fitzsimmons and his friends were coming off the golf course at La Costa, Charlie McGuire * was getting out of bed in the small brown shingle home he owned that looked out at the back of the Statue of Liberty from across a cemetery, a swamp and a turnpike in Jersey City, New Jersey. McGuire didn't have to pull up the window shades. He was so used to sleeping during the day that he hadn't pulled them down.

He slipped off his pajamas and put on one of the plaid work shirts and one of the pairs of jeans that he always wore on the job. At sixty, his brown hair had grayed and his bifocals had thickened. His skin had wrinkled and his shoulders had started rounding out. Yet his biceps were still thick and hard, though lined now visibly with winding blue veins, and there was a lot of meat on his chest that hadn't yet dropped to his paunch. Tying his boots, he walked downstairs to the kitchen, where Joanna was packing his box dinner.

Two hours later, McGuire pulled into the parking lot at a refrigerated warehouse on Enterprise Avenue at Frozen Food Plaza in Se-

* McGuire's name and some personal details have been changed to protect his privacy.

300

caucus, New Jersey. Taking a thick winter jacket and a pair of heavy gloves from the back seat of his green Plymouth, he walked in through a side door, found the punch card bearing his name, and slipped it into the time clock.

The giant Ace Refrigerating Company * warehouse, where McGuire worked, sits among dozens of similar, acre-sized structures camped across the Hudson River from the Empire State Building. These were the metropolitan distribution centers for products ranging from corn flakes to carpets to cat litter. Charlie McGuire's "barn" was different from the average warehouse; most of it was ten degrees below zero. The products McGuire handled as a selector, checker, sorter, and "authorized fork lift operator" (as the button he wore on his jacket collar announced) were all frozen foods—pot pies, orange juice, ice cream, vegetables and anything else that needed to go from farm to proceesing plant to kitchen table, while defying the laws of nature.

Freezing perishables and storing them in giant refrigerated warehouses before delivering them by refrigerated trucks to the supermarket had no doubt marked a tremendous breakthrough in supplying food to masses of people far from agricultural areas. But people had to haul the goods in and out of those warehouses, and human blood and skin don't do well shuttling in and out of -10-degree weather every couple of minutes. Dwarfed by the football-field–sized freezer and reduced to brittle clumsiness by the cold, McGuire and the others were intruders among the hundreds of yards of racks and rows of rock-hard cartons. As if to remind them, a huge blower, installed about fifty feet up near the ceiling to keep the temperature down when the door opened, lashed an extra wind-chill factor at them each time they entered the freezer.

"This is the coldest barn around," McGuire explained one night several weeks after the Seventh Annual Fitzsimmons Invitational, as he guided his forklift under a crate of Minute Maid orange-juice cans. "Here you need big boots, a hat, and a good coat. It's always minus ten degrees, plus there's the blowers that make it worse. Other barns are warmer," he continued, in an Irish brogue. "They can go as high as ten degrees above."

Holding down the speed of his yellow forklift vehicle to accommodate the numb-footed reporter walking alongside him, McGuire drove down three rows to find the Birdseye pot pies that were listed

* The name of the company has been changed.

next on the computer-printed shipping order he held in his right glove. The goods were destined to be shipped later that night to a wholesale depot in the South Bronx. "You see, you take a sheet like this from the box out there on the platform and you come in and get the stuff. It doesn't take too long, but you don't take your gloves off or anything like that. . . . To me, it's not too hard of a job. The only thing is, you're in and out of the cold all the time. The platform's kept cool, but not like the freezer. It's about forty or fifty degrees warmer. So, if you're a selector, you have to go in and out of the weather all the time. The other thing is that the job gets monotonous. Oh boy, it does. And you get disgusted. But somehow or another you don't let it faze you."

The job, in fact, had never fazed Charlie McGuire in all the years he had been doing it. Something else had: the seniority list that was posted on the bulletin board he walked past every day. It gave him credit for having been with the company since 1956. He thought he should have a 1951 starting date. For more than twenty years, he had been fighting to get the date changed to 1951. This meant, even now, that other men at Ace were so much higher on the seniority list than he was that he still didn't always get the priority choice when it came to choosing vacation dates. It also meant that many nights, like tonight, he had to work in the freezer as a selector instead of working outside on the platform as a "checker" (checking the orders the selector had gathered). Checking was easier work, and as he put it, "You just have to wear a light jacket and you don't need gloves."

But what infuriated McGuire more than the company's action was that his union, New Jersey Teamster Local 617, hadn't done anything for him. During the last few years they hadn't even answered the letters he had written about "my situation." By the time of the Seventh Annual Fitzsimmons International this had turned Charles McGuire—a quiet journeyman, blue-collar, lapel-flag wearer—into a dissident. Not a cocky young dissident; not a raving, ideological dissident, nor a crybaby dissident; not even a dissident with a Teamsters horror story to tell—as had the members who were loan-sharked into submission or "sweethearted" out of jobs in Provenzano-controlled New Jersey. He was an angry man, dissatisfied with his union because of a gripe that probably seemed trivial to anyone else. It had obsessed him for more than two decades; simply, he felt cheated out of what was rightfully his.

In this sense, McGuire was typical of a small but growing new type of Teamster, who was just plain dissatisfied with his union. Many were younger men, impatient with advances made on wages, benefits, or job conditions. But it seemed that more were, like McGuire, older workers who were fed up with years of reading and hearing about corruption among union leaders who weren't producing enough in the way of benefits, job conditions, grievances and attention to individual problems like McGuire's.

McGuire's problem was based on a tangle of job changes between 1951 and 1956.

In 1951 he had started work for Ace, his present employer, at their warehouse in Manhattan. His job was to sort and pack orders destined for A & P supermarkets. In 1953, A & P had given McGuire's particular type of work to a company called Reliable Trucking. McGuire and his co-workers kept their jobs but went on a Reliable payroll. As Reliable employees, they became members of a different Teamsters local. Then in 1955, Reliable was purchased by Ace. And in 1956 the A & P business—McGuire's work—was shifted back from Reliable Trucking (now a subsidiary of Ace, but still a separate company) to Ace. Accordingly McGuire went back on an Ace payroll and was put back into Local 617. But Ace refused to give McGuire credit for his past work and regarded his starting time for them as 1956. McGuire claimed that his starting time was 1951. He argued that the three years on Reliable's payroll was not an interruption of service requiring the new 1956 starting date with Ace, because he had been doing the same work and because Ace and Reliable were actually the same company. "It was all a paper shuffle," he asserted, "to deprive me and the other men of our seniority. Even in 1951 Reliable and Ace were the same companies. . . . One week I'd get a check from one, the next week a check from the other. It was all a fraud. My rightful starting time was 1951, and it wasn't interrupted except on their goddamned papers."

It was true that Reliable and Ace shared much of the A & P work at the Ace warehouse even in 1951. But corporate records examined twenty-five years later showed no evidence that the two corporations were actually connected in any way prior to Ace's purchase of Reliable in 1955. Also, McGuire's own Social Security records showed none of the intermingling of payroll checks he claimed. This would technically support Ace's claim for a 1956 starting date in calculating seniority rights. However, in such situations, technicalities usually didn't carry the day. What was curious about McGuire's problem was that his union hadn't fought to get him the 1951 date. In fact, according to McGuire, a Local 617 business agent had told him when he went on the Reliable payroll in 1953 not to worry "about whose name is on your check. You'll keep your 1951 date."

According to many other local leaders, such back-and-forth shifts between payrolls are common in the freight industry. But usually the union convinced the employer to make some accommodations, especially when the worker had been doing the same work in the same place during the years in question. As Ron Carey put it when told the facts of McGuire's case, "in that type of situation, we'd sit down and work something out on the starting date. You know, we have a stake in it too; if we didn't do anything in a situation like this, the guys would figure we sold them out." Two decades later, of the Local 617 officals who had been in charge of the union during the 1950s, some, including the man who had originally told McGuire not to worry, were dead. The others refused to be interviewed.

"Oh, I yelled," McGuire recalled more than twenty years later. "Every week I'd call someone or write a letter to the union. But, they never answered me." Soon, McGuire even started going to a priest who doubled as a labor-relations teacher at a local high school. This led to his filing a complaint with the National Labor Relations Board. They turned him down because he had filed his grievance too long after the company's award of the '56 date. On several occasions, he even turned down the vacation weeks he was offered, saying that to accept it "would be telling them I've given up." Still he got no help from his union. "For all these years the union was against me because I was a man fighting for what was right. Fighting for what was due him."

"Dad has fought a one-man battle against the company and the union for twenty years," his son Bob, also a Teamster, agreed in late 1976. "I'm just surprised the union hasn't tried to do anything to him." The same concern, in fact, had caused McGuire to pull one punch: "The one thing I never did," he explained "was go to an outside lawyer. I figured you never know what can happen to you if you go too far, knowing the way these guys at the union operate."

One afternoon McGuire sat at his kitchen table and talked at length about the union. To prepare for the session he had gotten up an hour early (at three in the afternoon), pulled out a tattered rubber-band-supported envelope from the drawer under the kitchen counter and arranged by date all the letters and papers he had collected over the years "about my case." As he sat there, his fat-cheeked Irish face looked more than a little like Fitzsimmons'.

Spread over his vinyl flowered tablecloth were seemingly endless copies of seniority lists, wage stubs, and hand-scrawled letters he had written to the union and the company. There were a few perfunctory answers from the bosses at Frozen Food Plaza. There was nothing from his local union or from the Provenzano-controlled joint council that supervised the local. They hadn't even answered him, he said.

Why did he think the union hadn't done anything about his problem? "Oh," he began with a chuckle, "because they've made their own deals with these companies. Pinto, [then the Local 617 president] got something for himself on this one. I can tell you that. . . .* These guys just want their own gifted positions. They don't care about me and the other manpower. They just want privilege. So if I complain and ask them to go against the bosses, why should they? Who am I, except a man who's never asked for a fuckin' gifted position but just wants what's coming to him?" There was no anger in his voice. He talked fast, and here and elsewhere he often used profanity for punctuation. But there was a no fist pounding, no veins popping in his neck, not even a raised voice, just a kind of lilting monologue in the deep brogue. Charlie McGuire—hard-working, system-following, time-clock-punching father of three and son of the Depression, who voted for Ford and Nixon—seethed rather than shouted as he sat in his Jersey City kitchen just outside the living room with the big head-of-the-house chair and the plastic-covered couch.

Though bitterly dissatisfied, he was quick to admit that "I have it much better than when I was a kid. Oh boy, that was something." His harder early years put his discontent in prospective. It didn't mean that he and other dissidents were ingrates. It suggested that they had a higher threshold for satisfaction and a greater willingness to fight for what they thought was theirs than a majority of their co-workers who were content to look back and see how far they'd come.

McGuire had been born in 1917 in coal country—near Scranton, Pennsylvania. The oldest of three sisters and two brothers, he had grown up during the worst of the Depression: "To tell you the truth, in them days you were lucky if you could go to school. I couldn't. I

---

* Again, it should be emphasized that no evidence supported McGuire's allegation of an actual "deal" in this case between the union and the companies involved.

had to stop after the sixth or seventh grade. You had to go help put the God-damned food on the table, so you were out looking, hustling some kind of money or another. Because, coming up during the Depression, if you had nobody working, you were really up against it.''

''Nobody was working in your family?''

''No, nobody at the time. Not steady. Not even my dad.''

''What was your first job?''

''Oh, we used to go out . . . and do a lot of apple picking and all that kind of stuff. . . . Then when I became eligible, I started working with the coal companies. . . . I was about twelve years old when I started for them as a slate picker. . . . [Slate picking] is when your coal has gone through a crusher and it's washed and everything. There's a lot of slate and rock involved, mixed in with it, and you pick the rock out of it.''

''So you weren't down in the mines?''

''Oh yeah I was. But not until I was about eighteen. My last job in Pennsylvania was in the mines. I got trapped. It was quite an experience. I decided I wouldn't ever care to go back into the mines again.''

After the mine episode, in 1941 McGuire left Pennsylvania and worked at a series of odd jobs. ''It was mostly going away and coming back. You'd take trips . . . I went to Michigan for a while and worked as a janitor or in restaurants washing dishes. Then I worked for a coal company outside the mines. I done lots of things.'' Another of those jobs, he added, was at a brass factory in Connecticut. In 1943 a metal press in the factory landed on McGuire's left hand, crushing several fingers. ''You see, the two fingers web here [they were permanently bent at the middle knuckle] and this knuckle is pushed down,'' he explained, extending the hand across the kitchen table. ''I had it operated on and everything else, but there was nothing they could do. . . . The doctor came from Yale, and he was one of the specialists, and he told me just to work it out as much as possible. I have a good grip in it. I have a very strong grip in it. . . . I have to, with the kind of work I do. . . . I still do a lot of private work, shoveling and things, around my house and for other people. So I need it.''

''Did the company give you any money for the accident?''

''Well, they paid the bills, plus they gave me a thousand dollars. . . . I was looking to get a guaranteed job out of them. But they weren't doing that. . . . I figured I was doing OK, because there were so many in that company who had their hands off.''

"Hands off?"

"Oh, yeah. Hands, and fingers, and other things. It was unbelievable with those presses."

One thing McGuire didn't do in the early '40s was join the war
effort. Though he had spent only a few years in the mines, his prein-
duction physical showed "something on my lungs," and the Army
turned him away. Thirty-five years later the lungs didn't bother him
much; in fact, as he put it, "I think the cold air in the refrigerator has
helped it. Before I'd feel all this congestion and sometimes I had
trouble breathing. Now, I feel OK most of the time."

McGuire had come to the refrigerators from a job on the loading
dock at a meat-packing company in 1944. He worked there for about
$40 a week, and then served a stint as a railroad brakeman—"I would
have stayed, but it just wasn't steady work"—before taking his first
refrigerator job in 1948. Social Security records show that he earned
a total of $3,203 from four different frozen-food warehouses in New
York and New Jersey that year. "Oh it was really such goddamn
cheap pay," he recalled. "It was unbelievable. I worked days, nights,
and weekends for that money . . . But at last I finally had steady
work. So I stayed."

And as he stayed, the Teamsters union he had joined made progress for him, first winning the right to negotiate a contract and then
winning steady pay increases. By 1955 he had saved up enough
money to buy the small shingle house, crowded onto a not-so-resi-
dential block in Jersey City. "I got the place real cheap—for seven
thousand. The whole thing. The yard and all. But it was in terrible
shape. I had to work on it full time for a few months just to make it
livable." By 1977 McGuire had raised three sons in the house, and
they had never gone hungry. Two are grown up and have moved out;
one is an over-the-road truck driver, and the other is a junior executive at a minerals company across the river at the New York World
Trade Center. "He tells me he can see the house from up there,"
McGuire beamed. "It's a real good job." The third son, thirteen, is
going to school and coming home every day to play with expensive
electric-guitar equipment. His father at the same age had been a 12-
hour-a-day slate picker.

In 1977 McGuire was earning $6.62 an hour for forty hours a week,
and averaging ten hours overtime a week, at $9.93 an hour. ("I get
home somewhere between five and seven every morning, but you
never know, with the overtime.") In a typical week McGuire grossed
about $365 and took home $248 after taxes. He had excellent health-

insurance coverage; a recent cataract operation hadn't cost him any-thing. He would be entitled to a $450-a-month pension when he re-tired. His plan was to move back to Pennsylvania with his wife: "We'll do it in three or four years after our last boy is old enough to move out on his own," he predicted. "I just hope Joanna will agree to it. Land is cheap there. But she likes to be near the city."

"Does she go into New York [a fifteen-minute drive] often?"

"Oh no. Never New York. We haven't been there in years. I meant Jersey City."

While McGuire's wages and pension were better than anything he had dreamed of as a boy, they were lower than those of Al Barkett and many other Teamsters around the country. The basic hourly rate for Barkett and for those in Barkett's company who did McGuire's kind of warehouse work was about two dollars an hour higher than McGuire's. Their pensions were a hundred dollars a month higher. (Also, at age sixty-five when McGuire started receiving Social Secu-rity payments, he would lose fifty dollars of the pension. Barkett and those in the Central States Pension Fund had no such reduction.) Even in New Jersey, McGuire pointed out, there were men in ware-house jobs "getting fifty or a hundred dollars a week more than we do."

McGuire also conceded that "there are lots of guys on these jobs who earn a lot less than me, too." The example he cited was one very close to home—his own "barn." At Ace, he explained, manage-ment had recently built a fence going right through the freezer divid-ing the place into two. When this happened, McGuire claimed, "Ace laid off half of the men—not me because I had seniority—but half of the men. They claimed they'd lost all of our A & P business to a company called Central.* That's why they had the layoffs. Well, right after that, Central started operations on that other side of the fence in *our* barn. They said they were renting the space from Ace. And they hired other guys who were members of *our* local at fifty or sixty dollars a week less to do the same work that our laid-off guys used to do. And these new guys, they only get a two-hundred-dollar-a month pension. The union says they can do that because it's another com-pany, but I know there's some kind of deal involved." In short, McGuire was claiming that Ace got out of its contract with the one hundred Local 617 men who got laid off, and then leased space to a different company, who hired new men at a lower wage to do the same work.

* The name has been changed.

Later checking found that McGuire's description and his salary numbers were correct, but that there was no evidence that any kind of "deal" was involved. For years, Teamsters contracts in the Provenzano-dominated New Jersey area have been a crazy-quilt of high-, low- and middle-scale wages and benefits. In most cases trucking or warehouse company executives whom I interviewed and who were paying less money for the same work attributed the differences to their better negotiating skills or to special conditions at their company—which, they had convinced the union officials, made lower wages necessary for them to stay in business. As to McGuire's specific allegation of a "deal" in the fence-dividing shuffle of work from Ace to Central, officials of both companies declined to be interviewed under any ground rules about their dealings with the Teamsters.

At Local 617, Frank Pinto, who was president of the union when the fence was built, had died of a heart attack. His successor, William McKernan, the local's long-time Secretary-Treasurer, did not return sixteen phone calls. When I finally stopped him in a hall at his headquarters, he declined to comment on why the new men working for Central were paid less and received smaller pensions, except to say that "they have different contracts because they're different companies. It's all very simple, and that's all I have to say. Next year maybe we'll do better."

McGuire had pointed out that contrary to usual practice, the one hundred men laid off by Ace were not the ones rehired when Central came in to do the same work at their new half of the Ace barn. This was critically important—many of the men who had been laid off had had contributions made in their names to the pension fund by Ace for several years. If they had been working for less than ten years, they had no right to any of that money; it stayed with the fund. Thus, with these men leaving and new men with no seniority coming on the job to replace them, one could say that the union's pension fund was made a gift of those years' contributions made for the laid-off men— a bonus for a pension fund like McGuire's, which was under questionable management.* "Why hadn't the same men been rehired by Central to work at their old jobs?" McKernan was asked. "I tried," he said, "but we couldn't arrange it. . . . You know, I don't even know you. Why should I tell you this?"

When he was asked more generally why McGuire was paid less than warehousemen in Al Barkett's Cleveland local and why others in New Jersey get even less, Joint Council 73 President Sam Proven-

* McGuire's was part of a group of Provenzano-controlled pension funds.

zano said, with no elaboration, "Here it's just different." Why hadn't he tried to standardize the contracts in the New Jersey area, as is done elsewhere, to prevent a situation like this one where Teamsters were laid off and replaced by other Teamsters working for less money? Provenzano replied that "to do that would drive all the businesses out of here."

Except for one employer who admitted a payoff to a New Jersey union official and another larger employer who said he had been solicited for a bribe, firsthand accounts of corruption in these erratic New Jersey Teamsters contracts were hard for a reporter to come by. Seemingly well-informed but secondhand allegations, though, were easy; even a few Teamsters vice-presidents and one top headquarters official who had long studied Teamsters contracts around the country asserted freely, on promises of anonymity, that, as the contract-wise official put it, "New Jersey is the worst sweetheart place we have. Some of those contracts are ridiculous."

To Charlie McGuire, the contracts were also invisible. As late as June 1977 he had never seen a written copy of the contract he had been working under since June 1975, even though he had requested it several times and even though the members were supposed to have ratified it by majority vote before it had been originally accepted. (They had ratified it, McGuire said, based on an oral description and a brief outline.) Nor had McGuire recently seen any business agents from his local visiting his "barn" to find out how things were and tend to any problems the men were having. You're lucky if you see someone from the union on the job once a year," he said. "And that's if you request him on a grievance. And even then, it doesn't do any good."

McGuire's local, Local 617, had long been considered the weak sister of Provenzano's home base Local 560. It has about 3,000 members. Although it is small—Ron Carey's local had 5,500 and is not much larger than average—the union's financial records revealed that its officers drew generous salaries in 1976. Pinto, the president and a long-time associate of the Provenzanos, collected $45,500 including expenses. Carey received $34,000. The vice-president of Local 617 made $35,000 and the secretary-treasurer $43,000. The same records showed someone named Vincent Gugliario on the payroll for $37,100. Gugliario was not known to McGuire and eleven other Local 617 members interviewed; all said they had never seen or heard of him. But in FBI files he was well known as Vincent "Vinnie The Sedge"

Gugliario, a New Jersey organized-crime soldier. Gugliario's job at Local 617 was listed as Trustee, the man responsible for auditing the activities and expenses of the other officers.

In another kitchen interview on a fall afternoon in 1977 McGuire talked more about his union. He began with a story of how, when he was a shop steward for a while in the '60s, Pinto approached him and asked him to continue the previous steward's job of taking numbers and other bets from the men on the job. "He told me I'd make money for myself, and be helping him out," McGuire recalled. "He even told me how I should arrange to collect what I got and send it over to the restaurant over in Hoboken, where all the action was taken. Well, I told him I'd rather not. You see, I knew that once you got involved with those guys then they had something to hold over you. And then they had you forever, you know, with the numbers and then letting out the loans." By "letting out the loans," McGuire was referring to the loan-shark operations that he said the union people also had a hand in, although he pointed out that it "didn't go on much in my barn. But some of the other barns! Oh boy. The stories you heard, you know, about people getting into trouble owing all kinds of money."

McGuire and, later, others in the local explained that owing such loans often led to the men being forced into pilfering operations for the loan sharks. "Oh, you wouldn't believe what gets stolen out of our place," he said, waving his good hand over his head. "Whole stacks of foods, even truckloads. Sometimes I just can't believe it."

Not that McGuire was a prude about it all. "I don't mind who steals what," he added. "It's only from the bosses, and they steal from everyone else, I guess. I just don't like it when it hurts the men."

This introduced the topic of Jimmy Hoffa as compared to Frank Fitzsimmons: "I never begrudged the union bosses anything," McGuire began. "More power to them if they can get it. But when they start trying to beat an individual who works for a living out of anything, then I have no use . . . for those officials. . . . I liked Hoffa. They claimed they should have built a monument for him. It was Kennedy that got him, I guess, and to me it seemed to be a personal grudge. But Fitzsimmons, he's like the rest of them. He doesn't do the manpower any good."

If everything was so bad, why did these local union officials keep getting elected and why did the contracts keep getting ratified by the members? "Because the men don't want to get involved." McGuire's voice rose for the first time. "That was my attitude until they took what was mine away from me. I've tried to lead them. But they don't give a damn as long as they're getting paid. Some of them can be bought for a drink. I've seen it. I've seen a guy who asked questions at a meeting be taken out for a drink by Pinto or someone and then he's back in line again. There's also fear," he added. "Even I don't want to go too far. My wife didn't want me to get involved at all. You know, the stories you hear. I could end up dead."

"Have you ever been threatened?"

"Well, I've been told by a steward or two not to make a certain move, like hiring a lawyer, because of my family and their well-being. But nothing right out in the open, no."

In 1976, McGuire did make one "move." He joined PROD, the Nader-backed Teamsters reform group. Soon, he was regularly putting their leaflets on the bulletin board at work (where they were promptly ripped down when he wasn't watching). "My son had gotten some of their literature and joined up," he recalled. "Then he told me about it, and once I found out that they were concerned about the warehouseman as well as the driver, I joined up, too."

A few years earlier, when it began, PROD had been concerned only with truck drivers and issues related to their safety. In 1971, after a study criticizing the Interstate Commerce Commission's regulation of the trucking industry, Ralph Nader convened a Washington conference on truck safety. Drivers who responded to questionnaires placed as advertisements in trucking magazines about the safety of their equipment were invited. According to the Nader ICC report, some 40 percent of the drivers who responded said their trucks were hazardous. When those attending the conference decided that the problem deserved continuing attention, the Professional Drivers Safety Council, PROD, was created. Originally the focus was on the ICC; they were the ones who were to be "prodded" into action, rather than the Teamsters. In fact, Nader had invited Fitzsimmons to participate in the 1971 conference and, afterward, to help in the new organization's work. In what was the first of a series of blunders that gave good publicity to the organization and steered it on a collision course with the Teamsters, Fitzsimmons declined, saying in a letter to Nader that the Teamsters had "spoken continually, and . . . effectively for all truck drivers in the area of motor vehicle safety."

From 1972 through 1975 PROD concentrated on relatively narrow truck safety issues, lobbying with the ICC and the Department of Transportation for technical rule changes. Run almost single-handedly by a $7,500-a-year lawyer named Arthur Fox, the group sputtered along with little more than fifteen hundred $20-a-year-dues-paying members, mostly from the 1971 conference and the original mailing list. They would not have survived without supporting grants from Nader's umbrella organization and Fox's almost maniacal determination.

"Gradually," Fox recalled, "we started getting into union affairs more and more. It wasn't my decision. Our members kept telling us that's where the real problems were—not just in terms of safety but in terms of their other rights, too. Whether it was a safety issue, like being fired for refusing to drive unsafe equipment, or any other issue, it was the union, through the [joint union-management] grievance committee that wasn't standing up for them." This transition was spurred by the public attention given the union following the Hoffa disappearance. "Then," Fox recalled, "we got the idea to do the book, and that really put us on the map."

The book was a PROD report entitled *Teamster Democracy and Financial Responsibility,* which it published and distributed to members, union locals, and the press, just prior to the June 1976 Teamsters convention in Las Vegas. Although it suffers from the zealous rhetoric that has marked Nader group efforts in other areas and more than the usual Naderite tendency to paint all who are not pure as purely evil, it marked a giant step forward in researching and presenting basic information about the Teamsters. The first part is an analysis of how the union was run and how, from the election of the general president down to the settlement of individual grievances, union democracy had gone by the wayside. The second part analyzes how the Teamsters spend their members' money. This was primarily the work of a young former warehouseman and sometime law student named John Sikorski, who practically lived in the Labor Department's file rooms for several months. Poring through the thousands of financial statements filed by the various Teamsters locals and joint councils over the years, Sikorski produced a list of the Teamsters who had benefited from high multiple salaries and from carefree nepotism practices. It was exhaustively detailed, and along with dozens of acerbic footnotes, it provided the first documented larger picture of Teamsters power and money being abused by upper- and middle-level leaders in every area of the country.* The press loved it, especially the easy-to-use salary charts documenting the multiple payrolls enjoyed by various local Teamsters bigwigs.

Even with the publicity from the book, PROD might have faded away—if it had not been for some help from Frank Fitzsimmons at the International convention a month later.

Fox followed up the book with a mailing to all Teamsters local leaders—they were the delegates to the convention—criticizing the way in which the mass of Fitzsimmons-sponsored 1976 constitutional amendments would be given to them for ratification only minutes before the vote, and suggesting that the delegates push for "reform" clauses in the constitution, which Fox had drafted and enclosed.

Apparently, the book, the mailing, or a combination of both, combined with all the bad press, were too much for Fitzsimmons. Rather than ignore Fox's fly-swatter tap at the giant union, Fitzsimmons startled the press and his own executive board by bitterly attacking Fox and PROD in his convention address. He said that "there isn't a local in the Teamsters that would hire him [Fox] as a janitor," and called him a "self-styled savior," who had "never worked at a craft but had gone to work for Ralph Nader," a man who "became a success because he said everything was unsafe." Then he rambled on, suggesting incoherently that PROD's funding must be linked either to antilabor groups or Communists or a combination of both and promising that "no damned Communist group is going to infiltrate this union." And, in a declaration that summed up his attitude and brought a standing ovation from the delegates, he bellowed that "for those who say it is time to reform this organization. . . . I say go to hell."

"That speech was the turning point for us," Sikorski recalled. "By naming Arthur [Fox], he . . . [Fitzsimmons] gave us publicity we never could have had. Plus the members really resented the go-to-hell statement when they read about it."

With the boost from Fitzsimmons, PROD was catapulted ahead of an equally small but more grass-roots dissident group known as TDU—Teamsters for a Democratic Union. More leftist and avowedly ideological than PROD and less concerned with PROD's nuts-and-bolts concentration on safety and other issues, TDU was peopled largely by truckers in the Midwest. Its leader, Peter Camar-

* Sikorski's work also suggested how the reports filed with the Labor Department could be used as a research tool—an innovation since used by many reporters, including this one.

ata, was beaten up while in Las Vegas. Through 1976 and 1977 TDU continued to make progress at the grass-roots level, leading wildcat strikes and even recruiting the officers of the largest local in Canada to their cause. (The new dissident leader of the local was quickly removed from office by the area conference chairman for calling an opponent a "turkey.") Nonetheless, in the public eye Fox and PROD became the number-one insurgent group. In part this was because of PROD's clever, hard-hitting newsletter and other literature that reported Fox's bread-and-butter legal victories in grievance suits. But it was mostly because after Fitzsimmons' outburst at the convention when the press needed to cover the "other side" of a Teamsters story, they usually went to PROD.

The process by which PROD became at least the "other half" of most Teamsters stories definitely overstated the group's importance and status among the rank-and-file Teamsters. By the end of 1977, they had grown from 2,000 to almost 5,000 members. But, as Fitzsimmons and other top Teamsters were forever pointing out, 5,000 out of 2,300,000 wasn't much. It was like having one dissident for every 460 members and, as Jackie Presser put it, "any large group will have a few nuts." But PROD's impact was greater than its numbers suggested. By 1977 it was impossible to find a local union where PROD activities weren't talked about frequently by the rank and file and where PROD sympathizers who were afraid or just not concerned enough to join weren't as numerous as actual PROD members. And though many who signed up were the kind of chronic malcontents or "nuts" who would join any opposition group, most were not.

It wasn't that they all had horror stories to tell about the union, but rather that there were men (and about a half dozen women) who, like McGuire, expected more from the union than they were getting in the way of basic representation. For example, there was the Georgia over-the-road driver who read about PROD in a trucking magazine in 1975 and joined because, as he told me, "my union wasn't doing anything but taking our dues. I never saw a business agent, and we never got any services." His biggest complaint had to do with drivers' seats. For him, even the air-ride seats were so insufficient in cushioning bumps that he'd been out of work for weeks at a time with back and prostate problems. His kidneys had been hurt so much by the jolts, he explained, that he occasionally urinated blood. By 1977, he was fighting the union on a new issue—its alleged inaction in preventing companies from making the drivers' cabs so small that, "your knees are against the dashboard and your head hits the roof when you go over a bump if you're more than six feet tall."

The week of the 1977 La Costa Tournament, this Georgia dissident was busy organizing for PROD in the Atlanta area where, he said, "new members were coming out of the woodwork now to join up." However, there was still no doubt that most Teamsters were easier to please than the Georgian and other PROD members. For example, when Barkett was asked about the Georgian's complaints about the size of the cabs in late 1977, he shrugged and said: "Ah hell, I'm six feet one and it doesn't bother me. It's not great but, shit, guys who complain about that stuff are just reaching. It's like a lawyer complaining about a client's after-shave lotion, even though the client pays him a lot of money. It's bullshit. These people [the trucking companies] are putting food on our tables. Why should we always be complaining?"

Of course, some PROD members had extreme grievances against the union. A trucker whom I talked to in a bar on the evening of one of the interviews with McGuire said he had been laid off his job in New Jersey in a Provenzano-inspired sweetheart deal and then threatened with broken legs and a dead family if he complained. Some of the men with the real horror stories, like the laid-off trucker, were afraid to join PROD.

Even as early as 1973 PROD's attacks on safety issues prompted Fitzsimmons to set up an International Health and Safety Department, which began addressing these problems systematically and with moderate aggressiveness. However, PROD did not make real progress in winning general reform of the Teamsters grievance procedure. Fox called it "a buddy system where management and the union hatch their own deals and the real interests of the members involved are ignored; it is the key structure in reforming the union."

While he didn't change the system, Fox did take on many individual cases for aggrieved members and was able to win significant National Labor Relations Board and court victories, overturning grievance decisions that union-management grievance panels had made. For example, he won a case for a UPS driver who, the grievance panel agreed, was to be fired for taking an unscheduled bathroom break during his 4½-hour drive. While unable to reform the union's authoritarian system of disciplining union members and officers, Fox did win several individual cases in which a PROD member had been thrown out of the union, fired from his job, or dismissed from low-level union posts because of his PROD activities. Also, Fox put together an excellent handbook outlining methods and legal rights for PROD organizers.

And always PROD was on the prowl for union misconduct. When the International delayed a scheduled increase in benefits paid to members on strike so that 18,000 United Parcel Service workers couldn't get it, Fox sued on behalf of a PROD member who was one of the strikers. Fitzsimmons quickly changed his mind and paid the increase. When PROD learned about sharply increased expenditures by the Central States Pension Fund for public relations—including a payment to a Chicago reporter to attend a PROD meeting surreptitiously and report back to the Fund's PR director—it fired off a letter to the Labor Department charging that public relations was not a necessary pension fund expenditure. The Department opened an investigation.*

The PROD effort was not without its faults. As with many of the groups that became part of the burgeoning Nader conglomerate, its work was often sloppy. Problems in this regard ranged from misspelling the name of the recipient of a transition memo to the incoming Carter administration, to misstating or overstating labor history or labor law in that and other memos and court papers, to making a few basic mistakes about names, salaries, family relationships and criminal records in the PROD book. Also as with other Nader organizations, PROD seemed to take on, in small but ironically noticeable ways, some of the qualities of those they were fighting. Criticisms of the union were often overstated or irresponsible. (A 1975 charge that only 10 percent of the members of the Central States Pension Fund received the pensions they applied for—repeated soon thereafter by *Newsweek*—is an excellent example.) Membership numbers were often overstated, as was the impact of various PROD initiatives. Letters to the editor of the newsletter were always pro-PROD and occasionally puffed-up before being printed.

Meetings of PROD's steering committee were closed to the press just as meetings of the Teamsters' executive board. At one such meeting they discussed whether the organization should continue to display a union label on their newsletter even though the newsletter was being produced at half the cost in a nonunion printing shop. (A counterfeit "bug," or union symbol, had been imprinted on the news-

---

* But, a year later, nothing had come of the investigation.

letter to indicate that it had been printed in a union shop.) The board members decided to continue the deception for the time being. And when Fox and Sikorski, like hundreds of others, including their Teamsters adversaries, were approached for cooperation on this book, they alone asked for remuneration (a contribution to PROD, not to them—which, Fox assured me, could be kept secret so as not to suggest any bias in the book).

PROD's positive impact outweighed these minuses. Working on a tiny budget—which, with all the mailings and lawsuits and organizing drives, never exceeded Fitzsimmons' salary—and out of a small, dingy $400-a-month suite two miles down Capitol Hill from the Teamsters headquarters, PROD, as Charlie McGuire put it "really kept those guys on their toes." Even a lawyer in the Teamster headquarters legal department conceded that "I have to say this for PROD. They've made my job here easier, because every time I'm worried about what someone's doing around here I tell them 'Look, it's not me. I don't care, but PROD will be all over us if we do that.' And they know it's true."

As the 1977 Fitzsimmons Invitational approached, things looked good for PROD. They had just passed the 5,000-membership mark and they were planning a series of organizing meetings around the country. There was no doubt that, among Teamsters, satisfaction with wages and apathy about everything else were still the most widespread sentiments, with fear of rocking the boat probably running a close second. So it was unlikely that PROD would soon become a truly powerful grass-roots organization. But it was destined for a wider, more significant role as a Teamsters gadfly and instigator of reform in worker safety and other areas. With membership increasing slowly but surely (and the leadership moving more toward TDU's nonelitist grass-roots orientation), there would be money for more staff, more litigation, and more lobbying and publicity efforts. A full-time health-and-safety director had been hired, and just a week before the 1977 Tournament she had been instrumental in providing the information for an NBC investigative report on unsafe trucking equipment, the dangers of driver fatigue and the government's and the union's inaction in attempting to correct either problem.

A month later, PROD assisted in a powerful article on the same subjects, in *The New York Times Magazine*. At the same time, PROD was also pushing the government in these areas, lobbying to improve the Department of Transportation's weak safety and driver-fatigue efforts, because, as Fox put it, "this is still the worst Teamster problem." There was, PROD Health and Safety Director Susan Ginsburg explained, only one inspector for every 23,000 large trucks on the road, even though the Department's own spot checks showed that as many as 40 percent of the tractor-trailers on the road were "imminently hazardous." The driver-fatigue situation was equally serious. "Drivers who have to stay on the road ten hours at a time get tired," Sikorski explained. "So they either fall asleep or they pop amphetamines to stay awake. Do you think anyone wants to be a forty-year-old amphetamine addict? You should see the letters we get."

Other letters PROD got and followed up on were from drivers who said they had been fired for refusing to drive unsafe equipment, drivers complaining about noise or about on-the-job motel accommodations, or drivers alerting the group to the dangers or discomforts of some new piece of trucking equipment. Another key problem PROD had begun to pester the union and employers about had to do with the time drivers were required to spend at home waiting for the company to call and tell them what time they had to be in for work. Since the calls could come over a period spanning several hours, even the driver's off-duty time was not totally free. (This was one issue about which Al Barkett did *not* think PROD was complaining too much. He hated having to wait at the phone, he said.)

PROD was also keeping up the pressure on Fitzsimmons, Presser, Provenzano and other top Teamsters over their salaries and other personal dealings. On the morning Fitzsimmons teed off for the 1977 La Costa Tournament, there were internal charges pending against him brought by PROD. The charges, filed officially by rank-and-filers with the International's executive board, accused Fitzsimmons of squandering union funds, condoning nepotism, and consorting with organized-crime figures, and asked the board to remove him. There was no chance that the board—of vice-presidents, the secretary-treasurers, and Fitzsimmons—would remove Fitzsimmons. But on advice from their lawyers, the board had agreed at least to appoint a panel to hear the charges. (Otherwise, Fox would have a better chance in court to appeal their ultimate decision, their lawyers warned.) That had encouraged more news coverage of PROD and the charges. Not only that, but some of the ambitious vice-presidents, especially Presser, were using the charges as one of many subtle pressure points in their efforts to get Fitzsimmons to step down, or to persuade other board members to encourage him to step down.

The group that Frank Fitzsimmons had breathed life into by attacking, was now strong enough to be assisting in his undoing.

That did not mean that, even with a new Teamsters general president, PROD would shed its gadfly role. Presser, Roy Williams or any of the other likely next presidents had all been targets of PROD's multiple-salary and nepotism watch, and targets of PROD's scathing press releases and newsletters. They hated PROD, and PROD was not likely to turn these future presidents or their union around. The legacy of the Beck-Hoffa-Fitzsimmons years, when most Teamsters had been lulled into shoulder-shrugging acceptance of wholesale nepotism and corruption—as long as *their* pay envelopes were large enough and steady enough—was not about to end simply because the name at the top was probably about to change. "PROD will be good keeping them on their toes and speaking up to stop some things," McGuire predicted at another kitchen-table interview the afternoon the 1977 La Costa festivities began. "But, they're never gonna change the union until the workingmen change, or the government comes in and takes over."

Charlie McGuire that afternoon was more hopeful than he had been in years that he was finally going to win his 1951 starting date. McKernan, the long-time secretary-treasurer, had just taken over as president of Local 617 following Frank Pinto's death. And, McGuire explained, "Now I think they're gonna do something for me. I tried to call McKernan and I got him right on the phone, and he said he'd try."

If that happened, I asked, would McGuire still stay in PROD? "Oh, God, yes," he answered quickly. "Of course. You need them. Because tomorrow these guys at the union will be trying to take something else from me or from another working man that's rightfully his."

CHAPTER IX

Jackie Presser

Jackie Presser accepted the handshakes and the pats on the back that morning in 1976 at La Costa with a big, boyish smile. He had two reasons for the congratulations, a new job and a new look. A week before, Fitzsimmons had appointed him an International vice-president. And for several months he had been on a diet and was halfway through losing one hundred of his three hundred pounds. When his colleagues from around the country, seeing him for the first time since the June convention, told him he looked great, he smiled and believed them.

When they told him how glad they were that Fitzsimmons had picked him to replace his father, he smiled the same smile, but he didn't believe them. He knew they were jealous—these sixty- and seventy-year-olds whom he had joined at the top, and the forty- and fifty- and sixty-year-olds whom he had jumped over at middle and lower levels. He knew they hated the idea that at fifty he had made it to the executive board on his father's shoulders. He also knew that they knew that he had bigger plans to take the top spot from the man who had appointed him. And he knew that they would all try to stop

him. Many of them would get over their jealousy, especially the older
men who had come up with his father and could be softened on the
idea that Bill's kid wasn't so bad. As to the others, he would outplay
and outmaneuver them, just as he would outshoot most of them on
the golf course that morning. He was a competitor. Whether it was
the glass case full of golf trophies in his Cleveland office or the multiple salaries he had arranged that amounted to more money than
Fitzsimmons made, he had lots of proof that he could outdistance the
others. He worked harder, he was shrewder, and he knew how to
watch his back. Now he was set to do it on his own, not just as Bill's
kid.

Fitzsimmons wouldn't have nominated Jackie for his father's seat
on the executive board, nor would the board members have approved
him, if he hadn't been Bill's son. But he wouldn't have gotten the job
if he had just been Bill's son either. Teamsters International, joint
council, and local payrolls were filled with the sons of top Teamsters.
Unlike Jackie, these were by and large a ragtag group of overaged
ne'er-do-wells. Though they were in their thirties, forties or fifties,
the sons of men like Fitzsimmons or vice-president Joe Trerotola were
still regarded as "kids" by their elders, who had sponsored them,
and their contemporaries, who sneered at them. They had never done
much for their fat salaries except prove that some people can't be
embarrassed into doing a day's work, even if they collect fifty to
seventy thousand dollars a year to do it. Jackie Presser was a worker,
a mover and a shaker. He had been organizing and working in unions
since he was twenty-two, and he was, in his own words, "damn good
at it, mostly because I can't stop working."

In 1966 Jackie had ventured out on his own after a series of organizing jobs provided by his father and his father's friends. He founded
his own local in his father's Ohio fiefdom. Within a few years Local
507 had organized its way into scores of small, medium and large
plants and warehouses. By 1971, in addition to running 507, he was a
trustee of his father's immensely powerful Ohio Teamsters Joint
Council, a business agent for a Cleveland bakers union that had affiliated with the Teamsters, and the president of a bartenders local.
Even then he wasn't shy about collecting generous salaries; the four
jobs paid him $97,754 that year. But he didn't just pick up the checks.
He worked hard at those jobs, learning the terrain, the ropes, and
the deals that his father had worked over the years. In the process,
Jackie and his father, whom he had always idolized, became in-

separable confidantes. "Bill never stopped talking about Jackie," one of Bill Presser's old friends recalled. "And he brought him everywhere. He was grooming him, and Jackie wasn't at all reluctant about it."

In 1972 Bill Presser gave his son his first national post, persuading Fitzsimmons, who regarded Bill Presser as his closest friend in the Teamsters hierarchy, to make Jackie a $35,000-a-year International general organizer. At the same time, the son boosted his salaries back in Ohio. With his new International salary his earnings came to a total of $193,921, which was 50 percent more than Fitzsimmons got. When an embezzlement conviction in 1974 forced Bill Presser to quit his job as a trustee of the Central States pension and health and welfare funds for eleven months, he arranged that Jackie take his place until he could resume his position there as the most powerful trustee on the funds' boards. At the same time Jackie expanded his base and his profile by joining civic groups and giving newspaper interviews about the Teamsters' "image" problem that new leaders like him were anxious to correct.

In 1975 father and son speeded up the schedule. Bill Presser, by then sixty-seven, had had diabetes and cancer for several years, and he had undergone several debilitating stomach operations. Although the operations and the treatments seemed to have slowed, and at times even stopped, the cancer, by 1975 he was failing. According to one pension fund official, when the elder Presser arrived in Chicago for a Fund board meeting in early 1975, he had to be carried from the car, which had become badly stained with blood from his rectum during the 5-minute ride from the airport. In 1976 Presser grew worse. "You just can't believe how sick my dad was then," Jackie Presser recalled. "He had a stomach held together by wire mesh, a prostate operation—oh, it was terrible. We thought he was gonna go any minute." Still, Bill Presser hung on to his vice-presidency, allowing himself to be renominated and reelected by acclamation—with a floor demonstration orchestrated by Jackie—at the June convention. Fitzsimmons, near tears, called Big Bill "one of the greatest men that I have ever known" and declared that "[if it] is possible for one man to love another, that is our feeling."

Through the first half of 1976, Jackie Presser went after new, national responsibilities. First father and son convinced Fitzsimmons that Jackie's work organizing Teamsters retirees in Ohio into a political force should be applied throughout the International and that

Jackie should run it. Then they began talking to Fitzsimmons about the ideas Jackie had for a national Teamsters public-relations campaign—patterned after Jackie's work in Ohio. And, again, they explained, Jackie was the best one to run it. At the same time, the younger Presser became, as he later put it, "tired of looking like a thug with all that weight. I went on a crash diet so I'd look more presentable to people who thought all Teamsters looked like hoods." At the June 1976 convention, an already slimmed-down Jackie Presser was given the plum of being one of two head sergeants at arms, and his retiree program was adopted as the national model. Two months later, Fitzsimmons announced that he was to be in charge of an expanded public-relations drive.

On October 7, 1976, a week before the La Costa Tournament, the International executive board convened for its quarterly meeting in Los Angeles, Jackie made his formal public-relations proposal. Although he had worked out the package with a Cleveland ad agency, he was "nervous as hell. . . . I mean, this was really going to be my show. And there I was presenting it to my father and all the guys he had come up with in the union who were also like fathers to me." Like most executive board business, Presser's presentation was uneventful. He walked the board through it without a hitch. After only a few perfunctory questions through the cigar and cigarette smoke, he started to leave the room.

As he remembered it, as he reached the door, "my dad asked me to wait a minute. Then he looked up. There were tears in his eyes. . . . 'Fitz,' he said. 'There's something I want to say and I'd like my boy to hear it.' And then he told them he'd decided he had to retire, that he just couldn't go on anymore. Well, Fitz was really shaken up. I mean, these guys were best friends. They had come up together in the Hoffa days. . . . I was speechless. I couldn't believe it. He had talked about stepping down, and a few weeks before he had gotten some horrible pains in his head that . . . had caused him to lose his memory for a little while—you know, just all of a sudden he'd forget what he was saying and start talking about something else. But this, this was so sudden.

"Fitz didn't say anything for a minute or two, and my knees were knocking I was so weak. Then Fitz looked up and started talking about what a great man Dad was. But then came the real shocker. He turned to me and said to the other guys sitting around the table, 'I'd like to nominate Jackie to take his place. Are there any objections?'

Well, there were none, and that was it. I was a vice-president. I had no idea in the world it was going to happen."

Other board members who were at the meeting confirmed the basics of Jackie Presser's account. Yet those who would talk about it also suggested that Bill Presser had known for a while that he was going to step down, but had waited until after the June convention so that his replacement could be appointed by Fitzsimmons instead of having to be elected by the convention delegates. Also, there was unanimous feeling that Bill Presser must have discussed the appointment of his son with Fitzsimmons beforehand. In several interviews Jackie Presser denied that his father's decision to step down was anything but sudden (refuting the argument that the retirement was delayed until after the convention) or that his father had talked to Fitzsimmons about appointing him. But in a telephone interview a year after the appointment, Fitzsimmons said that "I'd known Bill was going to resign at that meeting for several months. In fact, I was aware of his retirement at least a year before." Fitzsimmons also said that Bill Presser had talked to him about giving his son the vice-presidency, but he added, "It wasn't just that Bill asked me . . . If you look at Jackie's record of what he had did, I don't know no more better equipped fella who's did more in actuality."

Whatever the circumstances, Jackie's appointment was greeted with a storm of indignation from the press and Teamsters critics. They saw it, as PROD's Arthur Fox put it, as "nothing less than the disgusting, shameless transfer of power from one corrupt generation to another. . . . These guys just don't give a shit what anyone thinks, do they?"

When it came to Jackie Presser, the critics actually had little specific to go on. He hadn't exactly been trained in unionism by the Boy Scouts, but he did have a clean record. His father was another story.

Bill Presser had come up in the hard world of Jimmy Hoffa. He was forever telling the story of how he had decided to go into union work when, as a kid, he saw his mother come home from beatings she had suffered as she walked picket lines in New York City's garment center. Bill Presser's dedication to the union movement was no doubt genuine when he began organizing fish and poultry workers in 1926. Nonetheless, by the early 1940s, according to FBI records and the McClellan Committee hearings, he had become involved in a juke-box racket in which he and a local owners' group in Cleveland used a Presser-controlled local union to make sure that those owners were the ones who had their juke boxes in the restaurants and bars most likely to yield the highest profits. At the same time he opened his own juke-box company with a Cleveland organized-crime figure named John Nardi.

It was also during the early '40s that Presser became one of the men closest to a rising Teamsters star named Jimmy Hoffa, though at the time his Cleveland juke-box union wasn't a part of the Teamsters. (Bill Presser knew Hoffa mainly through the underworld friends they had in common, Jackie Presser candidly recalled thirty years later.) In 1951, Presser took his juke-box operations into a newly chartered Teamsters local. He quickly became Hoffa's top Ohio lieutenant and a key source of the Midwestern support that would soon propel Hoffa to the union's presidency. At the same time Presser installed as his number-one aide at the Joint Council Louis M. "Babe" Triscaro, a former prize fighter whom McClellan Committee investigator Walter Sheridan later described in his memoirs as Presser's "liaison" with the Cleveland underworld.

In 1951 Presser expanded his juke-box operation to Youngstown, Ohio, where he hired Joseph Blumetti as a business agent. He was a former bartender who had served three years in federal prison on a white-slavery (promoting prostitution) conviction. Presser would continue to employ so many men of this sort in his expanding union empire that a 1971 Labor Department memorandum on organized-crime influence in the labor movement called Presser's joint council officers a "Who's Who of organized crime in Northern Ohio." The memo singled out, in addition to Blumetti, a convicted burglar and robber who served as the treasurer of Local 400; a convicted murderer who served as president of Cleveland Local 407 (Al Barkett's local); a convicted strong-arm robber who served as vice-president of Local 407; a convicted labor-law violator who was president of Local 293; and Nardi, his old Mafia-connected vending-machine partner who was secretary-treasurer of Vending Machine Service Workers Local 410.

The memo suggested an explanation for Presser's ex-offender employment program that had long been suspected by Cleveland Teamsters observers: that Presser was operating his unions in concert with the then alleged Cleveland crime boss Frank Milano. On the Local 410 payroll, the 1971 memo reported, was an attorney named Carmen Milano. The memo went on to report that "[Carmen] Milano states that he is retained to service grievances. Department of Labor investigation disclosed that few, if any, grievances have ever been filed in this local. Milano is also known by the Department of Labor to receive a $200 monthly retainer from Local 436 Teamsters for the same purpose, and it is believed that Milano is most probably getting similar retainers from several Teamsters locals. Milano," the memo continued, "is the nephew of Cosa Nostra kingpin Frank Milano." Adding to the alleged Frank Milano connection, the memo also noted that John Nardi was Frank Milano's brother-in-law. Five years after the Labor Department memo was written, a Cleveland newspaper article quoted Frank Milano's brother, Anthony, also an alleged underworld figure, as confirming that Bill Presser had been one of his "protégés."

Had Bill Presser gained and kept his Ohio kingdom by sharing the Teamsters action there with Milano's organized-crime family and employing many of their troops?

In 1977, Jackie Presser wouldn't answer that question for the record, except to say, "You draw your own conclusion about what it took to overcome all the goons and scabs and police harassment to start a union movement in those days."

Whatever it took, Bill Presser seems to have been able to do it without ever personally falling into truly serious trouble with the law. But he did have some minor scrapes. In 1953, as the executive secretary of the Tobacco and Candy Jobbers Association, he was convicted of restraint of trade, a misdemeanor, and fined $1,500. The following year, a House of Representatives committee headed by Ohio Republican George Bender began an investigation of Ohio Teamsters activities. When Presser was called to testify in Washington and was asked about his personal finances, he took the Fifth Amendment. Then a few months later, although Bender had announced an expansion of the Congressional probe, the investigation was abruptly dropped.

Years later, McClellan Committee investigator Walter Sheridan in *The Fall and Rise of Jimmy Hoffa,* reported that one Ohio Teamsters leader, James Luken, had told him that Presser and the others had talked openly about $40,000 of Teamsters money that was spent to "pull strings" to get the Bender investigation stopped and that Presser had soon thereafter abruptly switched the Teamsters' support to Bender in his 1954 race for the United States Senate. In a 1977 telephone interview, Luken reconfirmed the Bender story to me, as well as Sheridan's reports that Luken's Cincinnati local union had been harassed by the International and that his family had received personal threats (including having funeral wreaths delivered to their home) when he refused to toe the Presser-Hoffa line in the middle 1950s.

Luken's story is one of the more impressive sagas in Teamsters history. A milk-truck driver who had risen to be president of the local Cincinnati milk-drivers' union and then the president of the Cincinnati joint council, Luken was one of the few men who dared to oppose Jimmy Hoffa at the height of his power. In return, Hoffa and Presser threatened his family, sent in rival Teamsters locals to underbid him on contracts, tried to bribe his top aides, framed one of his lieutenants on a phony rape charge, and attempted to rig elections against him. As Robert Kennedy wrote in 1960, "threats, abuses, bribes, trumped-up charges—Jim Luken and his followers have faced them all and have not yet been beaten in their fight against Jimmy Hoffa and William Presser." * Kennedy did not live to learn how right he was about Luken's ability to survive. In 1961 Luken defied the strongest Hoffa-Presser opposition imaginable, not to mention the obstacles the International constitution put before him, and broke his union away from the Teamsters and into the AFL-CIO. By 1977, Luken's AFL-CIO union was thriving, and Luken was the mayor of Cincinnati.

Despite his alliances, Bill Presser's first and last tastes of prison weren't to come until 1960. In 1958 Walter Sheridan visited Presser's Cleveland office at the taxi drivers' local that he had taken over. Sheridan was looking for evidence to take back to Robert Kennedy and the McClellan Committee that might confirm Luken's allegation of a payoff to stop the Bender Congressional committee probe. Going through one file, he came across an envelope labeled "Christmas list." The list was an invoice for eight champagne buckets at $100 each that had been sent at the union's expense to, among others, Hoffa, Allen Dorfman, a federal judge, the Ohio Republican State Chairman and George Bender. Excited by what he thought might be helpful evidence, Sheridan told Presser he wanted to take the invoice list—which he could have done under the authority of a Senate committee subpoena. Presser didn't object, but asked that Sheridan come back later to pick it up so that he could first get it photo-copied.

According to Sheridan, when he returned a few days later, the names of those to whom the company had shipped the buckets had been torn off, and, as Sheridan later wrote, Presser told him, "You

* Robert Kennedy, *The Enemy Within* (New York: Harper and Brothers, 1960), p. 142

have your job to do, and I have mine." * Of course Sheridan was quickly able to get an original copy of the invoice with the names on it from the champagne bucket company, leaving Bill Presser clumsily exposed to an obstruction-of-justice charge for destroying evidence under subpoena. Two years later, in 1960, when Presser refused to tell the McClellan Committee whether he had destroyed the list, he was sent to jail for two months for contempt of Congress. Soon thereafter he was convicted of obstruction of justice. Following appeals, he spent another six months in federal prison.

Bill Presser's only other criminal conviction didn't come until 1971, when he pleaded guilty to eight counts of shaking down employers by making them buy ads in the joint council's newspaper in return for labor peace. While the shakedown was proved, it was never shown that the money went to Presser personally rather than to the union. Presser was fined, instead of being sentenced to prison, in part because no personal profit had been shown and in part because by then his health was starting to fail. Two years later, in 1973, Presser was again indicted, this time on charges that were later characterized by his son, Jackie, as "such chicken shit that they proved how far the government would go to harass him." The five-count indictment for embezzlement and falsification of records, alleged in one count that he had misused $86; in another that he had misused $381; in another that he had spent $767 of union money on personal airline tickets; in another that he had sold a union car to a retiring union official for only $1; and on the last count that he had falsified union records to cover up those four transactions.

"Do you think if my father was gonna steal, he'd steal eighty-six bucks or three hundred bucks," Jackie Presser asked in 1977, after explaining that the sale of the car for one dollar was a standard, though perhaps questionably generous, union severance practice that had been conducted openly. "Which of us," he added, "couldn't be indicted for spending fifty or a hundred bucks the wrong way on our expense accounts?" A federal prosecutor involved in Teamsters cases defended the seemingly trivial Presser indictments on the grounds that "If this is all you can get a guy like Presser on, you go ahead and try, because you know he's a crook anyway. So you take what you can get him on." Whatever the merits of that principle of prosecution, the federal judge in this case didn't believe that the

* *The Fall and Rise of Jimmy Hoffa*, p. 87.

government could even get Presser on those trivial charges. He dismissed the indictments before Presser's defense began, declaring that the government's presentation of its case not only didn't show his guilt but was actually so bad that it suggested he was innocent on all five counts.

Over the years the one other area in which Bill Presser had come close to, but escaped, serious trouble with the law had to do with his performance as a trustee of the Central States Pension Fund. He had been installed by Hoffa on the Fund's board in 1957. There was no doubt that he had had a hand in arranging the loans that Hoffa had authorized in the late '50s and early and middle '60s to the group headed by Moe Dalitz, the old-time gambler and syndicate boss and fellow Clevelander. With Presser's help, Dalitz embarked on a borrowing spree that began in Las Vegas and culminated in the loans that had built La Costa. In 1966 Presser had gotten Hoffa to go along with a $1,600,000 loan to build the Eastgate amusement center in Cleveland. The president and owner of Eastgate was a young union organizer named Jackie Presser. Four years later the place went bankrupt and Jackie Presser defaulted on the loan.

But as with Allen Dorfman, whatever real independent influence Bill Presser had as a member of the pension fund board did not come until March 1967, when Hoffa went to prison. Then, he became, in the words of another trustee "second only to Allen Dorfman in power at the Fund." This and other interviews, incuding one with Dorfman, suggest unanimously that it wasn't a case of Presser working under Dorfman but, rather, a matter of the two handling separate functions at the Fund. Presser and other trustees were always able to arrange a few loans for their friends. According to a source close to Bill Presser, Presser did indeed arrange the loans that were approved for the Bally Slot Machine Company, which was then largely owned by his close friend Sam Klein, who gave small gifts of Bally stock to Dorfman and Fitzsimmons and gifts totaling 3,750 shares to Bill Presser and members of the Presser family, including Jackie. Also, Presser had played a key role in suggesting Allen Glick as a front for Las Vegas loans. But, largely, Dorfman was still the man to see on loans.

Presser, as chairman of the trustees' executive committee, was, in title, the boss of the Fund. This not only made him a kind of front man who winked at and approved all of Dorfman's questionable loans; it gave him charge of all nonloan decisions at the Fund, such as how claims would be managed or how benefit rates would be set. The other trustees, especially Presser's close friend Fitzsimmons, ceded most of their interest and power to Presser on these issues.

It was in that management capacity that Presser was the key man in the Fund's decision to hire Dan Shannon as an administrator of the Fund; just as it was Presser who continually backed Shannon in Shannon's efforts to take more and more of the Fund's functions away from Dorfman. "Presser was the main guy who hired Dan and the guy who pushed for Dan and backed Dan up at every meeting," a source close to Shannon later recalled. "He was always there when Dan needed him, including those days when Dan was getting so much shit from Dorfman or [Dorfman aide Alvin] Baron that it looked like he'd have to resign or be killed."

Big Bill Presser's sponsorship and defense of Shannon adds a strong measure of ambiguity to his record—an ambiguity that is reflected still more sharply in his son. On the one hand he was capable, as in the Shannon case, of supporting a positive, honest approach to union business; on the other hand, he consistently supported Hoffa and, at a minimum, passively allowed organized-crime forces a piece of the Teamsters action. His Ohio kingdom was nothing like the jungle of sweetheart contracts that Tony Provenzano's New Jersey was; yet he was also the man who tried to crush Jim Luken in Cincinnati, and there is evidence—especially from his earlier years—that he and the gangsters he had hired from the Milano mob presided over some highly questionable contracts. He protected Shannon and was never himself prosecuted for any pension fund activities except the Labor Department's 1978 civil suit; but it was also true that he had brought Allen Glick to Allen Dorfman's attention and that he had allowed Dorfman to fleece the Fund with all those loans to the mob.

"My father went as far as he could," Jackie Presser said over dinner one night in 1977, trying to explain his father's inconsistencies during one of several candid interviews that repeatedly drifted from on-the-record to off-the-record and back. "He brought in Shannon when he thought he could, and he tried to build a good union in Ohio. But when you ask me why he didn't stop Dorfman, then I know you're not thinking. You're not understanding reality. The reality is that if he had tried to stop Dorfman he'd have gotten his head blown off."

That explained part of it. In another discussion the son went further, conceding that his father had "come up through the old school." In the Teamsters that meant "you had to deal with all those people—the Milanos, the Dorfmans, the Triscaros, the Nardis." It was not just a question of fear, but also, he asserted, a question of how you got things done and how you made your way in the world. Above all, the younger Presser explained, it was a matter of doing what you had to do to build a strong union. "My father cared about the union and those union people in it," he added. It is a point not disputed by Al Barkett and many other Cleveland Teamsters, who, unlike their counterparts' opinion of the Provenzanos, generally agreed that the elder Presser had been a hard-working, accessible union boss.

But Jackie's explanation ignored other unpleasant factors, such as the greed and the ambition that moved him to destroy evidence for Jimmy Hoffa, to float the loan for his son's amusement center, to go after Jim Luken, and to stay on the good side of Dorfman and his friends by letting the pension fund be raided by them.

"Bill Presser was no different than any of the old-time industrial robber barons like John D. Rockefeller," one Ohio politician and long-time Presser friend explained. "They [the robber barons] exploited people, broke some laws, made deals, and did everything else necessary to build something for themselves and their families. Well, that's what Bill did with his union work." Another Presser associate, who was also close to Shannon at the pension fund, agreed with the robber-baron analogy. But he added, "As Bill got sick and close to the end of his life that's when he brought Shannon in. He wanted a good, safe pension fund to be his memorial. He wanted, like the robber barons, to have respectability in his old age. And, he wanted to pass it all along to his son."

By La Costa Tournament day, 1976, the old man had passed most of it along to his son (though he was still alive and in title still retained control over the Ohio joint council and still drew so much money in multiple salaries that he had recently bought his wife a $40,000 Rolls-Royce.) It wasn't a Jimmy Hoffa-to-Jimmy Hoffa, Jr., transition, in which the father attempted to push the son into a different world altogether. Here the father was trying to bring his son into a better, cleaned-up version of the same world. In terms of education or polish, Jackie Presser was nothing like Hoffa junior. He had never made it to college; and although he was well tailored and a much softer personality than his gruff old father (and didn't write letters like one found in his father's old files, asking for "data pertinent to this guy's beefs''), Jackie Presser was not the soft-spoken, articulate young lawyer that Jimmy Hoffa, Jr., was. Nor was he part of any virginal new generation. He was a fifty-year-old overweight union boss who had spent twenty-five years—the years of Beck and Hoffa and Fitzsimmons and Dorfman and Bill Presser and Tony Provenzano—in union work. He knew about the deals, and he had been involved in his share of them.

But he didn't care now about more money. He had made himself a millionaire several years back by building a theater-nightclub in Cleveland that specialized in Las Vegas-type shows, and he was satisfied to live on the huge expense account and legal multiple salaries from various Teamsters payrolls that amounted to a quarter of a million dollars a year. If Jackie Presser was greedy for anything beyond those payrolls, it was power, not money. And the paramount truth that separated Jackie Presser's ambitious world of 1976 from Bill Presser's world of 1946 was that, as Jackie saw it, staying clean was how he could get the greatest power prize the Teamsters had to offer—the presidency.

As Presser teed off that morning at La Costa, he was certain that he had one advantage besides age over the older board members, particularly Vice-President Roy Williams, who might compete with him when Fitzsimmons finally called it quits. He alone, he believed, understood that in the late 1970s, the government, with its new ERISA law, and the press, with its post-Hoffa-disappearance, post-Watergate bloodhound urge—were not going to let the Teamsters leadership continue to be riddled by corruption so brazenly. The next president would have to be clean enough to withstand relentless scrutiny from the government and the press. He had stayed clean, not pristine, but clean enough so that, despite constant federal investigations of his union and of his complex business deals, he had stayed out of grand-jury rooms and the organized-crime headlines so heavily populated by Teamsters. And he had thrown himself into his union work as never before, working eighteen-hour days negotiating good contracts in Ohio and pushing his national public-relations campaign from a suite at the Washington headquarters that he now used nearly as often as he used the Cleveland office.

Rising to the top wasn't simply a matter of staying clean. Presser had another flank to protect. If Fitzsimmons and the other powerful elders on the executive board and in the joint councils and locals around the country thought he was too straight or that he wouldn't help them continue to cut their deals, there was no chance that they would let him take over for Fitzsimmons. This was the tightrope Jackie Presser was mounting in October 1976. It was a dangerous balancing act. But if he could pull it off and end up on top, Presser's self-imposed schizophrenia could signal the emergence of the whole union as an institution stepping out slowly and reluctantly from its bad old robber baron days into a second generation in which power would be exercised, and corrupted, less openly and with greater sophistication as increasingly more energetic attempts at respectability became the order of the day. In the one national union function that Presser ran—public relations—the tightrope between yielding to old-line pressures and responding to new ones was already putting the Teamsters in an on-again, off-again posture of slowly being dragged kicking and screaming into a new world. To watch Jackie Presser's Teamsters public-relations campaign was to watch a man, and a union, struggling and stumbling and agonizing their way through a transition filled with inconsistencies, spasmodic regressions, and bitter internal strife. To watch Jackie Presser try to push that PR campaign as a way of pushing himself to the top was to watch a man living dangerously.

Jackie Presser's PR offensive had grown in part out of earlier efforts his father had made to win respectability in his later years. "Bill was a lot like Jackie by the middle seventies," a close friend recalled. "He thought it was time for the Teamsters to change their image as bad guys or outcasts, and I guess he passed it on to Jackie." Bill Presser "became a major Cleveland civic and political leader and one of those guys involved in every charity." Such was the elder Presser's prestige that by June 1974 the Cleveland *Press* could write an affectionate portrait of "the old wheelhorse" looking back on "50 tumultuous years in the labor movement." The article mentioned the apostolic blessing from Pope Paul and the Tower of David award from the Israeli government on his office wall, and described a charity dinner honoring him the next night. The dinner was sponsored by a civic committee that included two federal judges, five members of the Ohio Supreme Court, twenty-seven of thirty-four Court of Common Pleas judges, and five of six judges from the Ohio Eighth District Appeals Court, including the chief justice, who was serving as the dinner chairman. The next year, when Bill Presser hoped the Labor Department wouldn't make him step down from the pension fund board because of the requirement that a convicted labor-law violator not serve for five years following his conviction, he sought and received letters attesting to his good character from the governor of Ohio, the mayor of Cleveland, and the Chief Justice of the Ohio Supreme Court.

The "old wheelhorse" going public and picking up badges of respectability was an unsettling enough departure from the norm for Teamsters bosses around the country. His son's total abandonment of the old low profile in favor of an all-out public-relations offensive was absolutely shocking. A year after that 1974 Cleveland dinner honoring William Presser, there was an even bigger dinner in Cleveland honoring Jackie Presser for his extraordinary work in selling Israel bonds. Supporting Israel had been a favorite, if not the only, Teamsters public-relations strategy since the night in 1956 when Harold Gibbons convinced Hoffa that $265,000 collected at a testimonial dinner should be donated for the construction of a children's home in Israel. Since then, Teamsters had been the biggest union buyers of Israel bonds. By 1977, they had bought $26,000,000 worth out of total American union purchases of $100,000,000. Much of the $26,000,000 was sold in 1973 in conjunction with a dinner honoring Frank Fitzsimmons.* But other than the Fitzsimmons dinner, for which an Israel bond spokesman recalled, "the union went all out to get everyone to kick in who owed them something," Presser's June 15, 1975, bond dinner was the biggest in Teamsters history. Just about everyone who was anyone in Cleveland politics or business turned out. At the dinner, Israeli Ambassador Simcha Dinitz inducted the guest of honor into the Prime Minister's Club, a group made up of people who personally (or, in Presser's case, through his union) bought more than $25,000 worth of bonds.

By the time of the 1976 La Costa tournament, this was hardly the only club or charitable cause that Jackie Presser was part of. "Jackie Presser has become a goddamn socialite in this town," a top Cleveland lawyer remarked unhappily a few weeks after the tournament.

---

* In fact there was so much Teamsters Israel-bond-buying around 1975—even by such unlikely locals as Tony Provenzano's Local 560—that some suspicious law-enforcement people suspected something more than good will was involved. However, it seemed, after much checking, only that the bonds, as Israel Bonds spokesman Meyer Steinglass put it, had "great PR value. . . . These are people [the Teamsters] looking for respectability and this is one way to get it. . . . And, in this union the guys at the top can make the locals buy the bonds. I mean, you know what they say, 'You can find yourself under a truck if you don't obey.' " To be sure, the Israel Bonds people might not have been too choosy about whom they get their money from—for example, one bond-drive testimonial in 1976 honored Teamsters official Joseph Pecora, a New Jersey underworld associate of Provenzano.

"I mean any civic board, or any charity drive, or any testimonial dinner you hear about in Cleveland, you find that this big fat Teamster is on the committee sponsoring the thing. It's amazing how he's done it. But he's part of the establishment now in Cleveland." The morning at La Costa in 1976 Presser was a member of twenty-six significant local civic groups, including the Mayor's Economic Coordinating Commission, the board of directors of the Cleveland Convention and Visitors Bureau (where he cochaired two committees), the Cleveland Convention Center Advisory Board, the board of trustees of the Free Medical Center of Greater Cleveland, the Citizens League, the City Club, the Kidney Dialysis Program, and the Hunger Task Force, not to mention being the cofounder of a home for women alcoholics and a member of three subcommittees of the Greater Cleveland Growth Association.

Some of these were relatively meaningless groups. But some, like the board of the Convention Center (where Presser's Teamsters did most of the heavy work) weren't, and even those that were gave him generous public exposure. By 1976, the Teamsters in Ohio, especially Cleveland, had more of a stranglehold on commerce than they did nationally. Ohio is perhaps the state where the Teamsters had organized better than anywhere else. Teamsters in Cleveland included such key jobs as cab drivers and sanitationmen as well as everyone in the freight industry.

The Pressers had been smart enough to ally with unions representing bartenders, bakers, and restaurant workers. Thus, except for labor disputes involving Ohio's giant steel and auto industries, Presser, or his father, was the key labor power in the state. This gave Jackie Presser the kind of "big shot" status that allowed him to pick up a phone and reach anyone in the Cleveland power structure. It also gave him a great deal of political clout, which he used unabashedly, developing a strong statewide Teamsters political action organization. He also used it carefully. Sometimes he endorsed Democrats running for local or state office, and sometimes he endorsed Republicans.

The high profile was not Presser's alone. He also pushed his Teamsters into the charity and civic-affairs limelight. The month after the La Costa tournament in 1976 there was one of the more spectacular charitable events in Cleveland history, a "circus" night at the Cleveland Coliseum in which 17,000 attended the "Teamsters night at the Greatest Show on Earth," with proceeds going to support handicapped and underprivileged children. That same year Presser's Teamsters locals, joint council, and Ohio Conference contributed more than $300,000 to local charities, more than any other group in the state. Contributions went to a list of groups ranging from the Notre Dame Club of Cleveland, to the American Foundation for the Blind, to the Shaker Heights B'nai B'rith Women. Meanwhile, the *Ohio Teamster,* the union's monthly newspaper, that year developed a more aggressive and more professional style of singing Teamsters praises and giving attention to politicians the union supported. With 150,000 subscribers, it was one of the largest papers in the state.

By February 1977, Presser had brought his Teamsters so far that there occurred in Cleveland a remarkable first in Teamsters history— a two-part series of long, front-page feature articles in the Cleveland *Press* was so positive that Presser had them reprinted and distributed as handouts. The articles noted the past legal troubles of Bill Presser and others, as well as the potential for future abuses of power that could come, for example, from the union having a billion dollars tied up in Cleveland banks on any given day. But they also highlighted the brighter side that Jackie Presser had worked so hard to get across: that Ohio Teamster membership had grown a phenomenal 42.9 percent over the last ten years, while other unions' membership declined; that the union arranged for five thousand summer jobs each year for high-school and college students (by having them fill in for Teamsters on vacation); that the Central States Pension Fund paid benefits far in excess of pensions given to most non-Teamsters, and that many Teamsters leaders and rank-and-filers were active in a variety of charity and civic groups.

The *Press* articles could have pointed out also that Jackie Presser negotiated good contracts for his men. He read and reread proposed contracts long into the night to master every detail. Unlike New Jersey, Presser had pushed for statewide parity for wages paid to Ohio Teamsters, a certain way to curb most sweetheart deals. Also unlike New Jersey, each member promptly received copies of contract proposals. In Jackie Presser's Ohio, trucking company and other executives who employed Teamsters offered little of the not-for-attribution rolling of the eyes, or other more specific indications of wrongdoing when asked how Teamsters contracts were worked out. Union members there said that ratification votes were on the level, as were the union elections.

Still, through 1977, Jackie Presser's transition from pinky-ringed old-time union boss to socialite union leader was hardly perfect, and not without its skeptics on both sides. In Presser, in his union, and in his Ohio PR campaign, old warts and regressions gave reformers ample reason to continue to distrust him, even as the old-timers who had worked with his father began increasingly to resent him. In many cases this was the result of his trying to strike a compromise, which ended up pleasing neither side. For example, Presser's $200,000 a year in multiple salaries would seem to have been not only a logical outgrowth of his projection of himself as a labor statesman and leading citizen worthy of the compensation given to prominent men on the other side of the table, but also a plausible compromise between the values of the old-time union hoods and the reformers. The old-timers could still get a lot of money, but now could get it legally, while the reformers could accept the new professionalism and above-board, on-top-of-the-table way of doing things that high salaries would mean.

As Presser argued in an interview, "I think we've reached the point where we can and should take all our money in salary. We don't need to be crooked about it any more. We deserve that money." It was good theory, but in practice neither side liked the idea. The old-timers didn't like the attention such salaries would focus on them, nor did they relish the idea of paying taxes on the money. And, as Presser put it, "stealing for a lot of these guys is fun. It's a game. And they're greedy, so they'll steal even with the high salaries. That's why they resent it when I tell them, 'Let's take it all on top of the table in pay.' They're still looking under the table, too."

As for the reformers, by any standard that related to other unions' salaries, Presser was too greedy about the idea. "He may be good," explained PROD's research director, Robert Windem, referring to Presser. "But is he $200,000 good, with no real education and with even people he negotiates against not getting paid that much? Also, he's the king of severance plans. He's got five different severance and pension plans from the Teamsters covering him.* This is just a rip-off that avoids the embezzlement statutes." Presser had spread the above-the-table largesse around in ways that to the reformers seemed even less legitimate than his own salary. For example, Har-

---

* There were the International's family-protection plan, the International's affiliates plan, the Ohio Conference of Teamsters severance plan, the Teamsters Joint Council 41 Business Agents Pension Fund and the Teamsters Local 507 Pension Fund.

old Friedman, a Presser family friend and ally received $352,000 in multiple salaries from a Presser-controlled Teamsters union that he was associated with as well as from a Teamsters-affiliated bakers union local. He became the first union official on record to draw two different salaries of over $100,000 each. Also a father-son team of lawyers close to the Presser family received nearly $2,000,000 over a three-year period in fees for managing the Ohio drivers' health and welfare fund. The payments were so excessive that PROD filed a complaint with the Labor Department, which in turn sued to recover some of the money and ultimately forced much of it to be returned.

If "taking it in salaries" didn't win Presser new friends on either side of the Teamsters generation gap, neither did his attitude toward the organized-crime–connected people his father had set up in the union. When I got Presser talking over dinner he would happily concede that people like Babe Triscaro (his father's closest aide) and John Nardi were, in his words on two different occasions, "scum, low life," and "the kind of hoods we have to clean out of here." But he made no visible effort to clean them out. In fact, he appointed John Nardi's son, John junior, a business agent of Local 507 in 1974. And, when Nardi senior was murdered in 1977 in a gangland-style execution, Presser approved the merger of Nardi's Local 410 into Local 416, which was run by Nardi's brother Nick. According to FBI sources, this allowed the organized-crime forces to keep control of both unions and to perpetuate a racket in which the mob used the union to maintain a monopoly on cigarette-vending machines in the Cleveland area. Also in 1977, organized-crime figures were found by the Cleveland *Press* to have been installed as the operators of bingo games, supposedly run for charity at a party center owned by Presser's wife.

With names like Nardi still on the union payroll, and with Presser aiding the underworld in these ways, reformers and government investigators watching the Teamsters and trying to size up Presser as the possible next president had more than enough reason to be suspicious. Yet by badmouthing the underworld elements to some reporters, and by cutting some of their influence and taking personal control of more and more contracts, Presser had reason enough to be nervous. "If Jackie keeps that up," one FBI agent who was familiar with the Cleveland scene remarked in mid-1977, "he's gonna be dead soon. He's got to understand that they're not going to take it if he unglues the alliance his father made with the Italians in Cleveland."

In fact, throughout 1977 in Cleveland, one heard rumors of how the "boys from Murray Hill," as the Italian neighborhood was called, were getting fed up with Presser's "arrogance" or his "independence." Adding to feelings about Presser's precarious position in 1977 were the murders in Cleveland of Nardi in May and a Nardi associate in September. Both were killed by bombs left in cars parked next to their cars and set off by remote control. According to an FBI affidavit appended to the indictment of those charged with the second murder, the murders were committed because Nardi was competing with another faction "for leadership in the Cleveland organized-crime family," and Presser was believed to be allied with Nardi in the fight.

Did these murders scare him, I asked Presser in September, three weeks before the 1977 La Costa tournament.

"Not really," he answered matter-of-factly. "The murders had to do with drug traffic or something like that, not the union. And besides, if I spent my time being scared, I'd get nothing done. Sure it's a risk, but I'm not scared."

That night when we walked from Presser's office out to his Cadillac, the car was parked in a tightly fenced-in private lot on the union property where no strange car with one of those remote-control bombs could possibly park next to it. The walk, itself, was a scene out of a Grade-B gangster movie: four burly "business agents," each big enough for any football team's front line (one, in fact, was a former professional tackle) surrounded us during the ten-yard stroll. Only after Presser had unlocked the burglar alarm and slipped behind the wheel of the telephone-equipped velour-lined caddy, did they grunt "see ya, boss" and stroll away.

Those wide-bodied business agents personified much of the ambivalence that marked Presser's life during the year following the 1976 Invitational.

Their tough-guy sneers and swaggers, and their part-time bodyguard duties, embodied the old-world side of Presser's act; on the other hand, their single-minded devotion to the crack-of-dawn systematic schedule Presser had laid out for them to visit union job sites every day illustrated the new dedication to union work he was trying to effect. There were other reminders of contradiction and confusion—large and small. Presser wore a diamond bracelet spelling out "Jackie," which warred with the custom-tailored wools that might otherwise have made him look like a well-heeled Wall Street lawyer. One of the "executives" of a public-relations firm that he had hired allegedly had organized-crime ties, and had spent twenty years in prison for participating in the murder of two police officers.

Also, despite his wealth, Presser insisted on making more money in ways that produced conflicts of interest with his union duties. He was part owner of a vehicle repair and body company that received nearly a quarter of a million dollars in business in 1976 from trucking companies that employed Teamsters. His wife owned a large restaurant that employed members of the bartenders and restaurant workers union he had also run until mid-1976. As required by law, Presser had filed reports of these conflicts with the Labor Department; therefore, nothing about these side interests was illegal on its face. But they crossed ethical boundaries that many leaders of other unions would have stayed clear of; and as a millionaire seeking the union presidency, he'd have been willing to forgo these extra incomes had he been wholly dedicated to the clean image he was trying to project.

Another symbolic throwback—one that emphasized how far Jackie Presser and his union had to go—was Presser's Cleveland office. Except for one wall where there was a bookcase and an electric paper shredder, the office was lined with plaques and trophies and other testimonial trivia. "That office tells you more about Jackie Presser than anything else," declared a close Presser friend who knew Presser in his role as a civic leader and political power. "He and all the other Teamster guys have inferiority complexes. No big business president has to have a plaque on the wall from the National Conference of Christians and Jews saying he's a nice guy. But I bet he did, twenty or thirty years ago. That's where Jackie is. He's insecure now. He doesn't think he's arrived yet. But he's trying."

For all his insecurity and the problems and tensions, stirred by the tightrope walking, Presser was still doing pretty well as the 1977 Fitzsimmons Tournament approached. The same friend who alluded to his inferiority complex remarked that "two years ago here in Cleveland the phrase was 'go see the fat man' if you needed something done politically or with labor. Now that Jackie's lost so much weight it's 'go see the man.' He's got more power than ever now, even with all the dissidents and all the guys from the old Italian families going against him." Presser's real challenge, the friend suggested, wasn't the opposition at home, but in Washington, where by 1977 he spent more than half his time working on the national PR campaign, and on his own campaign to succeed Fitzsimmons. "He's been telling me that 'Here I'm a big fish, but when I get to the

Washington office I'm a guppie compared to some of the sharks there.' "

But perhaps it was more a case of a lone shark against the other sharks. From the 1976 tournament to the 1977 tournament the infighting was fierce: the old-liners, led by Vice-President Roy Williams, tried to undercut Presser, as Presser tried to use his public-relations drive to hoist himself above them. "Things are getting pretty rough around here," a top headquarters staffer with a good ear for gossip remarked during the summer of 1977. "The old guys are all trying to cut up Jackie, but he's using his father's friendship with Fitz to fight back. He's also scaring Fitz into backing him, by telling him that without Jackie's PR campaign the government will be able to force him out. Personally, I think Jackie's using the PR campaign to force Fitz out himself."

Talks with other knowledgeable headquarters officials yielded a clear impression that Fitzsimmons was backing Presser without realizing that Presser was actually trying to use his position to jettison Fitzsimmons by creating a climate in which it would be difficult for Fitzsimmons to survive. On a few occasions, Presser set up situations involving Fitzsimmons and the press that seemed designed to make Fitzsimmons look bad. In April 1977 he helped Fitzsimmons plan that meeting in Washington to which all local union officers were hastily summoned only to hear Fitzsimmons say he wasn't going to resign and offer a patently false explanation for his having left the pension fund board. The meeting impressed no one and embittered many local union officials who had had to cancel plans for Easter vacations in order to attend.

Sources close to Fitzsimmons, as well as Fitzsimmons himself in an interview, later claimed that Presser had urged that the meeting be closed to the press. That night, the evening news featured film clips of the press being pushed back from the door. Presser later confided to others and to me that he had urged Fitzsimmons to open up the meeting, but that Fitzsimmons had refused. This, it turned out, was part of a pattern of confiding conflicting or negative information about Fitzsimmons to some members of the press. To one shrewd executive board member "Presser's whispering," as he put it, was predictable. "You don't take a guy who's looking to take over your job and make him your PR man," he explained. "That's just stupid."

Not that the Teamsters didn't need a good, nationwide public-relations program. For two decades Teamsters PR work had ranged from Hoffa lending pension fund money to William Loeb's Manchester *Union Leader* to Hoffa spitting at Des Moines *Register* reporter Clark Mollenhoff the day Hoffa went to jail. There had been little professional attempt to get the Teamsters story across, except for occasional Hoffa testimonial dinners, or the legislative conferences with key politicians as speakers.

The one real try at sustained communication, begun in 1972, ended the following year in a fiasco. Television personality Ed McMahon had approached the Teamsters with an elaborate $1,750,000 program, including a network special that he would produce and lend his name to, a high-school essay contest, and a truck caravan to travel around the country under the theme "America on the Move," which would celebrate the Teamsters' role in American life. A little more than a year later, with the caravan halted and the teen-age winners of the essay contest not paid (though the TV show starring Sammy Davis, Jr., Debbie Reynolds and McMahon was broadcast), the money had disappeared and the Teamsters were suing McMahon and his partner for diverting the funds to another business venture. By the end of 1977 the case was finally settled with McMahon, according to a Teamsters lawyer, "paying us a substantial amount." Other than that, until Presser came on the scene, the Teamsters PR program was nil.

The public-relations director at the Washington headquarters was a gruff and craggy Fitzsimmons lookalike who had few press contacts and was so in the dark about union affairs that on one occasion he didn't know Fitzsimmons had scheduled a rare press conference until a reporter told him about it a few hours before. His main job was editing the *Teamster* magazine, a dull, old-fashioned journal of puffery. The magazine, in fact, was a profound illustration of the way the Teamsters had ignored the potential communications clout the largest and richest union in the world could muster.

When Bill Presser convinced Fitzsimmons to let Jackie take his PR effort nationwide things began to change. By the end of 1977 the magazine, sent at an annual cost of $2,668,000, to a monthly audience bigger than that enjoyed by all but a handful of America's largest publications, was still mostly a waste of postage and paper. But an overhaul was in the planning stages. And in other media areas major initiatives were underway. Beginning in the fall of 1976 the union budgeted nearly a quarter of a million dollars per season to sponsor college and professional football games on a nationwide radio network. According to the advertising records, the ads, carrying messages about Teamsters benefits and the diversity of Teamsters membership, reached more than three million adults each broadcast. During one Saturday halftime, Presser himself could be heard telling the fans about everything the Teamsters had done for sports and charity. Billboards were put up in several cities carrying the message that Teamsters membership was "America's best buy," and that "It's not easy being Number One."

On the day before President Jimmy Carter's inauguration, full-page ads were purchased in major city newspapers wishing him well and presenting a long summary of Teamsters goals and principles. About a month later Presser arranged for a carefully controlled appearance for Fitzsimmons on a late-evening Sammy Davis, Jr., network television show. Soon after that, working on another front, Presser sent a busload of Ohio retirees to Washington to attend a Congressional hearing so that, for once, the crowd at such events would contain more rank-and-file supporters than PROD dissidents.

As the October 1977 La Costa tournament approached, Presser had bigger plans in the works for the purchase of TV time and the use of a nationwide citizen-band radio network to sing the Teamsters praises. One night, about three weeks before the tournament, he sat in his office and read aloud to me a message he planned to deliver personally the following year on radio or TV explaining why Teamsters dues were "the best bargain in America."

Most of these PR efforts, especially the inaugural newspaper ads, the Fitzsimmons TV appearance, and Presser's proposed speech, were clumsy by sophisticated Madison Avenue standards. But that was part of the transition. Similarly, as with Presser's Ohio posture, his performance in Washington was marred by lapses back to the old style. Like Fitzsimmons, he couldn't bring himself to refrain from attacking PROD and implying that they were somehow a Communist front. Nor could Presser control himself one day outside an executive board meeting when he saw NBC reporter Brian Ross, who had done some scathing reports on the Teamsters. Within earshot of other reporters he cursed Ross out bitterly. Presser, in fact, was light-years ahead of others in the union in dealing with the media. Most other Teamsters officials routinely ignored reporters' inquiries, while others went out of their way to impugn reporters' motives or integrity.

"Sure they're not very good at PR yet," one of Presser's friends and public-relations advisers conceded. "Most of the stuff, like the inauguration ads, is still pretty amateur. But that's because they're an institution going through an evolution. It's like General Motors years ago. You remember, they created Ralph Nader by attacking him. They even had him followed. But then they learned basic PR, how to get a message across by not being paranoid. How to talk to the press. Well, it's the same with the Teamsters. They created the Nader offspring, PROD, by attacking them. But now, ever so slowly, they're learning how to react and how to communicate. It's all part of an evolution. You watch, in three years they'll have the slickest, best magazine and the best advertising money can buy.''

For Fitzsimmons, three years probably isn't soon enough. And even if it is, what he didn't realize was that that kind of aggressive, sophisticated public profile and his own survival weren't compatible. He is a symbol of the corrupt past, and the more Presser conveys the image of a strong, new, community-minded union, the more out of place Fitzsimmons will look sitting at the top, and the bigger, more tempting target he'll be for prosecutors frustrated and egged on by Teamsters advertising themselves as good guys. If that process doesn't happen naturally, Presser could help it along with leaks to reporters and to friends in the union about how incompetent and out of touch Fitzsimmons has been. Indeed, as the Eighth Annual Fitzsimmons Invitational neared in October 1977, such messages from Presser were becoming increasingly frequent.

Still, Fitzsimmons continued to support Presser and the expanding PR program that increased his influence and exposure. He thought, wrongly, that a Teamsters PR campaign was a Fitzsimmons PR campaign.

Pride and the way simple family loyalties and concerns affect pride were major ingredients overlooked in many attempts by observers over the years to analyze the Teamsters leaders' behavior. Many of the actions that seemed incredibly brazen or illogical or unrealistic could be explained by understanding the world they went home to every night. According to one member of Fitzsimmons' family, the aging union president was terribly troubled by all the reports in the press of his dishonesty and incompetence. To Fitzsimmons, Presser's PR campaign to set the record straight offered some comfort for him and his family.

For Presser, too, the PR offensive was partly rooted in pride. For years his four children had been plagued by the Teamsters reputation. ''We used to ask him [one of Presser's sons] if we could come over to his basement and see Jimmy Hoffa's body," a classmate of one of his children recalled in 1977. Unlike Fitzsimmons, Presser's efforts to make Teamsters a respectable word meant more than justifying his career to himself and his children. It was a way of justifying the career of his father, who, as Presser put it, was "the human being I admire and love more than anyone else on earth." There was also special pressure on Presser from the women in his life. His mother and his wife were not the stereotypical unknowing, unseeing, all-innocent Teamsters boss's wives: Mother Faye was a shrewd, sharp woman who had been the closest thing to "one of the guys" at any Teamsters gathering; and Wife Carmen owned that bingo parlor in Cleveland that used mob gamblers to help run the games. Nonetheless, by 1977 both women were seriously ill, and Presser's PR campaign, as well as his quest for respectability, could in part also be attributed to his desire to set things right for them.

Though Fitzsimmons supported Presser's PR offensive, most of the other members of the executive board hated it. For them, pride was handled Provenzano-style—by tuning out criticism and creating for your family a different world to live in. "Jackie's ideas are OK, I guess," Sam Provenzano said glumly one morning. "But it's a waste of money. Hell, we know we're honest."

"Why do we need to look good and nice," veteran New York Teamsters organizer and lobbyist Nicholas Kisburg bellowed during a late 1977 interview. Kisburg, who significantly was the man closest to Eastern Conference head and International Vice-President Joseph Trerotola, added "Be sure to write that I said Jackie Presser is a clown. . . . He's watched too much TV and has seen you can sell horse shit. And that's what he thinks he can do with us. . . ." Or as Allen Dorfman put it, "Fuck Jackie Presser. . . . who gives a shit what people think of us. We've come this far being attacked by the press and the government, haven't we?"

Presser knew that many top teamsters didn't like his PR ideas simply because they were Presser's. They resented him, and they didn't like the notion of his being involved in anything that would give him a leg up on the union presidency. In view of this hostility, it was hard to imagine how Presser expected to get this board to choose him as the president if Fitzsimmons resigned before the 1981 convention. (The union constitution provides that in the event of a vacancy the board chooses the president to serve until a convention can be called.) It seemed that Presser would be better off trying to keep

Fitzsimmons in place, so that Fitzsimmons could survive until the next convention. Then Presser, perhaps even with Fitzsimmons' endorsement, could try to get the convention, rather than the board, to choose him.

"No, that's not his thinking," a veteran board member explained. "Jackie's not worried about what the board will do, because he figures enough of them hate [Roy] Williams enough to choose him [Presser, over Williams]. Some of the guys on the board like [Edward] Lawson [from Canada] like Jackie. Besides, even if the board chooses one of the old-liners like Williams, Jackie figures he'll be able to beat him at the convention, which will have to be held within six months of the board's choice. Also, he figures the longer Fitz stays in, the more likely it is that some real clean reformer will gather support. Or that one of the old-liners, like Williams, will have more time to make deals to put him over the top. Then there's also the fact that Fitzsimmons would be too scared to endorse anyone at the convention anyway, and even if he did it might just hurt the guy."

Another possibility, discussed by some top Teamsters at the 1977 La Costa tournament, was that Fitzsimmons would resign soon, but that the board would pick a compromise—an inoffensive interim president. The top prospect for such an interim spot was Trerotola, the aging, New York-based International vice-president. Trerotola's personal honesty yet studious tolerance for others' dishonesty was the reason that in 1966 he had been made president of New York's Joint Council 16 in another compromise between factions. This scenario called for a decentralization of power to the regional vice-presidents under the hapless Trerotola even more pronounced than the power shift that had marked the Hoffa-to-Fitzsimmons transition.

However things worked out, it seemed clear that ultimately Presser would be squaring off against Roy Williams, the Kansas City-based sixty-two-year-old ninth vice-president whom Fitzsimmons had appointed to the key job of Central States Conference director in 1976. Williams is an old-time Teamsters boss. In the words of Jimmy Hoffa, Jr., he is "a lot like my dad in the sense that he loves power and is very physical—very hard driving. He was a protégé of my father's." Apparently Williams had learned not only Hoffa's love for power but also his method of teaming up with organized crime to get it. FBI agents, Labor Department investigators and other law-enforcement people were certain, as one put it, "that Roy's been tied in with the mob for years," and that as another Teamsters vice-president (but *not* Presser) explained, "Roy's not a free citizen, he has to do what these guys tell him."

According to the FBI, the "guy" who told Williams the most was Nicholas Civella, the long-time Kansas City organized-crime chief. A 1971 Labor Department memo (the same one, ironically, that detailed the mob associates and employees of Bill Presser) declared that "it was also learned that Roy Williams is under the complete domination of Civella. Williams will not act contrary to the wishes of Civella, apparently because of both self interest and fear." The memo also attributed Williams' rise in the union to Civella's original sponsorship of him.

As the fall of 1977 approached, Williams, who had twice before been charged with but acquitted of embezzlement, was again in trouble. One of the Central States Pension Fund loans that the Justice Department was reportedly looking at for prosecution possibilities was a loan to build the Landmark Hotel in Las Vegas. Williams, a Fund trustee until the Labor Department forced him to resign earlier in 1977, reportedly arranged for the 1966 loan to the Landmark in return for Civella getting a "finder's fee."

None of Williams' vulnerabilities had been lost on Jackie Presser. Presser took every opportunity he could find during 1977 to remind the members of the executive board that going along with a man who had a record like Williams' would mean no easing of the pressure on the union from PROD, from the public, or from all the government investigations. It was a plausible argument, even though it didn't take into consideration that putting the name Presser at the top wouldn't exactly wipe the slate clean either. Presser also tipped off at least one reporter to Williams' involvement in a prepaid-legal-services scheme in which Williams' Kansas City union members would sign up for a prepaid plan and part of the fees reportedly would be for kickbacks to organized-crime figures. (The twice-indicted Williams had even prepared a letter to sell the reportedly crooked plan to his members by citing his knowledge of the virtues of good legal protection, since, "as you know, I have been through many legal battles.") When federal investigators got word of the scheme and began asking about it, the plan was scrapped. Presser also spread the word, accurately, that it was Williams who had spearheaded the drive in the spring of 1977 to get the Central States health and welfare fund to renew Allen Dorfman's lucrative claims-processing contract.

Williams, for his part, reminded those who he thought needed reminding that Jackie might be Bill's kid, but that he had grown too arrogant now and was too young and too willing to sell the old-liners down the river just so he could ride to the top on that new "image bullshit of his," as he was heard characterizing Presser's PR campaign on one occasion. Besides, Williams argued, Presser was a buffoon, and all that public-relations stuff was "just a lot of crap." In making his case, Williams' top ally was the Teamsters number-two officer, Secretary-Treasurer Ray Schoessling.

Presser countered such thrusts, not with high-minded ethical arguments about honesty, but by reassuring even the most crooked of the board members that his new image-building would actually protect them.

This suggests that even if he were to win the presidency Presser would still walk that tightrope between pleasing the crooks and appeasing the reformers and government investigators. In one candid conversation in late September of 1977 he conceded that the balancing act would be tough, perhaps even impossible. "You know," he began, "that chair Fitzsimmons sits in isn't a throne, it's an electric chair. They [government prosecutors] got the last two men who sat there [Dave Beck and Jimmy Hoffa] and sent them to jail, and it wouldn't surprise me if they got Fitz on something soon. They're sure trying. On the other hand," he continued, "if you're totally honest and if you try to clean up the union like you say I should, and you try to do it fast enough and without making accommodations so the government won't get you, the other guys—the hoods—will get you. Just like they got Hoffa when he threatened them. So that's a death chair either way."

When I asked other top Teamsters, they offered essentially the same view of the union presidency. Harold Gibbons said, "Williams and Presser are crazy to be fighting over that job. It's a shortcut to the shithouse. Look what happened to Beck and Jimmy." But all those who expressed that view, including Gibbons and Presser, would take the job in a minute. Almost like the Presidency of the United States or the mayoralty of a big city, the top Teamsters spot is testimony to how the promise of power and fame overcomes any logic or rationality that argues that the job can be self-destructive.

Through the 1977 La Costa Tournament the jockeying between Williams and Presser continued. Like the plaques on Presser's wall back in Cleveland, most of the soap-opera intrigue of innuendo and in-fighting was not terribly subtle. Of course, neither Williams nor

Presser could really be sure who was lining up on who's side. All the board members they courted wanted to end up siding with the winner. And some—including Gibbons and Joe Morgan from the South, and maybe even Jesse Carr from Alaska—still harbored their own dreams of the presidency.

For Presser, more so than Williams, the campaign was a big gamble. He couldn't really tell whether he might be threatening them too much. Was he, he often wondered, pushing so hard against the old-liners and not doing enough quietly to reassure them, that they'd have him killed? Back in Ohio, he had the same problem, and the same fear. These worries—combined with the work he was plunged into, also on two fronts, of negotiating contracts in Ohio while running the PR campaign out of Washington—had given him a brutal first year as a Teamsters vice-president. He had traveled endlessly between Ohio and Washington, trying in both areas to stay on top of things, to feel the pulse, and to do the necessary jockeying. He was also planning another nightclub-theater that he hoped would duplicate the success of the first one. More important, he had had the burden of helping his wife face her illness, helping his father and mother cope with their illnesses, and trying to find some useful employment for one of his daughters who had been slightly handicapped in a car accident. Even during the 1977 tournament itself, these pressures converged on him; he had to take an all-night plane after the last round of golf so he could be in Cleveland to take Carmen home from another of her hospital stays the next morning and then put in a full afternoon of work going over local contracts.

Four months after the tournament, on February 1, 1978, the government would add its own pressure, naming him as a defendant in its massive ERISA suit against the Central States Pension Fund. He had been a trustee for only eleven months during 1974 and 1975, when he was sitting in for his father (also named in the suit), and there was no allegation that he arranged any of the questionable loans listed. Williams, who had also been named in the suit, was much more vulnerable. But the charge that Presser hadn't met his fiduciary responsibility to prevent or protest the allegedly bad loans might be tough to beat, and immediately it endangered the credit that he was arranging to start his new nightclub with.

Still, professionally at least, the future looked good. He had come a long way from the grudging backslapping and congratulations they had given him the October before, when he was seen as a "kid" who had visions of being more than he deserved to be. They still resented him, but they could see now that he might just pull it off. A few weeks after the tournament he opened a new, giant public-relations complex in the newly built wing of the Washington headquarters. From there he would mastermind an elaborately expanded PR campaign that would give him still more clout and drastically increase his own public exposure as a Teamsters spokesman. The pressure would intensify as he got closer. There were certain to be more government investigations and more attacks from PROD. But he was sure he could ride them out. With the government investigating Williams and, along with the press, keeping the pressure on Fitzsimmons, Dorfman and the others, things seemed to be working his way.

The morning Presser got home from the tournament, Fitzsimmons called to say that, after all the golf scores had been tallied the day before, Jackie Presser had been declared the winner.

CHAPTER X

Gibbons

Harold Gibbons loves to play golf. It is a game he can play without being crowded, and it has a certain elegance. Yet for all the glorious golf in the offing at La Costa the morning of October 13, 1976, Gibbons resisted the wake-up call.

He was hung over. The night before at the bar he had faded back to the old days with old friends. The few loyalists among the Tournament-goers were still captivated by the magnetism that had carried Gibbons through hundreds of negotiating sessions and union hall assemblies. Freed from the realities by the drinks and the blurring of memory, they pretended with him that he was the hero that he might have been. They relived and embellished old glories all night, exchanging enough smirks and subtle quips to establish their tacit agreement that by rights Gibbons should have been top man. He looks the part.

Gibbons is still strikingly good-looking. He has a strong voice, he is crisp and precise. Tall and white-haired, he is usually tan. He spends his winters in Palm Springs. He is tastefully dressed.

On October 13, Harold Gibbons was strictly second-string. Fitzsimmons, not the smart, suave, Harold Gibbons, had made it to the top. Gibbons was a well-preserved sixty-seven-year-old might-have-been. He knew that the ass-kissers would push by him in the locker room and at the tee-off to get near Fitzsimmons. And he would have to pay his respects, too.

As he lit the first of the pack of cigarettes he would smoke by the end of the morning, he thought he would score a small point for independence by wearing the "Dean's List" button (named for White House Counsel John Dean), signifying that he had been on Nixon's enemies list. That would remind Fitz and the rest of them that he had refused to support Nixon in '72. But so what? He was going along now.

For the others in the Teamsters hierarchy, Fitzsimmons' limitations were a source of behind-the-back jokes. Still, they all seemed to like him. Gibbons hated Fitzsimmons with an intensity that was difficult to control on mornings when he actually had to face him. Fitzsimmons had displayed a viciousness against Gibbons that he rarely exhibited in dealing with others. He castrated Gibbons publicly in 1973 and sent him out to pasture.

In many respects, Harold Patrick Gibbons had little to sulk about. He had come a long way. Sixty years earlier, when he had a hard time getting up in the morning, his mother used to have to wash his feet just to coax him out of bed. But those really were hard times. He was the youngest of twenty-three brothers and sisters sired by a father named Patrick Gibbons who included Patrick in all their names. The family lived in a coal-mine camp in northeast Pennsylvania called Archibald Patch. Things were bad for the average family, let alone one with twenty-three kids. Gibbons' father and all his brothers (in 1977 he had forgotten how many brothers there were) were coal miners. Often, when the miners went through one of their regular multi-month strikes, Harold ate a potato for breakfast, lunch, and dinner. His first full-time job, at seventeen, was as a dishwasher in Scranton. He worked twelve hours a day, seven days a week for ten dollars.

Fifty years later, being the second vice-president of the largest union in the world—even if Fitzsimmons made sure he didn't get much work to do—and having to play a round on one of the country's best golf courses might have been nothing to complain about. But you couldn't convince Gibbons. He knew that he could have been the most important American labor leader of his time.

When Gibbons' family drifted out to Chicago, he took a job as a short-order cook; then he took another in a machinery warehouse. But he was more than an ordinary blue-collar worker trying to survive the Depression. He had set high sights for himself and decided to get an education. During the summer, when he was twenty and twenty-one, he won a YMCA contest that paid for him to go to an industrial-workers' summer school at the University of Wisconsin.

Summer school intensified his enthusiasm for intellectual things, and turned him in a new direction. More than four decades later, Gibbons remembered that he had seen "a society divided between those who own and those who work." He described his learning process this way:

"I was going to be an engineer and I was going to be a rich guy. This may be very self-serving, but it's actually the truth. I went up to the University of Wisconsin and there's a bunch of socialist kids there. And after we became acquainted . . . they used to take me . . . into their dormitory and they'd lock the door, and you'd stay right there and listen. And they'd pound and pound away on me. . . . Then . . . I got in this economic discussion group. We were studying . . . capitalism and socialism . . . The result was that a lot of the things that were part of my childhood growing up in the coal fields came back to me in a flood. . . . I came away from there with a conviction that if I had any talent, any energies, any brains, I'm gonna devote it to the have-nots and not the haves. . . . It was just that simple . . . Like they used to say about John L. Lewis, he was in the dues manufacturing business, but if he was in the business of manufacturing sewing machines he would have been a success there, too. And I suspect that I could have made a living in other ways, but I've never had a desire since those summers to do anything but be a trade-union man."

After the University of Wisconsin, Gibbons enrolled in a New Deal worker-education program at the University of Chicago. Soon, the twenty-two-year-old was teaching other workers there and writing textbooks. ("I was smarter and better read than the others and I convinced them I could do the work.") Gibbons joined a socialist discussion group. ("Boy, I'm surprised I ever escaped jail in those days. We were crazy. Running around the streets agitating on every issue. But it really gave me a consciousness that I've kept.")

The young socialist organized his first union, a local consisting of his fellow adult-education teachers. A year and a half later, at a

Teachers Federation convention—where he showed himself to be a fiery speaker—Gibbons was elected a vice-president of the teachers national union. Two years later, in 1936, he got involved through some socialist friends in a Congress of Industrial Organizations (CIO) taxi drivers' strike. First he was the editor of the strikers' newspaper, then he became assistant director of the Chicago branch of the CIO. At the CIO, he led dozens of other strikes, including one involving women textile workers who threw themselves in front of police cars that were trying to break through their picket lines. "I worked on textile problems and anything else that came up," Gibbons told me at the side of the pool at his home in Palm Springs. "We used to send a crew out just to walk the streets and find the sit-down strikes that were taking place in the restaurants, factories, and anywhere else. Then at night I taught school."

In 1938, at age twenty-eight, Gibbons became a regional organizer for textile workers in five states. Now based in Louisville, he worked for a salary of $35 a week, although, "we were usually so short of money in the union that I worked for half pay." Gibbons went on the first of what he estimated to be "more than a hundred trips from the picket lines to the shithouse," the local jail. "We were outlaws. If you could have seen the way the cops treated us in those days you'd understand a little more about why we became so cynical and disgusted about law and the establishment."

Gibbons met Ann Colter at a Socialist-sponsored peace rally in 1938. She was the chairwoman, and he had been invited to speak. They married three months later.

In 1941 Gibbons shifted to another union job: running the Retail, Wholesale and Department Store Employees Union of the CIO (1,200 members in six tiny locals and one joint council) in St. Louis. In 1947 he broke with the CIO and merged the locals into an independent distribution workers union. It wasn't until early 1949 that Gibbons became a big power in St. Louis and finally had the chance to put his socialist politics to work. In January of that year he signed a pact to merge his distribution workers into an 8,000-member local of the Teamsters Union. Under the merger agreement all of Gibbons' workers were folded into Teamsters Local 688; the then-president of the Teamsters local retired; and Gibbons became president of the union. Ultimately he expanded the local to 16,000 members including a large group of brewery and soda factory workers.

Within two years, Local 688, under Harold Gibbons, became so much of a workers' ideal that twenty-five years later it still looked revolutionary.

Gibbons' workers got free, unlimited hospitalization and medical care for themselves and their spouses and children—a benefit virtually unheard of in 1951. "Other workers, if they had any health protection at all," Gibbons explained, "had insurance. But that had limitations. If you had to have an appendectomy the insurance gave you $75. But the doctor charged you $150, so you were stuck. That was no good. Some of the guys I was organizing were making 35 cents an hour, and they couldn't afford that. So we built our own Labor Health Institute with its own doctors [57 of them working part-time by 1951] that handled everything. It was the first prepaid health plan as far as I know, and the employers paid for all of it." Gibbons' members also got free dental care (except for bridgework and dentures, which they got at cost.) They got free home nursing services, drugs and eyeglasses at cost, and free legal advice. By 1951 they also had pension benefits—at least four years earlier than other Teamsters locals won them.

When food prices rose rapidly that year, the union opened a nonprofit grocery for its members. A few years later, Gibbons persuaded the employers to pay for a recreation center as part of the employee health program. Wholly financed by employers, it had become, by the early '60s, an unparalleled complex that included an indoor swimming pool and gymnasium center for winter recreation and a 300-acre outdoor swimming, camping, tennis and golf-course complex in suburban St. Louis. In short, the workers had the same kind of country-club facilities that their bosses had. "Many of our members were from the slums," Gibbons said. "I saw the health-and-recreation camp as the only way to get their kids some fresh air and a decent place to play in. It was the first time recreational facilities were ever defined as part of a legitimate union health plan that the employers could pay for. For the members and children who were black, it was the only decent place they could go, because everything was segregated in those days."

Gibbons fought segregation in St. Louis. "We used the union as a social force." In January of 1952, two years before the Supreme Court's decision striking down school segregation, Gibbons published a union plan for the desegregation of St. Louis's public schools. At the time, public schools were required by the Missouri constitution to be divided by race. "It was just plain common sense.

But what a reaction the fuckin' thing got," Gibbons recalled. One St. Louis resident called it "a Russian booby trap," in a letter to a local newspaper. When the civil-rights struggle in the South opened on other fronts in the middle '50s, Gibbons thrust 688 into the battle headlong: "If you were black you couldn't get into a theater anywhere in the city of St. Louis except in the black community," he recalled. "And you couldn't find anywhere outside the black community for a black woman to eat or go to the john when she was shopping. Our Local 688 led that whole goddamn fight. We picketed the theaters. We broke 'em down. We went down and sat in restaurants while we were in drug stores. We raised hell. We busted the city wide open."

Civil rights was not the only social and political front into which Gibbons threw his union's muscle. A system of "community stewards" was established to put Teamsters power to work in the neighborhoods. In each ward with more than twenty-five Local 688 members, a community steward organized meetings where members expressed themselves about garbage collection, street lights and other local services, and pressured officials to take action. As Gibbons explained it, "If, let's say, we needed a playground in that neighborhood, we'd have the steward get all our members in that neighborhood together and start raising hell. We'd call a meeting, and you know when you're talking about a playground it isn't just for Teamsters members. So our guys would get every goddamn neighbor to go to the meeting, too. In the 24th Ward, which was our best ward, we'd have 1,500 or 2,000 people, when the ward committee man might get 150 to *his* meetings. He'd die. And you know he'd listen to us."

The union tackled citywide issues as aggressively as it did neighborhood service problems: "The streetcar companies were raising their fares and cutting back on service. Well, we have an initiative deal in Missouri where you can get up petitions and put something on the ballot. I mobilized the membership to sign petitions, and we got enough to put it on the ballot. The result is we socialized the goddamn transit system. . . . We now have a bistate agency that runs all the busses. . . . When a private company fucked up the sewerage system in the county, we went out and got all the signatures necessary and got a metropolitan sewer district—established strictly on the basis of 688's activities. . . . When our people couldn't afford to send their kids to college—they had no community colleges in St. Louis or even a branch of the state college—we went out, agitated, passed resolutions and everything else, and we now have three community colleges in the city, plus a branch of the state university.''

The way the union was governed in those days was as singular as its civic activities. Attendance at union meetings was compulsory. Unexcused absences, which were rare, brought fines, which were donated to charity. Even more remarkable, the rules, while they fostered unity and tight discipline among the ranks, were not used as tools for dictatorial control by Gibbons. If anything, it was just the opposite. In 1952, the year of the desegregation plan, Gibbons earned $90 a week, plus $5 a day for expenses. Every staff member received the same salary. All raises had to be negotiated through a steward's subcommittee, headed that year by a platform loader at a shoe company's warehouse. The raise then had to be approved by a 500-member steward's council which took its work seriously. The same council approved union expenditures—after another subcommittee had approved them—and any major union initiatives, such as the desegregation proposal.

At least part of the secret of Gibbons' success in achieving unprecedented benefits and sizable increases for his members, and in winning numerous membership-recruiting drives in the early '50s, came from the unity and discipline that the governing structure fostered. A Local 688 strike was a group effort. It was fueled by a genuine feeling of participation by the members and by the political ideology that Gibbons preached to them at stewards' meetings and membership rallies. His eloquence and charisma flowered.

Twenty-five years later, dozens of veteran warehouse workers interviewed would still remember Gibbons, in the words of one of them, as "the most impressive man I ever saw in my life speaking to an audience." Gibbons, the socialist from Chicago, marched to the class-war drumbeat with more fervor than anyone in the audience. This too was part of his success: he worked longer and harder than most union leaders. In an average week in the early '50s Gibbons might have had two or three dozen picket lines going at three or four strikes, and it was not unusual for him to begin his rounds at 4 or 5 A.M.

Gibbons brought the same personal magnetism to the negotiating table. Employers were impressed by him, and impressed that he could and would pull his men out of their plants if an agreement wasn't struck. Beyond that, he was intelligent enough to absorb complex contract issues quickly and find solutions both sides could live with. Then there was another element: Gibbons was honest. No portion of management's settlement of a deal went under the table; it all came across the top to finance the wages, benefits and civic activities of Local 688's members.

By the early '50s, Local 688—with its Labor Health Institute, "community stewards," petition drives, free legal advice, civil-rights fights, compulsory attendance at meetings, stewards council, and other special features—had become the nation's model of progressive unionism. Labor leaders and academics came from all over the country to tour Gibbons' local. The State Department put it on its list of sites for visiting dignitaries. Gibbons was a superstar in labor circles. The local press did close-ups of the tall, handsome young unionist and his good-looking young family. He was invited to lecture at Harvard, invited to tour Europe to give his assessment of how the Marshall Plan was helping workers (he said it was "failing miserably") and invited to tour Israel and assess labor relations there.

Gibbons' brand of Teamsterism would not have been so noteworthy had the Teamsters of the '50s and '60s been faithful to their past. The phenomenal growth of the Teamsters union in the 1930s and '40s into a major labor organization had been effected by a small group of devout socialists and communists whose political fervor and commitment to the class struggle exceeded even Gibbons' concept of unionism as an engine for radical social and political change.

The Team Drivers International Union was founded in Detroit in 1899 as an arm of the American Federation of Labor (AFL). It had 18 locals and 1,200 drivers. By 1902 the union had grown quickly and violently to 30,000 members. They were involved that year in about a hundred lockouts or strikes. This was the early, brutal first half century of the American labor movement. Unions were seen by business interests, the police, and most of the press as organized extortion rings of have-nots who deserved no better lot in life and certainly weren't going to get it by disrupting the natural order of things by withholding work. For the Teamsters, the biggest battle in 1902 was a thirteen-day strike of drivers who worked out of Chicago's meat-packing houses. There was almost continuous rioting as police clubbed picketers and Teamsters tried to block the goon-guarded meat and bakery wagons. In those early days of horse-drawn wagons a teamster strike was immediately a cause of community panic; there was no such thing as frozen foods, and the team drivers were a city's daily life line. Teamsters membership buttons were reversible, with one side to be used at parades and a black side to be worn at members' funerals.

In 1902 a splinter group, the Teamsters National Union, was formed. But in August 1903 the two teamster organizations, yielding to a plea from the AFL, had joined at a Niagara Falls convention to found the International Brotherhood of Teamsters. Two months later the first headquarters was opened in Indianapolis, with Cornelius Stein installed as president at a salary of $150 a month. This was also the year the Teamsters got their first taste of terrible publicity: on December 30, 1903, 1,200 striking livery drivers (seeking two dollars a day for twelve hours) were accused in the press of "jeering at the holocaust," "loafing in saloons" and "laughing at the call for volunteers" while the great Chicago Iroquois Theatre fire killed 602 people, mostly women and children. Two years later Chicago was the scene of another of the bloodiest Teamsters strikes, in which several hundred blacks were imported from the South, given rifles, and paid by the employers' association to drive the Teamsters' wagons. There were mass riots and a great deal of bloodshed.

In 1907 "Big Dan" Tobin was elected the general president of the union. During the next twenty years the union expanded gradually—organizing drivers, stablemen and warehouse helpers in major cities around the country. Tobin, a key figure in the AFL, was content to let the big-city Teamsters fiefdoms run themselves independently, while he dabbled in AFL politics. In the 1920s and '30s there were more local strikes and more violence as horse drivers, stablemen, and an increasing number of motorized-truck drivers took to the streets demanding wages of 25 to 40 cents an hour. A strike of all the Teamsters in Philadelphia at Christmas time in 1933, for example, caused a near-panic as food shortages developed. All milk trucks, taxis, bakery trucks, laundry wagons and other vehicles bringing goods in and out of the city were halted. Crowds of Teamsters pummeled strikebreaking drivers and tried to stop trains. The police and hired goons responded in kind.

It was during these hard, violent times that many of the big-city Teamsters locals and joint councils made their first alliances with local gangsters. Decades later, when it would seem as if the Teamsters had originated the idea of mob involvement in labor affairs, a compelling truth would often be forgotten: the Teamsters had gone to the mob for muscle because the other side had done so first. As union activity spread through the first half of the twentieth century, it became an almost common management practice to use organized-crime goons to break strikes. That the Teamsters—in Detroit with the "Purple Gang," in Chicago with Al Capone, in Cleveland with the Milano family, in any city—went to the same source, is not surprising.

Throughout the '30s and '40s there were local investigations of racketeering in the Teamsters and other unions. (One of the more celebrated was the New York conviction of Joseph "Socks" Lanza for his Teamsters extortion activities at the Fulton Fish Market.)

In the decade prior to 1933 Teamsters membership declined from 76,000 in 1924 to 75,000 in 1933. Things were not going well; the union was little more than a motley crew of local drivers, dwarfed by dozens of other labor organizations. But, beginning in 1934, the union began growing by leaps and bounds. In part the sudden growth was the result of the new rights that all labor enjoyed from the federal Norris-La Guardia Act in 1932, and the New Deal's National Industrial Recovery Act in 1933, and in 1935 the Wagner Labor Act, which solidly established the National Labor Relations Board. But more directly it was the result of a Teamsters strike in Minneapolis, Minnesota, led by a militant group of Communists.

The leader in Minneapolis was Farrell Dobbs, an avowed Trotskyite, the wing of the Communist Party founded in 1928 to support Leon Trotsky against Joseph Stalin. In the United States, the Trotskyite party was called the Socialist Workers Party. If the Teamsters who relaxed at La Costa in 1976 owed their wealth and power to one man and one group, it was Farrell Dobbs and the Socialist Workers Party.

In May of 1934 Dobbs, along with a fellow SWP member and local Teamsters leader Ray Dunne, called a strike of all Teamsters in Minneapolis. They were seeking 42½ cents an hour for warehousemen, 52½ cents for drivers, and union recognition for both. Smart and practical militants, Dobbs and Dunne had prepared for the fight carefully. They had organized their own newspapers, sound trucks, and hospital, plus a network of union members serving as volunteer organizers to solicit support from other workers once the strike had begun. Employers and other nonunion people, calling themselves the "Citizens Alliance" (and described in the press as the city's "respectable element") were deputized by the police as special officers.

They armed themselves with badges and guns, while the truckers collected pipes and baseball bats.

Ten days later a riot broke out, and two of the special deputies, including one from one of the city's richest families, were beaten to death. The next day the police sent an armed convoy to escort a strikebreaking truck. Unarmed strikers tried to block it with their own truck. The police opened fire without warning, wounding sixty-seven strikers and killing two. The chaos continued for four months. The governor declared martial law, and the National Guard general in charge of enforcing it ordered what may be the most severe, though short-lived, curb on freedom of the press in modern American history: he banned the publication of "alarmist reports" or material "defaming" the state of Minnesota.

In September the employers slowly began to give in. Dobbs's militant struggle had succeeded: his union won expanded recognition, seniority rights and higher wages.

In the flush of victory, Dobbs looked for ways to expand his jurisdiction, and his dream of unionism as the trailblazer of Trotskyite-Communist revolution. Soon he had an idea—a "vision" Gibbons called it thirty-three years later—that ultimately became the key strategic factor in transforming the Teamsters from a ragtag federation of local delivery men in several cities into the nation's most powerful union.

The way to expand his union, and his union's political impact, Dobbs reasoned, was to organize the long-distance drivers who drove between cities. If those over-the-road drivers could be organized, Dobbs would have the missionaries he needed to carry his victories in Minneapolis, as well as his political message, to surrounding cities. Long-distance trucking was just then starting to compete with the railroads for long-haul freight. It was the right idea at the right time.

Dobbs had a plan for the perfect wedge to get things started: he would require that all drivers coming into his Minneapolis terminals, where he had organized the warehouse workers as well as the drivers, be union members working under a uniform union contract; failing that, nothing would move there. Then, he would organize warehousemen in other terminals and make the same requirement of the drivers who delivered or picked up goods at these terminals.

Teamsters president Dan Tobin opposed the plan. The union had always ignored the over-the-road drivers and the warehousemen, preferring to concentrate on local delivery men. To Tobin, the long-haulers and men in the warehouses were "trash." More importantly, organizing over-the-road men would end the insulation of the local fiefdoms and require centralized decision making. This was something that the meek Tobin was fearful of supporting for fear of offending the local Teamsters bosses who kept him in power. He preferred to spend most of his time on AFL affairs rather than preside over a centralized Teamsters brotherhood. This was also a time when Communist activity in unions was generating intense public pressure and government scrutiny, and Tobin wanted no part of Dobbs and his Trotskyites. To make things worse, Tobin was Franklin D. Roosevelt's closest labor supporter (closer to Roosevelt than Fitzsimmons would be to Nixon), and Dobbs's Socialist Workers' Party was fervently anti-Roosevelt.

After two years of skirmishing with the International leadership, Dobbs and several like-minded Teamsters leaders defied Tobin, who for the time being could do nothing about it. Dobbs pursued his over-the-road organizing by forming a central council of Teamsters to seek uniform wages in the Midwest. Using his Minneapolis terminal as a base, he leapfrogged from one strategic terminal to another. Organizing truckers, and the warehouse workers who would have to handle goods from other truckers who would in turn be targets of the organizing drives, he brilliantly exploited the vulnerability of individual companies to selective strikes, the disunity of the employer associations in the region, and the need for truckers shipping cross-country or even cross-regionally to use the terminals that he had selected for strike action. He succeeded beyond expectation. By the end of 1939, he had solid hold of all Teamsters drivers in the central states under the Central States Drivers Council, and Teamsters membership had grown from 75,000 in 1933 to 420,000. Most of the growth was in Dobbs's area or in areas, such as the Far West, where other Teamsters leaders, including future president Dave Beck, had borrowed his idea.

In early 1940 Dobbs suddenly quit the Teamsters to work full-time on Socialist Workers Party activities. (He ran as the SWP's presidential candidate three times.) It is fascinating to speculate about what might have happened had Dobbs not decided to devote his life to his party, and accepted Tobin's peace offering that he become an International vice-president and a possible heir apparent to the presidency. But it seems likely that Harold Gibbons in the early '50s might not have been a socialist side show within a group of nonpolitical power-hungry leaders.

Those were the union leaders who replaced Dobbs and furthered his plan of organizing over-the-road drivers and warehousemen at key terminals as levers for winning new members and forcing area-wide contracts. The most nonpolitical, power-hungry Teamster of them all ended up taking over Dobbs's Central States Drivers Council. His name was Jimmy Hoffa.

Hoffa met Dobbs in the middle 1930s, when as a Detroit organizer he was part of a group sent by Tobin to help Dobbs in his local strike. In 1939, he had been part of Dobbs's team working in Detroit on getting the first regional agreement. Dobbs later wrote that Hoffa was "eager to learn and quick to absorb new ideas." This was an understatement. Hoffa developed Dobbs's organizing techniques marvelously—especially his method of leapfrogging from one key area of vulnerability to another, then using the captured terminals as levers to keep nonunion-delivered goods out of these terminals, thereby winning new drivers, then coming back to win the drivers and the warehousemen at places in between, and finally ending up with an area-wide union contract. With Beck doing the same thing in the West and new federal labor laws helping all unions, Teamsters membership jumped from the 420,000 in 1939 to 1,100,000 in 1952.

Hoffa learned Dobbs's methods, but he disdained his politics. When Tobin finally purged the Trotskyites from Dobbs's Minneapolis local in 1941 (with the help of Roosevelt's Justice Department, which made the war-opposing Minnesota Trotskyite union leaders the first people imprisoned under the Smith Act) he sent Hoffa out there to make sure the purge was complete.

It is one of the more compelling ironies in American labor history that Hoffa used the groundwork that Dobbs and the Trotskyites had laid to build a cynical money-hungry, crime-allied, apolitical dictatorship. Or, more generally, that the union which used Dobbs's blueprint for expansion would, under Hoffa, open the widest possible gap between the wealth of the union leaders and that of the rank and file, and bestow its only two presidential endorsements in the following two decades on Republicans Dwight D. Eisenhower and Richard M. Nixon.

It is no less an irony that Hoffa's closest aide and confidante during that turnabout in the '50s and '60s was Harold Gibbons, the socialist pride of St. Louis.

The Gibbons-Hoffa alliance began in 1953, at a time when Gibbons' local was becoming a showcase of progressive unionism. The local was threatened with a takeover by the St. Louis organized-crime family controlled by "Irish" Workman. Gibbons had heard of Hoffa and of the way Hoffa had been able to get along with mobsters in Detroit, so he turned to him for help in fighting off the Workman gang. Gibbons remembered their first meeting this way:

"In those days it was common knowledge that the guys running the joint council [in St. Louis] were hoodlums [pronounced "who'd lums" by Gibbons]. One day one of my guys was grabbed in a bar by one of these hoodlums and told that either we put some of their people on the payroll of 688 or he was going to kill me. . . . Well, we didn't know a goddamn thing about hoodlums. But Dick [Cavener, Gibbons' number-two man at the local] knew Jimmy. So we went on over to Detroit and we talked with Hoffa. And Hoffa said, 'Well, you got no problems. Just put somebody on the payroll. They won't bother you. No one's going to get killed.' But, he says, 'At the end of six months you'll be taking orders from this guy you put on the payroll. And he'll be running the local.' He said the alternative is 'to get yourself a pistol and the first son of a bitch who walks in the door you shoot him in the head.' I said, 'Fine, goodbye' and went back to St. Louis and bought pistols."

Hoffa did more than offer good advice. According to Gibbons, "Jimmy offered to help. He came into town with his boys. You see he had the OK of the Chicago mob [the old Capone gang] and the Detroit mob to get rid of the Workman gang. And he told them [the Workman gang] that whatever they tried to do to us, he'd do double to them." He also installed bodyguards to protect Gibbons around the clock.

Before long, not only had Hoffa helped Gibbons to hold on to his local, he had arranged things so that Gibbons got to take over the whole joint council. He persuaded then-International president Dave Beck to put the gang-dominated joint council into trusteeship, and deployed enough muscle to St. Louis so that the overthrown leadership wouldn't object. Then he appointed Gibbons as the trustee in charge. It was not a question of benevolence. As with the Provenzano-assisted "paper-local" overthrow of the New York joint council, this was part of Hoffa's strategy to install people in key joint council posts around the country who were beholden to him.

The courtship of convenience between the tough, ambitious union boss from Detroit and the ideologue socialist from St. Louis became a permanent alliance and a deep friendship. Gibbons soon became Hoffa's premier Central Conference ally in the latter's drive to use that power base as a springboard to the union presidency. When Hoffa became president in 1958, the two, with Gibbons serving as Hoffa's executive assistant, ran the union. They roomed together in a Washington apartment when they were in the capital.

There is no evidence that Gibbons' political ideals rubbed off on Hoffa. But some of Hoffa's brass-knuckle, what's-in-it-for-me style of unionism rubbed off on Gibbons.

Soon after Hoffa intervened to help him in 1953, Gibbons hired his own gang muscle in Bernard Baker, a twice-convicted 325-pound thug who had been a prize fighter, a strong-arm man on the New York docks, a bouncer and an errand boy for mobster "Bugsy" Siegel. Baker was put on the payroll by Gibbons as a Central States "organizer," a job Robert Kennedy later described this way: "We heard testimony [at the McClellan Committee hearings] from union men around the country who told of Barney Baker's unique abilities when it came to organizing. Sometimes the mere threat of his presence in a room was enough to silence the men who otherwise would have opposed Hoffa's reign."

Baker's testimony before the McClellan Committee dramatized the two worlds Harold Gibbons now shuttled between. He related that Gibbons had closed the deal for hiring him at a dinner of the Americans for Democratic Action, the high-brow liberal political group of which Gibbons was an original board member. Baker also testified readily about his own mobster friends, delighting the Senators and spectators with his explanation that two of his buddies, "Cockeyed" Dunne and "Squint" Sheridan, had each "met his maker . . . through electrocution in the State of New York." Twenty years after the testimony, Baker could be found, his feet up on an empty desk, reading a racing form in a room marked B. Baker at Allen Dorfman's insurance-claim office at the Central States Pension and Health and Welfare Fund building in Chicago.

I had a chance to talk to Baker when Dorfman had him drive me to the airport after an interview. Cauliflower-eared, raggedly dressed, and appearing somewhat disoriented by old age, Baker got behind the wheel of a new Cadillac with a shield marked "Clergy," on the back bumper. The Cadillac was "a gift from Allen," he explained. As for the Clergy emblem "I arranged for that. . . . It keeps you from getting tickets." He also explained that he was now a "public-relations man" for Dorfman. Asked about the work he had done back in the '50s for Gibbons, Baker smiled and said "I did all kinds of shit for Harold. We had lots of fun."

Gibbons had also hired a convicted burglar and a half dozen other hoodlums as organizers. Twenty years later his explanations fluctuated from a professed desire to give ex-offenders a chance to be rehabilitated, to the claim that Baker was "a great public speaker and brilliant organizer," to the simple statement that "These are the kinds of people Jimmy and I needed to fight management."

As such men became part of Gibbons' union work, his brand of democratic unionism faded. The McClellan Committee later heard testimony about how James Ford, an outspoken Gibbons critic in St. Louis, had been brutally beaten and thrown over a stair railing after speaking out at a union meeting. Gibbons repeatedly denied any knowledge of the assault. In earlier days there wouldn't have been any assault to deny.

In 1958 Hoffa, as new International president, pulled the St. Louis joint council out of trusteeship and called for an election of a joint council president, which he assumed Gibbons would win. In the end, Gibbons won only because Hoffa added a carnival workers' local to the joint council, so that its officers could vote. (In joint council elections, local union officers vote.) The last-minute addition of the local clearly violated the International constitution—a point Gibbons was at a loss to dispute before the McClellan Committee.

The index of the McClellan Committee's thousands of pages of testimony reveals that Gibbons was mentioned more than anyone other than Hoffa. Most often he was cited as having been with Hoffa at a given meeting. At no time was Gibbons mentioned as being involved in taking payoffs. But on many occasions he was cited as having been Hoffa's man on the scene enforcing Hoffa's code. Gibbons led Hoffa's fight against Jim Luken and for Bill Presser in Ohio. Gibbons was sent to help with the paper locals in New York and make sure Tony Provenzano was kept in power in New Jersey. (In 1977 one of Provenzano's early campaign managers confirmed to me that "Harold was the toughest and most eloquent arguer for Tony.")

Gibbons began to have run-ins with the law that were more serious than his picket-line arrests. In 1954 he was jailed for four days for refusing to surrender his local's financial records to a federal grand jury that was investigating irregularities in his union's finances. He capitulated. Gibbons later remembered the jail experience this way: "It was terrible . . . I couldn't eat the slop they gave me. I would always take it and the other guys in the cell would divide it up. I was with three other guys. A bank robber and a couple of gasoline[-station] stick-up men. It was so funny—the class differentials. The bank robber wouldn't even talk to these other bastards. He says they're shitheels to go out and rob a fuckin' gas station. You know, there's a distinction; he robbed a bank . . . The other thing that hit you was that one kid in there was apparently a homosexual. Seemed to be seventeen, eighteen years old. That's where the shit was going on. They were following him in when he was taking a shower. Bullshit like that. It was the worst experience I ever had in my life.''

Gibbons later faced a more serious prospect of jail. He was indicted two different times for filing fake union financial records. One time he was arrested on the charges at a political dinner just after he had escorted the famously pure Illinois Senator Paul H. Douglas to the podium. "I thought Paul was going to die. But they did it to harass me. [Robert] Kennedy really wanted to discredit me and he put pressure on the prosecutors." Both times the charges were so meager that the judge immediately dismissed them before trial.

Kennedy harbored special contempt for Gibbons. As an old Kennedy aide said, "Bobby had a special thing for Harold. He kind of knew he was personally clean, but he couldn't stand the way Hoffa used Gibbons, the great liberal and intellectual, as his window dressing. He hated Gibbons, because he knew Gibbons could have done so much better for the union." Kennedy reserved a special viciousness for Gibbons. In *The Enemy Within* he wrote:

> Before our Committee hearings destroyed the pretty myth, Gibbons was pictured as the Teamster egghead, an intellectual and philosopher 'way above the everyday hurly-burly of union infighting and gouging . . . In running his little command, the Committee found, Gibbons is as ruthless as Hoffa. He talks about democracy, but completely disregards it even in his private life. His house outside St. Louis is plainly furnished and his family lives modestly. Gibbons himself, a tall and thin man with a cold superior look, has an apartment or a hotel room in the city and lives expensively and well. He wants to enjoy the finer things, and Teamster money is used to help him. . . . This bright, self-centered arrogant man is not popular within the Teamsters Union; he could not exist a day without Hoffa.

Seventeen years later Gibbons' daughter, Elizabeth Vasquez, listened as I reread Kennedy's charge. "Oh yes, I remember that well." She responded with a grin. "I was fifteen and in high school, and someone in the class gave a book report on Kennedy's book, not knowing that Daddy was the same Gibbons as the one in the book. Well, the whole class started to smile and shift around in their seats. They were embarrassed for me. But the teacher reacted differently. He told the kid who I was and then made him read to the class that part you just read. You should have seen the reaction. Most of the kids were insulted that Kennedy had put down our neighborhood as being 'modest.' And then another girl raised her hand and said that she didn't care what Bobby Kennedy said, Elizabeth's daddy is the nicest daddy I know.''

Gibbons had a special kind of marriage and a family life that could easily be disparaged. His wife, Ann, had been as devout a socialist as her husband. But unlike Harold, she had been brought up in middle- and upper-middle-class circumstances. She had had a taste of the good life and had rejected it. "Mom just didn't care about nice clothes or expensive meals or traveling, or any of that,'' Elizabeth Vasquez remembered. "But Dad did. You see, he hadn't had any of that when he was growing up. . . . He was so impressed with wealth and with nice clothes . . . I remember he used to always wear the nicest dark suits, because, he said, that when he walked into a nego- tiating room he didn't want the businessmen on the other side to be dressed better than he was. He was superimpressed by businessmen. Too impressed, I think.''

Gibbons was also a womanizer. "He had a special relationship with our mother,'' his daughter explained over lunch one day in 1977. "They loved each other dearly. I mean, he was totally destroyed when she died [in 1973]. Six months later he'd still instinctively dial her number from some hotel room at night. But as close as they were, sexual fidelity, at least on his part, was not part of their marriage contract. There's no use kidding about that.''

Operating out of an apartment in St. Louis's elegant Chase Hotel (which had a Central States Pension Fund loan), and later also from the Washington apartment that he shared with Hoffa,* Gibbons lived expensively. His expense-account bills became legendary in Team- sters circles. He traveled first class, ate at the finest restaurants, and found beautiful women wherever he went.

He was not bashful with his expense account, or his multiple sala- ries from the International and his St. Louis union. Yet no one ac- cused Gibbons of stealing a nickel. And, while he rode high with

---

* Gibbons' sexual cavorting was initially a source of friction with the devoutly faithful Hoffa until Hoffa later grew to tolerate it.

Hoffa and his corrupt cohorts, back home he kept his union hard at work pursuing its progressive goals and maintaining its showcase image. When the interests of his local members clashed with Hoffa's, Gibbons invariably stuck by his local. When he realized that his members would do better not to have their pensions be part of the corruption-marred Central States Pension Fund, he pulled them out and gave their pension benefits to an insurance company to manage. At home, whatever Gibbons' extracurricular pursuits, his children and his wife remained devoted to him, and in its own way his was an exceptionally close family.

In fact, the real relevance of his high living and sexual pursuits is that they offer an explanation for his curious alliance with Hoffa. The swaggering, fearless Jimmy Hoffa offered Gibbons a different class war. With Hoffa he could personally jump right over to the other side of the class barrier. He might have done that by going into business or a profession, but this way he could do it while still fighting for his workers and his socialist goals as a union leader. Hypocrisy and simple greed? Yes. But especially understandable in Gibbons' case. Here was Jimmy Hoffa, showing him that unionists could be brash and powerful and have lots of pocket money. That he yielded to the temptation to dominate men—and women—and took the chance Hoffa offered to ride high, live well, and play sexual conqueror in a world where he had been born as the last of twenty-three hungry faces in the crowd is not surprising.

Gibbons insisted to me that loftier ideals were involved in his alliance with Hoffa. Yes, he saw in Hoffa a man he could follow to the top. But he rode with Hoffa because Hoffa promised him that ultimately he would rid the union of the gangsters he had used to take it over and then vigorously pursue Gibbons' social goals. Gibbons pointed out repeatedly that as a man who had been a social outcast and was used to being on the receiving end of police work for his radical political activities and his militant picket-line confrontations, he was not terribly stuffy about the fact that Hoffa's friends had police records. Nor was he inclined to help the police do their jobs. (Once in 1961, when asked by a Congressional committee why he hadn't told police about an instance of corruption he had known about, he commented, "I've been running too long with the hares to start running with the hounds.") No doubt there was a great deal of truth to Gibbons' rationale for going with Hoffa, especially that he was not a snob about Hoffa's associates. But his explanation falls down. Hoffa never tried to clean up the union once he took over. Nor does his explanation acknowledge that, though the Hoffa alliance gave Harold Gibbons the chance to fight against the exploitation of the working class by day, it offered him expense accounts and women by night.

Joseph Rauh, the veteran liberal political activist and lawyer and, with Gibbons, a founder of Americans for Democratic Action, tells a story about a time Gibbons almost made a break with Hoffa and, by definition, the world Hoffa provided him. In 1958 during the Mc-Clellan hearings Bobby Kennedy tried to use Rauh as an intermediary to persuade Gibbons to testify against Hoffa and tell what he knew about Teamsters corruption. "Harold was a great man, and a great, great friend of mine," Rauh recalled nineteen years later. "And Bobby [Kennedy] had been talking to me about how he knew Harold could be the key to changing the union. He also said that Harold had records that he needed and that his testimony could be the key to all the hearings . . . Well, it was the weekend of our ADA convention, and all the board members had a dinner. . . . Harold was on the board. So I talked to him. I told him it was embarrassing to the ADA for him not to cooperate, and that it would be a great thing for the labor movement if he did. He was noncommittal, but agreed that we'd have lunch that Monday . . . So we met for lunch. And we talked and talked about all kinds of things. And after we each had three or four drinks he gave me his word that the records would be turned over and that he'd tell everything he knew. 'I'm going to prove to you and all my liberal friends that I've got nothing to hide,' he said. I'll never forget that. After a while we left, and I remember we shared a cab, and he had the cab drop him off at Eddie [Edward Bennett] Williams' office. [Williams was then the Teamsters' and Hoffa's lawyer.] Well, he left the cab and went up there to that office and that's the last time I ever heard from him. He never turned over the records and never cooperated . . . It's a tragedy. He was one of the great figures in the American labor movement. But he had a weakness for two-hundred-dollar suits, and for women; and I guess he just decided it wasn't worth giving that up. What a sad story."

Gibbons for his part did not remember the Rauh lunch when asked about it in 1977, and Williams—who became one of Gibbons' closest friends during those years—denied ever advising any witness not to cooperate in an investigation. But there was no denying that Harold Gibbons remained Jimmy Hoffa's man. "Harold and I and a few others were Jimmy's liberal window dressing," recalled Florian Bartosic, another liberal activist who served as the union's in-house counsel for a few years. "Jimmy kept us around to make him look good. You know, so he could look like a legitimate trade-unionist."

The window dressing sometimes yielded constructive by-products. By all accounts, it was Gibbons, for example, who got Hoffa to reverse his earlier track record in Detroit of tolerating Teamsters discrimination against blacks and to push courageously and successfully for integrated Teamsters locals, even in the most virulently racist areas of the South and Midwest. A Hoffa lunch with Martin Luther King, Jr., was arranged by Gibbons, as was a $25,000 contribution to King's Southern Christian Leadership Conference. But such initiatives were limited. Hoffa refused, despite all of Gibbons' pleadings, to speak at the King-sponsored March on Washington in 1963. And Gibbons' efforts to have the Teamsters take the lead in pushing for nondiscrimination and even affirmative action in hiring in the trucking industry were consistently vetoed by Hoffa. So were Gibbons' proposals to have the Teamsters use their growing treasury to sponsor low-income subsidized housing in Washington's ghetto, a massive project that, he told Hoffa, would be a great public-relations coup. Yet never was Gibbons heard publicly criticizing Hoffa for his failure to keep faith with what Gibbons saw as the political mandate of trade unionism. In 1960 Gibbons was a key Hoffa man behind a campaign to convince Teamsters and their friends to vote for Richard Nixon over Hoffa-enemy John Kennedy.

Nor did Gibbons publicly criticize Hoffa's toleration of men like Provenzano and Dorfman, who made his union an instrument in organized crime's exploitation of working people. On the contrary, Gibbons became Hoffa's most eloquent defender when Hoffa's ties with organized-crime figures were attacked by Kennedy and others: "They [the Teamsters gangsters] were tough unionists"; "they were being persecuted"; "they were temporarily necessary for Hoffa to keep control." So went various versions of the Gibbons speech.

Certain other signs suggested that Harold Gibbons had not been wholly bought off by Jimmy Hoffa. Through the late '50s and early '60s his Local 688 in St. Louis continued to be a model of exactly the kind of union the Teamsters, under Hoffa, could have been. Bread-and-butter wages and benefits were continually expanded as were the social services Gibbons had pioneered there in the early '50s. A giant two-building, 28- and 38-story apartment-house complex was built to provide the unions' retirees with good, low-cost, subsidized housing. The union's community-stewards system flourished. Gibbons threw himself into local drives for low-income, integrated housing to replace St. Louis' desperate slums, and for a new mass transit system.

Several vice-presidents recalled that beginning about 1963 Gibbons secretly approached them with ideas for democratizing the International by having the executive board of all the vice-presidents assert itself against Hoffa's one-man rule. Usually these were vague one-on-one conversations, often coming after a long night at a bar. In no instance did they proceed beyond the whispering stage into substantive action. Still, Gibbons was mindful of the problems presented by Hoffa's dictatorial reign and willing at least to try to recruit others in an effort to do something about it. But although he was the brainiest vice-president and the one who would have the most impact if he were to speak out, he wasn't willing to do any of this on his own. He was always looking unrealistically to one or more of the group of meek Hoffa cohorts to stand with him.

"There's one thing you have to remember about Harold," one of his closest friends at the time later explained. "He was terrified by Hoffa and his friends. These guys, these gangsters, weren't his element. He hadn't grown up doing business the way they had. He always used to talk about getting killed if he crossed Hoffa or any of the others. He never wanted to be seen as the stand-up guy against them because he thought they'd kill him." Other friends remembered Gibbons the same way, as someone who became afraid, not just for his expense accounts and his powerful position, but also for his life.

There was also a strong element of friendship and loyalty involved. As Gibbons said during one long interview, "sure, there were lots of things about Hoffa that I didn't like. But you know I came up with the guy, and I owed him. You have to factor that in to whatever you say about me." There was also the practical problem, as Gibbons emphasized, that "unless I could get the support of some of the guys on the executive board, I couldn't have done anything anyway. Hoffa would have just rolled right over me if I'd stood up by myself."

Whatever the mix of reasons, Gibbons stuck with Hoffa through the McClellan Committee hearings, through the early years of establishing the Central States Pension Fund as a bank for mobsters and cronies (which Gibbons kept his own union's funds and himself out of), and through the battles to set up and keep people like Provenzano in power. But finally there was a break.

When John Kennedy was killed in Dallas on November 22, 1963, Gibbons was having lunch in a Washington restaurant. His relationship with Hoffa had not been good in recent months. Hoffa, under incessant pressure from the Kennedy Justice Department, had been more arrogant and moody than ever, frequently throwing temper tantrums that invariably featured bitter, humiliating tirades against any lesser personage (which meant everyone, including Gibbons) who happened to be in the room. Hoffa seemed to be responding to all the charges of corruption, not by reforming, but by reaching out to the most corrupt elements of the union to dig in with him for the fight against the Kennedys. Dorfman, Provenzano, and others involved in Hoffa's underworld activities seemed to be around him more than ever. At one point, Gibbons even overheard parts of a conversation in which Hoffa discussed the possibility of having Robert Kennedy murdered.

"I came back to the office, after I heard [John] Kennedy'd been shot," Gibbons recalled nearly fourteen years later. "When I got back it was confirmed that he was dead. So I immediately told people to lower the flags and I sent a message of condolence to the family. You see, Hoffa was out of town, and I was in command of the operation when he was away. . . . Well, I reached out for Hoffa to tell him, and when he finally called in I mentioned to him what I'd done. He raised hell with me for having done it. He cursed the Kennedys— this was two hours after the guy'd been shot—and he cursed me. And finally, after he screamed for a while, I told him, 'When you get back get yourself a new boy because I'm not going to be here. I'm resigning.' This for me was the last straw." *

In early December, Gibbons' resignation as Hoffa's top aide was headlined in the St. Louis papers. While he told reporters in background discussions or through friends that a fight over his flag-lowering and Kennedy condolence message (as well as his order to close the union headquarters the day of Kennedy's funeral) was the cause of the split, his official statement was characteristically loyal; it was only a desire to get back to his union work in St. Louis, he claimed, that had caused him to leave the number-two International post.

Thus Gibbons went off the International's payroll as Hoffa's executive assistant (and Frank Fitzsimmons replaced him), while keeping his titles and salaries as International vice-president, St. Louis joint

---

* Two days later, Hoffa offered his public reaction to the Kennedy assassination, telling reporters that "Bobby Kennedy is now just another lawyer."

council president, and head of his St. Louis local. Yet he never really left Hoffa's employ. "I told Jimmy I wanted to quit," he later recalled, "but that if he needed me to help from time to time on something I would. Well, after trying through some emissaries to get me to stay, he came in to see me—I was still at the headquarters clearing away some things—and said, 'You said, you'd help out if I needed you. Well, I've got to go down South [to Nashville] for my [jury-tampering] trial. Will you at least stay until I get back?' So I said I would, but that I wouldn't take his money; I'd be paid by my St. Louis local. Then, after the Nashville trial, he had the trial [for mail fraud] in Chicago, and then he had his appeals. So I never really left until sometime in 1965."

Even then, Gibbons didn't burn his bridges completely. He still spoke out in the boss's defense and helped him with organizing and contract negotiations. One reason, undoubtedly, was that, though he no longer drew his executive-assistant's salary, Gibbons continued to draw a whopping amount in expenses from the International. Teamsters files show that in 1966 Gibbons collected a hefty $38,837 in reimbursed expenses. The same year, Hoffa, the twelve other vice-presidents, the four International trustees, and the International secretary-treasurer together collected a total of $20,841. At least as important as the expense money was the obvious opportunity that Hoffa's legal troubles presented. As Hoffa began to run out of appeals from his two convictions in Nashville and in Chicago, it became increasingly clear that he would soon have to go to prison—which, in turn, meant that he would have to name someone to stand in for him. On more than one occasion Hoffa had hinted to his right-hand man and roommate that he, Gibbons, would be the one to take Hoffa's place if his courtroom luck ever ran out and he had to go away for a while. Even after their falling-out over the Kennedy assassination, Gibbons still believed that this was likely as long as he didn't break with Hoffa totally.

He was wrong. In 1966 Hoffa announced that he had picked Frank Fitzsimmons for the new post of general vice-president, a job from which he would serve as acting general president in the event of Hoffa's imprisonment. For Gibbons, Hoffa's decision was crushing. "After all the years he and Jimmy had been so close," one intimate friend recalled, "and after the promises Jimmy had made, Harold just couldn't believe it. I've never seen him so down. And, what made things worse was that Hoffa chose this guy, Fitzsimmons, instead. A total nincompoop. A guy who'd been a total nonentity in the union. It was humiliating.'' Hoffa, of course, had his own reasons. He hoped to run things from prison if necessary. What he didn't want was a stand-in who might find some backbone or independence once he got the feel of the big chair at headquarters. Gibbons' blasphemy in honoring the assassinated President and then quitting over Hoffa's ensuing temper tantrum confirmed any suspicions Hoffa already had that Gibbons would be just that kind of ingrate.

We know now that Hoffa made the wrong pick. Fitzsimmons stopped taking Hoffa's orders from prison and refused to slip back into obscurity once Hoffa was ready to come back. For what it's worth, Gibbons swore in a table-pounding 1977 interview, "Goddamn it, if Jimmy put me there with the understanding that I'd step aside when he was able to come back, of course I'd have kept my word. That's the great irony of the thing.''

For a while Gibbons decided to fight Hoffa's decision by challenging Fitzsimmons' election as general vice-president at the 1966 convention. But, after a canvass of the other vice-presidents, he backed down. Even as he was on his way to jail, Hoffa's power over these top Teamsters, or at least their perception of his power, was such that none was willing to join a palace revolt.

To predict what would have happened had Gibbons been Hoffa's choice, or if he had successfully fought Fitzsimmons, is impossible. Perhaps he would have turned the union into a national version of his St. Louis showcase. Perhaps he would have followed Hoffa with all the loyalty that Hoffa had expected of Fitzsimmons. Or he might have been killed for not accommodating the mob the way Fitzsimmons did. What is certain is that the coronation of the man who used to get coffee for Gibbons and Hoffa while they ran the union left Gibbons a bitter man.

He reacted by turning most of his attention back to his St. Louis local and joint council; by becoming a source of contemptuous, behind-the-back whispers about Fitzsimmons; and by pursuing his expense accounts and the good, sexy life with an intensity that made his earlier Hoffa days seem austere. Teamsters records indicate that from 1967 through 1970 Gibbons collected $123,000 from the International treasury in reimbursed expenses, not to mention the use of a luxury car and the St. Louis apartment, and tens of thousands of dollars more from his St. Louis local and joint council. He got all this even though he was given little, if any, work to do for the International by Fitzsimmons. Almost every meal he ate—and they were all at the best places—and nearly everything else he did was reimbursed by the union. While Gibbons was drawing this $123,000 from the International, Fitzsimmons himself drew $17,000 in expenses, though much of his travel and eating admittedly was covered by International credit cards and other direct disbursements that would not show up on a statement of reimbursed expenses. During the same four years the other eleven vice-presidents, who unlike Gibbons usually had major substantive responsibilities as conference chairmen or organizers, drew about $7,000 or $8,000 each.

Gibbons faded as a national force in the union. Fitzsimmons, not oblivious to Gibbons' contempt and his lingering pretensions to his office, was not about to give him much to do. The only occasion on which Gibbons surfaced nationally was when he became involved in an ill-fated plan to set up a national unit to bind all Teamsters airport freight workers. Curiously, the plan might have expanded New York Teamsters gangster Harry Davidoff's control over other airports at a time when his corrupt activities at Kennedy airport were already drawing intense public criticism and law-enforcement attention, though Gibbons later asserted that Davidoff would not have benefited.

In 1971 when Fitzsimmons was scheduled to be elected as general president at the convention, Gibbons again contemplated a challenge. Most of the vice-presidents rejected his overtures for support, because they had been happy in the four post-Hoffa years. Yet, some responded positively. In fact, with the scattered hints of support he did get in the soundings he took of executive board members, and with the broader support he was likely to get from the convention delegates, it seemed that Gibbons had a real shot at overturning Fitzsimmons. On the other hand, in the seventy-three-year history of the union no member of the executive board had ever even challenged an incumbent leader, let alone defeated him. It was the most significant career decision Gibbons ever made.

He decided not to challenge. Close friends and one fellow vice-president later recalled that in the end Gibbons backed away for several reasons. First, he thought that with Fitzsimmons as acting president having control over the convention and having had four years of incumbency with which to call in a multitude of IOU's for past favors, he would probably lose. (The voters in this election were the local and joint-council officials who were delegates to the convention, not the rank and file.) And if he lost he knew that not only wouldn't he be an International vice-president anymore (he would be running for president and therefore not vice-president), he also would probably lose his St. Louis post. Fitzsimmons would take revenge by putting the local and the joint council in trusteeship. Gibbons was also afraid for his life if he won, or looked as if he could win.

In 1971, four years before the Hoffa disappearance, it may have seemed far-fetched to most people that as powerful and as public a figure as a Teamsters president could be the victim of a gangland murder. Not to Gibbons. Just as the poor boy from the coal mines of Archibald Patch, Pennsylvania, was so impressed with rich businessmen and their fine clothes, so too was the socialist ideologue "egghead" impressed by Teamsters-associated mobsters and the ease with which they resorted to violence. The year when Gibbons had to weigh these fears, in 1971, was the time when mob dominance of the union was at its absolute peak. People like the Provenzano family were in the saddle in many areas of the country, and Dorfman was at the height of his loan-dispensing glory. Gibbons considered the consequences of barging in on the arrangement of passive acceptance that Fitzsimmons had made with the mob. The thought left him more than a little reluctant. And, as if he needed it, at least two of the vice-presidents he consulted added their own warning that he would be killed if he had the bad luck to win and the bad sense to try to change things once he did.

As Gibbons weighed these thoughts, Fitzsimmons tipped the balance for him. In mid-1971, he offered Gibbons the key job of chairman of the Central Conference—Hoffa's old post. In return, Gibbons would have to agree to drop his presidential plans and run again for vice-president on the Fitzsimmons slate at the convention. The Central Conference job was a real sweetener. It would pay Gibbons an extra $37,000 a year, and it would once more give him something to do beyond the local level.

After some soul searching, Gibbons took the deal. In 1971 and 1972, his salaries and expense reimbursements from the St. Louis local and the joint council, and from the International vice-presidency as well as the new Central Conference job, totalled $118,841 and $107,977 respectively.

Gibbons flaunted it. He escorted his women to the poshest restaurants and best hotel suites in whatever city he happened to be in. He was seen ringside at the best boxing matches or front and center at opening night of the best nighclub acts. More than ever, he palled around with the show-business elite whose names were staples on the most glittering marquees of Las Vegas. Like Jackie Presser five years later, Gibbons in 1971 had a wall full of plaques in his office—only, in those days, Gibbons' office was bigger than Presser's ever was and the plaques were interspersed with photos of the great man sharing a golf game or a laugh with Frank Sinatra, Bob Hope, Dean Martin and Sammy Davis, Jr. He even bought a small house with a pool in Palm Springs near Sinatra's spread and next door to Sinatra sidekick Jilly Rizzo. At the same time, he dug in at the Central Conference, busily, and happily, negotiating contracts and running organizing drives.

All the while, he maintained a careful détente with Fitzsimmons and the corrupt elements that were enjoying their heyday. He was never heard to protest the corruption that thrived everywhere he went. And although membership on the board of trustees of the Central States Pension Fund and the Central States Health and Welfare Fund had been automatic for the Central Conference chairman, he stayed off the boards and out of the funds' affairs entirely—not participating in the mob's fleecing of his members' benefit funds, but not doing anything about it either. His relationship with Dorfman, in fact, was quite cordial whenever they ran into each other on the fairways of La Costa and at the other elegant resting spots that Gibbons frequented now more than ever.

Then, just as it looked as if any objective observer might forever close the book on the question of whether Harold Gibbons had been bought off, he acted with principle and selflessness.

It happened at La Costa in July 1972. La Costa room records show that the members of the International executive board, as well as other top Teamsters personages including Jimmy Hoffa, Jr., and Tony Provenzano (then still barred from officially holding office because of his labor-law-violation conviction) gathered there on July 14. (Most took two-bedroom suites at the hotel, although physical-fitness buff Provenzano took a double at the spa.) The main purpose of the meeting, Gibbons found out at the bar the night before business was to start, was the union's endorsement of Richard M. Nixon for reelection. It was to be Fitzsimmons' big gift for his friend, the President. The way the talk was going that night the board's unanimous vote for Nixon the next day was being taken for granted.

Fitzsimmons and the others might have known better. For several years Gibbons had been one of the most prominent labor leaders in the movement to stop the war in Vietnam. Since Nixon's election in 1968, he had been one of the most vocal labor critics of the Nixon-Kissinger Vietnam policies. In 1971, much to Fitzsimmons' displeasure, Gibbons had hosted a national meeting in St. Louis of labor leaders who opposed the war. And to Fitzsimmons' horror, Gibbons had actually gone to North Vietnam that year with some fellow doves in search of peace feelers. (Later he would also try to arrange for Hoffa to go with him on a second trip to North Vietnam; but Fitzsimmons, not wanting to be upstaged by Gibbons or Hoffa, would use his White House influence to get that mission scuttled.) Gibbons' dislike of Nixon, and his over-all political independence, should have been no surprise to Fitzsimmons and the executive board. Throughout the spring, Gibbons had been quoted as telling reporters that he was going to try to persuade the executive board to endorse either Democratic Senator Edmund Muskie or Democratic Senator George McGovern.

Though Fitzsimmons didn't know it, Gibbons had nearly split with the Teamsters—and Jimmy Hoffa—far more drastically in 1968: he had almost endorsed Robert Kennedy. Kennedy's antiwar and civil-rights views were enough to make Gibbons forget all that Kennedy had said and written about him and endorse him after Kennedy's anticipated primary victory in California. The planned endorsement had been coaxed out of Gibbons by several phone calls from Kennedy and one secret meeting Gibbons had had with Kennedy brother-in-law Stephen Smith. (In 1960, the Kennedys had tried and failed to get a Gibbons endorsement for John Kennedy; that attempt was made during a secret meeting Gibbons had with Joseph Kennedy, the candidate's father, which was arranged by their mutual friend Frank Sinatra.)

When the Nixon 1972 endorsement question came up at the bar that night, Gibbons told the others that there was no way he would support the President's reelection. All night, they pleaded with him to change his mind. Another vice-president, Einar Mohn of California, also voiced an objection. His problem with Nixon, according to Gibbons and another vice-president who was there, was that the White House's proposed legislation to prevent strikes in the transportation industry would, he thought, severely threaten the union. "How can I support a man whose bill will cripple our union?" Mohn reportedly asked. Charles Colson, Nixon's counsel and Fitzsimmons' chief White House hand-holder, was at La Costa to round up the endorsement for the boss and he heard Mohn's complaint. As one vice-president later told the story, "Colson looked up and said, 'What bill are you talking about?' Einar told him, and Colson said he'd take care of it. Well the next morning at eight Colson called him and said the legislation has been withdrawn.* Now that was just for one fuckin' vote on the Board. You can imagine what they'd do for Fitz's vote."

As for Gibbons, he held firm the next morning. "The other guys kept telling me how bad it was going to look to have one guy who wouldn't go along," he recalled. Some even took Gibbons aside and warned him that Fitzsimmons, who hadn't said a word to him about the endorsement, was boiling mad and would take revenge. It was, in fact, the first time in Teamsters history—or at least in the history any of the veteran Teamsters could remember—that any member of the executive board threatened to oppose the general president publicly on a major issue. Still, Gibbons refused. "I told them," he recalled, "that at least I can look at myself in the mirror, but you guys can't if you endorse that crook." And so it went. The executive board voted 19–1 to endorse Nixon.

Immediately following the vote, the twenty board members piled into a caravan of five limousines and drove the thirty miles from La Costa up the coast to Nixon's San Clemente home to present him with the news personally. A beaming Richard Nixon gave each of the visitors, including Gibbons, a barbecue lunch, drinks, a personalized presidential golf ball and a crack at his private three-hole course. That afternoon Gibbons' stubbornness didn't seem to cost him anything. "I was treated like a king, there," he remembered five years later. "I think I got more attention than anyone else. He [Nixon] knew about the vote, of course. . . . The President has a tee right on his property that shoots out 150 yards to the green—right alongside the ocean. So he picked up a club and hit one and said, 'Mr. Gibbons, would you like to try this.' He hit one on [to the green] and I hit one on. And then Fitz and a bunch of the others took turns. But they were all missing it. They just kept missing, and Nixon and I kept hitting it on. It was so funny."

The fun and games were short-lived. The month after the Nixon

---

* The Nixon bill was suddenly withdrawn, much to the embarrassment of the Republicans in Congress who had sponsored it for the President and were not informed beforehand of the sudden policy reversal.

landslide victory over George McGovern, Fitzsimmons moved to even the score. On December 10 he sent telegrams to the members of the executive board: "I have determined that it would be in the best interests of the International union to replace the director of the Central Conference of Teamsters." Losing the Central Conference job meant a loss in income for Gibbons of $37,000 and an end to his substantive union work outside St. Louis. He still held on to his International vice-presidency. That was an elected position, from which Fitzsimmons could not unilaterally remove him. But a vice-presidency alone paid only $18,000 if stripped of additional, presidentially appointed duties such as a conference chairmanship or an international organizer's title. Asked if his firing of Gibbons had been motivated by the Nixon-endorsement affair, Fitzsimmons told the press (and me four years later) that, on the contrary, it was because Gibbons hadn't "measured up to the job." He provided no specifics. He didn't have to; the union constitution gave him the power to give away and take back such appointments as he pleased as long as a majority of the executive board did not object. (True to form, the executive board silently approved Fitzsimmons' move. One of the vice-presidents who voted to support Gibbons—Edward Lawson of Canada—was quickly relieved by Fitzsimmons of the extra job he held as a general organizer.) At the same time, the word was passed to Gibbons that at Fitzsimmons' direction his huge expense-account vouchers would no longer be approved.

That was only the first blow. In early 1973, Fitzsimmons passed the word to St. Louis Teamsters officials that Gibbons had to be ousted there, also. They in turn went home and told Gibbons that if he didn't resign his Local 688 post (he was secretary-treasurer) and his joint-council presidency, he would be brought up on internal charges, and both organizations would be placed in trusteeship by Fitzsimmons. If that happened, he was warned, Fitzsimmons would pick a trustee who would begin to dismantle all that Gibbons had built there; also, he would take a careful look at the hefty life-insurance and severance-pay plans Gibbons had set up for himself to see if they couldn't be eliminated. His only choice, Gibbons was told, was to pick his successor in St. Louis and resign quietly—which is what he did. So, by mid-1973 he literally had no responsibilities anywhere—at the International, at the Central Conference, or in St. Louis. And he was earning only his $18,000 vice-president's salary and the few dollars a week in expenses and allowances they would allow him. He had gone from a $118,000-a-year big shot in 1971 to an $18,000-a-year discard in 1973.

His personal life was also falling apart. Ann Gibbons was dying. Through all the one-night affairs and high living on the road or at the downtown apartment while Ann stayed home with their three children, Harold and Ann Gibbons had somehow been an extraordinarily close couple. Rarely a night had gone by when he hadn't called her at some hour from some hotel room or phone booth to go over the day's work. And most weekends he had tried to make it home to be with her. "He relied on her for all his guidance," one source close to the family recalled. "I mean, with him spending all day with people like Hoffa or the others who didn't have his background or share his social beliefs, she was his one outlet and the one person he shared everything with—except, of course, the affairs." Now, Ann was dying of cancer; and Gibbons, wracked with sorrow and guilt, according to his daughter—and dismembered professionally and financially by Fitzsimmons—reached the lowest point in his life. When the three children along with one grandchild gathered in St. Louis for their mother's final days, Gibbons didn't have the money to put them up in separate rooms at the hotel; all including his daughter and her new baby shared the same single room.

According to daughter Elizabeth her father received offers from several businessman friends during this time. "They knew Father was in trouble and they offered him all kinds of deals," she recalled. "But he turned them down. I remember one night we talked about it, and he kept repeating, 'I can't go over to them. I'm a trade-unionist.' "

Instead, Gibbons went through three tormenting, bitter years. "I went from well over a $100,000 to $18,000, and it was not easy," he remarked, "but I chopped expenses like hell. The worst part was not the money, but having three years [1973 through 1975] with no job. You just can't imagine what that does to you. The only luck I had was that I still had enough friends to speak at union ground-breakings and stewards' meetings. Those invitations were all I had. At least, whoever invited me would pick up the expenses. So, once in a while I got to travel well again." As if things could get worse, Gibbons' support of McGovern also earned him a place on the Nixon "enemies list" that John Dean later revealed during the Watergate investigations. By 1974 a spot on the list was a badge of honor, but in 1973 it meant audits of Gibbons' 1971 and 1972 tax returns. (These resulted in a clearly unjustified $300,000 assessment involving his union-paid life-insurance plans. After a skirmish in Tax Court the government dropped all such claims, although he was assessed about $600 for unsupported expense deductions.*

There was one bright spot: the reemergence of the man who had taken him to the mountain the decade before.

Although Jimmy Hoffa had been released from prison at the end of 1971 it wasn't until the spring of 1973 that he began to put the word out that he was going to try to force his way back into the union. Until then he had been on parole and hadn't wanted to risk having it revoked. Even in 1973, he was subject to the Nixon-imposed restriction against engaging in union activity. Nevertheless, he began planning his campaign to take his job back at the 1976 convention. One of the first people he called was Harold Gibbons.

Forgotten was Hoffa's jilting of Gibbons in 1966. Forgotten was Gibbons' near-endorsement of Hoffa enemy Robert Kennedy in 1968. Gibbons and Hoffa needed each other, as they had in the past. When Hoffa began crisscrossing the country in 1974 (under the guise of speaking engagements sponsored by a prison reform group) in order to rebuild his old support, Gibbons tried to arrange speaking invitations to the same places so that he could be with him. The two were back together again; only, now both were on the outside looking in. This time, Hoffa promised Gibbons that as an outsider he, Hoffa, wouldn't be obligated to the gangsters he had tolerated before. This time, he really would wipe the slate clean once he took over, and turn the union into the kind of union Gibbons dreamed of. Did Gibbons believe him? Maybe. But that didn't matter. What mattered was that Hoffa offered him a ticket back to the top.

In 1974 and 1975 Hoffa was Gibbons' only hope. The two agreed that Gibbons would be Hoffa's campaign manager at the 1976 convention battle against Fitzsimmons.

Toward the middle of 1975 Gibbons began, according to several close friends, to get nervous about the fight they planned for next year. He would come back from board meetings or other encounters with men in the Teamsters hierarchy and tell friends that he had gotten vague signals that if Hoffa didn't back off something was going

---

* The Watergate investigation later turned up an "Eyes Only" memo from Nixon aide Colson to White House Counsel John Dean calling Gibbons an "all-out enemy" and asking that a tax audit of Gibbons be initiated. Colson, who was the White House liaison to Fitzsimmons, told Dean that "a well informed source" had told him that Gibbons had income-tax discrepancies.

to happen to him, and perhaps to Gibbons as well. After such meetings the only thing that calmed him slightly was Hoffa's own cocky assurance of his invulnerability.

Two intimate friends of Gibbons asserted to me two years later that in late June or early July 1975 Gibbons received a more specific signal from the forces trying to keep Hoffa out of the union. If Hoffa didn't call off his campaign immediately, they claimed Gibbons was told, he would be killed in a matter of weeks. Gibbons, these sources asserted, carried the message to Hoffa, who characteristically brushed it off. During more than a dozen interviews, Gibbons denied that he received such a specific message or that he had given one like that to Hoffa. But he didn't deny that he had come to fear for Hoffa's life and that he had discussed his fear with Hoffa. Nor did he deny that the day he got word from Jimmy Hoffa, Jr., that Hoffa had vanished, was the saddest and scariest day of his life. Two or three days after the disappearance, Gibbons got a call from one of the television networks asking "if they could come out to my house in Palm Springs for an extended interview. I said, 'What the hell do you want from me? Why the sudden interest?' And the producer said kind of sheepishly, 'Well, frankly Mr. Gibbons, we figure you may be next to go.' "

It didn't take a television producer to remind Gibbons of the possibility. The disappearance of Jimmy Hoffa, whom Gibbons had always thought fearless because he really could stare down all danger, reinforced all of Gibbons' old fears of, as he put it to one friend, "Going out of the union movement 'feet first.' "

Nonetheless, as in 1971, he now toyed with the notion of challenging Fitzsimmons at the convention. If not for the too-obvious physical dangers involved he would probably have done it. The climate was even better than it had been in 1971, with many old Hoffa loyalists urging him or Jimmy junior to run. He seemed to offer the perfect mix of qualities to many who would be delegates at the convention: long-time identification with what to many was the now-martyred Jimmy Hoffa; long-time visibility as Hoffa's number-one aide; and a reputation for personal honesty that in the period following the Hoffa disappearance might, to many of the delegates, offer a welcome reprieve from the bad press and law-enforcement heat. Of course, on the other side, Gibbons had to consider not only the risk to his life but also the possibility that too many of the delegates had their own corrupt stake in Fitzsimmons' continued reign. Also, Fitzsimmons, as the incumbent, probably held enough patronage and other power over the delegates to choke off any insurgent candidacy. Still, if there was ever a time when an insurgent had a chance to unseat Fitzsimmons, a Gibbons candidacy in 1976 was it.

Once again, it didn't happen. Once again, while Gibbons was in the midst of weighing the odds, Fitsimmons sealed the decision by making a deal with him.

"He called me to Washington one day to meet with him," Gibbons explained. "It was about three months before the convention. And when I got there he said, 'Harold, I'd like to have the same unified slate running with me this time. You've been talking about running on your own for vice-president, as if I wasn't going to put you on my slate again. You've even been talking about running for president. Well, what do I have to do to get you to run with me as a vice-president?' So, I told him I wanted a job. I didn't care so much about the money, but I wanted an assignment again. I wanted to be out there. And he said, 'OK, Harold, as soon as the convention's over I'll give you something.' And I said, 'Frank, I want something now.' And he said OK, and gave me an assignment." So, Gibbons dropped his plans to make his move for the top spot, confining his insurgent activities to a long, secret phone conversation he had with PROD's Arthur Fox. "We called him for help in drafting our constitutional reform proposals," Fox later explained. "And he was extremely helpful to us. I was surprised."

At the convention in June, Gibbons got a taste of what might have been had he made his move: by most accounts his nomination as second vice-president received a thunderous, standing ovation that exceeded that given to any of the other board members including Fitzsimmons. When the applause died down, Gibbons' eyes were watery as he looked out at the 2,200 delegates and accepted their designation.

Part of the new assignment Gibbons got from Fitzsimmons called for him to be the International vice-president in charge of overseeing union activities in the boondocks of North and South Dakota, as well as in his own St. Louis metropolitan area. It was a far cry from the responsibilities he had had as Hoffa's second-in-command or as Fitzsimmons' chairman of the all-important Central Conference, which encompassed the Teamsters bread-and-butter trucking-industry states. In fact it was as close to no assignment as any assignment could be. However, after the convention, Ray Schoessling, the general secretary-treasurer, who had always liked Gibbons, gave him another more interesting job: he was to go to California to try to work out some kind of settlement in the Teamsters' raging fight with Cesar Chavez' United Farm Workers.

In the late '60s Gibbons had walked picket lines in St. Louis with Cesar Chavez and given Chavez' fledgling farm workers' union all the support he could. Now, in 1976, Gibbons was sent to California as a representative of the major force—other than the farm owners and agribusinesses themselves—that was holding Chavez back from his drive to organize the poor, mostly immigrant men and women who worked for far less than the minimum wage picking lettuce, artichokes and grapes. Few objective observers saw the Teamsters' role in the farm-worker struggle as anything other than a disgrace to the labor movement. As one highly regarded observer and veteran labor activist who was sent in 1970 to arbitrate the dispute explained seven years later, "Chavez killed himself for ten years organizing these people. He came to them when they had nothing. Then, once he started to make progress the growers [the employers] ran to the Teamsters to sign up their workers with them. They knew the Teamsters would let them off easier than Cesar would. And instead of telling the growers to go to hell, the Teamsters accepted their invitation. It was a straight steal on the part of the Teamsters. They had been in the farming [and food-processing] industry out there [on the West Coast] for thirty or forty years and hadn't done a goddamn thing for these people. Then, after Chavez knocks his brains out for them, they tried to take it all from him."

The Teamsters made their move to usurp Chavez' newly organized workers in 1970, when it first looked like Chavez had turned the corner in his long fight. The growers had kept Chavez' people off their land and, thus, away from the workers. But the Teamsters were now invited in to sign up the laborers. Threatening workers with the loss of their jobs if they didn't drop Chavez and sign Teamsters contracts, and rarely hesitating to use violence to keep Chavez' organizers away or to break a Chavez-instigated strike, the Teamsters organizers began to whittle away at Chavez' contracts and membership rolls. Chavez fought back with renewed organizing drives, with appeals for public support of boycotts of nonunion, or Teamster-picked, grapes and lettuce (to which the Teamsters responded with ads urging workers to "Buy Lettuce" or "Buy Grapes") and with strikes against Teamsters-associated growers. The strikes were led by bands of organizers nearly mesmerized by their dedication to the cause. They were often met with such brutal Teamsters-instigated violence that in the press, at least, this became the classic struggle between the "good guys" and the big "bad guys."

The battle seesawed for six years. Three Teamsters agreements between Chavez and the Teamsters were worked out at various times, but all fell through at the last minute. In 1974 George Meany threw the AFL-CIO behind the grape and lettuce boycott and pledged financial support to Chavez' perennially poor union. He also asserted that the violence in the strike had "resulted solely and simply because the Teamsters imported goons."

Actually, Fitzsimmons and other International officials had little taste for the Chavez battle. It was a public-relations fiasco at a time when they were taking more than their share of public criticism and government pressure for activities that they had a much larger stake in—such as continuing corruption at the Central States Pension Fund. It was costing a great deal of organizing money, and the prospects of an eventual payoff were doubtful. But though the big Teamsters bosses didn't relish the fight, their problem was that this was a strictly local operation being waged by the locals and joint council in the California farmland area. And Fitzsimmons, unlike Hoffa, was not strong enough to put a stop to it. The Western Conference director, then Einar Mohn, was later described by observers on the scene as anxious to end the fight but unable to push the local people to a settlement.

In the meantime, the Teamsters cranked out their own side of the story from Washington, claiming that they had been involved in organizing West Coast farm workers since the 1930s (true, but they had organized only a handful in all those years); that the workers favored them over Chavez' union (not true, if you believed the overwhelming results of elections that had been allowed to go on free of violence or coercion, in which workers chose between the two unions); and that Chavez was a good crusader but not a good bread-and-butter union leader. The last point was partly true; Chavez had never been able adequately to "service" (that is, enforce and maintain grievance machinery for) his contracts; he had often filed incomplete financial reports with the government, or neglected to file the required reports at all; his pension and welfare funds had often been poorly managed; his insistence on going it alone, rather than as part of another, larger union had limited his potential; and his union meetings and other activities really did have more the flavor of a religious crusade than a trade-union drive. But to Gibbons, reflecting on the Chavez-Teamsters fight in 1977, these Teamsters arguments, however on target, did not state the case for driving Chavez *out;* rather, they argued, in Gibbons' words, "for trying to bring him in to our union as head of a new trade division for farm labor. He's the kind of guy who should be part of our union. We should be helping him, not fighting him. That's what I would have done."

That was not what Gibbons' marching orders were in 1976, nor is that how he argued. His job was to try to negotiate a settlement giving the Teamsters as much jurisdiction as possible, and Chavez as little, over the disputed workers. Although officials of Chavez' union harbored none of the bitterness toward him that they felt for other Teamsters officials and agreed that he had negotiated in good faith, they did remember that he had made the same arguments about the Teamsters having been there first and Chavez not being a good trade-unionist. When asked, Gibbons conceded the point; explaining that "I was out there trying in a fair way to present our side of the case, even though we weren't all right."

In the end, Gibbons was not able to pull off a settlement, and his efforts ended toward the end of 1976. In the words of one long-time farm-workers battle observer, "The time still just wasn't ripe for an agreement." Several months later, after the Teamsters lost a majority of the worker elections mandated by a new California labor law, the time became ripe; and an agreement with Chavez was reached in which he finally got uncontested jurisdiction over most of the field labor and the Teamsters kept their jurisdiction over cannery and food-processing workers.

Beyond the small assignments Fitzsimmons gave him and the work he did for a while in the farm-workers fight, Gibbons had not been busy with union work in the months preceding the October 1976 La Costa tournament. It was better than the three years before, when he had had no work at all. But it wasn't like the old days. To keep occupied, Gibbons threw himself into political and civic affairs in St. Louis. In early 1976 he toyed with running for Congress, but then changed his mind. He did run, unsuccessfully, as a Democratic convention delegate on the slate supporting the ill-fated presidential candidacy of liberal Congressman Morris Udall. He became chairman of the St. Louis Convention Center board and lent his name, and in many cases his time, to several other local civic or liberal cause groups. He also continued his participation on the boards of a variety of national civil-rights and liberal organizations, including the national advisory board of the American Civil Liberties Union. In St. Louis, he appeared so often on television programs discussing politics or labor issues that he became more well-known than ever in the city he had adopted as his home in 1941. Still, no amount of local television, or advisory boards, or spot assignments from the International could satisfy Gibbons' urge for the real power and real limelight he had once had. At the time of the 1976 Fitzsimmons Invitational, Gibbons was in the thick of his farm-workers work, and it was keeping him almost as busy and as well-traveled as the old days. But he knew it was a temporary assignment and that even if he were to resolve anything between Chavez and the Teamsters locals, Fitzsimmons would have the final say and take the credit for it.

Life for Harold Gibbons didn't pack much of a wallop anymore. He found himself thinking, and talking, more about the past than about the present or future. This was probably a transition that most sixty-seven-year-olds have already gone through. But for Gibbons, who despite his chain-smoking and drinking looked and felt younger than he was, it had sneaked up on him cruelly at a time when he still had to watch his old coffee-gopher contemporary fumble around with the power he knew he could have done so much with.

In many ways, the year following the 1976 Fitzsimmons Invitational was a better one. Gibbons was assigned the job of working out an extraordinary, transoceanic merger of the already-giant Teamsters local that controlled Alaska with the local that represented Teamsters in Hawaii. It wasn't exactly a high-visibility assignment, but it kept him jetting back and forth to two relatively exotic frontiers; and it kept him in close contact with a good friend and a uniquely invigorating companion named Jesse Carr, the former California truck driver who had driven up to Alaska one day in the middle '50s and built the strongest, richest and most powerful Teamsters local.

Meanwhile, between trips to Alaska and Hawaii and to the quarterly executive board meetings, Gibbons maintained a small office (tiny, compared to what he had had in the old days) in the union office building he had built across from the senior citizens housing complex and the health institute in St. Louis. There, he served as a kind of elder statesman, providing negotiating advice to the local officers and the joint-council officials who asked for it, and acting as the liaison between the St. Louis Teamsters and the International. (He also continued to act in the same liaison capacity for North and

South Dakota Teamsters.) However, while his office was in St. Louis and though he still kept the apartment at the Chase Hotel there, with a Lincoln Continental waiting in the garage, Gibbons actually spent most of his time at his home on the outskirts of Palm Springs in the exclusive community of Rancho Mirage.

In January of 1977 he announced his engagement to Toni Stein, a woman he had known for several years and whom he had met when she ran a posh St. Louis restaurant, where he regularly took his girl friends. Blond, beautiful, and about thirty-five years younger than Gibbons, she could have been mistaken for one of those girl friends. With this marriage ended the schizophrenic shuttle between his plain, simple home life and the glittering night life of expensive eateries, sexy women, and celebrity sidekicks. Toni had none of the ideological hang-ups that Ann had had. Unlike Ann, she shared little of Gibbons' background in political and social causes. But she did share his weakness for glitter. Now it became possible for Gibbons to be faithfully married to a woman he loved and enjoy the good life at the same time. Together, the old Socialist and his new bride danced across the Palm Springs society pages. Their engagement party in January was a celebrity-packed sit-down dinner for two hundred hosted by one of Palm Springs' wealthiest businessmen. Their March wedding was a star-studded Palm Springs affair given by the former owner of New York's El Morocco Club. As a photo spread in the society magazine *Palm Springs Life* reported, the ceremony and dinner party were followed by an entertainment spectacular put on by old Gibbons pals Barbara McNair, Billy Daniels, Ed McMahon and Frank Sinatra. (The Gibbonses were, in fact, so close to the Sinatras that only a last-minute change in plans kept Toni off the private jet that crashed carrying Sinatra's mother to a Las Vegas opening in January.) And through the year the new couple, as happy and devoted to each other as any two newlyweds ever were, were regular guests at Palm Springs' most exclusive dinner parties.

As Gibbons seemed to come to terms with his appetite for the good life, so too he seemed to come to terms with the hierarchy that had discarded him and worked him over so thoroughly. Fitzsimmons and all the other Executive Board members, including Sam Provenzano, were invited to the wedding; and at the pep rally Fitzsimmons called a month later in Washington, Gibbons was one of the most spirited, eloquent speakers. He seemed to have accepted his second-string status.

But a closer look found strong signs that he hadn't, that he still simmered with bitterness and still entertained thoughts of trying to turn the tables on Fitzsimmons and the others. As the Eighth Annual Fitzsimmons Invitational approached in October 1977, close Gibbons friends reported that he spoke now with more contempt than ever about Fitzsimmons' stewardship and with more bitterness than ever about not getting enough assignments to keep him busy. The week of the tournament he risked a new rupture in the détente between himself and Fitzsimmons by rejecting a request to use him as a front man to help Fitzsimmons hang on. According to a source in Secretary-Treasurer Roy Schoessling's office, that week, Schoessling, a Fitzsimmons ally, asked Gibbons to chair the subcommittee of the Executive Board that was to hear the PROD charges that sought Fitzsimmons' removal for a variety of misdeeds. The plan was for the subcommittee to exonerate Fitzsimmons. Fitzsimmons and Schoessling thought Gibbons would be the most credible exonerator. (There was no risk in his turning on Fitzsimmons, since the subcommittee would be stacked with loyalists. And its decision would have to be approved by the full Executive Board, anyway.) Gibbons rejected the offer, which implied a sweetener of some extra expense money. He told Schoessling, "I've never lied for that guy yet, and I'm not going to do it at this stage of my life."

Through 1977 Gibbons also was growing increasingly upset about what had happened to his St. Louis local since he had been forced out in 1973. An official International booklet distributed in 1977 lauded Local 688 as "one of the most visual examples of a local union engaged in social and community activities," and cited the union-built senior-citizens housing complex and the Labor Health Institute as exemplary Teamsters projects. In 1977 the retirees' housing project—two well-kept handsome apartment buildings with a fountain and sculpture plaza tastefully adorning the front entrance and well-equipped activity rooms and cafeterias occupying the first floors—was a model of comfortable, dignified senior-citizen housing. And the Labor Health Institute, supplemented by its extraordinary indoor and outdoor recreation facilities, was still unsurpassed in providing free health care to working men and women.

Other Gibbons monuments were also in place, such as the city's law school, for which he had had the union donate the land, and the training program for shop stewards and the minischool at the outdoor recreation center for rank-and-filers, both of which he had established. The local's over-all performance was still such that by the end of 1977 PROD could report only three recruits among Local 688's 16,000 members. Just about any St. Louis Teamster you asked about Harold Gibbons would reply with glowing superlatives.

Gibbons was nonetheless bitterly disappointed that many of his projects had been scuttled. Day-care centers he had opened and planned to expand were closed. The community-stewards system was gone. His "Twentieth Century Plan" to raise money for antipoverty work through collective bargaining with the city's major employers had been scrapped. Two neighborhood service centers that he had opened, one in the poor-white community and one in the black ghetto, were now gone. His Council Plaza union office building had defaulted on its Central States Pension Fund loan. A major reason for the building's insolvency was the rental income that was lost when, at the International's (that is, Fitzsimmons') insistence, the Central Conference had broken its leases with the building and moved its offices elsewhere. When that happened, as Gibbons put it, "The guys running the union didn't have the guts to tell the Fund that without that rental income they needed a new mortgage." To further harass Gibbons, the Fund, with Fitzsimmons' approval, had then sued the union for nonpayment of the loan and had repossessed the building— a toughness rarely displayed by the Fund when loans to its underworld friends went unpaid. Also, Gibbons' successors had not negotiated increases in employer contributions to the Health Institute, which were crucial to meet predictable cost increases. As a result, the facility's financial stability was threatened.

Ironically, it was trouble that Gibbons' successors had caused on another front—again, with Fitzsimmons' tacit approval—that ended up keeping Gibbons away from the Eighth Annual Fitzsimmons Invitational in October of 1977. The day the tournament opened, on October 14, Gibbons found himself in a St. Louis courtroom fighting to keep the men who now ran the local union from dissolving the life-insurance trust worth $200,000 that Gibbons had arranged for Local 688 to set up for him several years before.

By the end of 1977 Gibbons was so unhappy about the state of things in St. Louis that after he had given me a tour there he urged me to "Go to Alaska and see what Jesse Carr's done, because that's my real legacy. I gave Jesse all his ideas for social programs." That being the case, Gibbons has a lot to be proud of. Carr's Alaska Teamsters are the best-paid and best-treated blue-collar workers in the world. Carr, a bulky, former truck driver whose favorite motto was "When you have them by the balls their hearts and minds usually will follow," has a stranglehold on the state. In 1977 14 percent of Alaska's total work force were Teamsters, including all the oil-pipeline workers, butchers, bakers, surveyors, truckers, telephone operators, school principals, and many city police and state employees.

Carr has used that power well. By 1977 he had built the closest thing in the United States to a worker-dominated state where working men and women lived well and wielded the balance of economic and political power. In 1976 his pipeline workers earned $11 to $15 an hour. They received $1,500 to $2,000 a month retirement pay. All family medical expenses, including dental work and eye care, were absolutely free. All families were part of a prepaid legal-service plan, also free. Taking Gibbons' idea, Carr had built a magnificent hospital complex to which Teamsters-owned jet ambulances flew in patients in need from around the giant state. He had built recreation facilities on a scale that dwarfed Gibbons' initial efforts in St. Louis. These included indoor athletic facilities that offered his Teamsters free, the pleasures of the wealthiest country-club members—indoor pools, saunas, tennis courts and gymnasiums. Taking another cue from Gibbons, he had had the union build office buildings around the state.

Since he had first come to Alaska, Carr had remained steadfastly independent of the International union, except for small favors (such as arranging for Hoffa's son and later Fitzsimmons' youngest son to get summer jobs there). His pension fund had never been mixed with any other Teamsters fund. In fact, he had established a rule that required that all its money be invested in Alaska. By 1977, with more than $100,000,000 in the fund, he had more financial clout in Alaska than any individual banker. If one adds that clout to his ability to shut down the state's economy and the fact that Carr's members constitute 20 percent of the state's voters, you have a union that Farrell Dobbs or Harold Gibbons could admire.

But, although Gibbons could say off-handedly that his real legacy was in Alaska with Jesse Carr, that claim could not be wholly satisfying. Carr conceded that Gibbons has been an inspiration to him, but Alaska was Carr's doing, not Gibbons'. Carr had never attached any of Gibbons' political or social ideals to the raw power that he built for the workers there. Carr's is the politics of bread-and-butter union issues; to him unionism is a force for social change only in so far as it means more money and benefits for his workers. There is a certain vulgarity about the way he wields his power. In addition to the sheer force of that power—more than any corruption—this was what had offended the Alaskan press and local public-interest groups so much that they repeatedly attacked Carr and the Teamsters.

Carr's union has none of the democratic niceties in its governance that Gibbons developed during his union's heyday in the early '50s. In many respects the rise of the Teamsters in Alaska means power to Jesse Carr, not to the workers. Although Carr had never been convicted of any crime and all the evidence suggests that on the whole his is an honest operation, by 1977 questions had been raised about the integrity of some aspects of his work that might make Gibbons shrink from claiming Alaska as his legacy. The Alaska pension fund had always been thought to be perfectly clean, but in 1977 it was revealed that the fund had lent money to a Teamsters-run credit union, which in turn had made several loans at low-interest rates to Teamsters officials who worked for Carr. Carr's hospital-complex and prepaid-legal-service plans were widely acclaimed, but by mid-1977 an Alaska Ralph Nader public-interest group found that the union had paid far more for both than had been paid for comparable hospital or legal-service plans. They were asking government investigators to find out why. Also, there were repeated charges, denied by Carr, that Carr had tolerated corruption on the pipeline construction project and, in fact, even allowed organized-crime operatives to be installed as union shop stewards there.

The Teamsters and Gibbons in particular had much to be proud of in the workers' empire that Carr had built. But however "inspirational" Gibbons had been, Alaska wasn't his baby, nor was it a baby he would adopt without reservation.

The matter of what Harold Gibbons' legacy was—or what it might have been—raises the question of who Harold Gibbons really is. Is he a high-minded socialist, or a hypocrite who simply mouthed the slogans as he reached for the union credit card? Is he, as Al Barkett volunteered during our ride, "the only straight one I ever heard of among all the top bosses," or did the work he did for Hoffa and his to-the-end defense of Hoffa make him as crooked as the others? Was he too easily corrupted by temptations of the wallet and flesh, or was he a man blocked from doing good by forces he couldn't risk trying to buck, and who turned to expensive clothes and top night spots and the Palm Springs life only out of frustration and the need to reach for the kinds of consolation prize that a twenty-third child in a family of poor coal miners would treasure? Most important, did Gibbons cop out where a stronger man would have acted, or was his reluctance based on an accurate assessment of the forces that would have beaten him back or killed him?

To assess Harold Gibbons is to search for the answers to difficult human questions. To know Gibbons and try to understand him is to know and understand that there is no bottom line, no black-or-white verdict. Over the eighteen months I researched this story, after more than 300 interviews, not one person associated with Teamsters hinted that Gibbons ever took a payoff of any kind. In 1977 he alone among all present or former Teamsters chieftains had accumulated no real assets (except about $20,000 equity in his house and his life-insurance policies). That makes the question of how honestly he had done his union negotiating an easy one. The other questions were not resolvable; they rarely are, and Gibbons makes them particularly complex. Just when you had heard all the stories about his high living, you were reminded that he had quarreled with Hoffa when Kennedy was killed, and he had thus risked his position. When you stopped to admire his senior-citizens housing and the spectacular 1952 school-integration plan, you took pause that the same man looked the other way as the Central States Pension Fund was fleeced, backed up Hoffa in 1960 against Kennedy and defended Hoffa against the undoubted accusations that the boss tolerated, even encouraged, organized crime in his union. But then you remembered his community stewards, his Labor Health Institute, and his trail-blazing system of stewards' council governance.

It's not difficult to convince yourself that no man should have been expected to go against the kind of force stacked against him, let alone give up all those salaries and fringes. But Harold Gibbons, by his vote for McGovern over Nixon, had shown himself to be unafraid of many of the consequences of being a maverick in the Teamsters hierarchy. So you expected uncommon courage from him, and you were disappointed that he never made the ultimate break and decided, come what may, to take them all on in a fight to take over the union. You had to wonder, as he did, whether such a break would have been, figuratively or literally, a suicide mission. But in the end you suspected that the tragedy of Harold Gibbons—your bottom line on him—was that he never dared to find out. And, in the way he spent much of his sixty-eighth year in 1977 bitterly looking back, you sensed that he had rendered the same verdict on himself. You knew, and you knew Gibbons knew, that had he tried and had he succeeded the Teamsters union would have been a very different union than it became.

By the end of 1977 Harold Gibbons—with all the black, white, and gray marks and all the might-have-been possibilities—was as good an allegory as we can imagine of his union. It was a union that had done as much as any single organization in the nation's history to redistribute wealth from the rich into the pockets of working-class people like Al Barkett, yet it had probably presided over more under-the-table sell-outs to management than any other labor union. For people like Charlie McGuire, it was an uncaring, inaccessible corrupt bureaucracy. Elsewhere, under the leadership of men like Ron Carey, it was a model of honest, concerned representative democracy. Led by people like Allen Dorfman, it had sponsored gangster embezzlement from senior citizens. It was also the union that had sponsored, and was paying, the nation's most generous private blue-collar pensions. It had justifiably earned headlines as a profit center for the most corrupt, vicious elements in our society. It was also often the victim of a double standard that made light of the incredible temptations union leadership offered, and ignored the businessmen who were the unions' partners in most acts of corruption.

As with Gibbons, it is clear that the Teamsters union is one giant might-have-been. As the nation's largest, most powerful union it could have been the nation's largest, most powerful voice for real economic justice. Had its leaders had a social and political vision that extended beyond invitations to golf at San Clemente, it could have been the nation's toughest and most effective lobbyist for civil liberties, civil rights and other social-justice concerns. Had its leaders wielded its financial power honestly—particularly in the case of the pension funds, which ultimately promised to give workers more financial clout in our economy than that held by any other group—the union might have, in Gibbons' words, "remade the base of America by investing the money in ways consistent with our social goals." Instead, the moneys were handled so corruptly that ultimately control over them had to be passed right back to the insurance companies, banks and other big-business-establishment institutions that had held the balance of the society's economic power in the first place. The Teamsters had won improved wages and decent health care for Barkett and McGuire and most of the 2,300,000 others. But had this union set out to do the larger job that its numbers, its muscle and its money equipped it to do, had its leaders had that kind of vision, Gibbons' recreation facilities, health institute, community action projects, senior-citizens subsidized housing, and civil-rights crusades of the '50s in St. Louis wouldn't have been mere relics in 1978 of an idiosyncratic local leader's whims.

In the months before and after the Eighth Annual Fitzsimmons Invitational, Harold Gibbons contemplated once more the old dream. He sounded out several vice-presidents about support for the presidency if the rumors about Fitzsimmons resigning were true, or if Fitzsimmons died. He began planning how he might attempt to run for the job at the convention that would have to be called to elect a new president within six months of a Fitzsimmons departure. None of the vice-presidents gave him a commitment, and his convention prospects didn't look much better. Perhaps he would still give it a try, but it seemed that time had passed him by. Roy Williams or Jackie Presser had a better shot at it.

If Williams took over, a major clean-up of the union was not in the cards. He had been part of the corruption himself for nearly twenty years. If Presser won, the prospects for an end to Teamsters business as usual were nearly as far-fetched. Presser was not likely to be willing or able to clean up the fiefdoms.

It also was not likely that the government would clean things up. Occasionally they could make a good case against a top leader, but this accomplished little more than putting a few players on the sidelines briefly. Ever since 1957, when Robert Kennedy and the McClellan Committee turned law-enforcement attention onto labor corruption, this is exactly what had occurred. "We even got two of their quarterbacks," a frustrated Justice Department prosecutor said in late 1976. "But that doesn't matter. They just keep sending in replacements."

The prosecutor and other government labor-corruption specialists attributed their losing battle to a number of factors. Most labor-law violations are misdemeanors, not felonies; misdemeanors rarely result in prison sentences and are negligible deterrents. The Labor Department, which has primary responsibility for investigating labor-law violations, is ill-equipped for its task. Its investigators have little law-enforcement training, and they are drastically understaffed. Also, as the department whose constituency is labor and labor unions, the Labor Department cannot be expected to investigate unions as fervently as other law-enforcement agencies.

Changes in the law that would tighten enforcement are unlikely. Other unions would lobby against such action, since they would fear that tougher laws and enforcement procedures intended to clean up the Teamsters will spill over into increased government scrutiny of their operations as well.

One change in the law—the pension reform act, ERISA—had been helpful in cleaning up the pension and other trust-funds side of Teamsters activities. But its use of civil, as opposed to criminal, penalties, while offering leverage to encourage reform, raises serious crime-control questions. Still, the law might prevent corruption in extreme cases as in the Central States Pension Fund by taking the money out of the hands of the crooks. At the end of 1977 the personnel charged with enforcing ERISA and monitoring the financial reporting that the law requires were gravely understaffed and buried under millions of documents filed by 600,000 pension plans from all over the nation. There was no way of knowing whether corruption at the Central States fund hadn't shifted to other Teamsters pension funds.

Neither Roy Williams nor Jackie Presser nor the government offers hope for genuine change at the Teamsters union. That will take someone with the talent and the vision of a Harold Gibbons emerging from a group like PROD or from a frustrating local experience like Ron Carey's.

Even then, the rank and file will have to be moved to action. The overwhelming majority have always shrugged at corruption and cared little about union political activities or social action as long as their pay checks keep getting bigger. Perhaps the apathy is destined to continue. Maybe the notion of the labor union as a hard-driving social and political force and a scrupulously honest bargainer for the workers is a pipe dream in a union that can satisfy its workers with a good-enough pay day no matter how corrupt and how tunnel-visioned their union is. Maybe the Teamsters union is never going to change because the rank and file is never going to be moved sufficiently to change it.

If that turns out to be true—if good leaders never come forward, or if the rank and file choose not to be led no matter who tries—then the story of the Teamsters union will, like that of Harold Gibbons, continue to be one of some good deeds, and some bad deeds, and with a sad bottom line that it could have been much better.

Index

PHOTO CREDITS

Acknowledgment is due the following for permission to include the photos in the picture insert. The photos are credited, in the order of their appearance, to:
Wide World Photos, UPI, Wide World Photos, Plain Dealer, Wide World Photos, Wide World Photos, Wide World Photos, Wide World Photos, UPI, Wide World Photos, UPI, UPI, UPI, personal, no credit, UPI.